REVERSING
UNDERACHIEVEMENT
AMONG GIFTED BLACK STUDENTS

DONNA Y. FORD

D1604925

PRUFROCK PRESS INC.
WACO, TEXAS

Library of Congress Cataloging-in-Publication Data

Ford, Donna Y.
 Reversing underachievement among gifted Black students / Donna Y. Ford. -- 2nd ed.
   p. cm.
 Includes bibliographical references.
 ISBN 978-1-59363-487-2 (pbk.)
 1. Gifted children--Education--United States. 2. African American students. 3. Underachievers--Education-
-United States. I. Title.

 LC3993.9.F66 2011
 371.95'6--dc22

                         2010044687

Edited by Jennifer Robins

Layout Design by Raquel Trevino

ISBN-13: 978-1-59363-487-2

Prufrock Press Inc.
P.O. Box 8813
Waco, TX 76714-8813
Phone: (800) 998-2208
Fax: (800) 240-0333
http://www.prufrock.com

REVERSING
UNDERACHIEVEMENT
AMONG GIFTED BLACK STUDENTS

TABLE OF CONTENTS

ACKNOWLEDGEMENTS

Thanks with all my heart to my son Khyle, my mother, my sisters, my nieces, and my nephew for their encouragement and support. They are my reason for being. I am also in the difficult position of "thanking" gifted underachieving Black students, for without them, this book and my career would not exist. This work is dedicated to those Black students who, for one reason or another, have failed or are failing to reach their potential in school and life. To gifted Black students—diamonds in the rough—this work is devoted to you, for

Our deepest fear is not that we are inadequate. Our deepest fear is that we are powerful beyond imagination. It is our light more than our darkness which scares us. We ask ourselves—who am I to be brilliant, beautiful, talented, and fabulous? Actually, who are you to not be? (Williamson, 1992, p. 165)

PREFACE

On the fringes of most school environments gathers a shadow population of students whose motivation and achievement are stymied. These are the marginal students who are not being well served by our public schools. Precious little attention is given either to the needs of these young people or to their assets. They are viewed as deviants from the "regular" students, outsiders who are not productive members of the learning community. This persistent problem of increasing numbers of students who are not succeeding must be attacked because youth who fail on the margins are as deserving as those who thrive in the mainstream.

—Sinclair and Ghory (1992, p. 33)

The seeds for this book were sewn many years ago, while I was still in formal schooling—a ninth grader. In 1976, I received an academic scholarship designated for bright and promising economically challenged students. I remember sitting in the auditorium where the entire school gathered for this important event and taking the exam for the scholarship entitled "A Better Chance." Within a few months, my mother and I were summoned to the principal's office, at which time we were informed that I had been awarded a scholarship. I was given a number of private high school options from which to attend. Too many of my classmates were less fortunate. Those who suffered from test anxiety, who succumbed to peer pressure, who believed negative stereotypes about Blacks, who did not take the test seriously, and who had other priorities, for example, did not score at the designated level to receive a scholarship. I did.

After some discussion with my mother, I chose to attend a local private high school located not too far from my family and friends. I had never been away from my mother and sisters, so staying close to home and commuting each day was best for me. I thought this was the best choice for my family and myself—close to home meant that I'd be in a safe haven. This is where my story begins, for my life changed forever. Everything plummeted—my grades, self-esteem, academic self-concept, racial identity, and my dignity. My most pleasant memory about school was the food. I gained more than 50 pounds that year.

I attended a private school for females. In grades 9–12, there were only four Black females, including myself. I was the only one on scholarship and poor. I quickly learned that one could face discrimination based on not just race, but also socioeconomic status. I could not identify with my wealthy White classmates. They spoke a language foreign to my ears—vacations, housekeepers/nannies, inheritances, personal jets, swimming pools, yachts, Jacuzzis, Porsches, Jaguars, and Mercedes. I literally carried a dictionary with me to translate. I understood the language of my Black classmates, but they, too, had little in common with me. Although not rich, they were well off but they were lost racially and culturally, as will be discussed later; I was on scholarship. Further, they were, on the surface or superficially, part of the "community," having attended the school for a number of years. I was truly the proverbial fish out of water; I connected with neither the more privileged White girls nor the Black ones. I was low income, others were not. That was at school.

Back at home, there were other trials and tribulations. My "friends," whom I'd known for years, resented my being at that "uppity White" school. I was now deemed a "sell out," a traitor, who was "acting White," disowning my community and sacrificing my racial identity. Survival guilt weighed heavy on me as a teenager. I contemplated the myriad of sacrifices I was making to become successful as a gifted Black student who was also female, and low income and (but?) ambitious—and wanting so desperately to be accepted, affirmed, and to fit in . . . somewhere.

I vaguely remember my teachers, for I have a tendency to push to the subconscious unpleasant memories and thoughts. My English teacher had the most significant and negative impact upon me. She violated my trust and respect in her as an educator, professional, and responsible adult. One of our class assignments was to read *The Scarlet Letter* by Nathaniel Hawthorne. For the first time in my life, I learned the potency of bibliotherapy, of the catharsis one can get from identifying with a character.

Being in this school, I now realized that I, too, had a scarlet letter—the color of my skin. Some 30 years later, and more than five decades after legalized and legislated desegregation via *Brown v. Board of Education* (1954), I still get frequent reminders (sometimes daily reminders) that, because I am Black, little is expected of me, and I should expect little. However, unlike Hester Prynne, Hawthorne's heroine, I committed neither a sin nor broken the law; I was born into my circumstances—this was not a choice.

I wrote about my scarlet letter for a class assignment in which I analogized that my scarlet letter was being Black—it was a curse, along with being poor. My teacher was so "surprised that I could write so well" and was so "insightful" that she requested that I share it with the class, a group of 15 or so rich White females who I had so little in common with, females who lived in mansions, who drove the most expensive cars, and who had personal drivers, personal planes, and yachts. I refused. My teacher's request eventually became an order and ultimatum. The A+ eventually became an F for "lack of cooperation and comradeship." My teacher simply did not understand—and maybe did not care to understand. The reading and writing assignment had been a welcome relief, a mental and physical catharsis and implosion. I was able to vent, rant, rave, and scream in text; I felt relief but not vindicated. My paper was like sharing a piece of my soul and my diary, but it was me, a teenager, against an adult.

The school administrators are also fuzzy images. They often searched my person, my possessions, and my locker when money, jewelry, or other items were stolen or misplaced. They violated me in almost every respect—psychologically, physically, academically, and more.

It was not long, perhaps a month after school began, that I began to withdraw and show classic signs of educational disengagement or burnout—daydreaming, procrastinating, turning in incomplete assignments, and coming to class late or not at all some days. Eventually, I committed the ultimate act of educational disengagement and apathy; I dropped out of school, not physically, but socially, psychologically, and emotionally. This disenchantment and disconnect revealed itself in my lowered motivation and grades, which plummeted from A's to C's. I had never made a C in my life. To say the least, my mother was worried and distraught, but I blamed the low grades on everything else but the truth. I never told her about the academic and social and emotional hell and torture that I had to endure for 180 days. My mother (my number one fan) believed that the school meant or guaranteed a promising future; the first step on the social mobility ladder. I could not and would not disappoint my mother by telling her about my daily trials and tribulations at school.

After a year, I dropped out of that school and transferred to my neighborhood school—low income and overwhelmingly Black. I needed to be affirmed socially, culturally, intellectually, and academically. Had my mother insisted that I return to the private school, I would have dropped out completely. I felt like a soldier must feel after battle; both battle fatigue and survival guilt were common to me. I was suicidal. My self-esteem, academic self-concept, and racial identity had been shattered. I needed to be among students who shared my struggles, who looked like me, who talked like me, who understood (or wanted and tried to understand) me. The teachers did not have to look like me; they just had to care.

My less-than-rigorous neighborhood school had its share of problems. I remember being taught in the 11th and 12th grades what I had learned in the 10th grade at the private school. As I reflect, it is clear that I received what some educators and researchers consider an inferior education at my neighborhood school. Yet, the teachers (all White) were wonderful—caring, humanistic, energetic, and skilled. Over time and slowly, my love for learning and motivation began to return.

As with many adolescents, I also experienced a dilemma, a conflict between my need for achievement and my need for affiliation. The latter won out. Although teachers were caring, I felt unchallenged in school and was fearful of doing well; many of my Black classmates (male and female) accused me of "acting White" and threatened me physically. It had been too easy to make the honor roll, too easy to change the bell curve, too easy to win writing scholarships, and too easy to become President of the National Honor Society.

I graduated from high school with several academic scholarships. I decided to attend, on a full academic scholarship, a local, private university where I was majoring in mathematics/engineering. Before the semester ended, I dropped out. Two professors had convinced me of three things. First, I did not belong in math and science because I was a female. Second, and more importantly, I did not belong in math and science because I was Black. Third, I would never earn a degree from that university—they would see to it. Again, I found myself underachieving, and flight from academics was the only option I could see. I also found out that I would be a young mother at the tender age of 18.

I stayed out of college for one year, got caught in the vicious cycle of being a single mother, and tried to envision life without a college degree, life without a career in engineering or math. My mother, barely 40 years old, eventually gave me the most important ultimatum of my life: Get back in school or else. I was blessed! She agreed to take care of my son, her grandson.

In 1980, I enrolled in a different university. After changing my major four or five times (maybe more), I graduated within 4 years with a degree in both communications and Spanish. I barely had a 3.0 grade point average, and C's were familiar and even comforting to me, but at least I had not failed.

In 1986, I applied for and was accepted into a master's degree program. I worked hard and excelled academically, but I felt incomplete, still searching for who I was and what I wanted to be when I grew up. I was unfulfilled academically and did not think that a master's degree was enough to make an impact. I sought a doctorate. Even though my grades were excellent as a graduate student, I had barely scored at the mean of 1000 on the Graduate Record Examination (GRE). I felt lucky to have been admitted but also believed that the college would benefit in some way from my presence and experiences.

It was not until I entered the doctoral program that I began to feel comfortable and confident on personal, racial, and professional levels. I began to feel empowered. I majored in urban education and was challenged to explore education in the context of urban life; the focus on social justice was refreshing. I could identify with the issues discussed in class—underachievement; the achievement gap; tracking; low teacher and deficit expectations; irrelevant curriculum; achievement-affiliation conflicts such as peer pressure, poverty, racism, and sexism; and other ills that permeate society and plague its schools. I learned to consider, appreciate, and respect the importance of multicultural education or culturally responsive education, teacher diversity, gifted education and Advanced Placement (AP) classes, comprehensive educational and counseling services, family/caregiver involvement, and motivation for success in school and, ultimately, life.

Although my story has a positive ending, albeit not the kind that movies are made of, the told and untold stories of so many others are not. This is 2010, and while there are books, studies, speculation, and comprehensive treatises on underachieving students (including gifted students and racially and culturally different students), there is no such work on *gifted underachieving Black* students beyond what I wrote in 1996. This is, again, an ambitious book, but not overly so. It was developed with multiple audiences in mind, including educators, administrators, counselors, parents/caregivers, researchers, and practitioners. It is relatively comprehensive because it focuses on the psychological, social, familial, and cultural factors that influence the achievement of Black students who are gifted or potentially gifted—but also underachieving. It focuses on the respective and collaborative roles that families, educators, and children themselves must play in promoting the academic, social, psychological, and emotional well-being of these particular students.

Several premises guide this work. In defining giftedness, I have adopted the inclusive definitions espoused by the U.S. Department of Education (1993), Howard Gardner (1983), and Robert Sternberg (1985). These definitions and attendant theories contend that giftedness is a context-bound and culture-dependent construct that requires multidimensional and multimodal assessment measures and strategies. Equity *and* excellence are at the heart of these works and are what drive me to excel and advocate for the rights of gifted Black students. They acknowledge the impossibility of a "one-size-fits-all" test to capture this elusive and complex construct and that tests are academic electric chairs for far too many students.

A second premise is that no group has a monopoly on giftedness, regardless of its form and the group. It is illogical and statistically impossible for giftedness to be the prerogative of one racial, gender, or socioeconomic group. Nonetheless, gifted programs and AP classes represent the most segregated programs in public schools. They are disproportionately White and middle and upper income or class, and they serve primarily intellectually and academically gifted students. If all gifted and potentially gifted students are to receive an appropriate education, gifted programs and AP classes must become desegregated.

Third, predicting potential is as problematic and difficult as predicting the weather. Despite sophisticated instruments (i.e., intelligence, achievement, and aptitude tests), mistakes are still made. Some children score higher than we expect; others score lower. Tests touted to be highly correlated with school performance and high in predictive ability show huge discrepancies for some students. Students do well in college whose test scores predicted otherwise, and students with the highest test scores can and do drop out. I was such an example.

A fourth premise is that all school personnel (e.g., teachers, psychologists, counselors, tutors) have a professional, moral, and ethical responsibility to help students reach their potential in school; no child should sit or learn on the margins, feeling either physically, culturally, psychologically, or socially isolated from the rewards of learning and educational challenge.

A fifth premise is that parent/family/community/school collaborations are essential to students' school success. Parents are their children's first teachers; teachers are children's surrogate parents or caregivers. Separating parents and primary caregivers from the process of schooling is tantamount to removing oxygen from air. Without oxygen, air does not exit. Without parents and other primary caregivers, like grandparents and aunts, schools and students have a hard time succeeding.

The next premise is that educators must focus not only solely on identification and/or assessment, but they also must take great pains to recruit and retain Black students in gifted education and AP classes. It is not enough to place Black students in these programs; efforts must be made to *keep* them once placed. Recruitment is comprised of screening, identification and assessment, and placement; recruitment is comprised of the learning environment, programming, and supports.

Finally, underachievement is not a "sickness that can be cured"; however, underachievement can be reversed. Underachievement is learned and can be unlearned. No child is born underachieving! Deficit perspectives and blaming children for their failures do little to resolve underachievement. The potential and motive to achieve is inherent in all children. No talent or potential should be allowed to atrophy.

A preface permits the author to describe not only what a book is, but also what is not. Given this license, I shall end by dispelling any misconceptions about the goals and objectives of this book. The book does not cover the entire range of issues related to underachievement among gifted Black students. Even though I am revising this book after more than a decade, the literature on this topic is still too modest for this task. Nonetheless, it seeks to present a comprehensive and thorough discussion of the issues raised. The book discusses the educational plight of Black students, but it is not an attempt to castigate or indict the educational system for these problems. In fact, finger pointing would represent a significant waste of time and paper. Instead, I make a proactive, consistent attempt to emphasize that underachievement is a multifaceted phenomenon whose etiology is equally multidimensional and complex. I hope to unravel some of its mystery.

Personally and professionally, I have witnessed Black children, many of them gifted but not formally identified, floundering in school. We all see events through the lens of our personal ideology, but only those with myopic and near-sighted vision can overlook the crises facing Black students in general education, gifted education, and AP classes.

Racially and culturally different students are at the greatest risk of

XVI   REVERSING UNDERACHIEVEMENT AMONG GIFTED BLACK STUDENTS

being forgotten and discounted in the context of gifted education and AP programs. Gifted Black students are a minority within a minority—an anomaly in gifted education and AP programs. That is to say, the gifted population comprises a numerical minority of the school population, and within this minority is yet another minority, namely Black students. As a gifted Black student, I walked in and endeavored to negotiate two worlds. Illustrated, one could put my school experiences into a Venn diagram. Teachers had a difficult time understanding me, for I was gifted *and* Black *and* poor—I was an oxymoron to them, just as gifted underachievement appears paradoxical. The gifted part of me was supposed to be conforming, hardworking, obedient, and academically outstanding; the Black part of me was supposed to be disobedient, lazy, defiant of authority, and academically poor. The poor part of me was supposed to also be of low intelligence, low achievement, low motivation, and poor behavior. No child should experience this hellish confusion. No human being should.

As a gifted Black student who *learned* to underachieve in the aforementioned private school, I needed several things to ensure a healthy, effective school experience. I needed teachers and other school personnel to acknowledge and appreciate the changing demographics of students and to respond by:

- ❖ seeking substantive preparation in both gifted and multicultural education;
- ❖ changing curriculum and instruction to reflect diversity and cultural differences;
- ❖ understanding that racially and culturally different students have a number of battles to fight, including social ills such as poverty, racism, prejudice, and stereotypes that interfere with motivation and inhibit equal and equitable learning opportunities;
- ❖ conducting more studies on the dilemmas confronting underachieving gifted Black students; and
- ❖ developing theories and professional and personal views of giftedness that are sensitive and responsive to culturally and racially different students.

In gifted education years ago as a low-income Black student, I was an oddity, just as many Black and economically challenged students are even today. This book speaks to the paucity of research, theory, and practice currently available on Black students (both those gifted and potentially gifted) and determinants of their underachievement. Without adequate research and subsequent prevention and intervention, many gifted Black students will continue to underachieve and, thus, fail to reach their academic potential. This book is offered as a contribution to the limited data available relating social, cultural, familial, and psychological factors to achievement among Black students. Research that seeks to understand and then address social, psychological, familial, and cultural barriers to academic achievement is in great demand in our schools, gifted programs, and AP classes. The book, therefore, has several general objectives:

❖ to increase awareness and understanding of social, cultural, familial, and psychological needs of gifted Black students, specifically those whose potential and talents are untapped;

❖ to provoke or instigate increased research and funding, as well as advocacy, on behalf of underachieving and gifted Black students;

❖ to increase the support of broad and inclusive definitions and theories of both giftedness and underachievement; and

❖ to desegregate gifted classes, programs, and services and AP classes by increasing the representation of Black (and other children of color) in them.

My ultimate goal is to decapitate social and cultural inequities that rear their ugly heads in schools. Hopefully, the book, or sections of it, will serve to revitalize national interest in gifted education and AP classes, particularly the plight of underachieving and gifted Black students. I hope that it affords readers a broad understanding of how schools, families, and the social, cultural, and psychological matrix all interact to affect achievement. If this book contributes in any way to the discourse on educational equality and equity, it will have been well worth the effort.

CHAPTER ONE

INTRODUCTION

"Khyle is such a social and active child; if only he'd calm down, talk less, and be less social, he would be one of our shining stars. He's a leader who uses his talents in nonproductive ways, mainly as the class clown. I've also noticed that he thrives on individual attention, and does poorly on tests, but his projects and ideas are outstanding. Although I think he is gifted, and he makes mainly A's and B's, I don't think he's ready to be in gifted classes. In my classes, gifted students are pretty introverted; they wouldn't want to work with him."

"Kieran is very creative—so much so that we placed her one grade ahead in art. She's also very intelligent, but doesn't seem interested in school subjects other than art and writing right now. Her friends, journaling, and surfing the Internet consume her interests and time. Last year, she did quite well. This year she is barely making B's. I think we need to place her back in general education classes until she is more focused."

"Cynara is somewhat of a later bloomer, like me [her mother]. She is quite capable of excelling in school, but doesn't find much value or relevance in what school has to offer. I was like this. When reading Homer's *Odyssey*, she asked her teacher, 'What will I learn about myself after reading this book? What does this old dead man have to do with me? I am a young Black female!' I also have a hard time learning and getting interested when I don't see a personal connection. Cynara's performance fluctuates based on the course and her interest."

"Yvonne has always been a fast learner; things come so easy for her. Now that she's in college, she seems so unmotivated—little interests her and any assignment that requires effort is avoided. She thinks that smart people should not have to work hard or study. She is very shy and doesn't talk much in class, even when prompted; to hide, Yvonne immerses herself in technology and gadgets, finding the Internet to be her 'best friend.' I don't see how she can survive in a classroom with other gifted students who are more assertive. Teachers wonder how she keeps getting A's given her low effort."

"Christopher has one of the sharpest minds that I have encountered. He's like a human *Jeopardy* game, so full of facts and tidbits. His memory is incredible! But when it comes to school, he could care less. One year he was failing most classes. The next year, he made mostly A's and B's. Nothing seems to challenge him, so Chris does his own thing. I am not convinced that he'd benefit from being in AP classes."

"Karen is one of my brightest students, but she has priorities other than school. She puts more effort into socializing and partying or clubbing than into achieving in school. She is more outspoken and direct than classmates. Teachers complain that she is very talkative and this distracts them and her classmates. She is a handful. Why would I want such a talkative and aggressive student in my class?"

"Patricia shows a lot of promise for becoming a medical doctor, but her grades in science and math are less than desirable. She has little contact with medical professionals, but has been told that becoming a doctor is the best or only option for getting out of poverty. Patricia seldom comes to class and, when she does, she is not prepared. Right now, boys (not school) take up most of her thinking and free time. What can we offer her by placement in an AP class?"

"Noah's performance is inconsistent. He so smart, but he makes a C as easily as he makes an A. When he is interested in the topic, he does quite well; otherwise, he fails to pay attention. He doesn't get in trouble, like misbehaving; instead, he doesn't apply himself. He should be in AP classes but doesn't want to enroll, arguing that such classes are for nerds and geeks. If it weren't for his father, he'd be OK with average grades. I think that students who are self-motivated should be in gifted programs; the others need to mature."

These comments, whether from parents/caregivers[1] or teachers or both, illustrate that underachieving students come in many guises, yet someone has recognized the potential and promise, or untapped abilities, in these particular students. The focus of this book is on underachievers. I distinguish between the terms *low achievement* and *underachievement*; I do not use them interchangeably although they are related. Low achievement refers to below-average academic performance, specifically grades of D and failing and/or performing below the 50th percentile on an achievement test. Low achievement says nothing about how a student is capable of performing. However, underachievement does refer to a discrepancy. An underachieving student is one whose school performance is below what is expected. Students earning C's and/or performing at the 50th percentile are average achievers/performers. Irrespective of the term used, these students are educationally disadvantaged; frankly, their educational needs are not being met. These students are pretty much failing in school, and schools are failing these students.

In the above scenarios, underachievement is evident. Some of the students are also low achievers, and a few are high achievers but, by virtue of exerting low effort, they are not performing to their potential, making them underachievers.

For all of the students, academic disconnect is evident, and interests and priorities that do not include academic achievement are apparent. In these and other scenarios, self-esteem, self-concept, and/or racial identity issues; the classroom climate; curriculum and instruction; teacher expectations; and/or peer pressures inhibit students' motivation and achievement.

Underachieving students are not a homogeneous group. Some students have problems associated with poor peer or social relationships, depression, anxiety, defensiveness, or negative self-images. Too many

---

1   The terms "parents," "families," and "caregivers" are used interchangeably in this book. I adopt the broadest and most inclusive notion of parents, particularly when focusing on Black and other culturally different groups. In the Black community, the notion of family is broad, particularly as large numbers of Blacks live in extended families. Regardless of the specific term, I am referring to the individual or individuals who play the primary role in raising the child. In addition to the biological or adoptive parent, this could be a grandmother, aunt, or other adult.

Black students, including those identified as gifted, have identities that are disconnected from academics. They more often find their sense of worth in community and familial settings, as well as in sports and the visual and performing arts. Other students may lack motivation and are considered lazy, procrastinators, perfectionists, or nonconformists. A common perception is that students would not be underachievers if they would just try harder, pay attention, listen, and do as told. However, overcoming or reversing underachieving is not this simple and straightforward for many students, particularly those who have had little or no early intervention, those who lack basic skills to take advantage of educational opportunities, those with weaknesses in self-regulation and problem-solving skills, and those who have negative self-images. For gifted Black students, reversing underachievement may be especially difficult if underachievement is related to social barriers, such as racism or deficit thinking; to peer pressure; to low family involvement; and to environmental barriers, such as poverty and low socioeconomic status (SES).

As the above scenarios indicate, and as reflected in Figure 1.1, several major factors at the macro and micro levels must be considered and addressed when seeking to understand and reverse underachievement. These include social, familial, school, and individual factors. Each of these factors is discussed in further detail in later chapter. Some students underachieve due to one or more variables in either of the rings; others underachieve due to the interrelatedness of two or more of the four major rings. Thus, if a student is facing low teacher expectations or low family involvement, this must be the target of intervention[2] For Khyle, Karen, and Kieran, interventions should target the social factors related to peer influences, as well as individual factors, because need for affiliation is greater than need for achievement. For Yvonne, Christopher, and Noah, a focus on work ethic ought to be addressed; for Patricia and Cynara, addressing academic self-concepts related to STEM (science, technology, engineering, and math) areas should be the focus. Having said this, educators ought not to use these as excuses to not refer and/or place Black students in gifted and AP classes. *Every* student who is underachieving, whether identified as gifted or otherwise, will need support and problem-specific interventions to perform better.

In conceptualizing and creating Figure 1.1, I wrestled with adding a cultural ring of influence. After deliberation, I concluded that, in one

2   Given that underachievement already exists with students in these scenarios, the term *intervention* is used. Ideally, efforts should focus on the prevention and early intervention of underachievement (and low achievement).

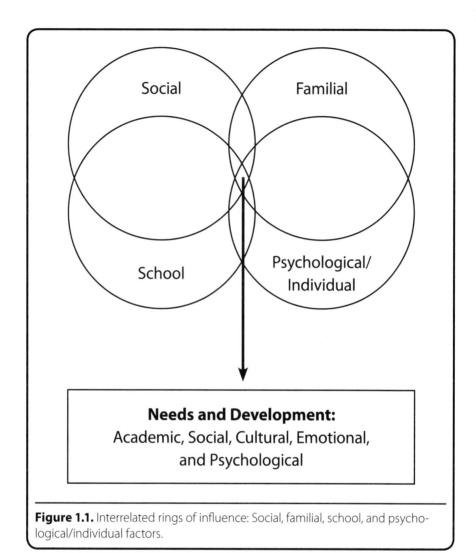

Figure 1.1. Interrelated rings of influence: Social, familial, school, and psychological/individual factors.

way or another, culture is a part of all of the rings. Having said this, Chapter 3 presents an overview of culture and cultural differences; this chapter is shorter than the others because, in all of the other chapters, there is a content/topic-specific focus on culture and cultural differences. It is impossible to discuss schools, homes, peers, testing and assessment, underachievement, underrepresentation, and so forth without great consideration to culture and cultural differences.

At some point, all students are vulnerable or at risk for underachievement. A portion of students in every school, AP class, and gifted class, program, or service consistently shows a lack of academic, psychological, emotional, cultural, and social skills necessary to take full advantage of educational opportunities. Often, these students become "in-school dropouts" who are physically present but otherwise disillusioned or dis- enchanted with school or academics, as reflected by poor motivation, dis- interest, boredom, daydreaming, acting out, tardiness, or truancy. Some Black students openly reject schools, as reflected in the high dropout rates nationally. Describing these students as lazy, unmotivated, or disin- terested in school and learning fails to explain why some students flee or retreat from educational institutions and resist learning opportunities. It also places the blame for underachievement squarely on the shoulders of Black students, many of whom are the victims of larger social and envi- ronmental ills—at home, in the community, and at school.

I have made several changes to this edition, attempting to update and fill in missing links from some 15 years ago. In the first edition, a major oversight was evident in the discussion of underachieving gifted Black students: not situating underachievement within the context of the achievement gap. A major purpose of the second edition is to correct this shortcoming. I wish this particular topic were unnecessary, that we had made more progress in improving Black students' achievement such that the gap had, at minimal, narrowed and, at best, closed! Although it may be difficult to accept, decades of data indicate that Black students, on average, fail to achieve at the same levels as their White counterparts, even when students are from the same income and/or socioeconomic class. More specifically, Black high school students tend to perform 4 years behind White students in reading and math.

Another change in this edition is terminology. I have moved away from the term racially and culturally *diverse* to that of *different* to com- municate the reality that *everyone* has a culture; it is my belief that dif- ferences in culture too often and, unnecessarily so, contribute to clashes and disharmony. Another oversight was not focusing on gifted students in K–8 settings, and little attention was given to what happens to these students in AP classes. Where appropriate, AP is included, so the focus is on what is (or is not) happening at the high school level. Having said this, I must admit that I do not believe that AP is best way to serve gifted students in high schools. Relatedly, in this revised book, I argue that the achievement gap cannot close unless two major issues are reconciled: More Black students must be placed in gifted education and AP classes and, conversely, fewer must be placed in special education. Borrowing from the blunt statement of Reverend Lowry on C-SPAN in 2006, "We must be as diligent about closing the achievement gap as we were about creating it."

Other changes to the book include more attention to testing Black

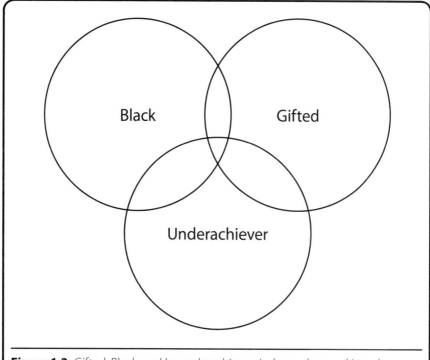

Figure 1.2. Gifted, Black, and/or underachiever: Independent and interdependent identities.

students and the ongoing and new problems and concerns, including issues like stereotype threat discussed by Claude Steele, work by Janet Helms and A. Wade Boykin on the impact of culture and cultural styles on test performance, and the promises that nonverbal measures hold for increasing identification, found in the work of Jack Naglieri.

The focus on programs also has changed. In the original book, I highlighted the Javits program. This book highlights gifted and general education programs found to be effective with identifying, placing, and serving gifted or potentially gifted Black students. Although other minor but important changes will be noted by readers, the final major one is the replacement of the original chapter on my research with gifted Black underachievers to a more recent study that focuses more on the notion and problem of "acting White" among gifted and potentially gifted Black students. This study first appeared in *Urban Education* (Ford, Grantham, & Whiting, 2008a). My work on "acting White" was inspired, so to speak, years ago by Signithia Fordham and John Ogbu.

Students comprising three demographic variables, illustrated in Figure 1.2, are the focus of this book: (a) Black, (b) gifted, and (c) underachiever. These variables operate independently and interdependently. It is a sad reality that little work exists on students who are gifted *and* (*but?*) underachieving. This is an oxymoron for many—how can one be gifted and underachieve? Likewise, little work exists on students who are gifted *and* Black. It can even be said that this is an oxymoron to some. On the other hand, there is a great deal of work on students who are Black *and* (*but?*) underachieving. This seems to be expected.

Underachieving students, especially if gifted, fall into a gray area in education. Those students who manifest specific identifiable academic/learning problems (e.g., learning disabilities, behavioral disorders, emotional problems) may qualify for special education programs and assistance. Students who manifest more subtle educational problems are likely to receive little or no meaningful assistance. Specifically, underachieving gifted students with subtle or nonspecific problems are seldom evaluated for learning difficulties and special services, primarily due to high intelligence or achievement test scores. Subsequently, they may slip through the cracks in standard diagnostic screening procedures and muddle through school.

Most descriptions of underachieving students focus on academic and intellectual underachievement. One is more likely to hear of a student who has poor motivation in math, reading, and science, for example, than in creativity, leadership, and other areas of giftedness, as in a few of the scenarios above. Yet, we all know people gifted or exceptional in the art of persuasion who use this skill in nonproductive or socially unacceptable ways (e.g., gang leaders, corrupt politicians). We all know students who show great skill in the visual and performing arts, but are too shy or anxious to perform for an audience.

Most descriptions of underachievers also support a deficit perspective: poor or lack of study skills, task commitment, motivation, organization, memory, self-concept, self-esteem, racial identity, and so forth. These characteristics, however, focus on the child/student and the symptoms of underachievement, rather than the etiology of underachievement. The result of focusing on the student, of blaming the victim, is that he or she is considered less desirable, less salvageable than other students. Unfortunately, educators are unable to deal with students who deviate too much from the norm and stereotypes; schools are designed for and cater to students who hold social capital and who are independent learners who excel, achieve, and fulfill the expectations of teachers, other educators, and parents/caregivers.

Students who underachieve are not born lazy or unmotivated. Many children *learn* to underachieve. For example, because of keen insight, an ability to note inconsistencies, as well as sensitivity to social injustices, many gifted Black students are aware of the contradictions between their academic learning and lived experiences. They grow critical and wary of the meritocratic ideology promoted in schools, and they are cognizant of race, class, and gender prejudice and discrimination in schools. This constant feedback can demotivate Black students and wreak havoc on their desire to participate in a system perceived as unresponsive, unjust, and otherwise discriminatory.

Despite widespread problems associated with underachievement in schools, the study of gifted underachievers is relatively new. Terman and Oden (1947) contended that "Circumstances [that] affect the fruition of human talent are questions of such transcendent importance that they should be investigated by every method that promises the slightest reduction of our ignorance" (p. 352). Yet, resolving underachievement among gifted students does not appear to be a high priority in the educational arena, including gifted education. Comparatively speaking, too few articles, books, and empirical studies have appeared in the professional and scholarly literature on gifted underachievers. Even fewer have appeared on underachieving gifted Black students.

PURPOSE

This book has several objectives, the overriding of which is to maximize learning opportunities and outcomes among Black students who have been formally identified as gifted, but are failing to reach their potential, and among Black students whose potential is undiscovered or unrecognized. Given their lack of formal identification and access to services for gifted students, undiscovered gifted students become underachievers. Like muscles, talent that is undiscovered or ignored will likely atrophy; figuratively speaking, if you don't use it, you lose it. This is not to say that gifted students become "ungifted," but instead, that their interests, motivation, and skills weaken. Thus, the students are less likely to demonstrate their gifts, and they are less likely to be recognized as gifted or highly capable or having great potential.

Although effective academic instruction serves as a primary and important method for promoting students' success, there are other methods of maximizing learning opportunities and outcomes for gifted and potentially gifted Black students. These methods include controlling or eliminating the effects of social, educational, familial, cultural, and psychological factors that inhibit the learning and potential of capable and promising Black students.

Sadly, schools appear to permit some degree of marginality; that is, a disconnection between students and the conditions designed for learning. In other words, schools allow individuals or subgroups to develop and sustain faulty, incomplete relationships with other school members and programs. Most schools tolerate the existence of a fringe population that is not fully involved in the mainstream school life. These marginal[3] students learn to contribute only a fraction of what they can; they use only a portion of their potential at school (Sinclair & Ghory, 1987).

BLACK STUDENTS

Life on the margins is an all too familiar reality for Black students. More than other racially and culturally different students, Black youth face social and environmental problems that inhibit their achievement motivation and educational outcomes. Racism is alive and well in many schools, and stereotypes about Black students, especially Black males, persist among teachers and school personnel. Such social problems exacerbate and are exacerbated by educational problems. When Black students fail to achieve at high levels, a vicious circle ensues. In the minds of some educators, these Black students fit into stereotypic roles assigned to Blacks; when they fail to achieve in school, they are destined to a life of social and economic disadvantage, unemployment, and underemployment. Society can avoid the costly problems associated with social and educational issues by investing now to develop the potential of all students. As noted by several authors in the aptly titled book *Overlooked Gems: A National Perspective on Low-Income Promising Learners*, edited by VanTassel-Baska and Stambaugh (2007), we can and must look for gifts and talents early among students, particularly among low-income and/or low-SES students. Ultimately, the cost of poor educational experiences and outcomes is significantly higher than the cost of good or excellent schools and schooling.

What are indicators of effective schools and educationally well children? Healthy children achieve to their potential in school because their talents (be they academic, leadership, creativity, or the arts) are recog-

---

3   Such students have also been called underachievers, low achievers, economically disadvantaged students, dropouts, and so forth. Irrespective of the term used, these students are educationally disadvantaged, and their educational needs are not being met. These students are failing in school, and schools are failing these students.

nized and nurtured. They hold positive self-attitudes and self-images as learners and racial or cultural beings, as well as positive attitudes toward their families and school. These children also have positive relations with teachers and peers (e.g., see Search Institute, 2010).

Healthy schools adopt prescriptive and proactive measures designed to increase students' well-being (e.g., Carter, 2000). Children with different needs (academic, social, cultural, psychological) are achieving at high levels. Teachers hold high expectations and positive attitudes toward students irrespective of their gender, race, language, income, and/or socioeconomic status. There is consistent and substantive collaboration between the home and school. Student motivation and interests are high, and teachers are prepared to work to meet students' academic and nonacademic needs. Administration, faculty, and staff are respectful and accepting of individual and group differences. They have a healthy respect for culture and cultural differences. Culture is defined as the collective beliefs, attitudes, traditions, customs, and behaviors that serve as a filter through which a group of people view and respond to the world (Ford & Harris, 1999; Hall, 1959, 1976; Hofstede, 2001; Shade, Kelly, & Oberg, 1997). Culture is a way of life, a way of looking at and interpreting life, and a way of responding to life. Although culture is dynamic and ever-changing, group members often have shared beliefs, attitudes, traditions, customs, and behaviors (e.g., Storti, 1999). Chapter 3 devotes more attention to culture, and it is discussed throughout all chapters in some way or another.

To meet the needs of Black students, gifted education and AP courses must be pluralistic and culturally responsive (see Figure 1.3). Specifically, when schools are culturally responsive (rather than color- or culture-blind or assaultive): (a) the learning environment (e.g., ambiance, visuals) is examined and changed to be welcoming and supportive; (b) educators' philosophy includes respect for and acceptance of cultural differences; (c) the curriculum (e.g., books and materials) is multicultural and relevant to students' lives, as well as free of biases and stereotypes; (d) instruction is modified to affirm and address learning style differences that are culturally based; and (e) assessment is comprehensive, dynamic, and reduced in biases[4] and unfairness (e.g., Banks, 2006; Boykin, Tyler, Watkins-Lewis, & Kizzie, 2006; Ford, Grantham, & Whiting, 2008a, 2008b; Ford & Harris, 1999; Ford & Kea, 2009; Gay, 2002; Ladson-Billings, 2009).

---

4   Much controversy surrounds this issue of test bias; some scholars adopt the position that tests are no longer biased; others disagree. I support the position that tests will always be biased; the best we can do is to select and use tests with the lowest amount of bias and the highest degree of psychometric integrity—those that are valid, reliable, and normed with culturally different groups.

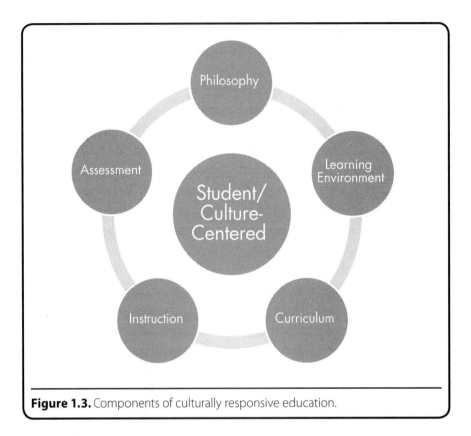

Figure 1.3. Components of culturally responsive education.

The degree or extent to which schools work to reduce or eliminate impediments to achievement is a barometer of their wellness. Contrary to popular opinion and practice, test scores are not necessarily the most important indicator of school wellness.

As described below, research is consistent in its findings that many Black students do not manifest the characteristics of educational well-being briefly described. Specifically, they are overrepresented in educational and social situations that place them at risk for educational disadvantage (e.g., special education, school suspension, dropping out), and underrepresented in educationally, economically, and socially advantaged situations; that is, in educational settings (e.g., gifted education, AP classes, prestigious colleges and universities) and situations that have a lot of social capital (e.g., graduation, college attendance).

AREAS OF UNDERREPRESENTATION

Numerous reports and studies describe the dismal educational status of Black students in schools. The Carnegie Corporation of New York

(1984/1985), the College Board (1985, 2002, 2008, 2009), Governors' Commission on Socially Disadvantaged Males (1989), Schott Foundation for Public Education (2006, 2007, 2008, 2009), U.S. Department of Education (e.g., 2002, 2003, 2004, 2006b, 2008), and other reports have revealed the dismal educational status of Black students in schools. Black students, particularly Black males, face a high probability of being referred to and placed in special education (Donovan & Cross, 2002), but are only half as likely to be placed in a class for the gifted (U.S. Department of Education, 2006b, 2008) and AP classes (Barton & Coley, 2009; College Board, 2009; Education Trust, 2009). Specifically, in 2006, Black students were underrepresented by 47% in gifted education; Black females were underrepresented by 35% and Black males by 55% (U.S. Department of Education, 2006b). This 47% equates to more than 250,000 Black students (101,000 Black females and 153,000 Black males) who were not identified as gifted (see Figure 1.4). Suffice it to say, no other group of students is as underrepresented in gifted education and AP classes as Black students (especially Black males).

As also shown in Figure 1.4, not only are Black students under-enrolled in gifted education programs, they are underrepresented in AP classes (College Board, 2009; U.S. Department of Education, 2006b, 2008), high-track groups, high-ability groups, and academic programs at all educational levels: kindergarten through grade 12, baccalaureate degrees, and graduate degrees. Moreover, the higher the level of education, the greater the degree of underrepresentation and the lower the graduation rate. In terms of academic courses, Black students are less likely than White students to be enrolled in math, physical sciences, and social studies; if enrolled in higher level classes such as calculus, algebra, trigonometry, and geometry, they are less likely to have the same number of years of such coursework as White students (Barton & Coley, 2009; College Board, 2009). The College Board (2009) reported that Blacks represented 14.4% of graduating students in high schools but only 7.8% of those taking AP exams. Further, AP courses were less likely to be offered in urban than suburban schools; specifically, Black students are the most likely to attend schools that do not offer any AP programs. Nineteen percent of Black students attend such schools, compared to 6% of Asian American students, 12% of Hispanic American students, and 14% of White students. In addition, fewer AP classes are offered in schools with high minority populations.

Regarding the equity index, the greatest discrepancy was for Black students, and in only one state—Hawaii—are Black students propor-

OCR Civil Rights Data Projections 2006

Data Items	Sex	American Indian/Alaska Native		Asian/Pacific Islander		Hispanic		Black (non-Hispanic)		White (non-Hispanic)		Total	
		Number	%	Number	%	Number	%	Number	%	Number	%	Number	%
Membership	M	305,536	0.63	1,196,644	2.47	5,074,850	10.46	4,222,890	8.71	14,107,371	29.09	24,907,290	51.36
	F	294,725	0.61	1,134,384	2.34	4,821,882	9.94	4,085,872	8.42	13,253,614	27.33	23,590,477	48.64
	Total	600,261	1.24	2,331,028	4.81	9,896,732	20.41	8,308,762	17.13	27,360,985	56.42	48,497,767	100
Gifted and talented	M	14,997	0.46	148,485	4.59	202,910	6.27	128,142	3.96	1,084,470	33.50	1,579,004	48.78
	F	16,365	0.51	155,731	4.81	211,148	6.52	168,004	5.19	1,106,740	34.19	1,657,988	51.22
	Total	31,362	0.97	304,216	9.40	414,058	12.79	296,146	9.15	2,191,210	67.69	3,236,992	100
Enrolled in AP	M	3,638	0.22	81,900	4.95	88,960	5.37	47,102	2.85	499,499	30.17	721,098	43.56
	F	5,124	0.31	93,736	5.66	131,752	7.96	84,165	5.08	619,631	37.43	934,408	56.44
	Total	8,762	0.53	175,636	10.61	220,712	13.33	131,267	7.93	1,119,130	67.60	1,655,506	100
AP Mathematics	M	973	0.22	35,038	7.98	25,111	5.72	10,151	2.31	153,405	34.96	224,678	51.20
	F	1,019	0.23	32,853	7.49	25,490	5.81	13,923	3.17	140,887	32.10	214,172	48.80
	Total	1,992	0.45	67,891	15.47	50,601	11.53	24,074	5.49	294,292	67.06	438,850	100
AP Science	M	1,120	0.25	35,445	7.91	25,313	5.65	11,722	2.61	144,494	32.23	218,095	48.65
	F	1,289	0.29	34,381	7.67	28,666	6.39	18,918	4.22	146,987	32.79	230,241	51.35
	Total	2,409	0.54	69,826	15.57	53,979	12.04	30,640	6.83	291,481	65.01	448,336	100
AP Foreign Language	M	333	0.15	8,548	3.75	33,725	14.78	4,142	1.81	39,756	17.42	86,504	37.90
	F	463	0.20	12,343	5.41	52,166	22.86	8,817	3.86	67,921	29.76	141,710	62.10
	Total	796	0.35	20,891	9.15	85,891	37.64	12,959	5.68	107,677	47.18	228,214	100
AP other subjects	M	3,328	0.23	69,853	4.80	76,101	5.23	42,674	2.93	421,766	28.98	613,722	42.17
	F	4,998	0.34	85,889	5.90	108,456	7.45	78,001	5.36	564,227	38.77	841,571	57.83
	Total	8,326	0.57	155,742	10.70	184,557	12.68	120,675	8.29	985,993	67.75	1,455,293	100

Figure 1.4. Demographics of gifted education and AP: Gender and racial representation. Adapted from U.S. Department of Education 2006 National and State Projections (http://ocrdata.ed.gov/Projections_2006.aspx).

tionately represented in AP classes (College Board, 2009). Similarly, in terms of college studies, Black students are underrepresented in the vast majority of degree areas, especially STEM areas—science, technology, engineering, and math (College Board, 2002, 2008, 2009). These injustices have not gone unnoticed by the Office for Civil Rights (U.S. Department of Education, 2008).

AREAS OF OVERREPRESENTATION

Black students are consistently overrepresented in special education, in the lowest ability groups and tracks, and among high school and college dropouts, the underemployed and unemployed, and, accordingly, the economically disadvantaged. In terms of college enrollment and degree areas, Black students are underrepresented in *all* fields of study *except* the social sciences and education (Barton & Coley, 2009; College Board, 2009; Education Trust, 2006, 2009).

In the case of low-track and low-ability classes, gifted education has been met with criticism (National Association for Gifted Children [NAGC], 1997, 2009). The field has been charged with elitism. Regarding ability grouping, research has consistently found poor quality of curriculum and instruction, a negative classroom climate, as well as poor teacher interaction and low student expectations (Kozol, 2005; Oakes, 1982, 1983, 1985, 1987, 1988, 2005, 2008; Orfield & Frankenberg, 2007; Orfield & Lee, 2007; Peske & Haycock, 2006). Lower track classes foster lower self-esteem, lower educational aspirations, lower levels of cognition (e.g., critical thinking, information processing, making inferences, synthesizing material), and, ultimately, few(er) opportunities for academic, social, and economic mobility.

All of the aforementioned educational problems fall under the umbrella of the achievement gap, which includes a myriad of contributing factors or correlates in some way or another (Federal Interagency Forum on Child and Family Statistics, 2009). This Federal Interagency Forum on Child and Family Statistics (2009) report identified indicators of children's well-being, categorizing them as (a) family and social environment, (b) economic circumstances, (c) health care, (d) physical environment and safety, (e) behavior, (f) education, and (g) health (see Figure 1.5).

In their comprehensive work, Barton (2003) and Barton and Coley (2009) reviewed hundreds of studies and, by way of meta-analyses, identified the top 14 (in 2003) and 16 (in 2009) correlates of the achievement gap. These gaps cluster into three major categories (home, school, health), as reflected in Figure 1.6. Of these 16 correlates (which overlap with those presented in Figure 1.5), lack of rigor in the curriculum ranks as number one. Acknowledging that *all* of the factors need to be addressed in their own right, for purposes of this book, I focus on two of the three major categories of factors. Chapter 6 focuses on the school factors, and Chapter 7 focuses on home factors.

CONCLUSION

The collective results suggest that Black students are less likely to be educated for self-determination, independence, and social empowerment than are White students; relatedly, they are more likely to be prepared for vocations that promise a life of dependency in the economic and social underclass (Children's Defense Fund, 2008; College Board, 1985, 2002, 2008, 2009; Education Trust, 2009; Schott Foundation for Public Education, 2009).

Many factors contribute to the poor participation of Black students in gifted education programs and AP classes. Without increased attention and substantive commitments to redress these issues, gifted programs will continue to be racially and economically segregated. Black students will continue to be underserviced educationally, unidentified as gifted, and underrepresented among formally identified gifted students.

This book seeks to ensure equity in access to educational opportunities for gifted Black students. Despite the *Brown v. Board of Education* (1954) landmark decision, Black students still find themselves at serious educational disadvantage in many schools, and gifted programs continue to be racially and economically stratified. Nowhere is this lack of access to equity more evident than in gifted education and AP classes, where Black and economically disadvantaged students are significantly underrepresented and, thus, underserved.

Indicators of children's well-being	Specific indicators
Family and social environment	Family structure and children's living arrangements; births to unmarried women; adolescent births; child care; children of at least one foreign-born parent; language spoken at home and difficulty speaking English; child maltreatment
Economic circumstances	Child poverty and family income; secure parental employment; food security
Health care	Health insurance coverage; usual source of health care; childhood immunization; oral health
Physical environment and safety	Outdoor and indoor air quality; drinking water quality; lead in the blood of children; housing problems; youth victims of serious violent crimes; child injury and mortality; adolescent injury and mortality
Behavior	Regular cigarette smoking; alcohol use; illicit drug use; sexual activity; youth perpetrators of serious violent crimes
Education	Family reading to young children; mathematics and reading achievement; high school academic course taking; high school completion; youth neither enrolled in school nor working; college enrollment
Health	Preterm birth and low birth weight; infant mortality; emotional and behavioral difficulties; adolescent depression; activity limitation; diet quality; overweight; asthma

Figure 1.5. National indicators of children's well-being. Adapted from Federal Interagency Forum on Child and Family Statistics (2009).

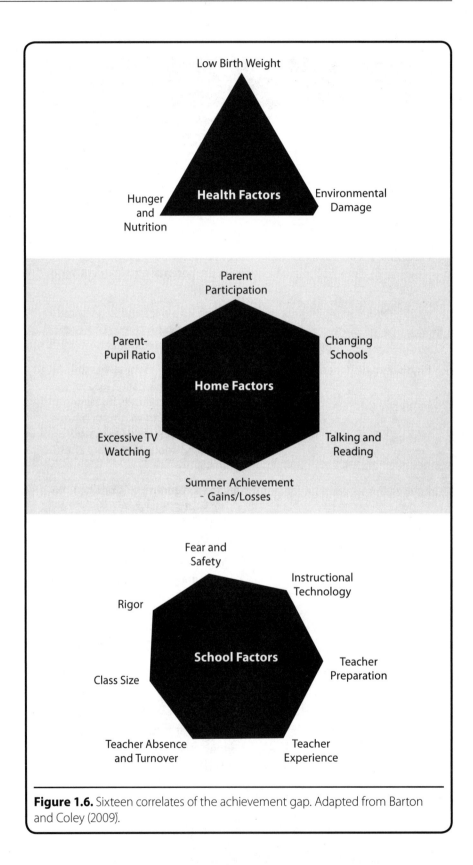

Figure 1.6. Sixteen correlates of the achievement gap. Adapted from Barton and Coley (2009).

CHAPTER TWO

LEGAL AND HISTORICAL PERSPECTIVES

*Few would deny that all human beings are due equal consid-
eration and respect. Few would deny that individuals should
enjoy the opportunity to rise as far as their talents and abilities may carry them.*

—Salomone (1986, p. 17)

Underachieving students were seldom studied prior to the mid-1950s,
perhaps because it was not until that time that measurement and prediction of ability and achievement were accepted; perhaps because social
and political interest had not focused on the problem (McCall, Evahn,
& Kratzer, 1992). In 1957, however, the Soviets launched the first satel-
lite into space, followed shortly by the United States' failure to duplicate
that feat. Subsequently, much concern arose about the current and future
technological ability of the U.S. and its most capable or promising students. Allegations ran rampant that schools were not preparing students
to compete on an international level. Social, political, and educational
attention turned to gifted achievers as well as underachievers—students
with superior intellectual ability who perform below the potential that is
expected or predicted.

This chapter focuses on how interest in both gifted students and poor achievers (low achievers and underachievers) has been cyclical and sporadic. It is primarily during times of crises and reactivity that gifted students are given increased attention, and that educators and policymakers call for reforms, excellence, and equity for gifted students, including those in AP classes. Relatedly, students in low-income and low-SES communities also are given greater attention in the context of reforming schools.

With the numerous reform reports of the 1980s and others since then, some attention has focused on low- and underachieving students, some of whom were gifted and many of whom are Black, as well as low income and/or low SES. There are two current foci of interest regarding the issue of poor achievement: low achievement and underachievement. As described below, the first focuses on economically challenged students, the majority of whom are minority or culturally different students; the second focuses on gifted students and those in AP classes.

QUESTIONS TO CONSIDER

❖ How similar have reactions been to gifted students and Black students relative to equitable educational opportunities? To what extent have both groups experienced a love-hate relationship in educational arenas and, ultimately, some form of benign neglect?

❖ Despite historical battles, so to speak, to achieve educational excellence and equity in school settings, why have the histories of gifted students and Black students been parallel rather than overlapping?

❖ What can be learned from legal/court cases that can and do inform gifted education practices relative to Black students?

HISTORICAL PERSPECTIVE ON LEGISLATION IMPACTING THE EDUCATION OF GIFTED AND BLACK STUDENTS

The road to educational excellence, equality, and equity, with its trials and tribulations, has not been smooth for three groups of students:

(a) gifted students; (b) low-income and/or low-SES students; and (c) Black and other culturally and racially different students. The respective histories of these students and their families have been and continue to marked by persistent battles to ensure that students formally identified as gifted (students requiring educational services beyond those normally provided in the schools in order to more fully develop and nurture their specific talents; U.S. Department of Education, 2003), low income and/or low SES, and Black and other racial and culturally different students receive the quality of services to which, as students and educational consumers, they are entitled (*Brown v. Board of Education*, 1954).

America has consistently shown a love-hate relationship with gifted students (Gallagher, 1988), mainly due to perceptions or misperceptions that special educational programs and AP classes for gifted students are elitist, inequitable, and undemocratic. The now-familiar argument of opponents is quite similar to the Matthew[1] effect (Stanovich, 1986), the-rich-get-richer-and-the-poor-get-poorer phenomenon.

There has also been resistance to special educational programs for economically disadvantaged students who are low income and/or low SES, as well as to racially and culturally different students. For example, when additional funding is allocated to the poorest schools (most often comprised of Black students), arguments supporting the Robin Hood effect mount and take a life of their own. Opponents contend that we are "taking from the rich, to give to the poor"—or some version of this position. This notion of who is "deserving" is akin to academic triage in the medical professional whereby those with authority or power believe that, to help one individual—based on perceived merit—is to sacrifice another of great value or worth. In school settings, academic triage is also evident when educators and administrators make decisions about who is "worth saving" or "salvageable": those with mild, moderate, or severe needs? Those who are low income and/or low SES versus high income and/or high SES? Those who are White versus those who are not? Do we intervene on behalf of one, two, or all three individuals or groups?

The result of the aforementioned beliefs and positions, arguments and conflicts is the pitting of students against each other; blaming them for their individual differences, cultural differences, and lack of "standardization" relative to the status quo. Stated differently, educators appear to

---

1   The concept of the Matthew effect originates from the Gospel according to Saint Matthew: "For whosoever hath, to him shall be given, and he shall have more abundance; but whosoever hath not, from him shall be taken away even that he hath" (13:12). "For unto everyone that have shall be given, and he shall have abundance: but from him that hath not shall be taken away even which he hath" (25:29).

be comfortable and complacent with standardization; it ensures routine and promises simple solutions to simple and/or complex or multifaceted problems. Our tolerance and reverence for variance among students is astonishingly mixed. Students are expected, for instance, to fit age- and culturally appropriate norms, curricular standards, and to meet test score means and procedures, but to not deviate far from the statistical hump of the normal or bell curve in any given area. Yet, like height and weight, deviation from the norm is normal and ought to be expected.

LEGISLATION IMPACTING BLACK STUDENTS

For the ancient Greeks, education epitomized a collective interest of the higher order. It represented the primary process by which society preserves and transmits its physical and intellectual character. Education in the United States borrowed its principles of democracy from this ideal of the common ethos, of the collective good.

To state the obvious, education is viewed as many things: the great equalizer (see the works of Horace Mann) that fosters critical thinking, socialization, upward and social mobility, and, ultimately, democracy. Given such views of education, it has been elevated in stature over the centuries, from a public benefit to a guaranteed right (Salomone, 1986) and a civil right (Banks, 2006).

Prior to the mid-20th century, the federal government treaded reactively and gingerly on educational territory. During this time, the United States witnessed a cataclysmic event that changed the power and focus of education, namely, *Brown v. Board of Education* (1954). In 2009, the United States commemorated the 55th anniversary of one of the most significant rulings in the history of the U.S. Supreme Court. In *Brown*, the Court recognized that "education is perhaps the most important function of state and local governments" (p. 493). Further, the Court ruled that the "segregation of children in public schools solely on the basis of race, even though the physical facilities and other 'tangible' factors may be equal" (*Brown v. Board of Education*, 1954, p. 493) not only deprived them of equal educational opportunities, but also violated their right to equal protection of laws guaranteed under the Fourteenth Amendment to the United States Constitution. *Brown* is the foundation upon which all subsequent developments ensuring the legal rights of the disenfranchised rest.

Brown represents a legal and moral imperative grounded in the principle of equality, the principle that all children should receive an education on equal terms. Not only did the mandate acknowledge the inherent worth of Black students, it argued that desegregated and/or racially segregated schools are unequal and unjust—as well as "un-American." The seminal case of *Brown* laid the foundation for equality and guided, directly and indirectly, a litany of educational decisions affecting Black students into the next century. The decision was based on the premise that racial discrimination violates our national sense of morality and equity.

The 1960s ushered in compensatory educational programs designed to redress inequities in learning opportunities for economically challenged students, particularly racial and culturally diverse students. Programs such as Head Start and Title I had the expressed goal of closing the educational gap (or gulf) between economically challenged and advantaged children and students, between poverty and plenty. The ultimate goal was to ensure the educational success of all students, regardless of their racial, cultural, income, and socioeconomic background, by equipping them with the skills necessary to compete in educational and social arenas.

The mid-1960s experienced the War on Poverty and Great Society Programs, which represented dramatic calls to reform education based on the equality principle. The Great Society Programs were justified on a theory of education as an "investment in human capital" (Schultz, 1961); rhetoric regarding the "wasted talented" flooded the educational scene, including gifted education programs at the elementary level and AP at the high school level.

In 1964, Congress enacted the Civil Rights Act. Title VI prohibits discrimination on the basis of race, color, and national origin in federally assisted programs. The act put teeth into the enforcement of the *Brown* mandate (Salomone, 1986) by helping to achieve substantial school desegregation, particularly in the South.

By the late 1970s, the United States witnessed a groundswell of opposition to both the equality and equity principle, specifically the reforms it generated. Salomone (1986) asserted that, to a society that valued merit and talent, we added the criteria of need and social neglect. And, in the process of meeting that national agenda, individual choice and community preference became all but irrelevant in the wider educational policy arena. As laws were passed to protect the rights of culturally different and economically challenged students, backlash mounted. Opponents demanded a greater deference to the individual rights of the majority. Fingers pointed to court-ordered busing to achieve racial balance, the redistribution of funds to achieve fiscal equity, and compensatory and bilingual education programs as culprits for various educational evils, including low achievement scores (Ford, 1996; Salomone, 1986). Albeit a legal case from the business field, also important to the discussion is the court case *Griggs v. Duke Power Co.* (1971).

Before the passage of the Civil Rights Act of 1964, Duke Power had a long-standing policy of segregating employees according to race. Namely, at its Dan River plant, Blacks were only allowed to work in its labor department, which constituted the lowest paying positions at Duke Power. After the Civil Rights Act was passed, the company changed its policies, namely adding a requirement of a high school diploma or a minimum score on an aptitude test for positions or promotions in areas other than the labor department. This decision had the effect of eliminating many Black applicants. The Supreme Court ruled against the policy used by Duke Power in selecting employees for such transfers and promotions based on a high school education and qualifying scores on an aptitude test. It was found that Black applicants, less likely to hold a high school diploma and averaging lower scores on the aptitude tests, were selected at a much lower rate for these positions compared to White applicants. In sum, given that the aptitude tests and the high school diploma requirement were broad-based and not directly related to the jobs in question, Duke Power's policy was found by the Court to be in violation of the Civil Rights Act. That is, the Court found that under Title VII of the Civil Rights Act, if such tests disparately impact racial groups, businesses must demonstrate that they are "reasonably related" to the job for which the test is required.

In the 1980s, a wave of educational reform movements highlighted the nature and extent of underachievement nationally. Goodlad (1984), Sizer (1984), and Boyer (1983), for instance, described the dismal state of education for gifted students and racially and culturally different students, including underachievement on both national and international levels. For example, the reports revealed that at least 50% of gifted students were failing to reach their academic potential (National Commission on Excellence in Education, 1983). Other reports have found similar results. Issues surrounding the "rising tide of mediocrity" and the nature and extent of the "imperiled educational system" resulted in renewed, but reactionary and temporary, fervor for change and action (e.g., reform).

Legislation and calls for reform are ongoing. Many of the advances regarding desegregation in public schools settings are being reversed such that some school districts are as segregated or more segregated than they were in the 1960s. Unfortunately, regression rather than progression is becoming all too common in the 21st century as schools reconsider rezoning and the efficacy of desegregated classrooms.

Issues regarding diversity in educational settings do not stop at the high school levels. In recent years, there have been many collegiate cases. Allegations of reverse discrimination cannot be ignored in gifted education and AP classes as we seek to increase access. It is becoming increasingly clear that the Supreme Court has grown more and more skeptical of affirmative action programs in recent decades, and affirmative action remains a controversial political issue today.

One of the most telling and debatable cases of reverse discrimination is *Regents of the University of California v. Bakke* (1978). Despite Allan Bakke's victory on the specific issue of his admission to medical school, the *Bakke* decision actually served to solidify the use of racial classifications within carefully constructed affirmative action programs. In the decades since, the Court has suggested that programs like these are under mounting scrutiny and require increasingly narrow construction and interpretation. For example, in *Wygant v. Jackson Board of Education* (1986), the Court held that a contract that gave minority teachers more protection against layoffs than White teachers was unfair. Similarly, in *City of Richmond v. J. A. Croson Co* (1989), the Court struck down a municipal program that set aside 30% of all public works contracts for minority businesses. In both cases, the Court found inadequate proof of specific, local discrimination to warrant the use of racial classifications. It insisted that affirmative action programs employing racial classifications were still permissible, but only when constructed as a remedy for proven and specific discrimination in the past.

In 2003, the Court returned to the issue of affirmative action programs in higher education by considering two cases involving the University of Michigan. Specifically, *Gratz v. Bollinger* was concerned with the use of race in undergraduate admissions, and *Grutter v. Bollinger* was concerned with the law school admissions process. The result was another split decision that served notice that affirmative action programs employing racial classifications, while still acceptable, will be subject to very close scrutiny by the Court in the future. If racial classifications are applied too heavily, as was the case with Michigan's undergraduate admissions policies, according to the Court, they will be struck down. If race is used more carefully, along with many other factors in order to achieve diversity, the Court would accept it. However, Justice Sandra Day O'Connor added that the Court's support for even these more narrowly constructed programs was not endless or without boundaries.

Justice O'Connor's suggestion that the Court's patience for affirmative action was limited has been echoed in the political arena by state initiatives seeking an end to racial classifications in college admissions and public hiring. By way of illustration, in 1996, California voters passed Proposition 209, which made it illegal to grant preferential treatment to any individual or group on the basis of race, sex, color, ethnicity, or national origin in the operation of public employment, public education, or public contracting. The state of Washington passed a similar initiative in 1998, Nebraska did so in 2008, and the Florida legislature also prohibited the use of racial classifications in college admissions in 2000.

Undeniably, these events portend the end of a misguided and unfair strategy to redress past discriminatory practices. According to some critics, granting preferential treatment to minorities violates the rights of majorities. By separating performance from reward, affirmative action threatens America's educational and industrial superiority. It leaves a cloud of suspicion hanging over the achievements of all Blacks, and it may stall or prevent the development of a truly color-blind society.

On the other hand, proponents of affirmative action argue that, without it, America's colleges will never overcome the centuries of racial oppression. They remind of us the substantive decline in racially different students' enrollment at the University of California after the passage of Proposition 209. And, they argue that advocates of a racially neutral, level playing field ignore White privilege, meaning Whites still enjoy certain cultural and economic advantages—their own form of affirmative action. Whites have always benefited and continue to profit from racial preferences (Shmoop University, 2010).

Despite the proactive or reactionary calls for equity, however, many misconceptions permeated the reform efforts to make excellence and equity for economically challenged Black and other culturally different students difficult. First, excellence was equated with quantity rather than quality of school experiences. For instance, reform seemed to focus extensively on cognitive performance (e.g., higher test scores and graduation rates) at the expense of the quality of students' school experiences, an issue that is particularly important when discussing underachievement among Black and other racially and culturally different students.

Second, reformers often supported a common core curriculum that, by its very nature, promoted conformity and uniformity—a one-size-fits-all and culture-blind approach. In general, a common curriculum ignores individual group/cultural differences in learning, particularly the academic needs of gifted, culturally different, and underachieving students.

Third, the reform reports supported the erroneous belief that opportunity to achieve the recommended standards of excellence is equally distributed and within every child's reach. In essence, the reports virtually ignored the educational limitations posed by low socioeconomic status, minority status (racial and cultural differences), family influences, handicapping conditions, and racial and gender prejudices (American Association of Colleges of Teacher Education, 1984, 2006). The net or cumulative effect was a retreat to the nonproductive belief that focusing on group differences was anti-intellectual and anti-democratic. No longer were students viewed as individuals with different needs. In attempting to be democratic, reformers ignored the importance of research on group differences (e.g., gender, race, socioeconomic status) as general guidelines from which to educate students, especially racially and culturally different students. This research includes the reality that students attend school with different levels of access, resources, and readiness; and that students of the same socioeconomic background, family structure, community, age, and gender can and do achieve differently.

Finally, the surge of reform reports of the 1980s virtually ignored issues surrounding school desegregation, cultural and racial differences, gender, and special education (including gifted education). Equally problematic, the reports gave little attention to the educational and social implications of increasing racial and ethnic demographics in the schools (e.g., Planty et al., 2009).

IMPLICATIONS

Notwithstanding legal mandates and calls for educational reform, the problems facing gifted Black youth continue today as they did when I wrote the first edition of this book (Ford, 1996). Albeit almost two decades ago, the U.S. Department of Education (1993) brought to the nation's attention and, hopefully, conscious, problems that continue to plague gifted education. Among the concerns were the underachievement of gifted students and the persistent underrepresentation of culturally and racially different children, as well as economically challenged students in programs and services for gifted students. For instance, students whose family income fell into the lowest quartile constituted only 9% of students formally identified as gifted, students whose family income fell into the upper quartile constituted 47% of formally identified gifted students, and racially and culturally different students constituted 8.9% of participants in gifted education programs and services. U.S. Department of Education (2006b) data show little progress for Black students specifically.[2] These problems and injustices require continued, consistent, proactive, and assertive efforts to redress the attendant inequities.

Brown v. Board of Education (1954) represented a monumental decision for race relations in American schools. Gifted education can ill-afford to ignore this legislation. This mandate for educational equality has grown into increased demands for radical and substantive changes in social and educational institutions, particularly schools. In some ways, *Brown*'s mandate was modest in scope because it called merely for "equal treatment of equals" in the terms of respect for the dignity of all human beings (Salomone, 1986, p. 30). *Brown* neither guaranteed nor automatically produced behavioral changes in the real world. Attitudes, it seems, cannot always be legislated. It was not until the 1960s that the principle of equality truly served as a basis for broader and more far-reaching social reform through educational reform. The War on Poverty went beyond equal treatment and represented a commitment to proactively and aggressively redress the effects of historical social and educational inequities. President Johnson, in his graduation speech to Howard University, affirmed "We seek not just freedom but opportunity, not just legal equity but human ability, not just equality as a right and a theory, but equality as a fact and a result" (see Eastland & Bennett, 1979).

In short, President Johnson recognized that inequities run deeper than unequal educational resources. For instance, although numerous reform efforts have been ushered in to reverse poor educational outcomes for Black students, the problems have been stubborn to change. Due to various social, cultural, and psychological issues, Black students often face seemingly insurmountable hurdles that decrease their chances for success both during and after school life. At the same time, these barriers increase their probability for academic burnout. Likewise, these factors decrease the probability that Black students, particularly economically challenged students, will be identified as gifted in grades pre-K–12 and participate in AP classes in high schools.

The outlook is equally bleak for gifted students. Gallagher (1988)

2   Data from the U.S. Department of Education (2006b) indicate progress relative to Hispanic and American Indian students' representation in gifted education over several years. Conversely, Black students are the *only* group for whom progress is not evident. This reality cannot and must not be ignored or discounted.

described the love-hate relationship with gifted students, in which the products of talent are valued, but educational programs and services to gifted students are viewed as elitist and anti-democratic. The "threats" posed by the Soviet Union and Sputnik in the late 1950s and, more recently, by the rigorous Japanese educational system marshal reformers to redress the shortcomings in gifted education and AP classes. With the U.S. Department of Education (1993) report on the status of gifted education, attention to gifted students was expected to increase. The report revealed that gifted seniors in the U.S. ranked among the lowest of 13 countries studied: biology (ranked 13th), chemistry (13th), algebra (13th), physics (9th), and calculus and geometry (12th). More recent reports present similar findings. Sadly and frankly, after the threat or impending doom has passed, those programs wither away. Such reactive responses are inadequate and have the effect of sustaining an overall low regard for the needs of gifted students, especially during longer, less tumultuous times. As described below, if gifted education is ever to receive adequate attention, strong support must come from the federal government and from much greater proportions of the professional and lay citizenry.

AN OVERVIEW OF KEY LEGISLATION IMPACTING GIFTED EDUCATION

The major initial impetus in protecting the rights of students with disabilities may be found in two federal trial court rulings, *Pennsylvania Association for Retarded Children (PARC) v. Commonwealth of Pennsylvania* (1971, 1972) and *Mills v. Board of Education of the District of Columbia* (1972). Although far from identical (*Mills* was brought on behalf of Black students when the District of Columbia sought to ignore the educational rights of perhaps as many as 18,000 exceptional children), both cases were consistent with the reasoning of *Brown*; both were decided on the basis of equal protection and due process under the Fourteenth Amendment.

The educational or academic needs of students with disabilities have deservedly and rightfully garnered attention and protection over several decades. Yet, federal initiatives on the rights of gifted students have progressed only modestly and tentatively. For example, a 1969 bill was proposed, as a result of a White House Task Force on the Gifted and Talented, but suffered an initial defeat; however, it won passage as part of the Elementary and Secondary Education Amendments of 1970. This law called for the development of model programs for the gifted and talented, and made such programs eligible for federal financial assistance under Titles III and IV of the Elementary and Secondary Education Act (ESEA, 1965).

Acting on recommendations in the Marland Report (1972), which offered the first federal definition of the gifted, Congress established the United States Office of the Gifted and Talented. In the same year, amendments to the ESEA, Title IV of the Special Projects Act, made categorical funding available for gifted education. But the actual amount allotted came to about one dollar a year for each eligible student. According to the Davidson Institute for Talent Development (2009) and NAGC's (2009) *State of the States in Gifted Education*, little has changed. Progress is slow.

Progress appeared to be on the horizon when the Gifted and Talented Children's Education Act of 1978, extending the funding provisions of the Special Projects Act, became law. Yet, the optimism was short lived as it was repealed by the Omnibus Budget Reconciliation Act of 1981. The Budget Act also closed the Office of the Gifted and Talented, eliminated categorical funding from federal sources, and combined authorizations for gifted education and 29 other programs into a single block funding while reducing the funding by more than 40% (Karnes & Marquardt, 1991; NAGC, 2009).

As a wave of educational reform swept the nation in the early 1980s amid concerns over the growing tide of mediocrity, support for gifted and talented programs once again grew. The Jacob K. Javits Gifted and Talented Students Act of 1988, Title IV, Part B of the ESEA, marked the culmination of the efforts of gifted education proponents. The Javits Act reinstated and both expanded and updated the programs cut 7 years earlier.

> Its goal is to provide financial assistance to State and local educational agencies . . . to initiate a coordinated program of research . . . designed to build a nationwide capability in elementary and secondary schools to meet the special educational needs of gifted and talented students. (Sec. 3062 (b))

Also, it "shall give highest priority" to students who are economically disadvantaged, limited English proficient, or "with handicaps" (Sec. 3065 (a)(1)).

As needed, overdue, and welcome as the Javits Act was (and is), however, it has two major shortcomings from the vantage point of gifted education advocates who are also working on behalf of Black students. First, although it recognizes the importance of gifted education, it fails to mandate the creation of programs. Second, it includes none of the substantive or procedural due process safeguards available to students with disabilities and other special education needs. For substantive, effective due process to be satisfied, a governmental (or in this case, public school) policy or action merely needs to be rationally related to a legitimate governmental goal. In the absence of a national policy on gifted education, however, the rationality standard remains subject to continual interpretation and neglect. Further, because there is no federal policy on the identification and placement of gifted students or on challenges to a student's (inappropriate or non-) placement (NAGC, 2009), one must look in vain for even a rational basis for such a policy. These loopholes not only deny parents/caregivers and students the procedural safeguards they ought to enjoy, but also give rise to equal protection and equity issues. Consequently, all of its good intentions aside, states or localities that place a low priority on programs for gifted students can easily ignore the Javits Act.

Following the precedents set by the Supreme Court in *Brown*, *PARC* and *Mills* reflected a general awareness that the denial of education to students with disabilities violated their rights to equal protection. Thus, laws were enacted to secure their rights. Reasoning by analogy, one can suggest that because gifted students are inadequately served by existing programs, then equal or equitable protection demands that they, too, be provided with placements suited to their special talents and abilities. Moreover, because the Supreme Court's ruling in *Board of Education of Hendrick Hudson Central School District v. Rowley* (1982) refused to extend the coverage of the Education for All Handicapped Children Act (EAHCA, 1975) beyond the minimum required by law, one is left to ponder how to address giftedness, which now lacks federal statutory protection.

IMPLICATIONS

More than 50 years after the Supreme Court's monumental ruling, the promise of *Brown* remains unfulfilled for gifted students. Only one major federal law, the Jacob K. Javits Gifted and Talented Students Act of 1988, acknowledges their needs. Yet, it stops short of mandating the creation of special programs. State laws on gifted education run the gamut. In its recent report on the status of gifted education, NAGC (2009) reported that six states fully mandate gifted education, two states mandate gifted with unspecified funding, five states mandate gifted education without funding, and 19 states mandate gifted education with partial funding. Fifteen states have no mandate for gifted education. Historically, special attention to the needs of gifted students has been sporadic, reactionary, and ad hoc. What sporadic interest there is seems to have begun with the national reaction to the 1957 Sputnik launch. That era implicitly made gifted students the prime benefactors of major curricular reform, because it was propelled by the need to redress underachievement among highly capable students. Albert (1969) reported that, among all articles published on gifted students between 1927 and 1965, more than 90% appeared after the launch of Sputnik.

The initial and comparatively brief emphasis on gifted education raised many of the problems advocates of gifted education face today: underfunding, understaffing, benign neglect, and a sort of studied inattention to the discrete needs of gifted students. As Zirkel and Stevens (1987) reported, of the estimated 2.5 to 3 million gifted children[3] in the nation, only 1.2 million participate in programs for the gifted. Thus, even those districts providing gifted education often fail to serve all of their qualified students.

Less than half of the states mandate the establishment of programs for the gifted (Coleman & Gallagher, 1992a, 1992b; Davidson Institute for Talent Development, 2009; NAGC, 2009), and state guidelines tend merely to describe rather than mandate what is desirable. Even if gifted education is mandated, there is no funding in several states. Gallagher (1988) identified four factors contributing to this problem: (a) narrow definitions of gifted and subsequent identification procedures; (b) a lack of offerings at certain grade levels or in certain subject areas; (c) superficial provisions rather than substantive programs; and (d) a lack of understanding of the many and varied needs of gifted students.

This scarcity of high-quality programs is exacerbated by the fact that no mechanism exists to require mediocre programs to improve. Compounding the problem further are the pervasive inconsistencies in the shape and comprehensiveness of existing state and local initiatives. Some gifted students receive as little as one hour a week of special

---

3   This figure is based on students who score in the top 3% to 5% on intelligence. It, therefore, underestimates the number of gifted students in general, as well as those not served. If one adopts a talent pool perspective, the number of gifted students would be greater. The figure also ignores gifted students with strengths in creativity, visual and performing arts, leadership, and academics.

instruction, primarily in the form of pull-out programs (more accurately, provisions) that cannot possibly meet the range of the needs of many of these students (NAGC, 2009).

The dilemma confronting gifted education is complicated still further by the fact that many existing programs are illegally arbitrary (Alvino, McDonnel, & Richert, 1981) in so far as they inadequately address the equal protection and due process rights of students. The rapid growth in the literature relating to program content for the gifted has outstripped interest in the legal and educational problems associated with the identification and placement of these students (Shaw, 1986). Support services also are absent for formally identified gifted students. Legislative initiatives primarily support research and development, demonstration projects, personnel preparation, and studies of children with handicapping conditions (Gallagher, 1988). The Javits Act, the primary source of federal funding available for this subgroup of special education learners, fails to mandate the development of programs. Hence, it and any programs it spawns remain vulnerable to budget cuts and being phased out.

Again, gifted students frequently face educational and benign neglect. The National Commission on Excellence in Education (1983) stated that the most highly gifted students need a more enriched and acceleration curriculum than other students of high ability. As Harrington, Harrington, and Karns (1991) emphasized, these needs extend beyond cooperative learning, heterogeneous grouping, and the dumbing down of the curriculum. Rather, gifted students require a more intensive and individualized curriculum, more challenging tasks, increased opportunities for creative expression and enrichment, and practical guidance and experience.

Despite legislative shortcomings, a Gallup Poll commissioned by the National Association for Gifted Children ("Gallup Poll Finds Public Support," 1992) found substantial support for gifted programs. Sixty-one percent of respondents believed that schools should do more to challenge the "very smartest" students. Concomitantly, 77% supported programs for "slow" learners. Eighty-five percent would support funding for gifted programs only if it did not reduce the amount offered to average and below-average learners. This qualification is a familiar one, reflecting a perception similar to the Matthew effect described earlier.

A SPECIAL NOTE: THE OFFICE FOR CIVIL RIGHTS

The Office for Civil Rights (OCR), a division of the U.S. Department of Education, enforces five federal civil rights laws prohibiting discrimination on the basis of race, color, national origin, sex, disability, and age by recipients of federal financial assistance (see Title VI of the Civil Rights Act of 1964 on prohibiting discrimination based on race, color, and national origin). According to the U.S. Department of Education (2008), "These civil rights laws represent a national commitment to end discrimination in education programs and activities. Because most education institutions receive some type of federal financial assistance, these laws apply throughout the nation" (p. 1). These civil rights laws extend to:

- ❖ 17,618 public elementary and secondary education agencies;
- ❖ 4,276 colleges and universities; and
- ❖ thousands of institutions conferring certificates below the associate degree level, such as training schools for truck drivers and cosmetologists, and other entities, such as libraries, museums, and vocational rehabilitation agencies. (U.S. Department of Education, 2008, p. 1)

Consequently, these civil rights laws protect millions of students attending or seeking to attend our education institutions. In certain situations, the laws also protect persons who are employed or seeking employment at education institutions. Overall, these laws protect:

- ◇ more than 49.8 million students attending public elementary and secondary schools; and
- ◇ more than 18.2 million students attending degree-granting institutions, such as colleges and universities. (U.S. Department of Education, 2008, p. 2)

Enforcing these laws is critical to carrying out the mission of the U.S. Department of Education to promote student achievement and preparation for global competitiveness by fostering educational excellence and ensuring equal access. More than half (51%) of court cases are based on discrimination regarding disabilities; 16% of cases are based on race discrimination (U.S. Department of Education, 2008, p. 19).

SUMMARY

Many education reform reports highlight the major problems associated with underachievement nationally. Although they do not devote attention to gifted underachievers, it is clear that no student is exempt from failing to reach his or her potential. There are numerous studies on underachievers in general, yet the study of gifted underachievers is a relatively recent or novel phenomenon. A greater paucity of data exists regarding gifted Black students who underachieve.

The nation is indeed at risk for at least two reasons. First, gifted students are underidentified, underserved, and exploited during national and international crises. Second, the fastest growing segment of the school population, mainly Black students, is being systematically and effectively excluded from the benefits of educational opportunity (Irvine, 1991). Nowhere is this exclusion more evident than in gifted education and AP classes in which Black students, especially Black males, are unacceptably and unnecessarily scarce. Should business continue as usual, the chances of Black students being formally identified and served will remain dismally small, and the current educational economic and social conditions of gifted Black students will remain gloomy. Equality enjoys popular appeal in all education reform initiatives, but there is often too little attention to the fact that a quality education (e.g., as promised since *Brown v. Board of Education* in 1954) cannot *and* will not be achieved without equity and a commitment to social justice.

CHAPTER THREE

CULTURAL FACTORS AS CORRELATES OF UNDERACHIEVEMENT AND ACHIEVEMENT

In a sense, everything in education relates to culture. . . . Just as hammers and languages are tools by which we get things done, so is culture; indeed, culture can be thought of as the primary human toolkit.

—Erickson (2010, p. 35)

The topics of culture and cultural differences have had a significant impact on current research and practice, with data pointing to an ever-increasing cultural gap between teachers and students. In 1972, culturally different students represented 21% of the public school population; three decades later (as of 2006), data indicate that these groups, combined, comprised 42% of the public school population (Planty et al., 2009). This percentage is expected to increase. Such current and increasing diversity requires teachers and other educators to become culturally competent and, hence, responsive.

The term *culture* is often used and misused. Historically, the term was associated with aesthetic pursuits such as art, drama, ballet, and literature. These pursuits are typically referred to as *high culture* as opposed to *low culture*, which describes the more popular art of hip hop music and mass media entertainment. A second use of the word culture includes terms such as *hip hop culture*, *adolescent culture*, *drug culture*, and *culture of poverty*, suggesting that distinct groups possess certain characteristics that are common among members; accordingly, they are referred to as *subcultures*. A third use of the word refers to the process of growing material in a chemical laboratory. Culture is also used to refer to a society (e.g., British culture; Bullivant, 1993). This chapter takes culture to mean values, beliefs, attitudes, and norms common to a group bounded by race, gender, age, geography, religion, income, and/or social class. A major premise of this chapter is that educators must be culturally responsive in their beliefs and practice. To be culturally responsive is to be proactive and assertive at recognizing, addressing, and understanding students' cultural needs and development. Cultural competence includes dispositions, knowledge, and skills.

Shade and Edwards (1987) defined culture as the collective consciousness of a community with its own unique customs, rituals, communication style, coping patterns, social organization, and childrearing attitudes and patterns. Shade and New (1993) defined culture as an accumulation and aggregation of beliefs, attitudes, habits, values, and practices that form a view of reality. Similarly, Manning and Baruth (2010) defined culture as "people's values, language, religion, ideals, artistic expressions, patterns of social and interpersonal relationships, and ways of perceiving, behaving, and thinking" (p. 25). These patterns function as a filter through which a group of individuals views and responds to environmental demands. Cultural patterns are generally invisible and silent; they are experienced by individuals in terms of thinking, feeling, behaving, and being (Hall, 1959). Everyone has a culture. No one is born with a culture; instead, the culturalization process begins at birth—culture is learned or acquired as a function of being raised: first, in a family and community and, then, in a school or other social milieu.

> Culture shapes and is shaped by the learning and teaching that happens during the practical conduct of daily life within all the educational settings we encounter as learning environments throughout the human life span—in families, in school classrooms, in community settings, and in the workplace. (Erickson, 2010, p. 36)

Erickson (2010) goes on to emphasize that culture is dynamic rather than static, stating, "We continue to learn new culture until we die. Yet people learn differing sets and subsets of culture. And they can unlearn culture—shedding it as well as adopting it" (p. 36). When individuals have competence in and function effectively in more than one culture, they are bicultural.

It is generally agreed that academic achievement is one byproduct of the socialization process, and that the survival of an individual or group of individuals depends on the type of environment(s) faced. Haggard (1957) stated that academic achievement is an expression of the extent to which children are responsive to socialization pressures and are in the process of acquiring skills, attitudes, and so on that are prized in their sociocultural group. When one's culture is in sync with the status quo, that individual or group has cultural clout. These include expressive lifestyles (e.g., social interactive skills; styles in dressing and walking; language and communication styles). (For more information, see Boykin, 1994; Boykin, Albury, et al., 2005; Boykin, Tyler, & Miller, 2005; Boykin et al., 2006.)

As the following sections indicate, just as social and psychological factors affect students' academic engagement, motivation to achieve, and school performance, so too do cultural forces, particularly when they conflict with those of the predominant culture, defined herein as middle-class White Americans. When the values of the two cultures mesh, Black students are likely to reach their academic potential. However, when the values are different, antithetical, or even conflicting, underachievement may prevail.

QUESTIONS TO CONSIDER

❖ Why does culture matter in teaching, learning, and assessment?

❖ How can educators create learning environments where students feel a sense of membership?

❖ How can educators build trusting and nurturing relationships with students who come from culturally different backgrounds?

❖ How can educators create learning environments that honor the worth and dignity of marginalized students—students on the fringes?

❖ How do I as an educator benefit by becoming culturally competent?

THE NATURE AND IMPORTANCE OF CULTURE IN THE UNITED STATES

The United States is comprised of an overarching core culture, often referred to as the macroculture, as well as smaller cultures, referred to as microcultures (Banks, 2006, 2010). This distinction between various cultural levels is important because each culture influences the values, norms, and behaviors of its members. A key, idealistic characteristic of the macroculture is described in the Declaration of Independence—the belief that all human beings are created equal; that all individuals are endowed with certain unalienable rights, including life, liberty, and the pursuit of happiness. Other mainstream cultural values, beyond liberty, freedom, and democracy, include competition, power, and money.

Generally, three strands of theory attempt to explain the school performance of racially and culturally different groups: (a) cultural deficit, (b) cultural difference, and (c) cultural conflict theories. All of these theories carry different implications for the educational outcomes of gifted Black students.

CULTURAL DEFICIT THEORIES

Cultural deficit theories (Gould, 1995; Menacha, 1997; Valencia, 1997; Valencia & Solórzano, 1997) hold that the culture in which Black students are reared is inadequate and substandard relative to socialization and education. The culture and all that it represents and espouses is deemed not just different, but inferior. These theories carry a "blame the victim" orientation, and supporters look upon Blacks and other racially different groups as not only culturally but also intellectually inferior. Bernstein (1982) observed that:

> scientific evidence of racial inferiority simply allows some people to do with better conscience what they would have found a way to do anyway. . . . It would be good to report that all this belongs to some "medieval" past. But as we all know, the spirit of Yerkes and his ilk persists. (p. 20)

Relatedly, Erickson (2010) stated:

American anthropologists developed culture as a social science concept in the early 20th century. They invented it as an alternative to *race* as an explanation for why people around the world differed in their action and beliefs. The prevailing belief was that people around the world differed in their actions and beliefs. The prevailing belief was that people acted as they did because of genetic inheritance and that the "civilized" ways of Western Europeans made it evident that they were racially superior to non-Western peoples. (p. 34)

Further, it is difficult to forget and ignore the absurd assertions or polemic contentions of Herrnstein and Murray (1994), who proposed that Blacks were socially and "culturally disadvantaged."

Ogbu (1988) contended that the lives and accomplishments of different groups in the United States must be examined in light of their history and status in this nation. Specifically, immigrants or voluntary minorities come to the U.S. with a frame of reference that is often optimistic and supportive of the American Dream. They tend to believe that being in the U.S. presents greater opportunities for success and upward mobility than in their original country. Thus, they are more willing to assimilate and to give up those cultural variables that hinder progress in the U.S.

Differently, slaves and their Black ancestors are viewed as involuntary minorities—they neither immigrated to nor chose to come to the U.S.; they did not come to the U.S. seeking the American Dream or with an attitude of assimilation or even accommodation. Because Blacks were incorporated in the country involuntarily, they frequently have a caste-like minority status in which they are relegated to menial positions educationally, socially, culturally, and vocationally. They are often degraded and treated by Whites as inferior. According to deficit theories or perspectives, "different" is equated with deficient, inferior, and substandard. To wit, educators may cite cultural deficits as a reason for the disproportionately low achievement and intelligence test scores of Black students and, hence, their underrepresentation in gifted programs and AP classes.

Shade (1978) argued that social science has been able to alleviate any social guilt that might be generated by placing the blame for the academic difficulties on Blacks themselves. Specifically, apologists for our current educational practices are able to ground their conclusions in stigma theory, enabling them to define the problem in terms of bored, unmotivated, and apathetic children influenced by a less-than-adequate home environment. If the home environment were not at least initially stimulating, these children would come to preschool and kindergarten bored and apathetic. But they do not. Whatever their environment, nearly all children initially enter their school experiences with this sense of wonder and awe of which Aristotle reminded us. They are bright-eyed, curious, and ready to learn (Bitting, Cordeiro, & Baptiste, 1992).

CULTURAL DIFFERENCE THEORIES

Herskovits (1958) was a forerunner in identifying values that are prevalent in the Black culture, including, but not limited to, childrearing practices, religious practices, songs and beliefs about music, beliefs in magic, and the concept of time. His work negated the prevailing belief that Blacks lacked a unique culture. Instead, he argued that Blacks retained much of the African culture even after slavery, agreeing with cultural anthropologists and educational scholars such as Boykin (1994); Boykin et al. (2006); Ford and Harris (1999); Hale (2001); Hilliard (1991, 1992, 1997); Irvine (2002, 2003); Ladson-Billings (1994, 2006, 2009); Shade, Kelly, and Oberg (1997); and others.

Cultural styles and orientations represent patterns learned at an early age, as one grows up in a given family and community context. As individuals move out of the context of this primary socialization, they respond to new situations with previously learned behaviors and styles. When individuals encounter cultural patterns that are different in the new situation, they may have difficulty making a cultural transition, which is also known as cultural shock (see Oberg, 1954, 1960). For gifted Black students, this new situation, or cultural shock, may include being placed in a gifted program or AP class where students, teachers, and school personnel may not understand their cultural styles and orientations. It is hypothesized that the less congruence between the home and school, the more difficult the cultural transition, and students' educational outcomes will be more negative (Abi-Nader, 1990; Delpit, 1995; Eisenhardt, 1989; Ford & Harris, 1999; Vogt, Jordan, & Tharp, 1987). The shock of moving to a foreign country or interacting with others from a different culture often consists of distinct phases, although not everyone passes through these phases and not everyone is in the new culture long enough to pass through all four:

❖ *Honeymoon phase*: During this period, the differences between the old and new culture are seen in a romantic light, wonderful and new. For example, in moving to a new country, an individual might love the new foods, the pace of the life, the people's habits, the buildings, and so on.

❖ *Negotiation phase*: After some time (usually weeks), differences between the old and new culture become apparent and may create anxiety. One may long for food the way it is prepared in one's native country, may find the pace of life too fast or slow, may find the people's habits annoying, and the like. This phase is often marked by mood swings caused by minor issues or without apparent reason. Depression is not uncommon.

❖ *Adjustment phase*: Again, after some time (usually 6–12 months), one grows accustomed to the new culture and develops routines. A person knows what to expect in most situations and the host country no longer feels all that new. One becomes concerned with basic living again, and things become more "normal."

❖ *Reverse culture shock* (also known as *re-entry shock*): Returning to one's home culture after growing accustomed to a new one can produce the same effects as described above, which an affected person often finds more surprising and difficult to deal with than the original culture shock.

Boykin (1994) has studied extensively the cultural styles of African Americans. Although he and others (e.g., Shade et al., 1997) do not focus specifically on *gifted* Black students, it is only reasonable to conclude that they, too, may have adopted such cultural styles or modalities. It is also important to note that many of these characteristics can be aligned to Gardner's (1983) multiple intelligences. Boykin (1994) described the following styles:

❖ *Spirituality*: This style is an approach to life that is vitalistic rather than mechanistic, with the conviction that nonmaterial, religious forces influence people's everyday lives. It connotes an acceptance of a nonmaterial higher force that pervades all of life's affairs. One is faithful, optimistic, and resilient. (Related to intrapersonal intelligence.)

❖ *Harmony*: This style embodies the notion that one's fate is interrelated with other elements in the scheme of things, so that humankind and nature are harmonically conjoined. It implies that one's functioning is inextricably linked to nature's order and one should be synchronized with this order. One values a sense of membership and community, is effective at reading the environment and nonverbal messages well, and is effective at noticing inconsistencies between what is said, how it is said, and what is done. (Related to naturalistic intelligence, interpersonal intelligence, spatial intelligence, and musical intelligence.)

❖ *Movement*: An emphasis on the interweaving of movement, rhythm, music, and dance, which are considered central to psychological health, is representative of this style. It connotes a premium placed on the interwoven amalgamation of movement, (poly)rhythm, dance, and percussion embodied in the musical beat. One is active, physical, and tactile. (Related to spatial intelligence and musical intelligence.)

❖ *Verve*: A propensity for relatively high levels of stimulation and to action that is energetic and lively is characteristic of this style. It connotes a particular receptiveness to relatively high levels of sensate (i.e., intensity and variability of) stimulation. One is tactile and kinesthetic; demonstrative and nonverbally expressive. (Related to spatial intelligence and musical intelligence.)

❖ *Affect*: With this style, there is an emphasis on emotions and feelings, together with a special sensitivity to emotional cues and a tendency to be emotionally responsive. It implies the centrality of affective information and emotional expressiveness, and the equal and integrated importance of thoughts and feelings. One is impulsive, emotional, and sensitive. (Related to interpersonal intelligence and intrapersonal intelligence.)

❖ *Communalism*: Communalism represents a commitment to social connectedness that includes an awareness that social bonds and responsibilities transcend individual privileges. This style represents a commitment to the fundamental interdependence of people and to the importance of social bonds, relationships, and the transcendence of the group. There is a strong need for affiliation. One is social, extraverted, family oriented, and community-oriented. (Related to interpersonal intelligence.)

❖ *Oral Tradition*: A preference for oral modes of communication in which both speaking and listening are treated as performances is common with this characteristic. Oral virtuosity—the ability to use metaphorically colorful, graphic forms of spoken language—is emphasized and cultivated. It connotes the centrality of oral/aural modes of communication for conveying full meaning and the cultivation of speaking as performance. One is talkative, blunt, and direct. (Related to linguistic intelligence.)

❖ *Expressive Individualism*: This style includes the cultivation of a distinctive personality and a proclivity for spontaneity, and genuine personal expression. It denotes the uniqueness of personal expression and personal style that is creative and dramatic. (Related to musical intelligence.)

❖ *Social Time Perspective*: This is an orientation to time that is treated as passing through a social space in which time is recurring, personal, and phenomenological. It denotes a commitment to a social construction of time as personified by an event orientation. Time is social, the event is the master, and time management and being on time can be a challenge. (Related to naturalistic intelligence.)

Boykin (1986) believed that the frames of reference held by Blacks and Whites are incommensurable. And, although they are not quite polar opposites, they have fundamental incompatibilities between them:

> The African perspective emphasizes spiritualism, whereas the Euro-American one emphasizes materialism. The former stresses harmony with nature; the latter stresses mastery over nature. The first relies on organic expressive movement, the second on mechanistic ones [which] contrast with a compressive orientation toward impulse control. One culture emphasizes interconnectedness, whereas the other puts a premium on separateness; one values affect, and the other places reason above all else. . . . In African culture there is an interplay between expressive individualism and communalism, so that possessions belong to the community at large, and uniqueness is valued. Euro-American culture juxtaposes possessive individualism and an egalitarian conformity: private property is an inalienable right, and sameness is valued. (Boykin, 1986, p. 63)

Collectivism is a primary characteristic of the Black culture. Collectivism among Blacks is akin to individualism among Whites. Historically, Blacks have defined success for one as success for all Blacks. Further, success has meant that Blacks must succeed as a people rather than as individuals. This kinship symbolizes a sense of peoplehood that has risen in opposition to that which threatens the group. As described below, this "groupism" has contributed much to the formation of extended families among Blacks. Blacks stress interdependence and a world view of collectivism. Black students are, therefore, taught to think, feel, and act in ways conducive to a cooperative or interdependent view of life.

Moreover, Black students are encouraged to view themselves as a central part of the family and the larger social community. Cooperation, obligation, sharing, and reciprocity are essential elements of social interaction. Unfortunately, these values are antithetical to the individualistic tendency of the dominant culture. The values espoused by Black students (e.g., collectivism or interdependence) do not mesh well with our nation's ideas and ideals of competition, independence, and autonomy.

Patton and Sims (1993) identified three components of a Black philosophical system that offers promise for guiding theory relative to developing constructs of intelligence and giftedness, as well as assessment practices. They contended that three orientations (metaphysics, axiology, and epistemology) reflect historical and classical African-oriented world views and ethos that lay the foundation for cultural themes among many Black students. *Metaphysics* concerns an individual's holistic view of reality and tendency to engage in synthetical and contextual thinking. Thus, emphasis is placed on viewing the whole (the forest) and then understanding the interconnectedness of parts (the trees). Other scholars have referred to this style of perceiving, thinking, and understanding as field-dependent, relational, and global.

Axiology concerns an individual's preference for person-to-person interactions and developing strong social bonds. Hale-Benson (1986), Hale (2001), and Fordham (1988) referred to this phenomenon as "fictive kinship." This preference is also seen in large, extended families that are common among African Americans and other children of color (Anderson & Allen, 1984; McAdoo, 1988). This need for social interaction and bonding may also suggest a preference for group work, cooperative learning, and other social learning experiences.

Epistemology represents the individual's emphasis on emotions and feelings, as well as his or her sensitivity to emotional cues (Patton & Sims, 1993). This preference is also evident in interpersonal intelligence (Gardner, 1983) or emotional intelligence (Goleman, 1995), whereby Black students may have an especially strong need for a supportive and nurturing classroom environment to functional optimally and thrive in school settings.

In many respects, Black students are in a triple quandary. They must learn to assimilate and accommodate, while still maintaining their racial identity as a Black person. This self-maintenance is essential when one is a victim of racial and economic oppression. Educators familiar with and sensitive to cultural themes, differences, and strengths, both across and within cultural groups, should be more effective in working with gifted

Black students. There is a critical need to decrease the potential cultural gap between teachers and students, and to deliver excellent and equitable services to children who probably do not live in the same neighborhoods or share the same cultural values and beliefs as teachers and other educators.

CULTURAL CONFLICT THEORIES

Unlike deficit theories, conflict theories acknowledge and respect cultural and individual differences. These theories hold that resistance to assimilation is a form of self-protection. As indicated earlier, the socialization processes of Blacks and Whites may differ significantly. Racially different students have distinct cultural values that may conflict with the dominant culture, which can negatively affect the educational process and subsequent achievement of Black students. Thus, unlike White students, Black students must simultaneously manipulate two cultures that may be quite diverse. Students unable to make this negotiation are likely to confront additional problems in schools.

Underachievement is more likely to occur when the values, beliefs, norms, and attitudes of members of the Black culture are inconsistent with those espoused by the majority culture (and most schools). In many instances, academically unsuccessful Black students are those whose cognitive and social development are at odds or not in sync with the majority culture. These children's acquisition and use of skills, knowledge, and orientation are in conflict with those of the formal classroom. Boykin (1986) suggested much the same when he stated that the hegemony of Euro-American values persists in all aspects of the mainstream culture— a hegemony that defines that which is different as illegitimate, and those who are different from the mainstream are viewed as inferior along a single linear dimension of human perfectibility. With this prevailing social homogenization ideology, differences are also treated as deficits. Jones (1981) captured this phenomenon best with his descriptor "cultural racism," defined as the attitude characterized by ethnocentricism, coupled with the power to make normative one's ethnocentric values. These differences make it difficult to identify Black students as gifted and having greater potential than they currently demonstrate.

CULTURAL FACTORS AND UNDERACHIEVEMENT

When Black students enter the educational arena, they do not shed their cultural backgrounds and orientations. Too many Black students who achieve poorly experience cultural incompatibility or discontinuity, social-code incompatibility, and difficulty shifting their cultural styles to fit school norms and expectations. The result is a gap between the contexts of learning and the contexts of performing (e.g., Gay, 1990, 2002; Ladson-Billings, 1990a, 1990b, 1994, 2006, 2009).

BEHAVIORAL STYLE

School cultural norms are most often grounded in the cultural styles and orientations of middle-class White America. These norms consistently include conformity, cooperation, passivity, quietness, individualized instruction, independence, competition, and teacher-directed instruction. In a seminal study, Goodlad (1983, 1984) examined the practices of teachers in more than 1,000 elementary and secondary schools. Goodlad and Oakes (1988) reported that the modus operandi of the typical classroom is still didactic, practice, and little else. Specifically, almost 70% of the total class time involved verbal interaction, with teachers outtalking students by a ratio of 3 to 1. Barely 5% of instructional time was spent on direct questioning, and less than 1% of that time was devoted to open-ended questions. In addition, more than 95% of classroom affect was neutral, and the majority of student participation in the learning process was passive. Most instruction was total class (67% to 75%), less than 5% of students worked independently, and less than 10% worked in small-group or cooperative situations. Although the data were not reported specifically relative to either gifted or minority students, it seems reasonable to assume that these students were represented in the study. Given this assumption, it also seems safe to conclude that the learning style preferences of many gifted Black students went unmet and that there was a conflict between teaching styles and learning styles.

The model student sits quietly in his or her seat, asks few questions, works passively and independently, completes assignments in the prescribed manner, and otherwise does not challenge the teacher. In general, however, these behaviors may not represent the behaviors most comfortable for Black children. For instance, Black children tend to have more difficulty staying in their seats and otherwise being immobile. DellaValle (1984) found that almost half of the Black junior high school students in the study could not sit still for protracted periods of time, 25% could sit still when interested, and only 25% engaged in teacher-preferred passivity.

Black students also tend to be more socially oriented and extraverted than White students. Extensive research by Boykin (1986, 1994) and Boykin and colleagues (Boykin, Albury, et al., 2005; Boykin et al., 2005; Boykin et al., 2006) highlights the behavioral verve that seems common among Black students. Specifically, Black students tend to reside in environments that condition them to expect a variety of social interactions, including kinship networks and extended families. The school failure of Black students can be attributed, at least in part, to their inability to master social codes of mainstream behavior—codes they are expected to adopt, but are seldom taught, in school.

COMMUNICATION STYLE

Brice Heath (1983) maintained that styles of speaking among Blacks are characterized by expressiveness and affect; these styles are more persuasive and theatrical, show great emotion, and demonstrate faster and higher levels of energy. Further, students ask more questions and are more challenging, particularly when inconsistencies and injustices are noticed. Similarly, the communication styles of Black students are often (mis)interpreted as confrontational, particularly when verbal communication is accompanied by nonverbal communication (e.g., body language, facial expressions, intonations) that adds strength or momentum to their words.

Racially and culturally different students learn early in school, both directly and indirectly, that their communication and behavioral styles are significantly different from those espoused by the school, a finding that can negatively affect their school achievement. The most obvious indications of communication differences are bidialectalism and bilingualism. Schools advocate for and reward English-only and standard dialect orientations, as do standardized tests. Students who are unable to code-switch and who are not proficient in standard English often have difficulty achieving and demonstrating their potential in school. For instance, for some Black students, frustration and cognitive overloads result when they have difficulty translating two languages or dialects.

LEARNING STYLES

One of the most promising areas of research in education centers on learning style preferences among students. Learning styles have been defined as the way individuals concentrate on, absorb, and remember new and difficult information. McCarthy (1990) defined learning styles as approaches to cognitive, affective, and psychological factors that function as relatively stable indicators of how one concentrates on, perceives, interacts with, and responds to the learning environment. Keefe (1979) also viewed learning styles along affective and psychological domains. These researchers argued that students' learning styles demand an eclectic approach to curriculum and instruction; this approach accommodates individual differences in learning by using multiple approaches, models, and strategies—concrete and abstract, whole-to-part and part-to-whole, visual and auditory, hands on—that reflect the diverse ways students' acquire knowledge.

Several researchers have found differences in learning styles between Black and White students (e.g., Boykin, 1994; Dunn & Dunn, 1992; Dunn, Dunn, & Price, 1984; Dunn et al., 1990; Hale, 2001; Hale-Benson, 1986; Hilliard, 1992). Black students, for example, are often field-dependent, global, relational, visual learners who have high mobility, tactile, and kinesthetic needs and preferences (Boykin et al., 2006; Saracho & Gerstl, 1992).

Torrance's (1977, 1978) characteristics of gifted culturally different groups acknowledged how these differences are strengths that can be used to identify and nurture their gifts and talents. These differences and characteristics have numerous implications for the identification of gifted Black students. The degree to which Black students are global versus analytic learners, visual versus auditory, highly mobile versus less mobile, and less peer-oriented versus more peer-oriented will affect their learning, achievement, motivation, and school performance. Accordingly, it also may inhibit their identification, placement, and retention in gifted programs and AP classes. Because Black students tend to be global and visual learners, they may not be identified by teachers and assessed adequately by standardized tests, which do to tap into these skills.

PEER GROUP INFLUENCES ON UNDERACHIEVEMENT

Maslow's (1962, 1968) hierarchy of needs may shed further light on gifted Black students' strive for achievement. Maslow's theory suggests that basic needs are the primary influence on a person's behavior. Certain needs determine an individual's behaviors, and the goal of behavior is to reduce the need, or at least the discomfort and tension created by the need. Once lower or deficiency needs (such as food, water, safety, and shelter) have been met, a person is freer to pursue higher order needs (such as affiliation, love and affection, skill accomplishment, education, and self-actualization). Individuals striving to meet basic survival needs may find it difficult, if not impossible, to fulfill higher order needs of education and self-actualization, for example, in their daily struggles.

Further, due to cultural style differences, students' needs may vary. The need for affiliation and to have a sense of belonging is important for many racially and culturally different students. Lindstrom and Van Sant (1986) argued that gifted culturally different students often find themselves caught in a quandary, an achievement-affiliation conflict. One participant in their study lamented, "I had to fight to be gifted. Then I had to fight because I am gifted" (Lindstrom & Van Sant, 1986, p. 586). Fordham (1988), Fordham and Ogbu (1986), and Ogbu (1990) reported that Black students underachieve to avoid being ostracized by peers and other members of their community; they underachieve to avoid being accused of acting White, of being raceless[1], or of rejecting the Black culture. Some gifted Black students want no part of school, particularly when it is perceived as benefitting Whites rather than Blacks. Therefore, some Black students, especially males, would rather excel in athletics than in school.

Olszewski-Kubilius and Scott (1992) maintained that economically disadvantaged culturally different students may be pressured by their nongifted peers not to do well academically. Black adolescents who achieve well in school risk being accused of "acting White" (Ford et al., 2008a; Fordham, 1986; Fordham & Ogbu, 1986). When one adds race to the issues confronting gifted learners, the complex problems confronting

---

1   Fordham's (1988) article, published in the *Harvard Educational Review*, presents a cogent explanation for the dilemmas associated with racelessness. However, the topic is not new and is described in the works of W. E. B. DuBois and many other African American scholars. Essentially, the argument is that, for some high-achieving and or gifted Blacks, becoming raceless is a Pyrrhic victory; for others, it is a pragmatic strategy.

gifted Black students are twofold. To some of these children, outstanding school achievement is perceived as the "man's game" (Passow, 1972, p. 28)—a game that is unworthy of pursuing by poor and/or minority learners. This anti-achievement message is often an effort to maintain racial and cultural identity and allegiance, and to avoid social isolation. Such students, for instance, may become class clowns to camouflage their intellectual and academic abilities and fit in.

In essence, the need for affiliation may override the need for achievement (Whiting, 2006a, 2009), making students susceptible to negative peer pressure. Negative peer pressure is a primary and potent influence on the school performance and motivation of gifted Black students. The possibility that gifted Black students may sabotage any chance they have of succeeding in school is a critical problem in education.

RECOMMENDATIONS

The world we have created is a product of our thinking; it cannot be changed until we change our thinking.

—Albert Einstein

As Dewey (1963) contended, it is the role of educators (and, by extension, other school personnel) to change conditions until opportunities for action and reflection are created that promote student learning and growth. The following recommendations are offered for helping to ensure that educators are better prepared to meet the needs of gifted Black students who seek their guidance and assistance.

CONTINUING PROFESSIONAL EDUCATION AND DEVELOPMENT IN WORKING WITH GIFTED STUDENTS

School personnel must seek extensive and substantive training in working with gifted (Black) students to understand and appreciate the heterogeneous nature of this group. Suggested courses include those related to underachievement, counseling, psychoeducational interventions, and social and emotional needs. Ideally, more teachers, counselors, and psychologists will pursue specializations such as certification, endorsements, minors, or undergraduate or graduate degrees in working with gifted and culturally different learners.

SUBSTANTIVE CULTURALLY RESPONSIVE OR MULTICULTURAL EDUCATION PREPARATION

School personnel also are encouraged to seek extensive and substantive multicultural training to understand better the differential and perhaps unique needs of gifted Black students. Because educators traditionally lack sufficient professional preparation in culturally responsive or multicultural education (e.g., teaching, curriculum and instruction, assessment, counseling, psychology, family studies), they may be unable to recognize that Black and other culturally different students encounter distinctive barriers to achievement. This less-than-optimal grounding in the development and needs of gifted Black students may hinder the skills, ability, and willingness of educators to respond effectively to their needs.

INCREASED INFORMATION GATHERING

School personnel are urged to gather more demographic data on their students. Cumulative records or transcripts (including grades, test scores, and anecdotal information) should be requested from all students seeking (or being referred for) assistance so that school counselors can begin to understand the past school experiences of gifted Black students relative to achievement and underachievement, and to their academic strengths and shortcomings. This information gathering requires increased communication and sharing among educators at the pre-K–12 and postsecondary levels.

INCREASED AND CONSISTENT CONTACT AMONG TEACHERS AND COUNSELORS AT ALL EDUCATIONAL LEVELS

The line of demarcation between high school and college counselors may itself contribute to negative educational outcomes for students (Grites, 1979; Neill & Medina, 1989). Therefore, teachers and counselors at all educational levels are urged to work collaboratively and consistently to ensure gifted students a smooth transition from one school level to the next. Educators at all levels must share relevant information with each other to help ensure a positive educational experience for gifted learners. Counselors also must join forces with teachers to find meaningful ways to serve gifted Black students who have not found sufficient reason or means for achieving academic and/or personal success. This collaboration promises to ensure that gifted Black students have as many support mechanisms as possible to learn and achieve. The problems confronting gifted Black students are so complex and diverse that simple approaches and programs, as well as isolated efforts, will have little success.

INCREASED ATTENTION TO THE SOCIAL, EMOTIONAL, AND PSYCHOLOGICAL NEEDS OF GIFTED BLACK STUDENTS

For increased understanding, insight, and awareness, counselors and teachers should explore social and emotional issues (e.g., peer pressure, peer relationships, social supports) and psychological concerns with gifted Black students. Hence, counselors must focus on the importance of understanding: (a) social and emotional needs such as the desire to belong or not to feel different, (b) social needs such as peer friendships, and (c) psychological needs such as racial identity, self-esteem, and self-concept. Moreover, cultural needs such as the ability to live in two different societies are special concerns for some gifted Black students. Ideally, counselors will be empathetic with, sensitive to, and knowledgeable of the realities that are associated with being gifted and be cognizant of the reality that being a gifted Black student compounds the aforementioned difficulties. With this knowledge base, teachers and counselors can help ensure that gifted Black students do not become marginalized.

RECRUITMENT OF CULTURALLY AND RACIALLY DIFFERENT SCHOOL PERSONNEL

Culturally and racially different school personnel represent important mentors and role models for gifted Black students. These educators also can serve as cultural translators who are likely to understand the needs and concerns of Black students. Given the changing demographics nationally (Hodgkinson, 1988, 2007; Planty et al., 2009; U.S. Census

Bureau, 2006), it seems only logical and natural that school personnel reflect this diversity.

ENHANCED EFFORTS DIRECTED AT THE RETENTION OF BLACK STUDENTS IN GIFTED PROGRAMS AND AP CLASSES

As asserted earlier, the underrepresentation of Black students in gifted programs and AP classes may be, in part, a function of their decision to leave the classes. For instance, feelings of isolation and alienation among gifted Black students and a lack of multicultural sensitivity and awareness by staff/personnel and students may contribute to this attrition.

Counselors and teachers are in an ideal position to serve as catalysts for change; they must seek to integrate, collaborate, and implement change. To the extent possible, counselors can serve as advocates for gifted Black students by training all school personnel (teachers, staff, and administrators) and students in multicultural awareness and creating culturally responsive settings. Counselors can also work with teachers to involve more Black families in the educational process. Equally important, counselors can help initiate a systematic and comprehensive needs assessment to understand the unique culture of their particular school or district. What are the multicultural needs of students and the school? In what ways do course schedules and grouping practices, for example, contribute to (or reinforce) gifted Black students' isolation and separation? To what extent do culturally different students participate in school activities? How positive are interactions or interpersonal relationships among students, as well as teachers and Black students (and other racially and culturally different students)? In what ways do curriculum, pedagogy, and counseling promote or reinforce biases and stereotypes? How much are Black families involved in schools? Is this participation substantive (e.g., teaching, planning, decision making, site-based management) or superficial (e.g., fundraising, bake sales)? How comfortable are Black students in gifted programs and AP classes? How do teachers and classmates feel about racially and culturally different students? Is there racial tension in the school, AP classes, and gifted classes?

Counselors also can work collaboratively with teachers to establish human relations opportunities for all students (and school personnel). Promoting understanding and awareness within all students requires interactions that are egalitarian, culturally sensitive, systematic, and comprehensive. A human relations group or committee, for instance, could be developed and meet consistently to discuss issues and instances of oppression, inclusion, exclusion, and separatism in the gifted program and school. Similarly, the group could develop a conflict resolution program in which problems are discussed and resolved by a supervised and neutral peer board that has received substantive training in conflict resolution and culturally sensitive conciliation skills.

SUMMARY

The chapter focused on some of the primary issues facing gifted Black students, specifically underachievement, racial identity, and social and emotional issues. It was emphasized that counselors and teachers have many roles and responsibilities that call for increased attention to barriers to gifted Black students' achievement and motivation. It was also stressed that learning styles, lack of motivation, poor peer relations, low self-concepts, weak racial identities, and environmental risk factors can work to the detriment of gifted Black students. Finally, it was emphasized that counselors should recognize both individual and group differences among *all* students.

Gifted Black students are first and foremost human beings in need of understanding, caring, respect, and empathy. With this basic awareness and appreciation, counselors can begin the process of effective counseling. It is incumbent upon school personnel to help gifted Black students to manage and appreciate their gifts, to manage negative peer pressures, to make appropriate educational choices, to learn effective coping strategies, to accept failure, and to set realistic goals and expectations.

Given the nation's changing demographics, educators are experiencing increased contact with Black and other culturally different students. With an understanding of their needs, teachers, counselors, and, hopefully, all school personnel can better serve this student population by celebrating diversity and advocating for the human rights of all students.

The strategies, interventions, and philosophies espoused throughout this chapter emphasize the importance of developing the whole child. This includes focusing on the needs and concerns of gifted students in general (e.g., high anxiety and stress, low self-concept, poor peer relations) and Black and minority students (e.g., racism, low teacher expectations, disproportionate dropout rates, learning style differences, racial identity). There are no easy solutions to the many problems facing gifted

Black students. It is clear, however, that with counselors and teachers as cultural brokers, advocates, and mentors, gifted Black students will be better prepared to achieve in school and life.

Social and cultural capital is elusive to many Black students in school settings. Most educators do not teach culturally different students how to survive and succeed in school, including how to study across cultural learning styles, how to adjust communication styles, how to interact "appropriately" with school administrators and teachers, and how to identify and adjust to the rules for functioning in different instructional classrooms (Gay, 2000). Specifically, the prevailing assumption is that school codes of behavior are common knowledge acquired from living in the macroculture or mainstream culture that surrounds schools. What too many educators fail to remember is that many racially and culturally different students live on the margins of the mainstream culture; they have neither a heritage nor tradition of success in predominantly White schools.

The core cultural ideals of equality, justice, freedom, and democracy carry far-reaching implications for the education of gifted Black students and the quest for human rights socially. A major function of schools should be the adoption of pluralism, which entails helping all students, but especially racially and culturally different students, to acquire the knowledge, skills, and attitudes needed to function effectively within the mainstream macroculture, their own microcultures, and within and across other microcultures (e.g., Asian Americans, Hispanic Americans, Native Americans).

CHAPTER FOUR

GIFTED STUDENTS: DEFINITIONS, THEORIES, AND ASSESSMENT

If the definition of giftedness is not a useful one, it can lead to unfavorable consequences of many kinds, both for society and its individuals. If the definition of giftedness is not valuable, talents may be wasted, and less valuable ones fostered and encouraged.

—Sternberg and Davidson (1986, p. 4)

Definitions of giftedness reflect the attitudes, beliefs, and values of the times, and those in power (i.e., the status quo and those with the greatest social, cultural, and economic capital) lead the way in determining what is gifted, how giftedness will be identified or assessed, and how such students will be served. In a Stone Age society, giftedness likely would have included the ability to hunt effectively; in ancient Greece, it might have been defined as skill in rhetoric; and in modern society, giftedness often involves mastering the skills demanded by advanced technology (Freeman, 1983).

The concepts of achievement, intelligence, high potential, talent development, and, accordingly, giftedness are interrelated, and have been widely studied and assigned a number of definitions in education, counseling, psychology, and other fields. Over the years, theorists have debated whether giftedness is primarily a cognitive entity or a function of some other construct, such as experience and exposure. More recently, attention has been directed toward the suggestion that giftedness is a multidimensional concept, and that educators should seek to identify, promote, and nurture potential among intellectually and academically gifted students, as well as among students who are gifted or showing potential in creativity, leadership, and the visual and performing arts, and who are intellectually and academically gifted (e.g., Ford, 1995, 2004, 2007a, 2007b, 2010; Ford & Harris, 1991; Frasier & Passow, 1994; Harris & Ford, 1991; Sternberg, 2007). If potential is to be fostered, it must first be discovered. These contemporary definitions suggest, both directly and indirectly, that it is naïve and fruitless to homogenize gifted students and characteristics.

In a compelling monograph entitled *A New Window for Looking at Gifted Children,* Frasier, Martin, and colleagues (1995) stated, "Manifestation of characteristics associated with giftedness may be different in minority children, yet educators are seldom trained in identifying those behaviors in ways other than the way they are observed in the majority culture" (p. 33). This statement was confirmed by Frasier, Hunsaker, Lee, Finley, and colleagues (1995) in a study that targeted teachers' perceptions of giftedness among racially and culturally different students. Sternberg's (2007) more recent work shows that we still have a way to go in the field:

> Different cultures have different conceptions of what it means to be gifted. But in identifying children as gifted, we often use only our own conception, ignoring the cultural context in which the children grew up. Such identification is inadequate and fails to do justice to the richness of the world's cultures. It also misses children who are gifted and may identify as gifted children who are not. (p. 160)

This chapter discusses conceptualizations of giftedness and presents an overview of both traditional and contemporary definitions. It draws implications for these definitions relative to underachieving and gifted Black students, including those in AP classes. Theories of giftedness and underachievement are also described, along with a brief overview of social, school, familial (or cultural), and psychological (personal) factors that influence identification and assessment[1] practices. These factors, in isolation or collectively, emphasize the importance of moving beyond decontextualized definitions and conceptions of giftedness. The chapter concludes with promising and equitable practices relative to increasing the representation of Black students in gifted programs and AP classes.

QUESTIONS TO CONSIDER

❖ How do notions of intelligence influence ideas, definitions, and theories of giftedness?

❖ How do notions of intelligence contribute to underrepresentation among Black students in gifted education and AP classes?

❖ In what ways have traditional definitions of intelligence and/or giftedness been misused or abused in education? How have definitions and theories of giftedness contributed to the underrepresentation of Black students and underachieving students in gifted education and AP classes?

❖ How have definitions and theories of giftedness changed in recent years, and what are the implications of such changes for gifted Black students, potentially gifted Black students, and gifted underachieving Black students?

❖ In what ways do testing and assessment practices and other identification practices (e.g., checklists, nomination forms) influence the representation of Black students in gifted education and AP classes? Why is testing such a controversial issue in gifted education?

❖ What are some of the strengths of Black students that can be used to recruit and retain them in gifted education and AP classes?

❖ What are the components of promising and equitable identification and assessment practices? What cautions and concerns exist about social, cultural, and gender biases and unfairness in testing and assessment?

❖ How can education move from simply testing to assessment, which is comprehensive, diagnostic, and prescriptive, and how might gifted Black and underachieving students benefit from this philosophical change?

---

1   I use the terms *identification* and *assessment* differently. Identification is simplistic, using one measure to address a closed-ended question that requires a yes/no response, while assessment is comprehensive, diagnostic, and prescriptive. It responds to an open-ended query. More than one instrument and source of data/information is collected and used; it is multidimensional and multimodal.

WHAT IS INTELLIGENCE?

We have all too often behaved as though intelligence is a physical substance, like a house or an egg crate composed of rooms or cells; we might better remember that it is no more to be deified than attributes like beauty or speed or honesty.

—Wesman (1968, p. 267)

Throughout history, the terms *giftedness* and *intelligence* have been used interchangeably, especially in educational and psychological settings. When students are referred to AP classes and gifted education programs and services, it is most often because they are viewed specifically as intellectually gifted students. This begs the question: What is intelligence, and how does it differ from or resemble giftedness?

Despite the overwhelming volume of research on intelligence, there is little consensus on a defensible and culturally responsive or inclusive definition. In their book, Sternberg and Detterman (1986) presented some two dozen definitions of intelligence. In general, the definitions were categorized based on the notion that: (a) intelligence resides within the individual (e.g., biological, motivational); (b) intelligence resides within the environment (e.g., cultural, societal); and (c) intelligence is an interaction between the individual and the environment. A sample of definitions examined by Sternberg and Detterman include:

- ❖ Intelligence is behavior that is adaptive, representing effective ways of meeting environmental demands as they change. Adaptive behavior is contextually determined, resulting in intelligence as a pluralistic concept (Anastasi).
- ❖ Intelligence is learning capacity, innate ability, problem-solving ability, and knowledge systems (Baltes).
- ❖ Intelligence is threefold: academic, technical, and social and practical. Intelligence differs in laboratory (schools) and real-world (practical and social) settings. Intelligence is determined at the societal level (Carroll).
- ❖ Intelligence is the repertoire of intellectual knowledge and skills available to a person at a given point in time. The content and process of intelligence need to be understood given its complexity (Humphreys).

❖ Intelligence is a general factor obtained from factoring an inter-correlation of numerous diverse mental tests, particularly tests assessing relation induction, and mental manipulations or trans-formations of stimuli in order to achieve a correct response. Intelligence is biological, but can be studied in laboratory and real-world settings (Jensen).

❖ Intelligence must be understood relative to the nature of the individual's value systems; intelligence is determined by the interaction of the individual's cognitive processes with his or her social-cultural environment (Pellegrino).

❖ Intelligence is adaptation in our everyday lives of striving to solve small and large problems confronted daily; intelligence is a func-tion of cognitive processes, neurological processes, and individual differences. Intelligence has biological determinants (Scarr).

Samuda, Kong, Cummins, Lewis, and Pascual-Leone (1991) also examined definitions of intelligence. Included in their examination are definitions espoused by test developers, such as Binet and Simon, Wechsler, and Vernon. Binet and Simon defined intelligence as the capacity to judge well, to reason well, and to comprehend well; Wechsler defined intelligence as the aggregate or global capacity of the individ-ual to act purposefully, to think rationally, and to deal effectively with the environment; and Vernon defined intelligence as the outcome of the interplay of innate potentiality and of conditions such as good emotional adjustment and appropriate educational stimulation.

At least three themes emerge from the various definitions just described. One of the most common themes is that of the ability to *adapt* to the environment and to changing situations and contexts. That is, many of the definitions relate to social or practical intelligence, also referred to as social competence. A second theme is that of the ability to reason abstractly. Third, several definitions indicate that intelligence is culture- or context-bound and socially determined. Thus, two different cultures may have different definitions of intelligence, and the value of different types of intelligences varies by culture and context (Sternberg, 2007). Given such different definitions, some more concrete than others, some more amenable to testing and assessment than others, one is left to wonder what intelligence tests really measure. Do they measure social intelligence? Practical or tacit intelligence (i.e., common sense, street sense, or wiseness)? Moral development? Test-taking skills and test wise-ness? What about differential exposure, experience, and opportunity? Do such tests measure schoolhouse intelligence or the kinds of intelligence needed to succeed in the real world?

Assumptions and definitions regarding intelligence often are inflammatory, unsupported, inconsistent, and contradictory (Onwuegbuzie & Daley, 2001). During my tenure in higher education, spanning more than two decades, I have asked college students to define intelligence or to describe an intelligent child. The following descriptors are common among each class at four universities. Intelligent children or individuals: (a) have a large vocabulary; (b) do well on tests and do well in school; (c) have IQ scores higher than 115; (d) are fast learners; (e) think rationally and systematically; (f) read well and have a large/extensive vocabulary; (g) have a good/powerful memory; (h) are curious, probing, and insightful; (i) are independent workers/self-initiators; (j) have a long attention span, are intense; (k) have complex thoughts and ideas; (l) are widely informed about many topics; (m) have good judgment and logic; (n) understand relationships and comprehend meanings; and (o) produce original or unusual products/ideas.

Too often, we forget or negate that these also are the characteristics of many gifted Black underachieving students. Given the aforementioned definitions and perceptions, including those among laypersons, one is also left to ponder what intelligence tests measure. Do they measure social or interpersonal and intrapersonal intelligence—the ability and skills to use one's intelligence to facilitate interactions with others or to facilitate understanding of oneself? Do they assess practical or tacit or commonsense intelligence—the ability to perform one's job effectively, to survive outside of educational settings (i.e., to survive or even thrive relative to daily aspects of living)? Do these tests measure or assess adaptation to or overcoming adverse life circumstances, also referred to as resilience?

DEFINITIONS OF GIFTEDNESS

Giftedness is another term that eludes definition and consensus in many ways. Since Terman (1925) presented his unidimensional definition of giftedness, traditional definitions of giftedness have been operationalized primarily in two ways: (a) by high scores on IQ tests (130 and higher) or (b) by high scores on achievement tests (often 92nd percentile or higher). Terman believed that gifted students were in the top 1% on the normal distribution curve of the Stanford-Binet, and his cutoff score for giftedness was an IQ of 140. Terman's definition is grounded in the assumption that giftedness is synonymous with intelligence and that intelligence can be measured accurately and effectively by standardized tests. Both of these assumptions ignore the difficulty of defining a complex term such as intelligence and finding valid, reliable, and fair measures—measures that are equitable and otherwise culturally responsive (Ford & Whiting, 2009; Whiting & Ford, 2009). Not only is the jury out, so to speak, on professionals' and layperson's definitions of gifted, so too is the federal government, as described below.

As reflected in Figure 4.1, the federal government has adopted six definitions of giftedness since 1970. The respective definitions have been both promising and harmful to the successful identification of underachieving and gifted Black students.

The 1970 definition, which was added with the Elementary and Secondary Education Amendments, is very vague and general. It offered little guidance to states and school districts and mentioned only intellectual and creative giftedness. The Marland (1972) definition specifically listed six types of giftedness: general intellectual, specific academic, creative or productive thinking, leadership, visual and performing arts, and psychomotor. However, in the most commonly adopted definition, one modified from the Marland definition in 1978 (Cassidy & Hossler, 1992), psychomotor giftedness was not specifically listed due to the belief that those with these gifts could be served under the visual and performing arts category. The 1988 definition found in the Jacob K. Javits Gifted and Talented Students Education Act strongly resembles the 1978 definition, with the exception that emphasis also is placed on gifted youth. The 1993 U.S. Department of Education definition addressed two historically ignored points specific to Black and other minority students: (a) students must be compared with others of their age, experience, or environment and (b) outstanding talents are present in individuals from all cultural groups, across all economic strata, and in all areas of human endeavor. The 2001 definition of gifted and talented in the No Child Left Behind (NCLB) Act is less philosophical than the 1993 definition; it resembles earlier definitions.

In addition to the federal definitions, it is important to consider state definitions. According to the *State of States in Gifted Education* report (NAGC, 2009), the following areas of giftedness are included in state definitions: intellectual (n = 34), creativity (n = 26), performing/visual arts (n = 25), academics (n = 23), specific academics (n = 17), and leadership (n = 17); some states also include cultural diversity (n = 10) and

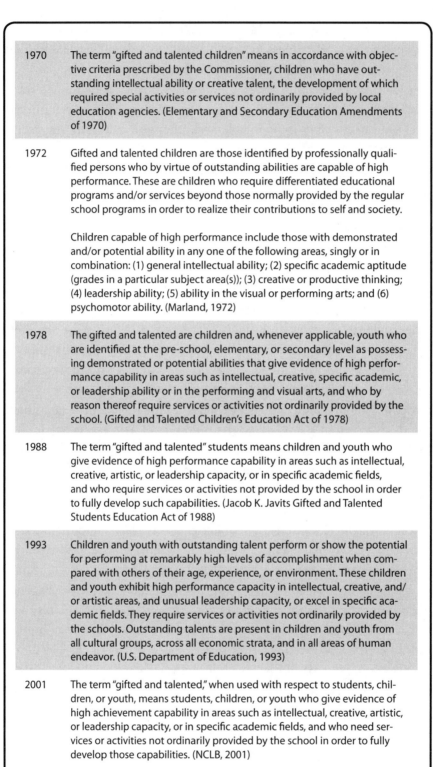

1970	The term "gifted and talented children" means in accordance with objective criteria prescribed by the Commissioner, children who have outstanding intellectual ability or creative talent, the development of which required special activities or services not ordinarily provided by local education agencies. (Elementary and Secondary Education Amendments of 1970)
1972	Gifted and talented children are those identified by professionally qualified persons who by virtue of outstanding abilities are capable of high performance. These are children who require differentiated educational programs and/or services beyond those normally provided by the regular school programs in order to realize their contributions to self and society. Children capable of high performance include those with demonstrated and/or potential ability in any one of the following areas, singly or in combination: (1) general intellectual ability; (2) specific academic aptitude (grades in a particular subject area(s)); (3) creative or productive thinking; (4) leadership ability; (5) ability in the visual or performing arts; and (6) psychomotor ability. (Marland, 1972)
1978	The gifted and talented are children and, whenever applicable, youth who are identified at the pre-school, elementary, or secondary level as possessing demonstrated or potential abilities that give evidence of high performance capability in areas such as intellectual, creative, specific academic, or leadership ability or in the performing and visual arts, and who by reason thereof require services or activities not ordinarily provided by the school. (Gifted and Talented Children's Education Act of 1978)
1988	The term "gifted and talented" students means children and youth who give evidence of high performance capability in areas such as intellectual, creative, artistic, or leadership capacity, or in specific academic fields, and who require services or activities not provided by the school in order to fully develop such capabilities. (Jacob K. Javits Gifted and Talented Students Education Act of 1988)
1993	Children and youth with outstanding talent perform or show the potential for performing at remarkably high levels of accomplishment when compared with others of their age, experience, or environment. These children and youth exhibit high performance capacity in intellectual, creative, and/or artistic areas, and unusual leadership capacity, or excel in specific academic fields. They require services or activities not ordinarily provided by the schools. Outstanding talents are present in children and youth from all cultural groups, across all economic strata, and in all areas of human endeavor. (U.S. Department of Education, 1993)
2001	The term "gifted and talented," when used with respect to students, children, or youth, means students, children, or youth who give evidence of high achievement capability in areas such as intellectual, creative, artistic, or leadership capacity, or in specific academic fields, and who need services or activities not ordinarily provided by the school in order to fully develop those capabilities. (NCLB, 2001)

Figure 4.1. Federal definitions of gifted and talented students.

underachieving students ($n = 5$) in their definitions. Having said this, however, many respondents to the survey (39%) reported that underrepresentation is a negative force in gifted and talented education.

A CLOSER LOOK AT FEDERAL DEFINITIONS

Cassidy and Hossler (1992) found that most states use either the 1978 federal definition outright or a modification of it, and no states reflected the more contemporary definition advanced by Sternberg (1985) and Gardner (1983). They added that 30 states had made no definitional revisions in at least a decade, and only 15 had made revisions in the last 5 years; more recent information indicates that only 10 states include cultural diversity in their definitions (NAGC, 2009).

Given that the federal definitions, particularly the 1978 definition, tend to guide school practices more than other definitions and theories of giftedness, a closer examination of their implications for Black students is in order.

Intellectual ability. The student evidences or shows potential for high levels of abstract reasoning, advanced vocabulary, advanced academic performance, excellent memory, and an accelerated rate of learning. Other characteristics include abstract and logical thinking, the ability to store and retrieve a wide range of information, the ability to deal with complex and abstract problems, and resourcefulness in managing the environment.

Individual or group intelligence tests are usually administered for identification or assessment purposes. Based on IQ scores, there are several levels or categories of intellectually gifted students. An IQ score of 130 (top 2%) is usually required for formal identification or further placement consideration. Highly gifted students are those with IQ scores of 145 or higher, and students of superior intelligence score 160 or higher. If we define gifted students as those with an IQ of 180 or higher, there may only be one child in a million identified.

The primary measurements are standardized tests of general intellectual ability. The most commonly used individual intelligence tests include the Wechsler Intelligence Scale for Children–Revised, the Stanford-Binet Intelligence Scale, the Peabody Picture Vocabulary Test–Revised, the Slosson Intelligence Test, and the Raven's Progressive Matrices. Commonly adopted group tests include the Cognitive Abilities Test, the Otis-Lennon Mental Ability Test, the Lorge-Thorndike Intelligence

Tests, the SRA Primary Mental Abilities Tests, and the Test of Cognitive Skills.

Instruments purported to be more culturally sensitive include the Naglieri Nonverbal Ability Tests I and II; the Universal Nonverbal Intelligence Test; the Matrix Analogies Test; the Raven's Progressive Matrices; the Test of Nonverbal Intelligence; the Kaufman Assessment Battery for Children; the Program of Assessment, Diagnosis, and Instruction; and the System of Multicultural Pluralistic Assessment.

General and specific academic ability. The student demonstrates or shows potential for high levels of academic achievement (e.g., mastery of content area or subject matter), particularly in an area or areas of interest. These students learn quickly, are curious, have long attention spans, and enjoy challenging schoolwork. Contrary to popular opinion, students are not gifted in every subject area. It is possible to be gifted in math and/or science but not language arts and vice versa.

Achievement and aptitude tests are most often used to identify and/or assess general and specific academic ability. Achievement tests presumably assess students' knowledge and skills acquired as a result of school experiences, specifically instruction. Commonly used achievement tests include the California Achievement Test, the Comprehensive Tests of Basic Skills, the Iowa Tests of Basic Skills, the Peabody Individual Achievement Test, the Stanford Achievement Test, the Metropolitan Achievement Test, and the SRA Achievement Series.

Aptitude tests are also considered to be measures of achievement and school-based learning; however, they are used to assess ability in specific areas and the test taker's potential to learn something in the future. Such tests include the Cognitive Abilities Test, the Differential Aptitude Test, and the Test of Cognitive Skills. Grades, grade point averages, class rank, work samples, teacher observations, and self-completed instruments (e.g., checklists, inventories) are also administered for identification and placement consideration. Achievement tests carry less controversy and stigma than intelligence tests because they are acknowledged to be highly related or dependent upon learning, experience, and exposure; there is less attention to the origins of intelligence—whether genetic or environment or both (see Ford, 2004; Onwuegbuzie & Daley, 2001)—with achievement tests. The validity and reliability of achievement tests rest a great deal on their being aligned with the school curriculum—if the test does not measure what has been taught, then students are likely to do poorly on it.

Creativity. The student demonstrates or shows potential for high levels of performance in areas such as divergent thinking, elaboration, originality, and fluency. These students perform above average on divergent rather than convergent thinking activities and exercises. They may be proficient in solving problems using skills such as finding facts, generating ideas, identifying multiple solutions and alternatives, and evaluating the solutions and outcomes. Creative students tend to be very probing, highly imaginative, experimenters, risk takers, and independent. Creative students also are considered nonconformists and nontraditional; they may be uninhibited in their opinions, and are sometimes radical and spirited in disagreement.

Standardized measures of creativity are less common than those of achievement and intelligence. Measures of divergent thinking are contradictory to the notion of standardized testing, which is based on convergent thinking—giving one answer or the "right" answer. However, frequently used instruments include the Torrance Tests of Creative Thinking, the Creative Tests for Children, Thinking Creatively in Action and Movement, the Creativity Attitude Survey, and Sounds and Images, as well as personality checklists and inventories of creative behaviors and analyses of students' work and portfolios. Although less valid and reliable, and clearly more subjective and biased, some schools identify and label students as creative based on teacher checklists or nomination forms. The efficacy or utility of this practice is questionable and, like all subjective measures and procedures, can contribute to underreferral and consequent underrepresentation (Ford et al., 2008b).

Leadership. The student demonstrates or shows potential for high levels of performance in organization and management, persuasion, communication and public speaking, interpersonal relations, and interpersonal relations and skills. Sternberg and Kolligian (1990) referred to leadership as a component of social intelligence, while Gardner (1985) considered leadership ability under both inter- and intrapersonal intelligences. Socially gifted children are able to understand people's motivation, have positive social relationships, are sensitive to the feelings of others, and effectively manage everyday problems. Persons with such strengths include those in sales and marketing, public relations, communications, mental health, teaching, and other social service professions. Other students look to them for ideas and decisions; they are frequently sought after by peers. They interact easily with others and participate in clubs, especially as leaders/officers and decision makers. Students gifted in leadership exude vision, confidence, and charisma; they inspire, initiate, and mobilize others.

Measurement of leadership often focuses on interpersonal and social skills and development. Sample instruments include the Vineland Social Maturity Scale and the California Preschool Social Competency Scale. Sociograms may also be used to examine popularity, along with memberships in school and community clubs and organizations.

Visual and performing arts. The student demonstrates or shows potential for high levels of ability to perform in areas such as dance, music, drama, and art. Students gifted in music are often identified by an unusual sense of pitch or a singing voice; others play a melody almost flawlessly without formal training. Dancers may be identified by the fluidity of their movement, while students with strengths in the dramatic arts are able to express themselves with unusual energy and emotion.

Visual and performing arts assessments include the Basic Motor Ability Test, Developmental Test of Visual and Motor Integration, and the Purdue Perceptual Motor Survey. Although tests and inventories are available, a panel of experts is used more often to evaluate such performances. Portfolios of artwork, music, plays, skits, and the like also are used in the identification process. Perhaps more than the other areas of giftedness, identification and assessment practices in the visual and performing arts are likely to be dynamic, performance based, and authentic.

IMPLICATIONS FOR GIFTED AND UNDERACHIEVING BLACK STUDENTS

The 1978 federal definition is often misinterpreted and misused by practitioners who give primary or first entrance consideration to specific academic and general intellectual giftedness and who treat the five areas of giftedness as if they are exhaustive. The federal definition merely lists potential areas of giftedness, as indicated by the term *such as*. The definition is also misused by those who retrofit students to the gifted program, rather than develop the gifted program based on community needs.

The 1978 definition eliminated psychomotor ability as an area of giftedness. Yet, as Gardner (1985) indicated, psychomotor ability is a legitimate type of intelligence. It is a talent in which many children excel and require special services outside of those normally provided by the schools. When one combines Gardner's theory with that of Boykin (1986) who focused on movement and verve, it seems even more necessary to give great attention to this type of intelligence (Ford, 2007a, 2007b, 2010). These gifted students are unusually coordinated and capable of athletic feats such as world-class figure skating, gymnastics and dance, basketball, and other physical tasks requiring a combination of dexterity, sensory acuity, and intellectual ability. How would the gifts and talents of persons such as Arthur Ashe, Serena and Venus Williams, Tiger Woods, Jacqueline Joyner-Kersee, Pelé, Michael Jordan, and Florence Griffith Joyner have developed without recognition, nurturance, and special guidance? One can only wonder whether their abilities would have atrophied.

Equally important, preferences for learning by and communicating though psychomotor activities (hands on, tactile, kinesthetic) often is evident among Black students, particularly males. This need is often so powerful that many Black males are (mis)labeled hyperactive and behaviorally disordered. This discussion is given greater attention in Chapter 10 on gender differences and issues.

The most encouraging aspect of the 1978 and 1993 federal definitions is their inclusion of the "potentially" gifted. They recognize the critical need to serve those students who, for various reasons, have yet to manifest their gifts—that is, students who might otherwise go unrecognized. These students tend to include underachievers, racially and culturally different students, economically disadvantaged students, students with learning and behavioral disorders, and students with physical disabilities. The emphasis on potential represents a progressive, future-oriented definition by denoting students' potential for becoming critically acclaimed performers or exemplary producers of ideas in spheres of activity that enhance the moral, physical, emotional, social, intellectual, or aesthetic life of humanity (Tannenbaum, 1983).

This most philosophical federal definition of giftedness (U.S. Department of Education, 1993) continues to offer much promise, including increased equity, for identifying Black and other culturally different students. The 1993 federal definition moves beyond a monolithic academic definition so long embraced. It also recognizes a broad range of ability and, for the first time, specifically mentions that no racial, cultural, or socioeconomic group has a monopoly on giftedness.

Irrespective of one's definition, emphasis on the cognitive and academic aspects of giftedness prevails in American schools and among professionals and laypersons alike. Intellectuality dominates our conceptualization of giftedness. Students who score low on standardized intelligence and achievement measures are not likely to be placed in gifted programs. A national survey by VanTassel-Baska, Patton, and Prillaman (1989) revealed that only 12 districts reported using definitions of "disadvantaged" gifted students. Of those, nine districts reported a definitional construct and four included culturally different, minority, and poor students. One definition reported by the researchers follows:

> those children regardless of race or ethnic group who may have language patterns and experiences, cultural backgrounds, economic disadvantages and/or educational disadvantages or differences that make it difficult for them to demonstrate their potential using traditional identification procedures. (VanTassel-Baska et al., 1989, p. 10)

CONSIDERATIONS OF CULTURAL DIFFERENCES IN THE MANIFESTATION OF GIFTEDNESS

The strengths that Black students bring into the classroom too often become weaknesses in school settings. To desegregate gifted programs and AP classes, we need to recognize the strengths of these students.

Gifted students from all cultural backgrounds share certain characteristics of giftedness, including the ability to meaningfully manipulate some symbol system held valuable in the subculture; the ability to think logically, given appropriate information; the ability to use stored knowledge to solve problems; the ability to reason by analogy; and the ability to extrapolate knowledge to new or novel situations (Frasier, Hunsaker, Lee, Mitchell, et al. 1995, Frasier & Passow, 1994; Gallagher & Kinney, 1974). In addition to these characteristics, gifted Black and other culturally and racially different students learn quickly through experience and retain and use ideas/information well. They are adept at generalizing learning to other areas, seeing relationships among apparently unrelated parts, and at solving problems in resourceful ways (Frasier, 1989; Torrance, 1977). Other characteristics include persuasive language, language rich in imagery, humor rich with symbolism, creativity, social intelligence, psychosocial sensitivity (particularly to inequities and social injustices), and sensitivity to movement and action (Boykin, 1994; Boykin, Albury, et al., 2005; Boykin et al., 2005; Boykin et al., 2006; Horowitz & O'Brien, 1985).

Torrance's (1977, 1978) list of creative positives captures many of the strengths gifted Black students bring into learning and assessment situations: unusual ability to express feelings and emotions; ability to improvise with common materials; articulation in role-playing and storytelling; enjoyment of and ability in music and rhythm, performing arts, creative movement, dance, and dramatics; expressive speech and sense of humor; expressive body language, including responsiveness to kinesthetic experiences; concrete thinking; and problem centered. Many of these characteristics and strengths appear in Boykin's research and are discussed throughout this book.

In addition to some of the characteristics listed by Torrance (1977, 1978), Gay (1978) noted that manifestations of giftedness in Black students include the ability to pick up quickly on racial attitudes and practices, being effective at reading behavioral cues and their implications, being independent and original, having a large vocabulary, and having multiple interests. Gifted Black students may also ask questions that teachers consider wrong or inappropriate, and use language that is considered inappropriate for school. They are experiential, perceptual, and concrete learners; however, all of these strengths may be hidden due to inferior educational experiences.

Black students often prefer inferential reasoning to deductive or inductive reasoning. They focus on people rather than things; have a keen sense of justice and are quick to analyze perceived injustices; lean toward altruism; prefer novel ideas and freedom (particularly relative to music, clothing, and speaking); and favor nonverbal communication modalities. My own experiences suggest that gifted Black students are:

❖ *Proficient at logic and solving problems*, especially daily and real-life problems, and meeting basic survival needs; they exude mental toughness and resilience.

❖ *Socially competent and sophisticated* (e.g., have social reasoning skills; learn through experiences; transfer learning from one situation to another; are flexible and resourceful in solving daily and authentic or real-life problems; effectively handle responsibilities outside of school; use common sense to deal with problems; deal effectively with conflicts and frustrations associated with social injustices).

❖ *Psychologically clever and intellectually playful*, with a unique sense of humor that is often misunderstood and unappreciated by educators—those unfamiliar with humor displayed through teasing, ribbing, jiving, playing the dozens, "dissing," and so forth may misinterpret such behaviors as a form of cruelty, insensitivity, or immaturity.

❖ *Insightful and perceptive*, often seeing inconsistencies (e.g., are adept at noting discrepancies between verbal and nonverbal cues; are sensitive to social injustices and other inequities, such as prejudice, discrimination, and racism communicated verbally and/or nonverbally, and be it covert or overt).

❖ *Creative, inventive, and resourceful*, as they see alternative perspectives. They are nonconforming, questioning, and opinionated; use ordinary materials in different ways; and have vivid imaginations.

❖ *Psychomotorically inclined*, as they prefer and get great satisfaction from active involvement and hands-on, experiential learning opportunities that allow them to engage with materials.

❖ *Social and interpersonal leaders*, because they are effective at persuasion, communication, and empathy, and read people and motives well.

❖ *Risk takers* who will challenge the status quo and accept the repercussions of expressing ideas, thoughts, or feelings; they find uncanny and memorable ways to capture attention and express ideas.

To repeat, gifted Black students share many of the strengths of gifted students in general—they retain and recall information well; enjoy complex problems; can tolerate ambiguity; are creative; are extremely curious, perceptive, evaluative, and judgmental; and interested in adult and social problems. The aforementioned characteristics serve as general guidelines from which to identify and assess gifted and potentially gifted Black students and those who are underachieving. To better understand and appreciate the strengths of these students, educators and other school personnel must get to know them as individuals and cultural beings, as well as use their strengths for prescriptive and proactive educational purposes. To do otherwise allows these strengths to become weaknesses in the classroom, promotes underachievement, and contributes to the persistent underrepresentation of Black students in gifted education and AP classes (and to these being racially segregated classes or programs).

THEORIES OF GIFTEDNESS: IMPLICATIONS FOR BLACK STUDENTS

Numerous theories of giftedness exist and have been described in detail elsewhere in books and publications in gifted education (e.g., Clark, 1991; Colangelo & Davis, 1991, 2003; Davis & Rimm, 1994, 2004; Davis, Rimm, & Siegle, 2010). Three contemporary theories of giftedness, however, are in the forefront of efforts designed to develop equitable and culturally responsive perspectives of giftedness: Renzulli (1986), Sternberg (1985), and Gardner (1983, 1985).

THREE-RING CONCEPTUALIZATION OF GIFTEDNESS

The three-ring theory indicates that giftedness consists of the interaction among three clusters: well-above-average ability, task commitment, and creativity. According to Renzulli (1986), no single cluster of variables or characteristics makes "giftedness"; rather, the interaction among them is a necessary ingredient for gifts and talents to develop. He advised that educators give equal attention to all three clusters in his theory in the identification process, and that giftedness be assessed in a natural setting, a real-life situation.

Renzulli (1986) contended that students with well-above-average ability constitute 15% to 20% of the school population. These students serve as a talent pool from which to further assess gifted students. General ability is the capacity to process information, to integrate experiences that result in appropriate and adaptive responses in new situations, as well as the capacity to engage in abstract thinking (e.g., verbal reasoning, spatial relations, memory, word fluency). Specific ability is the capacity to acquire knowledge and the ability to perform in one or more activities in a specialized area (e.g., chemistry, ballet, math, sculpture, photography). Each specific ability area or category can be further subdivided into even more specific areas (e.g., portrait photography, photojournalism, and so forth).

Renzulli (1986) noted that task commitment is not equated with motivation. Task commitment represents energy brought to bear on a particular task or specific performance area. Related terms include perseverance, hard work, dedicated practice, and endurance. The third and final cluster of giftedness, creativity, is evident in divergent and original thinkers. They show ingenuity and are able to set aside established conventions.

Implications. Renzulli's (1986) theory broadens the identification net from the traditional 3% to 5% of the population to 15% to 20%. Talent pools support the notion of potential and talent development—that a golden chromosome does not exist for giftedness (Reis & Renzulli, 2009; Renzulli, 1977, 1986, 1987, 1997, 2002). Talent pools acknowledge that lower test scores do not automatically equal lower intelligence or ability, and that many talents are resistant to formal testing. The notion of talent development is a contemporary view of giftedness that is dynamic and relative, rather than static and absolute.

The inclusion of task commitment in the definition of giftedness has many implications for underachieving students. Although Renzulli's (1986) theory has been criticized on this component, he does not contend that task commitment is synonymous with motivation, that it is global, or that students are gifted in all areas. The theory focuses on what fuels students in their area(s) of giftedness.

TRIARCHIC THEORY OF INTELLIGENCE

Sternberg's (1985) Triarchic Theory of Intelligence posited three kinds of intelligence: componential, experiential, and contextual. Componential intelligence, most valued in schools, is characteristic of students who routinely achieve high test scores and take naturally to analytical thinking. Experiential intelligence describes creative thinkers who can combine disparate experiences in insightful ways without necessarily achieving high test scores. Finally, those who possess common sense and practical intelligence and are "street-smart" (i.e., have learned how to "play the game" and how to manipulate the environment), but who do not test particularly high, have what Sternberg called contextual intelligence.

The Triarchic Theory proposes that: (a) intelligence cannot be understood outside of a sociocultural context and what is gifted in one culture or environment may not be gifted in another; (b) intelligence is purposeful, goal-oriented, relevant behavior consisting of the ability to learn from experience and adapt to one's environment; and (c) intelligence depends on information processing skills and strategies.

Implications. Unlike other theories of giftedness, Sternberg (1985) focused on social intelligence and competence. According the theory, gifted individuals shape their environments and, perhaps more importantly, do not necessarily boast high IQs and achievement test scores. The theory acknowledges that schoolhouse giftedness does not guarantee success in the real world. By focusing on intelligence both inside and outside of schools, Sternberg recognized that talent comes in different forms and is context-specific. Sternberg (2007) argued that giftedness and/or intelligence must be viewed and valued through a cultural lens.

THEORY OF MULTIPLE INTELLIGENCES

Gardner's (1983) theory of multiple intelligences maintained that intelligence resembles a constellation of at least eight discrete competencies: musical, bodily kinesthetic, logical-mathematical, linguistic, spatial, interpersonal, intrapersonal, and naturalistic:

❖ *Musical intelligence* represents an unusual sensitivity to pitch, rhythm, and timber. These students understand and appreciate the power and complexity of music. They are rhythm and melody oriented.

❖ *Bodily kinesthetic intelligence* requires cognitive intelligence and problem-solving skills. These students exercise great control over their bodies and over objects; they are aware of and sensitive to timing, and behaviors in their particular talent area are reflexive-like. They are able to control their body movements and to handle objects skillfully. They excel in fine-motor activities and crafts and achieve self-expression through body action and touching things to learn about them. They are physically oriented.

❖ *Logical-mathematical intelligence* is a remarkable ability to solve problems; it is the archetype of "raw intelligence." This type of intelligence has been heavily investigated by traditional psychologists and is found on traditional, standardized intelligence tests. Logical-mathematical students are proficient at abstract thought, organization, logic, and problem solving.

❖ *Linguistic intelligence*, like logical-mathematical, is held in high esteem by traditional psychologists and also measured on standardized intelligence tests. Students with such intelligence are sensitive to language, as well as the various meanings and relationships among words; sensitive to the sounds and rhythm of words; and sensitive to the different functions of language. They are strong in oral and written expression and understanding. In essence, they are word oriented.

❖ *Spatial intelligence*, such as the visual arts, employs intelligence in the use of space. For example, spatial problem solving is crucial for playing chess and navigating. These students have a keen sense of observation and are visual thinkers who learn best using mental images and metaphors. They also are holistic learners who often see the forest before the trees.

❖ *Interpersonal intelligence* requires a core capacity to notice distinction among others, particularly in their mood, temperaments, motivation, and intentions. Students possessing this type of intelligence are socially oriented; they are adept at reading both the overt and covert intentions of others. Social competence, solidarity, leadership, organization, persuasion, and communication are important elements of interpersonal intelligence.

❖ *Intrapersonal intelligence* requires access to one's own feelings and emotions and the capacity to discriminate among various affect. Eventually, these gifted students draw upon them as a way of understanding and guiding their own behavior. Self-knowledge, awareness, and sensitivity to one's own values, purposes, short-comings, and feelings are important qualities of intrapersonal intelligence. These students appear wise and philosophical; they are intuitively oriented.

❖ *Naturalistic intelligence* has to do with nature, nurturing, and relating information to one's natural surroundings. This type of intelligence was not part of Gardner's original theory of multiple intelligences, but was added to the theory in 1997. These individuals are said to have greater or stronger sensitivity to nature and their place within it, the ability to nurture and grow things, and a greater ease in caring for and coping and interacting with animals. They also are able to discern changes in weather, as well as changes in their familiar and natural setting.

Implications. Gardner (1983, 1985) has maintained that a person can be intelligent or gifted in one area, but average or below average in the others. The theory of multiple intelligences calls into question and opposes the prevailing belief that gifted students are globally gifted, that they achieve in all areas, and that traditional areas or domains are more valuable and valid than others. It is culturally fair in that it is inclusive—it does not appear to discriminate against racially and culturally different students. Further, intelligences in the noncognitive domains (e.g., interpersonal) are just as valid, valuable, and praiseworthy as competencies in those traditionally deemed "intelligent." For example, among the Puluwat Islanders in the South Seas, spatial intelligence is critical for navigating canoes (Gardner, 1983, 1985), and in Third World countries, moral and social intelligence are highly valued. Hundeide (1992) contended that culturally different students live in a unique cognitive world, and they seem to have developed those aspects of intelligence relevant for social survival. In other societies, interpersonal intelligence is valued in literary endeavors. Nonetheless, the ability to write poetry, play sports, present a convincing argument, or lead others is not reflected on standardized tests. Yet, as Hundeide asked, "How relevant is our conception of deductive-analytic ability to the pragmatic challenges of their everyday life at the subsistence level?" (p. 62).

Bodily-kinesthetic learners are likely to be (mis)labeled as hyperactive and unjustly medicated. For example, males and Black students are overrepresented among students identified as hyperactive. Similarly, spatial students who require vivid pictures and images for optimal learning may be mislabeled as having ADHD.

Historically, musically inclined students and other students whose strengths are in the visual and performing arts are likely to be labeled "talented" rather than gifted. Accordingly, they are less likely than logical-mathematical and linguistic children to be placed in academically rigorous programs. Similarly, interpersonally and intrapersonally gifted students are unlikely to be placed in gifted education and AP classes.

The intelligences just described—bodily-kinesthetic, visual and performing arts, and inter- and intrapersonal—represent important strengths of Black students. By way of example, more Black students than White students are oral/vocal, social/extraverted, spatial/tactile/active, and visual learners (Boykin et al, 2006; Hale, 2001; Shade, 1994, 1997; Webb-Johnson, 2002). Many Black students demonstrate social intelligence, for instance, by a desire to focus on people rather than things, and to focus on the social aspects of learning. According to Damico's (1989) research, *people* in school are more important to Black students than the *concept* of school. Similarly, Eato and Lerner (1981) found that Black students are better able to recognize faces and emotions than other racial groups, and they are extremely sensitive to social nuances.

Manifestation	Level	Type	Context
Potential	Above average	Visual and performing arts	School
Demonstrated	Gifted	Intellectual	Home
	Very gifted	Academic (general, specific)	Community/environment
		Creative	
		Social	
		Other	

Figure 4.2. A proposed multidimensional model of giftedness.

A PROPOSED DEFINITION AND CULTURALLY RESPONSIVE MODEL OF GIFTEDNESS

All of the definitions of giftedness described earlier offer some promises for defining, identifying, and eventually assessing giftedness and potential among Black students. Their collective perspectives suggest what the U.S. Department of Education (1993) federal definition indicated:

> Children and youth with outstanding talent perform or show the potential for performing at remarkably high levels of accomplishment when compared with others of their age, experience, or environment. These children and youth exhibit high performance capability in intellectual, creative, and/or artistic areas, possess an unusual leadership capacity, or excel in specific academic fields. They require services or activities not ordinarily provided by the schools. Outstanding talents are present in children and youth from all cultural groups, across all economic strata, and in all areas of human endeavor. (p. 11)

As Figure 4.2 illustrates, giftedness is multifaceted. Some students demonstrate their giftedness and others show characteristics of giftedness but they may not be formally identified due to low test scores, cultural differences, or other factors. The model also acknowledges the reality of various types of giftedness (as described by Gardner, Sternberg, Renzulli, and others) and its contextual nature. Two students, described below, place the model into perspective.

Student A: Jackie is a 8-year-old Black student who teachers describe as very gifted in creativity, primarily based on Jackie's performance outside of school. On the Torrance Tests of Creative Thinking (a teacher checklist), Jackie received a 48 (out of 50). In addition, she has written several books of poetry (two of them published). In language arts, however, Jackie consistently earns a C.

Student B: Myron is an 8-year-old Black student who teachers describe as very gifted in creativity, primarily based on performance in school. His language arts teacher rated Myron 48 out of 50. He has never written a book and shows no interest in poetry, but consistently earns A's in language arts.

The abilities and skills of Jackie and Myron are reflected in their creativity scores; whereas Jackie demonstrates her abilities outside of school, Myron demonstrates his abilities academically. Given this information, which student is likely to be admitted to a gifted program? Which student appears to require special services not ordinarily provided by the school? Is an intelligence test needed before a placement decision can be made for either student?

IDENTIFICATION AND ASSESSMENT PRACTICES

STANDARDIZED TESTS

A crisis exists in the psychoeducational assessment of minority group children.
—Jones (1988, p. 13)

Neill and Medina (1989) reported that U.S. public schools administered 105 million standardized tests to 39.8 million students (an average of 2.5 tests per student) during the 1986–1987 school year. This figure includes the administering of more than 55 million standardized tests of achievement, competency, and basic skills. Not counted are the 30 to 40 million tests administered to students in compensatory and special education programs, and the 2 million used to screen prekindergarten and kindergarten students. Nor does it include tests for the General Educational Development (GED) program, the National Assessment of Educational Progress (NAEP), and admissions to college and secondary school, which total an additional 6 or 7 million tests annually. Finally, these figures do not include tests used to identify students with limited proficiency in English, tests administered by private and parochial schools, or tests used to identify students for gifted programs.

The No Child Left Behind Act of 2001 solidified standards-based reform as a national priority, and required that every public school student in grades 3 through 8, and in one high school grade, be tested; the number of tests for this alone is estimated at some 45 million each year (Toch, 2006). It has also been estimated that during the 2005–2006 school year, those states (n = 23) that have not yet fully implemented NCLB's testing requirements administered approximately 11.4 million new tests. It is important to note that the above estimates are for tests associated with NCLB—not those used for screening, identification, and placement in gifted and AP classes.

As discussed in Chapter 2, Public Law 94-142, the Education for All Handicapped Children Act, requires that children be evaluated using instruments that are not racially or culturally biased. A major impetus for P.L. 94-142 was the overrepresentation of minority students in special education classes. Other legal battles have been fought on behalf of equity (or lack thereof) in testing practices for Black and other minority students (e.g., *Larry P. v. Riles*, 1979; *Hobson v. Hansen*, 1967; *Diana v. California State Board of Education*, 1970). These court cases were brought on behalf of legal, ethical, and/or social concerns for children of color. One of the most enlightening cases from the business profession that warrants discussion here is that of *Griggs v. Duke Power* (1971). This case focused extensively on the notion of "disparate impact" regarding tests. One question stemming from the case is as follows: If a group consistently performs poorly on a test, why do we continue to use it? In addition, we must be consistent in applying this principle across different types of groups. For example, if bias or unfairness exists in a test against females, then it should not be used; it places males at an advantage. Who would find this acceptable? So it is too with income, SES, and race. How can we (e.g., educators, decision makers) defend using a test that disadvantages one group while simultaneously advantaging another?

Bernal (1981) suggested that if identification techniques discriminate against Black students, it is because they rely on tests designed to measure the performance of persons from the dominant culture, of values generally espoused by White middle-class students. Sternberg and Kolligian (1990) found that standardized intelligence tests measure analytic abilities but ignore synthetic abilities. The tests do not describe in toto intelligence, personality, and achievement because they explain only 10%–25% of performance outside of school (Sternberg, 1985, 2007). Wagner and Sternberg (1985) reported moderate correlations between .4 and .7 between school achievement and ability, and other work has reported correlations of .7 between intelligence tests taken in early and later years (Bloom, 1964; Tannenbaum, 1992). Essentially, IQ scores account for only 16% to 50% of school achievement (Pelligrini & Glickman, 1990; Tannenbaum, 1992) and assess only a minute fraction of the 100 or more kinds of intelligence (Taylor & Ellison, 1968). In essence, academic skill assessments show little criterion validity, and their utility for making consequential decisions about students' futures are questionable. Academic and intelligence tests predict the results a person will obtain on other tests of the same kind. Nonetheless, testing is big business and massive standardized testing in the schools and gifted programs persist ad nauseam, and educators seem not to have heeded the sage advice of Tannenbaum (1992): "IQ in itself is far from a totally valid sign of any kind of giftedness, not matter how giftedness is defined" (p. 18).

SOURCES OF POOR TEST PERFORMANCE FOR BLACK STUDENTS

Worthen, Borg, and White (1993) noted:

Care should be taken not to attribute the biases in our society to the instruments that report their cumulative effects. In many respects, our tests are only a mirror that reflect the educational results of cultural bias; shattering the mirror will not solve the problem. (p. 38)

Many factors inhibit the performance of Black students on standardized tests of intelligence and achievement, specifically environmental factors, psychological variables, and problems within the tests themselves.

Environmental factors and test performance. McCall, Applebaum, and Hogarty (1973) found that Stanford-Binet scores changed on the average 28.5 points between the ages of 2 ½ and 17, with the largest change being 40 points (almost three standard deviations). However, for economically challenged students, scores tended to decrease with formal schooling. McCall and colleagues (1973) attributed the decrease primarily to the effects of environmental factors. Low-income and low-SES students, for instance, have qualitatively different and quantitatively fewer educational opportunities than middle- and high-SES students (e.g., Burney & Beilke; 2008; Stambaugh, 2009; VanTassel-Baska, 2010; VanTassel-Baska & Stambaugh, 2007). Because a disproportionate percentage of Black students live in poverty, they are especially vulnerable to low or poor test scores and to negative educational outcomes.

My own observations of intelligence and achievement tests reveal that many items assess moral rather than cognitive development, and they are heavily loaded with language and culture or experiences that place many students at a grave disadvantage. For example, on one popular standardized intelligence test, students are asked what they *should* do if they find a wallet containing money. Test takers must choose between returning and keeping the money. For economically challenged students, this can be a very difficult decision that is precluded by economic need rather than cognitive/intellectual or moral development (see Maslow, 1954, for information on basic or deficiency needs). Similarly, on a popular achievement test, students are asked to choose the "best" answer to common items found in a restaurant. Some children/students living in poverty have never been to a restaurant (fast food notwithstanding); therefore, the particular items listed are irrelevant and inappropriate. Sattler (1992) noted that "Items on intelligence tests represent important aspects of competence in the *common* culture" (p. 568). This notion of "common culture" represents the fundamental problems with tests that purport to be objective and unbiased. Sattler's statement begs the question: Test items represent aspects of competence in *whose* culture? Is there a *common* culture (Ford, 2007b)?

Per Table 4.1, much of this discussion about the test bias and fairness was captured by Flanagan and Ortiz (2001) and Flanagan, Ortiz, and Alfonso (2007), who reported that Black and other culturally different students may not do well on intelligence tests due to their cultural loading/demand and linguistic demand/loading. They show that performance on nonverbal subscales are lower on both linguistic and cultural loading than verbal subscales, which opens opportunities for Black

Table 4.1
Linguistic and Cultural Loadings on Subscales of Intelligence Tests

	Low degree of cultural loading	Moderate degree of cultural loading	High degree of cultural loading
Low linguistic demand	• Wechsler Matrix Reasoning • Stanford-Binet IV Pattern Analysis	• Wechsler Block Design, Symbol Search, and Digit Span • Stanford-Binet IV Memory for Digits, Matrices, and Bead Memory	• Stanford-Binet IV Number Series
Moderate linguistic demand	• Wechsler Object Assembly • Stanford-Binet IV Memory for Objects	• Wechsler Block Design, Symbol Search, and Digit Span • Stanford-Binet IV Memory for Digits, Matrices, and Bead Memory	• Stanford-Binet IV Equation Building
High linguistic demand			• Wechsler Information, Similarities, Vocabulary, and Comprehension • Stanford-Binet IV Vocabulary, Verbal Relations, Absurdities, and Comprehension

students and those in poverty to more fairly demonstrate their intelligence. Along these lines, Sternberg (2007) argued that IQ tests, to a large extent, reflect a cultural conception of competence. He went on to add that for a school to understand the child, the school must understand both the child and the community's concept of giftedness and the gifted child—and how the child stacks up in comparison to the norm of his or her peers.

Psychological factors and test performance. A large database exists regarding the influence of motivation and test anxiety on test outcomes. Students who have poor or weak academic motivation, are disinterested in the test, easily distracted, and excessively concerned about test outcomes tend to have lower scores on standardized tests than students who are motivated, interested, less anxious, and on task. These same concerns hold for students with low academic self-concepts, low self-esteem, an external locus of control, and other indices of low or poor academic self-confidence.

Cognitive styles such as attention to global versus analytical features of stimuli (also referred to as field-dependent and field-independent perceptual styles, respectively), the division of stimuli into large rather than small or discrete categories, intuitive and inductive thinking compared to deductive thinking, and impulsiveness versus reflectiveness influence test results in terms of speed, precision, and quality. For example, impulsive students are likely to make errors because they take less time to consider the problem and are affected by the distractors in the test items. Field-dependent students tend to have difficulty separating the stimuli from the background, are less analytical, and are more socially inclined (e.g., prefer group over individual learning experiences). Field-independent students tend to be analytic, independent learners, and intrinsically motivated. Because these are the values espoused in schools, field-independent learners have greater chances for school success than do field-dependent students. Further, field-independent students often favor mathematics and the sciences, thus they are likely to do well on intelligence tests that measure analytical abilities and abstract reasoning. Decades of research demonstrate that Black students are more likely to be field-dependent learners (i.e., relational, social, holistic, global learners) who approach learning situations intuitively rather than logically (Hale, 2001; Hilliard, 1979; Shade, 1994; Shade et al., 1997).

Stereotype threat and test performance. Stereotype threat refers to being at risk of confirming, as self-characteristic, a negative stereotype about one's group (Aronson, 2004). This social-psychological term was first used by Steele and Aronson (1995), who showed that Black college freshmen and sophomores performed more poorly on standardized tests than did White students when their race was emphasized during test administration. Conversely, when race was not emphasized, Black students performed better on the test and equivalently with White students. The results showed that performance in academic contexts can be harmed by the awareness that one's behavior might be viewed through the lens of racial stereotypes.

Similar effects had been reported earlier by Katz, Roberts, and Robinson (1965), but Steele and Aronson's (1995) study prompted a renewed exploration of the causes and consequences of stereotype threat. More than 300 experiments on stereotype threat have been published in peer-reviewed journals (see Nguyen & Ryan, 2008, and Walton & Cohen, 2007, for meta-analyses).

Since Steele and Aronson's (1995) study, research on stereotype threat has broadened in several important respects. First, research has shown that the *consequences* of stereotype threat extend beyond underachievement on academic tasks. For example, it can lead to self-handicapping strategies, such as reduced practice time for a task and reduced sense of belonging to the stereotyped domain (Good, Dweck, & Rattan, 2008). In addition, consistent exposure to stereotype threat faced by some racially different students in academic environments can reduce the degree that individuals value the domain in question (Aronson, Fried, & Good, 2002; Steele, 1997). In education, it can also lead students to choose not to pursue the domain of study and, consequently, limit the range of professions that they can or wish to pursue. Therefore, the long-term effects of stereotype threat might contribute to educational and social inequality (Good et al., 2008; Schmader, Johns, & Barquissau, 2004). Given the heavy or sole reliance on tests to make decisions about gifted education and AP enrollment, stereotype threat cannot be trivialized or ignored.

Culture, cultural styles, and test performance. Beyond or in addition to exploring the social-psychology of testing by way of stereotype threat, it is imperative that educators, test developers, and test users avoid being culture-blind in their development, interpretation, and use of the test scores of Black and other culturally different groups, particularly when making comparisons with White students.

As stated in Chapter 1, culture is defined as the collective beliefs, attitudes, traditions, customs, and behaviors that serve as a filter through which a group of people view and respond to the world (e.g., Erickson, 2010; Ford & Harris, 1999; Ford & Milner, 2005; Hall, 1959, 1976, 1983). Culture is a way of life, a way of looking at and interpreting life, and a way of responding to life. Culture operates primarily at the unconscious level (e.g., Erickson, 2010; Hofstede, 2001; Oberg, 1954, 1960).

Helms (1992) has provided another thought-provoking, conceptual treatise on the issue of how culture impacts test performance and, thereby, raises questions about the validity of tests when used with diverse groups (see Groth-Marnat, 1997, 2003; Miller, 1996; Sattler, 1992; and Sternberg, 1982, 2007, for other definitions of culture and the impact of culture on test performance). Helms (1992) maintained that the notion of cultural or functional equivalence must be considered when diverse students are being tested or assessed. Using Boykin's (1986) research on the modal characteristics of Blacks, Helms (1992) hypothesized how these

Afrocentric cultural dimensions or characteristics can and do influence the test performance of Black students (see Table 4.2).

As described in Chapter 3, Afrocentric styles delineated in Boykin's (1986) research include: spirituality, verve, movement, harmony, communalism, oral tradition; social time perspective, affect, and individual expressiveness[2]. Table 4.2 describes these dimensions with respect to the hypothetical testing responses of Black students. These dimensions affect students' communication styles, learning styles, thinking styles, and test-taking styles and skills (Ford, 2007a; Ford & Harris, 1999; Helms, 1992). For instance, students for whom movement and verve are strong dimensions of their being will be spontaneous, active, and energetic; they may have a difficult time sitting through lengthy tests. Students for whom orality (oral tradition) is strong may prefer to explain their answers or write essays rather than respond to multiple-choice items; students for whom time perspective is predominant may have difficulty managing their time when taking tests. When students have a communal orientation, they may prefer to work in groups rather than alone; this preference may be interpreted as immaturity, laziness, or cheating by educators who are unfamiliar with cultural styles and differences (Delgado-Gaitan & Trueba, 1985).

As noted in the previous chapters and others, the Afrocentric dimensions described by Boykin (1983, 1986) are research-based, and they describe many, but not all, Black students. The point here is that culture matters not only when students are learning, but also when they are taking tests; this reality should not be ignored, negated, or minimized when examining the test scores of diverse students. Accordingly, Helms (1992) asked:

❖ Is there evidence that the culturally conditioned intellectual skills used by Blacks and Whites generally differ and that these differences have been equivalently incorporated into the measurement procedures?

❖ Do Blacks and Whites use the same test-taking strategies when ostensibly responding to the same material, and do these strategies have equivalent meaning?

❖ If different strategies are used by different racial groups, to what

2   Boykin's (1994) data-based model of Afrocentric cultural styles has been examined and discussed in hundreds of publications; for a discussion of the cultural styles of Blacks, Hispanic Americans, Asian Americans, and Native Americans, see, for example, Baldwin and Vialle (1999), Castellano (2003), Shade et al. (1997), Storti (1999), Maker and Schiever (1989), Banks and Banks (1993), Callahan and McIntyre (1994), Cline and Schwartz (1999), Ford and Harris (1999), and Ford and Milner (2005).

Table 4.2
African Cultural Components in Cognitive Ability Testing:
Hypothesized Effects of Afrocentric Values and Beliefs

Dimension	Potential influence(s) on test responses
Spirituality	It may be difficult for a student to separate relevant aspects of the test stimuli from factors caused by luck or circumstances. The student may not study, choosing to rely instead on faith for positive performance.
Harmony	The ambience in which one takes the test may influence one's responses; the test taker may be distracted by events taking place during the test. Lower performance may result if the learning environment is negative or hostile.
Movement and verve	Active test-taking strategies may result in better performance than sedentary ones; the test taker may have difficulty sitting through and concentrating during lengthy tests. The student is likely to perform better when given breaks.
Affect	Feelings may facilitate or hinder test performance; the test taker may find it difficult to "understand" persons in test stimuli who act without feeling. The student may not do well if offended by test items, including words and pictures.
Communalism	Performance may be influenced when the test taker is anxious about the test scores being reflective of his or her cultural group and having negative consequences for the group. The student may get anxious or have test anxiety.
Expressiveness	The test taker may choose the more imaginative or creative response alternative; the student may be impulsive in choosing responses.
Orality (oral traditional)	Test performance may differ when the test taker is tested orally; the test taker may be frustrated by paper-pencil tests, preferring instead to take the tests orally or show knowledge and skills via performance, skit, debate, and the like.
Social time (polychronicity)	The belief that obtaining a "good" answer is more important than finishing on time may lead the test taker to "waste" or mismanage time; he or she may not begin responding immediately to the test or may be more concerned about the performance of friends than his or her own score/performance. The student may "cheat" to help friends do well.

Note. Adapted from Helms (1992). Also see Boykin (1986).

extent are these differences an aspect of test prediction and criteria?

❖ How does one measure the cultural characteristics of intelligence tests? (p. 1097)

The implications of these questions for educators is that, when differences in performance on intelligence tests are attributed to racial or cultural differences, educators must recognize this explanation for the non sequitur that it is. Instead of continuing to use such measures until something better comes along, educators must challenge the scientists on whose work their test usage is based to find culturally defined psychological explanations (e.g., culture-specific attitudes, feelings, and behaviors) for why such racial and ethnic differences exist (Helms, 1992).

Instrumentation. Few researchers and educational professionals would disagree that the most important aspect on any test is the degree to which it is fair, valid, and reliable. These characteristics determine the usefulness of the test; an instrument that provides inconsistent results lack usefulness. As McLeod and Crophy (1989) stated, no identification instrument acts like a crystal ball; it does not predict the future without a reference point.

Given that intelligence is not a fixed attribute, scores derived from intelligence tests cannot be assumed to be fixed. Patchen (1982) reported that, for Black students, the relationship between current grade point average (GPA) and IQ scores is .28 and that it is .47 for White students. Moreover, Patchen reported a correlation of .23 for occupational aspiration and GPA for Black students and .42 for White students. These figures and other data highlight the importance of examining the validity and reliability of standardized tests for Black students.

Sources of error affecting test reliability include trait instability, sampling error, scoring error, administrator error, and the test taker's health, motivation, degree of fatigue, and so forth. Other factors also influence the reliability of tests, including test length (the greater the number of items, the higher the reliability), group heterogeneity (the more homogeneous the group, the higher the reliability), and the spread of scores (the wider the range, the higher the reliability).

In this era of high-stakes testing, arguments against using standardized tests with Black and some other culturally different students have proliferated in recent years on the grounds that Black students are consistently assessed by tests that do not indicate the value of the reliability coefficient for their particular group (Ford, 2004, 2007a, 2007b, 2010;

Greenfield, 1997; Haney & Madaus, 1989; Helms, 1992, 1994; Hilliard, 1976, 1979, 1992, 1997; Samuda, 1998; Whiting & Ford, 2009). The tests only indicate how reliable the results are according to sample groups upon which reliability was first established. In essence, high reliability coefficients are only high for the reference group and those groups that approximate it. To illustrate, if a test is normed or standardized on a sample of predominantly White and middle or upper income or SES students, it will be less reliable for Black and/or low-income and SES students. Because the life experiences and educational opportunities between Black and White students may vary considerably (e.g., due to racism, prejudice, discrimination, as well as differences in culture), the reliability, validity, and ultimate utility of the test (or instrument) may also be questionable for middle and upper income and SES Black students due to cultural differences (Ford & Whiting, 2009).

Like reliability, factors affecting test validity are problematic in terms of using standardized tests with Black students. Regarding content validity, it is assumed that the test taker has been exposed to and is familiar with the information from which the tests are drawn, and that the language of the test (or test maker) is the language of the test taker. Samuda (1998), Flanagan and Ortiz (2001), and Flanagan and colleagues (2007) reported that the emphasis placed on the definition of abstract words, analogies, sentence completion, and so forth in the Stanford-Binet and other standardized intelligence tests presupposes a certain mastery of the comprehension and usage of standard English. Perhaps the most obvious example is that we continue to give students tests in English when their primary language is not English; or we test students on their command of standard English, when they communicate best in other languages and dialects (e.g., Black English, also referred to as Ebonics or African American Vernacular English). Although this latter example is controversial, current beliefs, values, and practices, nonetheless, equate command of the English language with intelligence, potential, and achievement. And, tragically, this is not likely to change.

Other tests lack cultural sensitivity in terms of format and presentation. For example, how valid are the results if a Black student takes a test in which none of the people depicted on the test are Black? The same question holds when females take tests in which males consistently play the dominant role, and females hold passive roles. Similarly, what impact does the race and gender of the examiner have on students' test performance? How important is the rapport between the student and test administrator? What about students' familiarity with the test format? What about the quality and presentation of instructions (e.g., oral, written, both)? What about students' test-taking skills? What about test anxiety and stereotype threat (Steele, 1997)?

In essence, the same issues affecting the validity and reliability of tests can result in biases and unfairness against low-income, low-SES, and racially different students; conversely, these tests are biased in favor of higher income and high-SES students, most of whom are White. An examination of standardized tests reveals that: (a) language differences exist between the test (or test maker) and the students; (b) the test questions center on the experiences and facts of the dominant culture, and the answers support middle-class values, which are often rewarded with more points; (c) the tests favor highly verbal students—those strong in standard English (they require, for example, a great deal of reading, word recognition, vocabulary, and sentence completion; many tests also require verbal responses); and (d) the tests do not consider the extent to which some students may not be oriented toward achievement. Poor academic motivation, task commitment, effort, and interest can and do compromise students' performance. The problem of test bias and unfairness is multifaceted. Laosa (1977) offered several relevant criticisms regarding testing practices:

- ❖ Standardized tests are biased and unfair to racially and culturally different students, as well as economically disadvantaged students. They do not reflect the language, experiences, or cognitive styles of these students.
- ❖ Standardized measurement procedures foster undemocratic attitudes by their use in forming racially, culturally, linguistically, and economically homogeneous classroom groups that severely limit educational, vocational, economic, and other societal opportunities.
- ❖ Assessments are sometimes conducted by persons who do not understand the culture and language of Black and other racially different students. As a result, they are unable to elicit a level of performance that accurately reflects the child's competence.
- ❖ Testing practices foster expectations that may be damaging by contributing to the self-fulfilling prophecy that ensures low levels of achievement for those who score low on tests.
- ❖ Standardized measurements rigidly shape school curricula and restrict educational change.
- ❖ Norm-referenced measures are not useful for instructional purposes.

- ❖ The limited scope of many standardized tests appraises only a part of the changes in children that schools should be interested in producing.
- ❖ Standardized testing practices foster a view of human beings as having only innate and fixed abilities and characteristics.

On this last note, Snyderman and Rothman (1987) found that more than half of the 877 measurement experts who responded to a survey on intelligence and aptitude testing believed that genetic factors contributed to Black-White differences in IQ scores. This belief is pervasive (Onwuegbuzie & Daley, 2001). A major reason for concerns about bias in mental testing is that it involves the specter of biological determinism—that the differences in test scores can be attributed largely to inherent differences. A second reason for this volatile issue is that tests play a pivotal role in classification or misclassification of students, particularly relative to special placements such as tracking, ability grouping, special education services, AP classes, and gifted education services. A third reason is that standardized test scores are highly correlated with family income; thus, tests are a major institution in preserving the status quo (Nairn, 1980).

The aforementioned sentiments or concerns about the potential and real harm of testing were captured in *Larry P. v. Riles* (1979), where the court ruled:

> If tests predict that a person is going to be a poor employee, the employer can legitimately deny the person the job, but if the tests suggest that a young child is probably going to be a poor student, a school cannot on that basis alone deny that child the opportunity to improve and develop the academic skills necessary to succeed in our society.

GRADING PRACTICES

Grades, one indicator of school achievement, serve many practical purposes in school and in identification practices. However, they lack standardization and are influenced significantly by students' motivation, classroom behavior, personal appearance, and study habits. Further, teachers' knowledge of students' IQ scores, income, SES, area of residence, and family structure contribute to stereotypes that are frequently characterized by low expectations (Rosenthal & Jacobson, 1992; Samuda, Feuerstein, Kaufman, Lewis, & Sternberg, 1998) and deficit thinking (Ford, Harris, Tyson, & Frazier Trotman, 2002).

The validity of grades is also questionable given that grading practices vary by the particular teacher, school, weights on assignments, and scales used. For example, my son attended three school districts with three different grading scales. At one school, the lowest grade for an A was 90%, at another it was 93%, and at the third, it was 95%. Similarly, 50% was failing at one school, while 69% was failing at another. One school had a 10-point scale, the second had a 7-point scale, and the third had a scale that varied (e.g., an A has a 5-point range, a D has a 7-point range).

Grades are also influenced by course difficulty and the quality of the school. Honor courses and higher track or ability group courses are more difficult/challenging than other courses. Grades received in courses that are less academically rigorous are quite different than those received in more academically rigorous courses.

NOMINATIONS

TEACHERS AS NOMINATORS AND IDENTIFIERS

Teachers often have limited or narrow notions of giftedness that fail to capture the strengths of Black and underachieving students. Exacerbating this problem is that checklists and nomination forms may be insensitive to the characteristics of gifted Black students. Yet, Tuttle, Becker, and Sousa (1988) noted that the most prevalent method of identifying gifted learners is to ask for teacher recommendations, a method they and others have found to be inadequate. Archambault and colleagues (1993) reported that teachers are also among the most highly used sources of referral and identification.

Early research by Pegnato and Birch (1959) found that junior high school teachers not only failed to nominate more than 50% of the gifted students in their school, but they also identified many average students as gifted. Jacobs (1971) found that primary teachers surveyed could identify only 10% of the students who had scored high on individual IQ tests. Although Borland (1978) found positive correlations between teacher ratings and students' IQ scores, he also discovered that teachers were more effective in identifying gifted females and gifted underachievers. Cox, Daniel, and Boston (1985) found that almost 38% of the third- and fourth-grade teachers in their study reported unidentified gifted students in their classrooms, yet 90% of school districts used teacher nominations for identification purposes.

A primary factor in the successful identification of gifted Black students is teacher attitude. High and Udall (1983) reported that racially different students were less likely than White students to be referred for gifted programs. They attributed this lack of referrals to teachers' attitudes and expectations. For example, teachers frequently emphasize behaviors such as cooperation, answering correctly, punctuality, and neatness when identifying gifted students. But these may not be the behaviors demonstrated by gifted Black and underachieving students. Similarly, there is often a mismatch between the learning characteristics of gifted Black students and those listed on many checklists completed by teachers. A perusal of several nomination forms indicate that characteristics of underachieving and minority students are noticeably absent, they lack both national and, perhaps more important, local normative data, and they focus on academic and cognitive characteristics.

Nomination forms should also gather information on the hobbies and interests of Black students, special talents, preferred activities when alone, and relationships with others, including older students and adults. Information on development and special needs (e.g., learning styles, medical, physiological), as well as learning opportunities provided by parents and other family members should also be gathered by teachers.

Given consistent findings regarding the difficulties teachers have in identifying gifted students, teacher nominations must be interpreted and used with caution. By focusing on the "model" gifted child (e.g., cooperative, well dressed, English speaking, teacher pleaser), many gifted students will be overlooked, specifically underachievers, nonconforming creative students, Black students, and other racially and culturally different students who face negative stereotypes. Stated differently, the subjectivity of nomination forms and the biases of teachers represent real threats to the successful identification of gifted and potentially gifted Black students.

Davis and Rimm's (1994) recommendation that schools develop their own teacher nomination forms must be taken with caution. Like any assessment measure, these forms must have respectable levels of reliability and validity and local norms, and they must include characteristics of giftedness among Black students and underachieving students. The Kranz Talent Identification Instrument (Kranz, 1981) has been recommended for use with students traditionally underrepresented in gifted education programs—Black, underachieving, and economically challenged students. Teachers rate all children on 10 dimensions (leadership and organizing talent, visual arts talent, performing arts talent, academic talent, psychomotor talent, spatial and abstract thinking talent, creative talent, one-sided talent, underachievement talent, and hidden talent).

When all is said and done, it cannot be denied that teachers play a significant and powerful role in Black students' underrepresentation in gifted and AP classes. Ford et al.'s (2008b) review of the literature found that *every* report or study on teacher referral (from 1971 to 2008) found that teachers underrefer Black students for gifted education screening and placement. This problem is noted throughout this book; underreferral contributes to both underrepresentation and underachievement.

SCHOOL PSYCHOLOGISTS AND COUNSELORS AS IDENTIFIERS

School psychologists and counselors are also heavily relied upon for identification and placement decisions for gifted and AP classes. Ironically, although school psychologists bear much of the burden for testing and/or assessment, there is little information on them regarding their role in or contribution to underrepresentation. They do the testing, scoring, and interpretation. To say the least, what they say, believe, do, and decide matters.

A few studies have explored public school counselors' awareness of issues confronting gifted students, as well as their training to work with this student population (e.g., Peterson & Morris, 2010). Findings indicate that few school counselors or psychologists are formally trained to work with gifted learners. For example, Klausmeier, Mishra, and Maker (1987) found that most school counselors considered their training in recognizing gifted students to be less than average and their training with culturally different, low-income, and low-SES groups to be below average or completely lacking. At the university level, Ford and Harris (1995a) found that only 10% of counselors reported receiving training to work with gifted learners, while 71% reported receiving some training in multicultural issues. They also found that the majority of the counselors were unaware of or indecisive about the issues hindering the identification and achievement of gifted students in general, and Black students in particular.

In their study of state certification endorsement for school counselors in special education, Frantz and Prillaman (1993) found that 11 states required at least one course in special education for their certification as school counselors, 17 were in the process of changing certification requirements for counselors and considering including a course in special education, and another 17 states neither required any courses nor were they in the process of considering changes in certification. This lack of training among school counselors and psychologists can contribute to misinterpreting information gathered from tests and teachers. It also may contribute to the underidentification and poor enrollment of Black students in gifted classes, programs, and services, and in AP classes.

FAMILIES/CAREGIVERS AS IDENTIFIERS

Because Black parents/families/caregivers share cultural values with their children, they may represent more effective sources of information than teachers. Families/caregivers, in general, are an excellent and reliable source of information about their children's strengths and weaknesses, yet they are seldom utilized in the identification process even though P.L. 94-142 requires parent participation in its guidelines. In a small and now dated study, Ciha, Harris, Hoffman, and Potter (1974) found that parents were more effective at identifying gifted students than were teachers. Specifically, parents nominated 75% of children accurately according to stated criteria, compared to teachers, who accurately nominated 22% of students. Ryan (1983) found that parents were more effective than teachers at identifying intellectually gifted Black students, as reflected by higher correlations with both the Stanford-Binet and Leiter International Performance Scale. Carroll, Gurski, Hinsdale, and McIntyre (1977) noted that:

> Family/caregiver involvement in assessment and programming adds a new dimension to the concept of assessment and accountability in education—the direct access of educators to the parents whose child they shape. In the context of culturally appropriate assessment, this accountability to parents is particularly meaningful since it implies accountability to the child's cultural and linguistic heritage as well. (p. 323)

Although families/caregivers represent important and reliable sources of information, nomination forms themselves may be unreliable. Families/caregiver nomination forms and checklists suffer from the same shortcomings as teacher nomination forms and checklists—poor or lack of reliability and validity data, no local norms, inaccurate or incomplete characteristics of gifted students, and a focus on intellectual or academic characteristics of giftedness. Forms must also be sensitive to reading levels. Families/caregivers who have difficulty understanding the forms are likely to over- or underestimate their child's ability, or fail to complete the forms altogether.

Information from grandparents or other extended family members should also be accepted in lieu of or in addition to parent nomination information. For instance, if children are reared by grandmothers or aunts (which is on the rise, according to the U.S. Census Bureau, 2006), these family members may be in a better position to describe gifted behaviors in Black children.

PEERS AS NOMINATORS

Cox and colleagues (1985) found that 25% of the school districts they surveyed used peer nominations for identification purposes. Many articles extol the virtues of peer nomination for identifying gifted students. Gagné (1989), however, reviewed 13 studies that used peer nominations and concluded that the scientific foundation for peer nominations is fragile. For instance, peer nomination forms tend to be monothematic—all of the items assess one ability. When nominations are plurithematic, researchers often combine the different subscales into a global score. This practice cancels the information gained from specific subscales. Further, peer nominations are often normed on a small sample; there is seldom reliability data (inter-judger reliability, pre-post reliability); there is often no data on construct and criterion validity. When construct validity data are provided, the nomination data are compared to IQ scores.

Although peer nominations are not sociograms, one must consider the extent to which they are appropriate for Black students when they attend predominantly White schools, gifted education, and AP classes. The lack of heterogeneity in such schools and programs calls into question the quality and quantity of peer relations (isolation, popularity), cultural differences, and economical differences. Further, to what extent are White students sensitive to cultural strengths of Black students? To what extent are peer nomination forms culturally sensitive or biased? To what extent do they contain characteristics of gifted underachievers?

SELF-NOMINATIONS

Self-nomination forms represent an important opportunity for unrecognized gifted Black students to be considered for identification and assessment. Renzulli (1987) indicated that high schools students in particular should be given opportunities to nominate themselves. However, as discussed in the next chapter, some gifted underachievers and Black students may not wish to be identified. For any student who wishes to hide his or her abilities, self-nominations are impractical. These students are not likely to nominate themselves. Much of this issue relates to negative peer pressures, which are discussed in several chapters in this book.

RECOMMENDATIONS

There is no "one-size-fits-all" intelligence or achievement test. To optimize identification and learning opportunities for gifted Black students, particularly underachievers, assessment must be comprehensive, dynamic, and culturally sensitive. Equally important, teachers and other school personnel must have substantive training in both gifted and multicultural education. There is also a critical need to progress from a culture of testing to a culture of identification, as well as to close the gap between research and practice.

FROM A CULTURE OF TESTING TO A CULTURE OF ASSESSMENT

The urgent need to move from a culture of identification to a culture of assessment is long overdue. Given the magnitude of testing, educators must be ever mindful of the important distinctions between identification and assessment. The purpose of identification is not a mere categorization of gifted abilities already fully manifest. Identification is actually a needs assessment for the purpose of placing students into educational programs designed to develop their latent potential. Identification is designed to confirm one's perception that a child needs special services (e.g., is gifted, underachieving), while assessment is prescriptive. Assessment is designed to give more specific information on the areas in which a student is gifted, as well as his or her strengths and shortcomings.

Assessment is defined as making an evaluation or estimation of development, the end product being a decision as to what intervention would be appropriate to facilitate the students' development. Because of its prescriptive nature, assessment conveys expectations about what is important for students to learn, provides information to students and parents about the students' progress, and helps guide and improve instruction. Because of its emphasis on multiple and diverse measures, assessment also provides information relative to accountability, guides policy decisions about school improvement and reform, and provides information for program evaluation.

Teachers must examine their evaluation practices and self-constructed tests relative to shortcomings. Such tests, according to Fleming and Chambers (1983), are most often short-answer and matching, but may also include true-false and multiple-choice items. Dorr-Bremm and Herman (1986) found that although teachers may use tests to report results to parents, identify students' strengths and weaknesses, group and place students, assign grades, and plan instruction, they are more likely to use their own opinions when judging student performance.

Despite the widespread use of teacher-made tests, little data exist regarding their quality. Carter (1984) and Gullickson and Ellwein (1985) reported that, too often, items are ambiguous, and teacher-made tests place a heavy emphasis on low-level thinking, namely, the simple recall of facts and information. Further, the tests are often too short to produce reliable scores, and teachers rarely conduct item analyses to improve the tests.

In ideal situations, assessment reflects the goals of the gifted program and AP classes and associated activities, mirrors the philosophy of the program, and actively involves students and their families/caregivers in the process. Assessment should not reduce or hinder student motivation or be used to filter out racially different, low-income, and low-SES students from gifted education and AP classes. And, as discussed below, assessments should be conducted by well-trained, culturally competent personnel who understand not only the instruments and their intended purposes, but also their shortcomings. All of these variables affect the quality and outcome of assessment practices, and they call for comprehensive, dynamic, and culturally responsive instruments and assessment.

Comprehensive and Culturally Responsive Assessment

The goal of comprehensive assessment is to generate an accurate snapshot of students' current level and mode of functioning within the context of their individual backgrounds and experiences (Ford, 2007b, 2010; Ford & Whiting 2009; Samuda, 1998; Whiting & Ford, 2009). Comprehensive and culturally responsive assessment provides information on students' specific learning styles, preferences, and needs such that it is diagnostic. Assessment must examine and gather data on students' culture, language, income, SES, self-concept, racial identity, and learning styles. At the same time, information should be gathered on students' strengths and weaknesses. Methodology needs to include surveillance—ongoing and consistent information gathering—that consists of qualitative data and observations, school and anecdotal records, personality assessments, and maturational and developmental information from families/caregivers and teachers.

Key objectives of comprehensive and dynamic assessment include examining students' potential, skills, and performance under familiar or novel tasks and situations. There should be observations of the strategies Black students use to perform and understand tasks, including information on learning style preferences (e.g., visual, auditory, kinesthetic, field-dependent, field-independent). Practices that do not acknowledge the complexity of assessment cannot be considered comprehensive and responsive.

Dynamic assessment was described by Vygotsky (1978), who contended that changes in performance are assessed in optimal ways by examining the interaction between learning and development. The zone of proximal development describes the relationship between the actual developmental level, as determined by independent problem solving, and the level of potential development, as determined by problem solving under adult guidance/supervision.

Valid and reliable instruments must be utilized in the assessment process. As Hansen and Linden (1990) and Sax (1989) advised, we must consider the purpose of the instrument, the target population, special considerations, and limitations of the test. These considerations are necessary to avoid exploiting students, to ensure equity, and not to invade the students' right to privacy based on thoughtless employment of dubious measurement devices.

The considerations listed in Figure 4.3 are essential for both formal and informal instruments. Accordingly, nomination forms and checklists for parents and teachers must be sensitive to all reading and educational levels, and include characteristics of Black students and underachieving students for clarity purposes. They should also contain examples and descriptors of the racially and culturally sensitive characteristics. Parents/caregivers and educators who are unable to understand the items on the checklist will have a difficult time responding accurately. Thus, we must make certain that both our formal and informal instruments are sensitive to parents and teachers. It would be informative if teachers and parents used the same or similar checklists so that decision makers can explore consistencies or discrepancies in the responses of parents and teachers. If discrepancies are significant, educators can examine the nature and extent of the differences. What do parents see that teachers do not (and visa versa)? Are there certain items in which inconsistencies are evident?

Culturally sensitive or responsive assessment is essential for identifying and assessing gifted Black students (Ford & Whiting, 2009). What are the strengths and weaknesses of assessment materials used for identification and placement decisions? What formal and informal mechanisms are used to assess, place, and provide programming for gifted Black and underachieving students? What barriers adversely affect the assessment and program opportunities of children because of race, cultural, ethnicity, and language? Is the underrepresentation of gifted Black students related to low teacher expectations, low student expectations, ethnocentric curriculum, discrimination or a hostile school and/or classroom climate, a mismatch between teaching and learning styles, lack of support services, and inappropriate assessment practices? To what extent are instructions presented in students' preferred mode of learning? Do students have opportunities to ask questions and clarify instructions? Has a good/positive rapport been established between the test administrator and student? Other questions to consider appear in Figure 4.4.

MULTIDIMENSIONAL AND MULTIMODAL ASSESSMENT PRACTICES

Numerous options exist for assessing Black students for placement in gifted programs; the most promising of these practices rely on multidimensional and multimodal assessment strategies. Unidimensional instruments such as intelligence and achievement tests do not reliably measure a multidimensional construct like intelligence, but multidimen-

Define the goals of the identification process:
1. List the major goals of the gifted program.
2. List the areas of giftedness to be served.

Assess the relevance of the instrument:
1. What does this instrument purport to measure?
2. Is this instrument relevant to the intended purposes? For example, does the instrument measure behaviors listed in the goals of the identification, assessment, placement, and programming/services process?

Review the technical components when selecting the instrument:
1. Is the instrument reliable?
   a. What types of reliability coefficients are reported?
   b. What are the reported reliability coefficients?
   c. What are the demographic characteristics of the population on whom the instrument was normed/validated?

2. Is the instrument valid?
   a. What types of validity evidence are presented?
   b. What are the reported validity coefficients?
   c. What are the demographic characteristics of the population on whom the instrument was normed/validated?

Use a variety of evaluation techniques:
1. What other evidence is available that can measure the constructs or behaviors of interest, and their relevance for identification of gifted students?
2. Are both quantitative and qualitative measures or methods used?

Look at the practical considerations:
1. Is the test efficient in terms of:
   a. scoring?
   b. administrative time?
   c. cost?

Assess the limitations of the instrument:
1. What are the limitations of the instrument (e.g., biases and unfairness relative to gender, race, type of giftedness, format, and instructions)?
2. Is the instrument acceptable in terms of community values?

Look at the potential benefits of using the instrument:
1. Are data already available from existing sources, thus reducing or eliminating the need for the instrument?

Consider the interpretation of instrument results:
1. Is there someone on staff who is knowledgeable about psychometrics, who can equitably interpret and use test results, specifically in a culturally sensitive way?
2. Are recommendations based on the results made by one individual or a panel of professionals familiar with testing, bias, and fairness and concerned citizens?
3. Are the test results interpreted in isolation of other data?
4. Are the test results weighed more heavily than other data?
5. Are the test results interpreted in a culturally sensitive manner?
6. How will the test results be explained to the parent/caregiver, both prior to and after testing? Is the parent/caregiver aware of potential risks to the student?

Know the risks associated with the test and results:
1. What are the chances/risk of students' suffering from embarrassment or emotional and psychological damage from taking the test and the results?

Ensure confidentiality of test scores:
1. How will students' rights to privacy be ensured?
2. Has parent/guardian consent to testing/evaluation been obtained?

Figure 4.3. Checklist of guidelines for selection of valid and reliable tests and instruments.

What is the school district's philosophy of Advanced Placement and gifted education, and what is its definition of gifted?

1. In what ways are the philosophy and definition inclusive? To what extent are the strengths of Black (and other racially and culturally different) students represented in the definition?
2. Do the gifted education program and AP classes reflect community needs and values? Are students retrofitted to the program or is the program reflective of student needs?
3. To what extent are contemporary definitions of giftedness, intelligence, achievement, and creativity adopted? Is potential included in definitions? Are policies procedures, and practices in alignment with definitions?

Are the gifted program and AP classes reflective of community demographics?

1. To what extent is diversity evident relative to gender, race, and socioeconomic status?
2. What, if any, discrepancy exists between the community and school demographic characteristics?

What opportunities exist for continuing professional development in gifted, AP, and multicultural/culturally responsive education?

1. Are faculty and other school personnel encouraged and given opportunities to participate in workshops, conferences, university courses, and the like on these topics?
2. Does a library exist for teachers? Does it contain up-to-date resources (e.g., newsletters, journals, books, posters, videos) that are multicultural/culturally responsive regarding identification and assessment, curriculum, and instruction?

Are assessment practices equitable?

1. Are the measures used fair, valid, and reliable for the student population?
2. What biases and unfairness/inequities exist relative to the selection process? What factors have a disparate impact on Black students?
3. How are instruments administered (individually or in group)?
4. Which instruments appear to be most effective at identifying and assessing the strengths of racially and culturally different students?
5. Is a combination of qualitative and quantitative assessment practices used? If so, is one given preference or higher weight than the other?
6. What are the primary purposes of assessment or evaluation?
7. Are personnel trained to administer and interpret test results in culturally sensitive or responsible ways?
8. To what extent are Black students' learning styles accommodated relative to test administration and instructions?
9. To what extent are Black students' home language, culture, and background reflected within the tests and other instruments (e.g., nomination forms, checklists)?
10. Are tests biased in favor of verbal students, high-income/high-SES students, and White students?

What, if any, mechanisms are in place to assess and address affective or noncognitive needs among students (i.e., psychological, social and emotional needs, environmental and risk factors)?

1. To what extent are support personnel and test administrators trained in gifted education and Advanced Placement?

Figure 4.4. Gifted program and AP class evaluation considerations.

2. To what extent are support personnel and test administrators trained in multicultural/culturally responsive education?
3. How diverse is the teaching faculty relative to race, gender, income, and SES?

To what extent are families involved in the formal learning process?
1. In what ways are parents/families/caregivers encouraged to become and remain involved?
2. How diverse are the parents/families/caregivers involved?
3. Are other caregivers and extended family members (e.g., aunts, grandmothers) encouraged to participate? How?

To what extent does the curriculum reflect a multicultural/culturally responsive orientation?
1. Is multicultural content infused throughout the curriculum?
2. Is the content pluralistic (i.e., reflects diversity relative to gender, race, culture, income, SES, and other sociodemographic variables)?
3. To what extent are learning style preferences/differences accommodated?

Figure 4.4, continued

sional assessment can increase the probability. These assessments take different forms; however, the essential components include both quantitative and qualitative assessment strategies. Using such strategies ensures that gifted programs and identification practices are inclusive rather than exclusive for potentially gifted students, underachievers, minority students, and other historically underrepresented groups.

As Table 4.3 suggests, quantitative identification instruments include both traditional and nontraditional instruments. The traditional tests include the Wechsler Intelligence Scale for Children, the Stanford-Binet Intelligence Test, the Comprehensive Test of Basic Skills, and the Peabody Individual Achievement Test–Revised, for example. Nontraditional, culturally sensitive instruments include the Raven's Coloured, Standard, and Advanced Progressive Matrices, the Matrix Analogies Test, the Naglieri Nonverbal Abilities Tests I and II, the Kaufman Assessment Battery for Children, and the Torrance Tests of Creative Thinking. Assessment models that result in profiles of giftedness among historically underrepresented students include the Baldwin Identification Matrix, the Frasier Talent Assessment Profile, the Program of Assessment Diagnosis and Instruction, and the Potentially Gifted Minority Student Project.

Qualitative identification strategies include portfolio assessments; reviews of students' transcripts; observational or performance-based assessments; nominations by parents, teachers, peers, or students themselves; interviews; and biographical inventories. Portfolios and bio-

Table 4.3
Sample Identification Instruments: A Multidimensional
and Multimodal Framework

Instrument/Index
Quantitative (traditional)
Wechsler Intelligence Scale for Children
Stanford-Binet Intelligence Test
Comprehensive Test of Basic Skills
Peabody Individual Achievement Test–Revised
Quantitative (nontraditional)
Naglieri Non-Verbal Abilities Tests I and II (1)
Universal Nonverbal Intelligence Test (1)
Raven's Coloured, Standard, and Advanced Progressive Matrices (1)
Kaufman Assessment Battery for Children (1, 2)
Matrix Analogies Test—expanded and short form (1)
Torrance Tests of Creative Thinking (3)
Torrance Tests of Creativity (3)
Tests of Creativity in Movement and Action (3)
Vineland Social Maturity Scale (4)
California Preschool Competence Scale (4)
Basic Motor Ability Test (5)
Developmental Test of Visual and Motor Integration (5)
Purdue Perceptual Motor Survey (5)
Qualitative
Portfolios and performance-based assessments (e.g., writing samples, artwork, audio or visual taping of classroom discussions, journals, projects) (1–5)
Biographical inventories (1–5)
Nomination forms and checklists (completed by parents, teachers, peers, self) (1–7)
Transcripts (e.g., explore strengths in certain subjects and areas, look for inconsistent performance)
Learning styles inventories (6)
Motivational and attitudinal measures (7)
Dynamic assessments
Promising assessment instruments for developing profiles
The Baldwin Identification Matrix
The Frasier Talent Assessment Profile
The Potentially Gifted Minority Student Project
The Program of Assessment Diagnosis and Instruction
System of Multicultural Pluralistic Assessment

Note. Adapted from Ford (1994). 1 = intellectual gifted; 2 = academic gifted; 3 = creative gifted; 4 = leadership; 5 = visual and performing arts; 6 = learning styles; 7 = motivation, self-concept, self-esteem, attitudes toward school, peer relationships.

graphical inventories represent two promising qualitative indices for identifying gifted Black students. Such practices and educational programs existed with many of the Javits projects (e.g., Baldwin, 1994; Callahan, Tomlinson, & Pizzat, 1993; Coleman, 1994; Ford, 1996; Kay & Subotnik, 1994; O'Tuel, 1994) at The National Research Center on the Gifted and Talented at the University of Connecticut and other universities.

The ultimate method of achieving equitable assessment is to adhere to ethical standards of testing, advanced by authors such as Sax (1989) and professional organizations such as the American Psychological Association (1974) and the American Educational Research Association, American Psychological Association, and National Council on Measurement in Education (1985). Specifically, any educator who uses or advises others in the use of standardized tests should:

- possess a general understanding of measurement principles;
- understand the limitations of tests and test interpretations;
- understand clearly the purposes for which a test is given and the probable consequences of scores resulting from it;
- be knowledgeable about the particular test used and its appropriate uses;
- receive training necessary to understand the test, its uses and limitations, and how to administer, score, and interpret it.
- possess enough technical knowledge to evaluate technical claims (e.g., validity and reliability claims);
- know the procedures necessary to reduce or eliminate bias in test selection, administration, and interpretation;
- advise examinees in advance of testing that they will be tested and of the purposes and nature of testing;
- keep all standardized test materials secure at all times so as not to invalidate present or future uses of the test;
- provide examinees with information about correct procedures for filling out answer sheets (the mechanisms, not the substance of responding); and
- keep test scores confidential. (Worthen et al., 1993, p. 49)

Other ethical considerations include monitoring the test-taking conditions for academic dishonesty, examining barriers to students' performance (e.g., high noise level, poor light, illness, distraction), and having personnel who are trained to work with minority students to interpret test results in a culturally sensitive manner.

CONSIDERATION OF NONCOGNITIVE FACTORS IN ASSESSMENT

Davis and Rimm (1989) asserted that:

the chief index of actual ability is test scores. Despite all the faults and problems related to testing, despite unreliability and measurement error, and despite all the biases that need to be considered related to low test scores, it seems apparent that children cannot score extremely high on tests purely by accident. (p. 304)

If students *consistently* score high on standardized tests, there may be some truth to this assertion. What is the likelihood that a child with an IQ of 130 or higher will be asked to repeat the test because the results may be inaccurate? Reasoning by analogy, just as low test scores can be attributed to test bias, measurement error, and test unreliability, so too can high test scores. Test scores are also affected by and related to level of test anxiety and learning styles preferences.

INCREASED EFFORTS TARGETED AT THE RETENTION OF BLACK STUDENTS IN GIFTED EDUCATION AND AP CLASSES

The majority of efforts in gifted education have focused on the identification and placement (i.e., recruitment) of Black students in gifted education and AP classes. Rarely have issues surrounding retention received attention. Once placed, gifted Black students need support services in place to ensure a goodness-of-fit with the program, classmates, and educators. The shortage of Black students and teachers in gifted education and AP classes translates into few role models and mentors for Black students. In one study, Ford (1999) found that Black teachers, like students, were underrepresented in gifted education classrooms. This shortage heightens the demand for cultural sensitivity and responsiveness by gifted education teachers and other school personnel, the majority of whom are White (Harmon, 2002; Planty et al., 2009).

Should gifted Black and underachieving students seek the guidance of psychologists and counselors, strategies must focus on helping them cope with the difficulties inherent in being part of a predominantly White and middle-class gifted or AP class: peer pressure, feelings of isolation from peers, and concerns about being different due to being one of few racially and culturally different students. Depending upon the students' strengths and weaknesses, and emotional and academic supports, tutoring by slightly older and achieving Black students may enhance their academic performance (Whiting, 2006a, 2009).

Gifted Black students who are low-income and/or low-SES often need financial and other supports for additional learning opportunities outside of school (e.g., on weekends, before and after school hours, during the summer); these would certainly promote success among gifted Black students and decrease underachievement. Such support might include scholarships to attend residential and nonresidential summer programs and institutes, and to participate in out-of-state competitions or other challenging and enriching learning opportunities.

Certainly, multiculturalism must consistently permeate the educational experiences for gifted students. A Black history month each February provides insufficient time to infuse Black students with pride in their racial and cultural heritage and the significant contributions of their ancestors to American history. All students, regardless of race, benefit from both multiethnic education (which focuses on race and culture) and multicultural education (which focuses on human diversity and individual differences in gender, race, socioeconomic status, and geographic origins). Gifted education and AP classes that are culturally responsive promote mutual respect and understanding, comradeship, collegiality, rigor, and social and cultural awareness. Ultimately, it also fosters a sense of collective interest in the well-being of the nation, and may very well help to retain Black students in programs for gifted and advanced learners.

SCHOOL PERSONNEL TRAINING/PREPARATION

Gifted education is not federally mandated. Instead, states take the lead (or not) on mandating and funding gifted education (Davidson Institute for Talent Development, 2009; NAGC, 2009). Just as unfortunate, the majority of teachers working with gifted students have little to no formal training in this area, not only at the college level but in professional development as well. Few teachers, counselors, psychologists, and other school personnel receive formal, consistent, or comprehensive training in gifted education, AP, or multicultural education. Further, textbooks on gifted students include a perfunctory chapter on gifted underachievers and racially and culturally different students (e.g., Clark, 1983; Colangelo & Davis, 1991, 2003; Davis & Rimm, 1994, 2004); and articles, theories, and research discuss and treat gifted students as a homogeneous or monolithic group, which is a naïve, unhelpful practice. Seldom do discussions of gifted Black students permeate books, studies, and articles in gifted education and AP classes (Ford, 1998, 2010). Although Maker and Schiever's (1989) edited book represented a departure from the norm in this respect, it contains derogatory and stereotypical information about Black and low-income and low-SES students. For instance, several tables list "absolute characteristics of giftedness" in comparison to values and behaviors of various racially and culturally diverse groups. For the most part, this format supports an either/or model of giftedness and the absolute characteristics presented are frequently in opposition to characteristics of minority students. For example, Black students are described by such negative stereotypes as "manipulative behavior," "immediate or short-term gratification," "mastery of minimum academic skills," "acting out," and "leadership in gangs" (Maker & Schiever, 1989, p. 210). More recent books on racially and culturally different gifted students are by Castellano (2003), Castellano and Frazier (2011), Cline and Schwartz (1999), Ford and Harris (1999), and Ford and Milner (2005).

This lack of integration in theories, training, and research, as well as inattention to negative stereotypes about gifted Black students significantly hinders referrals (or nominations) of Black students for identification and assessment (Ford, 2010; Ford et al., 2008b). This inadequate or insufficient attention to the positive characteristics of Black students oftentimes supports a cultural deficit perspective that contributes to or exacerbates the underrepresentation of Black students in gifted programs and AP classes. To avoid miseducating themselves and miseducating Black students, teachers and counselors must get substantive (rather than superficial) training or preparation in AP, gifted, and multicultural/culturally responsive education.

In terms of gifted education (and even AP class) preparation, Karnes and Whorton (1991) recommended a minimum of four courses in the psychology of the gifted, assessment of gifted students, counseling of gifted students, curriculum development for gifted students, strategies and materials for teaching gifted learners, creative studies, program development and evaluation, parent education and advocacy, and special problems of gifted students. They also recommended at least three courses in graduate-level research methodology, a minimum of three courses in an approved content area designed to develop specialization, and a practicum in gifted education under the supervision of a university faculty member. Beyond these recommendations, coursework in multi-cultural education is essential and practica should occur within a racially or economically different school community. Teacher education training must espouse a culturally responsive pedagogy for gifted Black students by using state-of-the-art research on the learning and cultural styles of different groups and evaluation strategies:

- ❖ Preservice teachers must gain classroom experiences with Black students (e.g., during practicum or internships).
- ❖ Teachers/school personnel must be trained to understand and respect students' cultural heritage and knowledge base, their worldviews, values, and customs. This training includes studying the history and culture of Black students and their families.
- ❖ Teachers and educators must understand students' communication skills and behaviors (e.g., body language, facial expressions, eye contact, silence, touch, public space, asking for help).
- ❖ Teachers and school personnel must understand and decrease their stereotypes, prejudices, apprehensions, fears, and overreactions to Black students, particularly males.
- ❖ Teachers and school personnel need to learn outreach, collaboration, and conflict resolution or compromising skills—specifically, how to work effectively with Black students, their families, and their community on behalf of students.
- ❖ Teachers and school personnel must gain a greater respect for individual and group differences in learning, achievement, communication, assessment, and behavior.

THE NEED FOR CONSISTENCY—MATCHING PRACTICE, THEORY, AND RESEARCH

Cox et al. (1985) reported that teacher nominations were most often used for identification (91%), followed closely by achievement tests (90%) and IQ tests (82%). Archambault et al. (1993) surveyed more than 3,000 third- and fourth-grade teachers regarding identification practices. Results indicated that most of the public school teachers used achievement tests (79%), followed closely by IQ tests (72%) and teacher nominations (70%). Whereas the percentages or rankings appear to have changed over the years, the three primary identification sources remain the same.

Negative educational outcomes for Black students that come from relying heavily on tests to identify giftedness among students have been described at length in earlier sections of this chapter. Given the numerous and urgent calls to find more comprehensive and equitable identification strategies and instruments, Gubbins, Siegle, Renzulli, and Brown (1993) conducted a study about educators' assumptions underlying the identification of gifted and talented students. More than 3,000 educators from 47 states responded to a survey distributed at the 1992 NAGC conference. Respondents also included Consultant Bank members of The National Research Center on the Gifted and Talented. There were five major findings. First, results indicated that educators disagreed that identification should be based on *restricted* identification practices (i.e., based on achievement and IQ tests, precise cut-off scores, restricted percentage, services for identified students only, and without teacher judgment/subjective criteria). Teachers of the gifted were more likely to disagree than were regular classroom teachers. Second, both educators of the gifted and those in the regular classroom agreed that identification practices should be *responsive and sensitive* to students' abilities to express their talents and gifts through various measures or observations (e.g., case studies, student-selected tasks, multiple formats, and nonintellectual factors such as creativity and leadership).

A third finding was that educators in both settings tended to agree that *ongoing assessment* was important in the identification process. They agreed that regular, periodic reviews; alternative identification criteria; judgment by qualified persons; and programming informed by identification information were essential factors in designing and implementing an effective and flexible identification system. Fourth, educators agreed that *multiple criteria* were important in the decision-making process. The respondents acknowledged that students express their abilities in diverse ways, that development can affect the expression of abilities, and that multiple types and sources of information should be gathered for an effective identification plan. Finally, teachers of gifted students agreed more strongly than other teachers that students' *cultural, experiential, and environmental backgrounds* provide important data on students' performance and, thus, the identification process. They acknowledged that locally developed methods, norms, and criteria should be used, and that services and activities should be informed by context-bound information with attention to cultural differences.

The findings indicate a clear need for more consistency among theory, research, and practice. Evaluation and follow-up studies are needed to explore the match between theories, research, and practice. Key areas to focus on include the school district's philosophy of gifted education and definition of giftedness; the degree to which the gifted program or AP class is reflective of community demographics; the opportunities for continuing professional development in gifted and multicultural education; whether assessment practices are equitable; the mechanisms in place to assess and address affective or noncognitive needs among students (i.e., social and emotional needs, environmental and risk factors); the extent to which families are involved in the formal learning process; and the extent to which the curricula reflect a multicultural or culturally responsive orientation.

SUMMARY

Americans are obsessed with standardization and intelligence testing. Standardized tests are used to identify and assess students for achievement or lack thereof. These tests are given enormous credibility in educational institutions; they are essentially reified, a state of grace only a little less gained by being deified (Hargis, 1989). In essence, there is a dogged insistence upon relying on standardized tests as the ultimate arbiter of educational value and success (Peterson, 1983). Hargis (1989) likened practices associated with standardization (e.g., norm-referenced tests, curriculum) to Procrustes's[3] bed—we force and squeeze students in various ways to make them fit the norm. Black students are too often casualties of Procrustean methods of dealing with students who vary from the educational norm.

The well-documented biases of standardized tests in predicting academic success among Black students has had little effect on educational policy and decision making. Black students have always been a puzzle to educators because of their unresponsiveness to standard measures of intellectual and academic performance—yet educators know they have substantial intellectual and academic ability and potential. This blind faith in tests and their use as the only (or even primary) criterion for giftedness is educationally harmful, unjust, and inequitable; such scores can reduce any chance Black and underachieving students have for place-

---

3   Procrustes was a legendary scoundrel from Attica who had an iron bed in which travelers were forced to sleep. Travelers who were too tall were shortened with an axe to fit the bed; those who were too short were stretched.

ment in gifted programs and, thereby, contribute to or guarantee their underenrollment in gifted education programs.

The problems associated with defining intelligence and achievement are made even more complex by several factors. The first factor is the value judgments placed on these constructs. That is to say, both achievement and intelligence per se are ubiquitous and relative terms such that what is viewed and valued as gifted or achievement to one person (or culture) may not be judged the same in another. Second, one's level of intelligence and achievement are frequently determined by some arbitrary, designated cut-off criteria on intelligence and achievement tests. Test scores frequently determine who is gifted or not gifted, and who has failed, achieved, or underachieved. In some schools, gifted Black students go unidentified because little, if any, consideration is given to the possibility that they may be highly capable students who are poor test takers or who have been given an inappropriate test. Further, no one instrument is adequate to identify gifted students. Gifted students are a heterogeneous group with a wide range of individual differences. Although educators are urged to be sensitive to such differences and the special characteristics of individual gifted students, most programs still persist in using traditional tests and methods of identification that rely on popular notions of gifted characteristics.

Perhaps the most educationally relevant individual differences relate to cognitive styles—the way individuals perceive and process information, and the strategies they use to carry out tasks. In essence, *how* underachieving and gifted Black students use and process information is as educationally informative as *why and how well* they do so.

To more effectively identify and assess giftedness, potential, and underachievement among Black students, educators must personalize testing and provide for differences and inequities. This means moving toward less standardization and more individualization with serious attention to culture. Included in this recommendation is the recognition that educators should adopt broader and more responsive theories, definitions, and assessments of giftedness, underachievement, and potential. Theories espoused by Renzulli, Gardner, and Sternberg were ahead of the times—all originating three decades ago, they embrace the ideology of inclusiveness and equity, and they acknowledge the influence of cultural and contextual variables on educational outcomes. In the final analysis, educators and other school personnel must work diligently to desegregate gifted programs.

CHAPTER FIVE

UNDERACHIEVEMENT: DEFINITIONS, THEORIES, AND ASSESSMENT

The status quo is not working for low-income and minority students. What goes on is a disgrace for children.

—Arne Duncan

Since the seminal works of Atkinson (1964, 1980), Bandura (1977), Maslow (1954), McClelland (1961), and McClelland, Atkinson, Lowell, and Clark (1953), educators and researchers have been intensely interested in those factors that motivate and demotivate students. Certainly, few situations are more frustrating and perplexing for parents/caregivers and educators than rearing or teaching a child who does not perform as well academically as his or her potential and expectation indicates. Alarmingly, cases of underachievement are becoming more common than ever, with estimates that some 15% to 50% of students underachieve. Among gifted Black students, I found that more than 75% were underachieving (Ford, 1991; Ford et al., 2008b).

The achievement gap in its many forms (school failure, dropping out, low achievement, and underachievement) is all too familiar in the approximately 17,000 schools districts nationally—including gifted programs and AP classes. Students of all ages and from all income and economic backgrounds and racial groups are wrestling with issues that threaten to promote, exacerbate, or maintain underachievement: cultural differences, gender issues, learning difficulties, learning style differences, low teacher expectations, peer pressure, family difficulties, fiscal problems, and confusion over goals and priorities. This is not an exhaustive list. Certainly, the phenomenon of underachievement is as complex and multifaceted as the students to whom this label is applied.

This chapter discusses the achievement gap and the concept of achievement in its various manifestations: underachievement, low achievement, nonachievement, and overachievement. Along with conceptual and operational definitions, theories of achievement and motivation are discussed. The chapter concludes with recommendations for the identification and assessment of underachievement among gifted Black students.

QUESTIONS TO CONSIDER

- ❖ What is achievement and its various forms (low achievement, underachievement, nonachievement, and overachievement)? How is underachievement measured?
- ❖ To what extent is underachievement a learned behavior and reactive response to situations?
- ❖ In what ways is underachievement the problem rather than a symptom of a larger problem, as in the achievement gap?
- ❖ What are the advantages and disadvantages of narrow versus broad definitions of underachievement?
- ❖ What factors contribute to the exclusive attention to academic underachievement and the inattention to underachievement in other areas of giftedness (e.g., creativity, leadership)?
- ❖ What factors contribute significantly to underachievement among Black students in general and those identified as gifted?

INTRODUCTION

In a 1987 letter to former presidential candidates, David T. Kearns,

Chairman of Xerox Corporation, charged America's public schools with turning out a product with a 50% defect rate. Kearns argued that the public schools are supplying a workforce—25% of whom have dropped out and another 25% who graduate with minimal skills such that they can barely read their own diplomas. Kearns added that Xerox expects defect-free parts from its suppliers; and while they get 99.9% perfection, they are still trying to correct that last tenth of a percent (Hargis, 1989).

The evidence continues to grow regarding poor achievement of students across all age, ability, skill, income, and socioeconomic status levels. For the most part, no student or group of students is totally exempt from the possibility of poor educational outcomes. However, middle-class and White students are less likely to have negative school experiences.

Life on the margins, however, is an all too familiar reality for Black students in classrooms in the past and today. It is an unfortunate reality that far too many Black students are overrepresented among poor achievers, dropouts, the lowest ability groups and educational tracks, and the otherwise educationally disenfranchised and disillusioned. High-achieving Black students are represented among those who drop out of high school. In a study of culturally different students who dropped out of school, the students ranked as the two primary factors (1) poor student-teacher relationships and (2) lack of relevance in the curriculum (Bridgeland, DiIulio, & Morison, 2006). Noteworthy is that more than 85% of these culturally different students had passing grades. Mounting data indicate that economically challenged and racially and culturally different students are first and foremost victims of defects inside and outside of the school setting. Manning and Baruth (2010) captured a key problem related to poverty quite well: "Regrettably, a person's socio-economic status is sometimes thought to indicate his or her ambitions or motivation to achieve" (p. 269). On a regular basis, curricular and instructional issues, testing practices, teacher-student relationships, low educator expectations, culturally assaultive or unresponsive classroom climates, and social and environmental factors all take their toll, either in isolation or collectively, on the social, emotional, psychological, and educational well-being of Black students, including formally identified gifted and potentially gifted Black students.

THE ACHIEVEMENT GAP: OVERVIEW AND RELEVANCE TO GIFTED BLACK UNDERACHIEVERS

A number of terms have been used to describe the comparative and differential performance of Black students and White students. In this book, the term *achievement gap* is used to cover a broad range of terms on this issue: rigor gap, expectation gap, opportunity gap, resource gap, funding gap, teacher quality gap, performance gap, cultural gap, and more. Terminology aside, all terms have in common the reality that, on average, Black students do not fare as well as White students in school/academic settings.

As briefly described in Chapter 1, some 16 correlates have been found to contribute significantly to the comparative and differential outcomes of Black and White students (Barton & Coley, 2009). Admittedly, students identified as gifted are not directly addressed in many of the reports; however, we cannot and must not ignore how gifted Black students are affected by the achievement gap and its correlates. Increasing access to gifted education and AP classes can only help to close the achievement gap (Barton & Coley, 2009; Ford, 2006).

There is no one or single achievement gap; it has many faces. These achievement gaps individually and collectively contribute to Black students performing less well than White students relative to grades, test scores, graduation rates, gifted and AP participation, and more. In essence, the omnibus achievement gap is a *symptom* of many other gaps, such as the funding gap, the resource gap, the teacher quality gap, the curriculum gap, the digital gap, the family involvement gap, and the expectations gap.

Essentially, the reasons behind the achievement gap are multifaceted and complex. The achievement gap starts at home, before children begin school, and then widens during the formal school years (e.g., Hart & Risley, 1995; Lee & Burkham, 2002). For example, at the kindergarten level, there tends to be a one-year gap between Black and White students; by the 12th grade, there is often a 4-year gap. It is counterintuitive that the gap *widens* while students are in school. Schools cannot place the blame solely on families; they cannot exonerate themselves from contributing to the achievement gap.

Many factors contribute to the achievement gap. Borrowing from the work of Barton (2003), Barton and Coley (2009), and Hodgkinson

(2007), I present an overview of the primary correlates (risk factors) of the achievement gap. Based on a review of several hundred studies that examined factors contributing to the achievement gap, Barton and Coley identified 16 variables that consistently and substantively contribute to the achievement gap[1.] At least three major factors and their subfactors or correlates—home, school, and health and nutrition—must be thoroughly examined to understand the achievement gap in a comprehensive manner. In this book, two of the three contexts are addressed: school and home. Attention is devoted to differences by income and race, for as noted by Barton and Coley (2009), "achievement differences across subgroups of the population have deep roots" (p. 8). These authors stated: "most of the risk factors are related to poverty and *all* poor children, regardless of race/ethnicity, are at risk of not fulfilling their potential" (p. 10). Essentially, race *and* income must be interrogated and deconstructed; it must not be assumed that these two variables (alone or combined) determine student achievement.

School Factors

Seven correlates found in school settings contribute to the math and reading achievement gaps. These school correlates must be considered in terms of their cumulative impact. For a total of 13 years, students attend school each year for approximately 180 days. Thus, what takes place in school has a major impact on students.

Rigor of the curriculum. Regardless of the term used to describe academic rigor (i.e., challenging curriculum, academic environment, or academic press; Barton & Coley, 2009), research shows consistently that students' academic achievement depends extensively upon the rigor of the curriculum; yet, the curriculum is frequently less rigorous for Black students than for others. Instructional rigor rests on teachers' expectations of students, as has been learned from research on teacher expectation-student achievement (TESA): When expectations are high, teachers challenge students. Rigor can be defined as high-level instruction and access to challenging programs, such as gifted education and AP classes (Barton & Coley, 2009; Handwerk, Tognatta, Coley, & Gitomer, 2008). Black students are less likely than White students to (a) have substantial credits in academic sources at the end of high school and (b) to participate in honors, AP, and gifted education classes. Whereas Black students

---

1   There is a great deal of overlap in the 15 risk factors listed by Hodgkinson (2007), the 14 correlates listed by Barton (2003), and the 16 correlates listed by Barton and Coley (2009).

represent more than 17% of the public school population, they represent only 8% of students participating in gifted education; even fewer are enrolled in AP and honors classes (U.S. Department of Education, 2006a). Publications by the College Board, Education Trust, Educational Testing Service, and other organizations describe more extensively problems regarding lack of access to rigorous instruction, classes, and programs, especially at the high school level.

Teacher preparation. The importance of teacher preparation and quality on student achievement cannot be ignored. Black students are more likely to be taught by teachers who are unqualified or poorly prepared, including teachers who lack certification, out-of-field teachers, teachers with the fewest credentials, and teachers with the lowest college and test scores (Barton & Coley, 2009; Peske & Haycock, 2006). In high-minority schools, 29% of teachers do not have at least a minor in the subject area in which they teach; in low-minority schools, this falls to 21% (Barton, 2003). Related to the previous issue of rigor, ill-qualified teachers will have difficulty teaching and challenging students; they are unlikely to raise students' achievement as they do not have the skills to do so.

Teacher experience. Inexperienced or novice teachers, those with fewer than 5 years of classroom experience, for example, are more likely to teach in urban than suburban settings (Barton & Coley, 2009). In schools with high percentages of Black students, 21% of teachers have fewer than 3 years of experience; in schools with low Black enrollment, 10% of teachers have fewer than 3 years of teaching (Barton, 2003). Further complicating this issue, data indicate that teachers working in high-minority schools often have low attendance rates, resulting in classes being taught by substitute teachers. Teacher attendance adversely affects the quality of instruction given to and received by Black students, contributing to their poorer school achievement compared to White students.

Teacher absence and turnover. Many minority and low-income students are more likely to attend schools with high levels of teacher absence and turnover. Relative to teacher turnover, 52% of Black students compared to 28% of White students had a teacher who left before the school year ended (Barton & Coley, 2009). In 2007, 8% of White eighth graders attended schools where 6% or more of the teachers were absent on an average day; this percentage was almost double (11%) for Black students. Being taught by different teachers, being taught by substitute teachers, and having inconsistency in their instruction impedes the learning of these students.

Class size. In schools where there are high percentages of Black students, class sizes are larger (Barton & Coley, 2009). For instance, in schools where Black students represent 50% or more of the population, the average class size is 23. In schools where Black students are less than 15%, class size average is 14 (Barton & Coley, 2009). Every educator knows that larger classes are more difficult to manage; more time is spent on behavior than teaching, resulting in students being denied the opportunity to learn at the same rates as their White classmates in smaller classrooms.

Instructional technology. This correlate concerns the digital divide; it includes access/availability, teachers' skills, *and* students' use of technology. Lack of access to instructional technology hinders students' learning. Schools with higher percentages of Black students are less likely to have computers in the classrooms, Internet access, and updated, high-quality software (Barton & Coley, 2009). Data indicate that 77% of teachers in low-minority schools versus 52% of teachers in high-minority schools were at the intermediate or advanced skill level (Barton & Coley, 2009). The third concern is that of how and whether teachers use technology in the classroom; 61% of students in low-minority schools are given assignments to conduct research on the Internet, compared to 35% for students in high-minority schools (Barton, 2003). As a result, Black students are less qualified to compete in situations where technological skills are essential, which is, clearly, in many cases.

Fear and safety. To state the obvious, learning is compromised when students feel unsafe. Classroom discipline, disruptions, and negative peer pressure (including gangs, bullying, and fears about fights at school) are reported more often by Black students than others (Barton & Coley, 2009). Students cannot learn in unsafe, threatening environments. They have difficulty concentrating and staying focused or engaged under such duress. Thus, many Black students may have poor attendance or drop out to avoid the stresses the come with violence, bullying, and negative peer pressures, which contributes to their poorer performance.

As just described, schools contribute to the achievement gap between Black students and White students in significant ways. However, they are not solely responsible for students' differential performance, as described next.

HOME FACTORS

I recognize that schools alone did not create the gap, nor can they close it without support from families and the larger community. Six additional correlates of the achievement gap, based outside of school—meaning in the home—must be addressed; these correlates are related directly to poverty, which is a "universal handicap" as noted by Hodgkinson (2007, p. 7). One third of Black children live in poverty compared to 10% of White children (Hodgkinson, 2007).

Parent-pupil ratio. The extent to which parents or primary care-givers are available to and spend quality time with their children varies by family structure and composition. A larger percentage of Black students (compared to White students) live in single-parent homes (Barton & Coley, 2009), and many of these are from low-income or low-SES backgrounds. For those living with mothers only, the rates are 17% for White children, compared to 49% for Black children (Barton, 2003). Hodgkinson (2007) reported more recently that

> regardless of race, the children in married couple families are much less likely to be poor (about 8%), while 29% of White children and 52% of Black and Hispanic children who live with a single mother are likely to be poor. (p. 10)

When parents are not present, students are left to make choices for themselves. This lack of supervision results in less structure and discipline for students; they may not spend their unsupervised time studying and/or participating in school-related activities, causing them to fall further behind White students.

Parent participation. The extent to which parents/caregivers are involved in their children's education affects students' achievement and behavior. Reports indicate that Black parents/caregivers tend to participate less in their children's education than others (Barton & Coley, 2009). According to Barton (2003), 44% of urban parents and 20% of suburban parents reported feeling unwelcome in schools. Approximately half of Black parents and three fourths of White parents attended a school event in 1999; approximately one fourth of Black parents and half of White parents volunteered or served on a committee. As with findings regarding lack of parent availability, student achievement suffers.

Student mobility. Hodgkinson (2007) raised several key concerns about transience; each year, 22% of children under the age of 5 move to a different house, with low-income families moving more often than higher income families (for more information, see Lee & Burkham, 2002). One harsh reality is that "large numbers of teachers may start and end the year with 24 students, but 22 of those 24 are different from the students they welcomed the first day of school" (Hodgkinson, 2007, p. 9). There are many negative consequences to changing schools; Black students, especially those who live in poverty, have the highest rates of changing schools (27% for Black students, and 13% for White students). Data indicate that 41% of students who change schools frequently are below grade level in reading, and 33% are below grade level in math (Barton, 2003). Gifted Black students are part of this highly mobile student population; like other students, their achievement is negatively affected and their educational experiences are compromised.

Talking and reading. Reading positively correlates with language acquisition, literacy development, test scores, and achievement. One longitudinal study (1993–2001) found that among 3–5 year olds, 64% of White preschoolers were read to every night in the previous week, compared to 48% for Black preschoolers in 2001 (see Barton, 2003; Hart & Risley, 1995). The consequences of poor reading skills are serious and long term, with students subsequently performing poorer on intelligence and achievement tests, and having difficulty keeping up in other subject areas.

Excessive TV watching. Minority students and those in poverty watch more TV. In 2000, 42% of Black and 13% of White fourth graders watched 6 hours or more of TV daily (Barton, 2003). Excessive and unsupervised TV watching negatively affects students' achievement, with students doing less homework and reading, and participating in fewer afterschool activities and intellectually stimulating activities.

Summer achievement gains/loss. Low-income and racially different students experience more loss academically over the summer than do their White and higher income classmates. Although trend data were not reported by Barton and Coley (2009), it is common sense that these students are less likely to perform to their potential. In the context of gifted education, high-income and well-educated families are more likely to enroll their children in summer enrichment programs, talent development programs, and other experiences to keep academics and achievement high.

HEALTH FACTORS

Although not the direct focus of this book, undeniably, health factors also contribute to underachievement and the achievement gap.

Hunger and nutrition. Hunger and nutrition (or lack thereof) are solidly related to income level. It is widely accepted and understood that the development of the mind and body is adversely affected when students are hungry and in poor health (e.g., underweight, overweight, sick, lacking vitamins). Food insecurity, a term used by the U.S. Department of Agriculture, refers to the availability of food and the ability of individuals to access it. A household is considered food insecure when its occupants live in hunger and fear of starvation. In 2005, 29% of Black children and 12% of White children were food insecure (Barton & Coley, 2009).

Low birth weight. According to Hodgkinson (2007), since 1990, a stubborn statistic has been that approximately 7% of babies have low birth weights, but for infants born to Black mothers, that rises to 13%. Even well-educated, middle-class Black mothers produce more low-birth-weight babies than the norm for all groups (Hodgkinson, 2007). Low birth weight often produces serious health problems that also increase being in many risk categories that hinder educational achievement, including learning disabilities.

Environmental damage. Research on the dangers and harmfulness of lead poisoning is well established, and in recent years, more attention has been devoted to the academic effects of mercury poisoning. Black students are disproportionately exposed to both. Lead that exceeds governmental standards can cause reductions in IQ and attention span and increased reading and learning disabilities and behavior problems (Barton & Coley, 2009). Black and low-income children have a higher risk of being exposed to lead from living in old houses or around old industrial areas with contaminated buildings and soil, in addition to having elevated levels of lead that is four times higher than for White children (Barton & Coley, 2009).

The effects of mercury are severe, impacting intelligence, cognitive thinking, attention, language, fine motor skills, walking, muscles, visual spatial skills, hearing, speech, and more. Blacks have higher levels of mercury than other groups. However, no trend or longitudinal data exist at this time (see Barton & Coley, 2009, p. 24).

SUMMARY

Despite the data just presented, many of these variables can be improved. If these 16 variables are the most powerful in contributing to and maintaining the gap, then it behooves us to address them in a proactive, systemic, comprehensive, and collaborative manner. Families, educators (e.g., administrators, teachers, counselors), community leaders, health professionals, policy makers, and others must collaborate to tackle this educational tragedy.

No one major factor or correlate contributes to or causes the achievement gap, which reinforces the reality that underachievement is complex and will take sustained prevention and intervention efforts to have an impact.

To say the obvious, educators, namely administrators, must ensure that Black students are taught by high-quality teachers and teachers with extensive experience in the classroom. School personnel and staff must receive formal preparation to work more effectively with Black students and, thus, raise their expectations for Black students, as has been proposed by advocates of multicultural and culturally responsive education (e.g., Sonia Nieto, James Banks, Linda Darling-Hammond, Geneva Gay, Gloria Ladson-Billings, Jacqueline Irvine). Further, to be as effective as possible, we must have highly trained and experienced educators, as well as smaller class sizes and schools. Teachers should also receive training in culturally responsive classroom management strategies. Educators must adopt and implement programs in their schools to address safety and negative peer relations and pressure. Conflict resolution programs and anger management programs would be helpful to students, both victims and the perpetrators.

In terms of homes and communities, families must understand the achievement gap and contributing factors, as well as their roles in contributing to it *and* closing it. They will need access to learning opportunities that educate, empower, and support them in working with schools and their children. Programs addressing family involvement and literacy are two timely topics. Community leaders should collaborate with schools and families to provide students and caregivers with mentors and role models. Finally, it is essential that schools, families, and businesses collaborate with resources such as social workers and healthcare providers to address problems like poverty, hunger, housing, healthcare, and environmental issues. Accountability and collaboration are key.

CONCEPTUAL DEFINITIONS

No concept can be applied without some attempt to define it, and the more complex the concept, the more difficult the task is of defining it. Similarly, the more complex the concept, the more likely the result will not satisfy all who ponder it (Kershner & Connolly, 1992). Such is the case with most terms in education and related fields, including achievement and its various manifestations: achievement gap, low achievement, underachievement, nonachievement, and overachievement.

WHAT IS ACHIEVEMENT?

Having patience, one must develop diligence, for accomplishment will dwell only in those who exert themselves. Just as there is no movement without wind, so success does not occur without diligence.

—Shantideva (1976, p. 52)

According to the *American Heritage Dictionary,* to achieve is to do, accomplish, or finish with success. Achievement means to attain or get with effort, as through exertion, skill, practice, or perseverance. Similarly, Chaplin's (1975) *Dictionary of Psychology* emphasized the importance of accomplishment and attainment with effort. These definitions embrace, either implicitly or explicitly, the notions of energy expended to overcome difficulties and perseverance to attain a desired goal or objective.

When students are referred to as achievers, it usually indicates that they have accomplished a task or met a goal, objective, or expectation. In many cases, this judgment is based on standards and opinions external to students (e.g., test scores, views of teachers and caregivers). In this regard, the extent to which one has achieved is relative and/or subjective. The expectations set by parents/caregivers may differ from those set by teachers. For example, a child identified as intellectually gifted who brings home a B- on a test may get different reactions from his mother, father, and teacher, depending on the expectations of each. A linguistically gifted student whose teacher encouraged him to submit a poem for publication consideration that is rejected by the editor will learn firsthand that people have different expectations for achievement. An academically gifted child whose GPA is less than 3.0 may find that her parents are unhappy, but her teachers are satisfied with her school performance.

Similar concerns relate to students whose talents are in creativity, leadership, visual and performing arts, and other areas of giftedness.

ACHIEVEMENT VERSUS UNDERACHIEVEMENT

When students are deemed to be achievers, it is believed that they are achieving at the level commensurate with their ability or intelligence. The notion of being on par comes to mind. Conversely, when students are underachievers, the notion of a discrepancy comes to mind. These students are not performing to some expected level. They should and can do better.

When performance is commensurate with predicted potential, students are said to be achieving to their potential. Motivation is one of the primary factors that distinguishes achievers from underachievers. When asked to describe "good" students, teachers typically list characteristics such as hardworking, cooperative, interested, and motivated. However, these characteristics alone do not guarantee that students will achieve to their potential. Other important factors include organizational skills, test-taking skills, study skills, and learning styles. Further, gifted students who lack academic motivation or have other priorities are as problematic and disconcerting for their teachers/educators as students who lack academic motivation. Specifically, if given the opportunity to work with hardworking, motivated, and relatively independent students who are not formally identified as gifted versus gifted students who are unmotivated, teachers would probably choose the former.

LOW ACHIEVEMENT VERSUS UNDERACHIEVEMENT

Low achievement is a failure to meet minimum standards of performance (e.g., the student is below average relative to grade level or group norm data). Low-achieving Black students may meet minimum standards, but still perform below their White peers. This issue relates to the achievement gap. Sinclair and Ghory (1987) indicated that 23% to 40% of the student population are low achievers. From a statistical perspective, low-achieving students represent those who rank at the 50th percentile or lower on the normal bell curve. Thus, frankly and unfortunately, 50% of students are destined to being labeled as low achievers.

In some cases, underachieving gifted students are also low-achieving students. For example, if a student ranks at the 39th percentile on an achievement test (or some other measure of achievement), she would not only be an underachiever, but also a low achiever. A gifted student who ranks at the 79th percentile, however, would not be described as a low achiever, as he is higher than average. Similar comparisons and conclusions can be drawn using grades or grade point averages.

NONPRODUCER VERSUS UNDERACHIEVER

Kessler (1963) distinguished between nonlearners and nonproducers, with the latter term being applied differently than Delisle's (1992) and Delisle and Galbraith's (2002) description of nonproducers. According to Kessler, nonlearners are children with identifiable learning difficulties (e.g., learning disabilities, ADHD) who score substantially better on standardized tests than their class performance indicates. Nonproducers have no discernable learning disabilities, yet they also perform lower than expected in school. Seemingly, nonproducers have difficulties resulting from motivational issues, which can be personal/psychological, familial, social, and/or school related. They *can* do the work, but *won't* or *don't*.

Delisle (1992) also distinguished between underachievers and nonproducers. Underachievers, he argued, are psychologically at risk, dependent and reactive, withdrawn, perfectionistic, and have poor academic self-concepts. They tend to evidence persistent achievement problems such that reversal and change are possible but difficult. On the other hand, nonproducers are described as mentally healthy, independent, and proactive students with positive self-concepts of ability. Their poor performance is situation specific or temporary, and their prognosis for intervention is more positive. For nonproducers, poor achievement is likely a conscious decision—they are unwilling to do the work. However, regardless of whether or not underachievement is a choice within one's control, the results are the same: The students are not working to their potential.

LEARNING DISABILITIES VERSUS UNDERACHIEVEMENT

Despite federal regulations, the definition of learning disabilities is still controversial. Hammill (1990) reviewed 28 articles and found 11 different definitions, all of which emphasized that a child with a learning disability is an underachiever. According to PL 94-142, a specific learning disability:

means a disorder in one or more of the basic psychological processes involved in the understanding or in using language, spoken or written, which may manifest itself in an imperfect ability to listen, think, speak, read, write, spell, or to do mathematical calculations. . . . The term does not apply to children having learning problems which are primarily the result of visual, hearing, or motor handicaps, of mental retardation, or emotional disturbance, or of environmental, cultural, or economic disadvantage.

Learning disabilities represent the largest percentage of students in special education. Some 1.5% to 4.6% of individuals have a learning disability (Mercer, 1986). Berk (1983) described gifted learning disabilities as a subcategory of underachievement, and Silverman (1989, 1993) appeared to use the terms interchangeably. Learning disabilities are apparent in areas such as oral expression, listening comprehension, written expression, basic reading skills, reading comprehension, mathematics calculations, and mathematics reasoning.

Like gifted underachievers, gifted students with learning disabilities are identified by an aptitude-achievement discrepancy. Children with learning disabilities may also have intracognitive and intra-achievement discrepancies (Aylward, 1994). Intracognitive discrepancy, also referred to as a disturbance in basic psychological processes, occurs in children who have a specific type of cognitive dysfunction (e.g., auditory processing, short-term memory, visual processing). These students may have difficulty retaining information that is presented verbally by the teacher, but can recall adequately information that is presented visually. All children may have a preference for a specific mode of instruction; children who are *unable* to perform adequately in one area compared to another may have a learning disability. An intra-achievement discrepancy reflects divergence or inconsistency in educational achievement performances. This particular discrepancy may occur between or across academic areas (e.g., reading, mathematics, science) or within an academic area (e.g., between reading decoding and reading comprehension; Aylward, 1994).

Berk (1983) proposed the following typology of learning disabilities: (a) students have at least *normal intelligence* (more specifically, the child is not mentally retarded); (b) *ability-achievement discrepancy*; (c) *academic disorder* (in reading, writing, spelling, math); and (d) *psychological processing disorders* (i.e., learning problems are associated with memory, perception, modality, sequencing, and closure). These factors inhibit, in meaningful ways, the development of processes or interfere with students' ability to process information effectively.

GIFTED UNDERACHIEVEMENT VERSUS NONGIFTED UNDERACHIEVEMENT

Traditionally, gifted underachievers have been defined as students who possess high or superior mental ability but lower performance than expected or predicted. In comparison, underachievers not identified as gifted tend not to have high intelligence and/or achievement test scores. The term nongifted underachievement is problematic, for there are many students who do not score well on standardized intelligence and achievement tests yet they are highly intelligent and high performers on school assignments. There are many gifted students, particularly Black students, who have not been formally identified because of poor test outcomes. This issue of their lower test performance is controversial. Debates about heredity versus environment are alive and well. We cannot ignore issues about test bias and unfairness (Ford & Whiting, 2009; Whiting & Ford, 2009).

WHAT IS OVERACHIEVEMENT?

Overachievers are often defined as students whose academic achievement performance is higher than predicted on the basis of their intelligence test scores. The independent variable (intelligence test) is compared to the dependent variable (e.g., achievement test score, GPA, teacher expectation, and/or caregiver expectation). If the intelligence test score is low, but academic performance is high, the student in said to be an overachiever. Mandel and Marcus (1988) highlighted the difficulty inherent in defining overachievement:

> The term "overachievement" contains perhaps the greatest logical inconsistency. How can one achieve above one's actual "ceiling" level of ability? How can one incapable of a certain activity nevertheless achieve above his or her actual potential for performing that task? Ordinary common sense tells us that "you cannot do what you cannot do" (i.e., you cannot do what, in fact, you are not capable of doing), and yet the term "overachievement" is applied on an everyday basis, and with a great deal of face validity. (p. 4)

Intentional or not, the terms underachievement and overachievement place much faith in the validity of standardized tests to identify ability and potential (or lack thereof). For example, these terms place greater emphasis on the value of the test than on students' school performance.

A CLOSER LOOK AT UNDERACHIEVEMENT

Operational definitions of poor achievement vary extensively, but many focus on motivation. Theorists have debated whether achievement motivation (or lack thereof) is a learned behavior based on experience, family factors, school factors, personality factors, or all four. Notwithstanding definitional difficulties, it is generally accepted that underachievement (manifested by poor grades, lack of effort, dropping out of school, or otherwise not reaching one's academic potential) is a serious problem among students in our schools, particularly among those in urban areas. The statistics on the number of students who drop out of school are disturbing, and they highlight the malaise in the educational milieu. Some schools report epidemic numbers: dropout rates from 30% to 80% (Bridgeland et al., 2006).

Contrary to popular opinion, educational disengagement is indeed experienced by formally identified gifted students. In *A Nation at Risk* (National Commission on Excellence in Education, 1983), it was reported that as many of 20% of students who drop out are gifted, and Renzulli and Park (2000) reported that dropping out among gifted students is more common than one might think or expect. Although Black students are overrepresented in the ranks of dropouts, the number of gifted Black students has often gone unreported. However, Ford (1991) found that 80% of formally identified gifted students were underachieving, primarily due to lack of effort and low teacher expectations. For these students, effort represented a double-edged sword, a pyrrhic victory. Further, Smith, LeRose, and Clasen (1991) reported that 30% of gifted Black students in their study who had been identified in high school had dropped out of college. More recently, Bridgeland and colleagues (2006) reported that 88% of culturally different students who dropped out of school had passing grades. Although the authors did not indicate whether any of the students in the sample were gifted, it is safe to assume some of them were.

The U.S. Department of Education (1993) and Renzulli (2003) noted that too many gifted students are unchallenged in school; subsequently, many get by with "effortless success" and their work ethic is compromised. It is often not until college that these students are challenged; by this time, however, they may not have acquired the basic skills needed for studying, organization, and test-taking.

Myriad definitions of underachievement can be found in the educational, sociological, anthropological, and psychological literature, with a few focusing specifically on gifted underachievers (e.g., Butler-Por, 1987; Ford, 1991, 1996; Raph, Goldberg, & Passow, 1966; Supplee, 1990; Whitmore, 1980, 1986, 1988). Generally (and to repeat myself), underachievement is defined as a discrepancy between some expected level of achievement and students' actual performance on one or more designated indices. For example, this gap can result from high scores on standardized tests, but academic performance that is comparatively low. Underachievement can also be defined as a gap between teachers' expectations and students' performance. That is to say, when teachers hold high expectations of Black students, but their performance is low or does not match the expectation, students may be labeled underachievers, learning disabled, or educationally handicapped.

Methods of operationally defining academic underachievement can be placed into three broad categories: (a) arbitrary absolute splits, (b) simple difference score, and (c) regression method (McCall et al., 1992). Researchers adopting the arbitrary absolute splits method define underachievers as having higher than a certain minimum on a measure of mental ability, but lower than a certain maximum on a measure of school performance. This definition is most often adopted relative to gifted students. For example, Saurenman and Michael (1980) defined gifted underachievers as having a Stanford-Binet 132 IQ or above and percentile ranking of 75 or below on the California Test of Basic Skills. Finney and Van Dalsem (1969) defined gifted underachievers as students who were in the top 25% of the Differential Aptitude Battery in verbal-numerical, but whose GPA was below the mean. Colangelo, Kerr, Christensen, and Maxey (1993) defined gifted underachievers as students with a composite score at or above the 95th percentile on the ACT and GPAs less than or equal to 2.25.

There are several limitations associated with the arbitrary absolute splits definition of underachievement (McCall et al., 1992). First, this definition lacks generalizability and comparability across studies because absolute values of scores or rankings are totally dependent on the instrument and/or sample. Second, there is no consensus on the particular instruments or splits to use, particularly given that identification and placement criteria for giftedness can vary considerably from one school to another (NAGC, 2009). Third, this method fails to consider the influence of noncognitive variables on test performance and subsequent scores.

The simple difference score method requires a common metric for ability and achievement, such as standard scores, grade level, or percentiles. Curry (1961) defined underachievement as a discrepancy of 10 or more points between T scores on the California Test of Mental Maturity and the California Achievement Test. According to McCall et al. (1992), statistical problems associated with regression to the mean affect interpretations of definitions based on this method. For instance, students who score high on one instrument are not likely to score as high on the other. Second, if the measures correlate weakly, a student who scores high on one instrument is likely to score low on the other. A third problem relates to the unreliability of difference scores. If the reliabilities for the two instruments are .80 and .90, and their correlation is .70, the difference scores will have a reliability of .51, which is relatively low or unstable (see McCall et al., 1992; Thorndike, 1963).

The most common and simplest method of conceptualizing underachievement is the regression method (Aylward, 1994). In this method, one calculates the regression of the achievement instrument on the ability measure, and then calculates the deviation of each student's score from the regression line. Students with a large negative deviation (most often one standard deviation or more) are considered underachievers. A major benefit of the regression model is that there is an equal probability that a discrepancy will be identified across all IQ levels. Given that the majority of referrals for poor school achievement involve children with lower IQs, use of discrepancy models results in underidentification of underachieving and learning-disabled children; however, use of regression equations may increase the identification rate by as much as 10% (Aylward, 1994).

As with the other methods described, the regression method has limitations. First, it assumes that the standard error of estimate is a constant value across the entire range of ability (McCall et al., 1992). Second, using one standard error is arbitrary and lacks empirical justification. At what point, for example, should one standard error rather than one and a half or two standard errors be used? Third, this method will always produce a given percentage of underachievers in a sample. Utilizing the statistical bell curve, 16% of students will automatically fall one standard deviation below the regression line. Despite these limitations, several researchers perceive it to be the most user-friendly (e.g., Farqhuar & Payne, 1964; Gowan, 1957; McCall et al., 1992). They contend that the discrepancies between the expected and actual scores are independent of the predictor variable (e.g., mental ability); as such, the method can be applied across the entire range of abilities. Second, the regression approach can be applied regardless of the particular instruments used. Finally, deviations from a regression line have better reliability than simple difference scores.

EXCLUSIVE VERSUS INCLUSIVE DEFINITIONS OF UNDERACHIEVEMENT

As described below, definitions of gifted underachievement can be categorized in at least two ways: (a) narrow and exclusive (culturally assaultive or blind) and (b) broad and inclusive (culturally responsive).

Narrow and exclusive definitions. Several problems are associated with narrow and exclusive definitions of underachievement. First, narrow definitions refer to gifted students who demonstrate well-above-average intellectual or academic ability on intelligence and achievement tests, but fail to develop or demonstrate their abilities. For instance, Raph et al. (1966) defined such students as those who rank in the upper third of the population in ability, but do not graduate from high school, do not attend college, or drop out of college.

Second, narrow definitions rely exclusively on standardized tests to identify and characterize underachievement among gifted students. For example, a discrepancy exists between an intelligence test and an achievement test (see Figure 5.1).

Third, there is a discrepancy between an intelligence test and a student's school performance. For example, the intelligence test score is high (at or above 130) but a student's GPA is lower than expected (e.g., one or two standard deviations below the level predicted). Fourth, defining underachievement as a discrepancy between an aptitude test score and a student's academic performance in school or on an achievement test is also exclusionary. A fifth example of a narrow definition of gifted underachievement appears when a student has high standardized test scores but teachers observe lower performance than predicted by the tests.

These definitions place great faith in intelligence tests to identify both giftedness and underachievement. In these examples, intelligence tests are used as the independent variable—*if* the intelligence test score is high, *then* the achievement level *should* be high. The aforementioned definitions ignore the impact of personal, cultural, social, and school variables on test performance.

Type I: Intelligence Test

- A child whose day-by-day efficiency in school is much poorer than would be expected on the basis of intelligence tests (Bricklin & Bricklin, 1967).
- A student who ranks in the top third of intellectual ability, but whose performance is dramatically below that level (Fine, 1967).
- One who evidences a long-standing pattern of academic underachievement not accounted for by learning disabilities, and giftedness only appears through intellectual testing or from remarkable discrepancies in reading and math (Fine & Pitts, 1980).
- A child achieving significantly below the level statistically predicted by his or her IQ (Newman, Dember, & Krug, 1973).
- A student whose language or nonlanguage IQ scores were 116 or above predicted potential and whose scores were at least one grade level below the achievement level expected and whose grades were B or less (Ohlsen & Gazda, 1965).
- Stanford-Binet IQ of 132 or above and percentile ranking of 75 or below on the California Test of Basic Skills (Sauernman & Michael, 1980).
- A student for whom a gap exists between achievement test scores and intelligence test scores or between academic grades and intelligence test scores (Gallagher, 1979).
- An individual who demonstrates well-above-average intellectual or academic ability on intelligence and aptitude tests, but fails to perform on school-related tasks at an equally high level (Hall, 1983).
- A student in the upper 25% of the population on the Pinter General Ability Test (IQ greater than 110) and who had earned a GPA below the mean of his or her class in grades 9–11 (Shaw & McCuen, 1960).

Type II: Aptitude and Achievement Tests

- A student who was in the top 25% of the Differential Aptitude Test in verbal-numerical and whose GPA was below the mean for all students at the DAT level (Finney & Van Dalsem, 1969).
- A composite score at or above the 95th percentile on the American College Testing Program (ACT) and a grade point average less than or equal to 2.25 (on a 4.00 scale; Colangelo et al., 1993).
- A student who demonstrates exceptionally high capacity for academic achievement and who is not performing satisfactorily for his or her levels of daily academics and on achievement tests (Whitmore, 1980).

Figure 5.1. Exclusive definitions of underachievement among gifted students.

Overall, the use of exclusive definitions results in an elite group of students being identified as gifted underachievers. By defining gifted underachievement from a psychometric basis only, and by limiting the definition to "high" test scores, many Black students (and other students who tend not to perform well on standardized tests) will be overlooked. Thorndike (1963) questioned the legitimacy of the concept of underachievement based on both psychometric and statistical bases, primarily because such measures are less than perfect predictors of potential and ability. Educators must be honest and clear about how they define underachievement, and recognize, as has Steele (1997, 1999), that tests contain biases and Black students are aware of this when being assessed. The notion of stereotype threat must be understood and considered when testing and assessing Black students.

Regardless of whether one adopts a definition of underachievement based on intelligence tests, achievement tests, school performance, and parent/caregiver and/or teacher expectations, the above definitions are exclusive and exclusionary because they focus only on academically and intellectually gifted underachievers. How is underachievement defined among gifted students whose strengths are in creativity, leadership, and the visual and performing arts, for instance?

Broad/inclusive definitions. Perhaps the broadest definition of underachievement among gifted students refers to those students who fail to develop their academic potential. The overreliance on psychometric assessment, high test scores, and focus on academic and intellectual giftedness are absent from inclusive and culturally responsive definitions. Culturally responsive definitions support the notion that if five gifted students of the same age and gender have the same IQ score, income, and socioeconomic status, they may achieve differently. One student may perform less than satisfactory in science, another in language arts, a third in music, a fourth in mathematics, and the fifth in physical education. In a different scenario, two of the five students may have the same GPA, a third student may be retained, a fourth student may have failed history, and the fifth student may have decided that school is meaningless and a waste of time.

Inclusive or culturally responsive definitions reflect a qualitative orientation that considers the extent to which motivation is present and effort is exerted. Moreover, emphasis is not placed so much on the discrepant test scores, but on the nature or etiology of the discrepancy. For example, a student's achievement test score can be lower than his or her intelligence test score because the student exerted little effort, did not understand the directions, the test was administered in a large group, the student was distracted, the teacher had low expectations, and so forth.

Culturally responsive definitions are based on a comprehensive, holistic assessment of intelligence, achievement, motivation, self-concept, anxiety, organization skills, and test-taking skills. Information is also gathered from parents/caregivers (e.g., checklist, nomination form, interview), teachers and other educators (e.g., observations, interview, checklist), and the student. In brief, culturally responsive and inclusive definitions support the notion that underachievement is a multidimensional construct that cannot be assessed with unidimensional instruments and tools.

PERSPECTIVES ON UNDERACHIEVEMENT

Underachieving students are not a homogeneous group. Some students have problems associated with poor peer or social relationships, lack of insight, depression, anxiety, defensiveness, and a negative self-image, for example. Other students may lack motivation and may be considered lazy, procrastinators, perfectionists, or nonconformists. A common perception is that these students would not be underachieving if they would "just try harder," "pay attention," "listen," and "follow rules." However, overcoming or reversing underachievement is not this simple for many students, particularly those who have had little or no early educational intervention, those who lack basic skills to take advantage of educational opportunities, and those who have negative self-perceptions. For Black students, reversing underachievement may be especially difficult if it is related to social barriers such as racism and peer pressure, and to environmental barriers such as poverty.

Unfortunately, most descriptions of underachievers support a deficit perspective: "poor" study skills, task commitment, motivation, organization, memory, self-concept, self-esteem, racial identity, and so forth. These characteristics, however, focus on the students and the symptoms, rather than the etiology of underachievement. This is why a focus on the achievement gap is essential in this discussion. The result of focusing on the student, of blaming the victim, is that the student is considered less desirable, less salvageable than other students. Schools are unable to "deal with" or work with students who deviate too much from the norm; schools are made for students who excel, achieve, and fulfill the (subjective) expectations of teachers and caregivers. A more productive or effective approach to understanding underachievement is to look at what contributes to low motivation and external motivation. Nowhere is the need to begin this proactive search more urgent than with Black students and those living in poverty—far too many are diamonds in the rough (Ford, 2010; VanTassel-Baska & Stambaugh, 2007).

THEORIES OF UNDERACHIEVEMENT

There are three things to remember about education. The first one is motivation. The second one is motivation. The third one is motivation.

—Terrell H. Bell

The issue of achievement motivation (or lack thereof) is under serious discussion by educators and psychologists alike. Motivation may be defined as those factors that incite and direct behavior. Dweck and Elliott (1983) defined motivation as the psychological factors that influence the direction, magnitude, and persistence of behaviors on a given task. They asserted that motivation is a function of assessments and inferences (e.g., Do I have the skills and can I complete the task successfully?), cognitive consequences (i.e., factors that affect attention and effort), and metacognitive skills (i.e., task analysis, strategy planning, and performance monitoring).

Several theories help to explain the nature and etiology of academic underachievement (e.g., social learning, need achievement, attribution). These theories vary in their orientation, but tend to agree that a lack of motivation contributes to low achievement and underachievement, and that a lack of achievement motivation is influenced by one's expectation of success and the value placed on achieving a desired end.

ACADEMIC UNDERACHIEVEMENT

Academic underachievement is often described in at least one of three ways: undifferentiated, specific, or hidden. *Undifferentiated* underachievement is general in nature. For instance, the student is not performing as well as her assessed aptitude would predict in most or all subject areas. With *specific* academic underachievement, the student does poorly in one or two specific or broad content areas (such as language-based, science-based, or math-based subjects). *Hidden* underachievement is perhaps the most difficult type to assess. In this situation, one student's performance on aptitude and achievement measures is consistently low; this student's abilities remain hidden because he is functionally untestable. Another student's achievement can be hidden by satisfactory performance when the teacher has little evidence that the student is capable of much higher performance.

In an early study, Roth (1970) categorized underachievement as follows: (a) neurotic—the student is preoccupied with his or her relationships with parent(s) and suffering from substantial anxiety and guilt over it, and subsequently, the student is paralyzed by concerns and cannot produce; (b) nonachievement syndrome—the student *chooses* not to make an effort and is failing; and (c) adolescent reaction—this is a development issue characterized by extreme independence seeking. The student works diligently to do everything his or her parent(s), teachers, and other adults oppose.

Whitmore (1980) studied underachievement specifically among gifted students and reported that types of underachievement can be categorized as: (a) aggressive—the student is disruptive, talkative, clowning around in class, rebellious, and hostile; (b) withdrawn—the student is uninterested, bored, and does not try to participate; and (c) a combination—the student is erratic, unpredictable, and vacillates between aggression and withdrawal.

Educators should also consider the context and duration of underachievement (see Table 5.1). Underachievement can be: (a) grade specific, such as the second- or third-grade syndrome among Black students, mainly males, in which they do well academically in early elementary but fall behind in upper elementary; (b) subject specific, in which students underperform in certain subject areas (e.g., math, science, language arts, social studies); and (c) teacher/classroom specific, in which students underperform when working with a particular teacher(s) or classroom, including poor relationships with peers.

Is underachievement acute (i.e., temporary/situational) or chronic (i.e., long term)? Situational underachievement results from a temporary period of disturbance (e.g., developmental issues such as adolescence, family problems, illness, new interests, moving to a new school, and personality conflicts with teacher and/or classmates).

Chronic underachievement is characterized by an established pattern, the student is usually below average in all subject areas, and there are no indications that it is being created by a temporary situation. This can include a student having a learning disability/challenge and problems

Table 5.1
Context and Duration of Underachievement

Duration	Context
Acute and short-term	• Poor teacher-student relationships • Social-emotional issues (e.g., poor relationships with class-mates—alienation and isolation; low and negative expecta-tions from classmates; bullying) • Transitional issues (e.g., moving to a new school or classroom; making adjustments socially or to fit in) • Interest and motivation related to nonacademic areas (e.g., sports and other extracurricular activities) greater than aca-demic interest and priorities • Family problems and issues (e.g., divorce, death) • Developmental issues (e.g., adolescence, racial identity changes)
Chronic and long-term	• Subject-specific poor achievement • Health issues and problems • Learning disabilities or challenges • Poverty (e.g., low income and/or low socioeconomic status) • Basic needs not met (e.g., food, shelter/homelessness, safety)

Note. Some of the acute and short-term contexts can become chronic and long-term, such as disin-terest in academics, obsessive interest in sports, ongoing peer pressure, and ongoing low teacher expectations and family issues. Relative to "basic needs," I am referring to Maslow's (1954) hierarchy of needs as one example.

with certain or all subject areas. It can also include living in poverty and being homeless, to name but a few.

UNDERACHIEVEMENT IN OTHER AREAS OF GIFTEDNESS

There is a growing body of literature on underachievement among academically and intellectually gifted students, but less attention has centered on other areas of giftedness, as described below.

Underachievement in leadership. Although gifted leaders can and do use their abilities in socially unproductive and unacceptable ways, we know little about such students. Adolph Hitler, Charles Manson, and Jim Jones were gifted "leaders" who went astray, to say the least. Insider traders, industrial and military spies, computer invaders and virus spreaders, and White collar professionals are described in the media as talented, intelligent persons. Before their downfall, most leaders have been respected for their abilities.

Underachievers in leadership choose unethical and expedient solutions to problems, they go with the group rather than against it, they compromise their values, they lack commitment to principles and causes, they do not identify with humanity, they do not feel compassion, they cannot admit to their shortcomings, and they are unwilling to accept societal norms.

According to Seeley (1984) and Seeley and Mahoney (1981), most of the literature on delinquency and giftedness centers on students with high IQ scores. Seldom do we focus on the full range of gifted students; rather, we focus on their strengths and positives, often ignoring their weaknesses. Seeley and Mahoney found that many students in the juvenile delinquency system were gifted, but their giftedness was not necessarily associated with high academic achievement. Most of the students scored poorly on tests that assessed fluid intelligence but performed well on achievement tests.

Although gifted students are generally rational thinkers who have high consciences and are often concerned about world and adult issues, they are not immune to using their gifts in nonproductive, destructive ways. Seeley (1984) explained the relationship between gifted students and delinquency in two ways: the vulnerability thesis and the protection thesis. The vulnerability thesis proposes that gifted students, because of their greater perceptual acuity and ease of learning, are more sensitive to environmental factors than other students. Subsequently, they are affected more by unfavorable environments. For instance, a gifted Black student may be vulnerable because he or she feels different from classmates and feels less able to fit in. To increase peer relations, this gifted student may do what is expected by peers to fit in. This thesis suggests that gifted students are more likely than other students to become delinquent because they are more likely to be adversely affected by negative environments at both home and school.

The protection thesis, however, views giftedness as a protection against delinquency. Gifted students have greater insight into their actions and those of others, and are better able to evaluate the long-range consequences of their behaviors than nongifted students. Consequently, gifted students are better able to understand and cope with environmental problems. As the antithesis of the vulnerability thesis, this perspective holds that gifted students are less likely to succumb to delinquent behaviors. Gifted students only become delinquent, Seeley (1984) added, when environmental conditions are exceptionally unfavorable. This statement carries important implications for Black students who are more likely than other students to confront racial discrimination, experience lowered teacher expectations, and live in conditions that place many students at risk for underachievement (e.g., poverty, living in a single-parent family).

Underachievement in creativity. Creative underachievers may have high test scores on measures of creativity, yet do not demonstrate many of the characteristics of creativity: divergent thinking, elaboration, fluency, and originality (see Torrance, 1973). Such students may produce many ideas, but lack initiative or follow through. Similarly, creative underachievers can demonstrate creative behaviors, but standardized tests can fail to capture the students' strengths. Specifically, with their emphasis on convergent thinking and paper-pencil evaluations, intelligence and achievement tests are antithetical to creative and divergent thinking.

Personality characteristics of nonconformity, resistance to adult domination, independence, risk taking, and indifference to rules can also hinder creative students' performance and teachers' evaluation of these students. Similarly, if these students are considered "weird" and nonconforming, neither teachers nor classmates may nominate them for identification.

Using Kohlberg's (1972, 1975) theory of moral development, Tan-Williams and Gutteridge (1981) studied the relationship between creativity and moral development among adolescents gifted in creativity. Kohlberg's theory proposed that moral development occurs in three levels, each with two stages: Level 1, preconventional moral reasoning (punishment-obedience orientation; personal reward orientation); Level 2, conventional moral reasoning (good-boy-nice girl orientation; law and order orientation); and Level 3, postconventional moral reasoning (social contract orientation; universal ethical principle orientation).

Tan-Williams and Gutteridge (1981) found that creatively gifted students were most likely to perform at Kohlberg's conventional level, although their scores were higher than adolescents not identified as gifted. At Level 3, "good" is equated with "nice," and this is determined by what pleases the individual and what is approved and sanctioned by others; at Level 4, laws are considered absolute, authority is respected, and the social order must be maintained. The authors concluded that the gifted students in their study were underdeveloped in moral development, especially considering their intellectual and creative skills.

Underachievement in the visual and performing arts. Research indicates that public speaking is one of the most common fears of people in general, ranking high with fear of death and losing loved ones, for example. It comes as no surprise, therefore, that many gifted students who are introverted, shy, or have low self-esteem may have difficulties performing for an audience, going to an audition, or submitting work for contests.

Also, low-income and/or low-SES students may not have the experiences and resources to seek professional training, mentors, and other opportunities to develop and nurture their abilities, skills, and interests (Books, 2004). Without formal training, students gifted in art, drama, music, dance, and other areas have a lower probability of being referred and identified, and having their needs met. Further, it is quite possible that males will be discouraged from pursuing interests in these areas due to societal expectations and misperceptions that dance, for example, is a feminine attribute and career.

TOWARD A MODEL OF UNDERACHIEVEMENT AMONG GIFTED BLACK STUDENTS

CULTURAL DIFFERENCES

For decades, Ogbu (1994, 2003, 2004, 2008) has proposed that the type of minority status one holds has a significant impact on students' learning and educational outcomes, along with the expectations held of them. According to his theory, there are three types of minority statuses: autonomous, immigrant/voluntary, and caste-like/involuntary. *Autonomous minorities* are minorities in number only. They include Jewish, Mormon, and Amish groups. Because there are no non-White autonomous minorities in the U.S., this section focuses on the remaining two groups. *Voluntary minorities* (e.g., Asian Americans) moved/immigrated to the U.S. because of their desire for greater economically and political independence, as well as greater overall opportunities. They have come to the U.S. in search of the American Dream. *Involuntary minorities* were brought to the U.S. against their will. Historically, groups such as Blacks, Native Americans, and Hispanic Americans have been denied equitable educational and employment opportunities; they have been relegated to menial social positions that keep them submerged in the underclass and among the educationally disadvantaged.

Both voluntary and involuntary minorities have primary cultural differences that existed prior to forced migration or voluntary immigration, such as communication, cognitive or learning style, interaction style, child-drearing practices, and values. However, involuntary minorities developed secondary cultural differences in reaction to contact with Whites that is characterized by superior-inferior or dominate-subordinate status. An important feature of secondary cultural differences is cultural inversion—the tendency to regard certain behaviors, events, and symbols as inappropriate for Blacks because they are characteristic of Whites. In other words, in reaction to oppression, Black students may choose to react in opposition to the values espoused in schools. Consequently, Black students hold two opposing frames of reference. By opposing those values, behaviors, and attitudes associated with White students, Black students develop a stronger social or collective identity.

Primary cultural differences do not develop in response to opposition, nor to protect one's collective identity, self-worth, or feelings of security. Voluntary minorities do not always perceive school achievement, for example, as threatening or as giving up their collective, group, or social identity. Rather, they perceive themselves as accommodating without assimilating—compromising. In effect, they appreciate or accept biculturality and code switching, and they believe that "playing the game" by the rules will yield short- and long-term gains: employment, upward mobility, and the realization of the American Dream. With these beliefs, voluntary minorities are able to cross cultural boundaries.

The picture is different for involuntary minorities who hold a dual and opposing frame of reference. These differences are perceived by involuntary minorities as part of a collective identity—not as barriers to be overcome. A lack of fluency in mainstream English, intergroup conflicts, and conflicts between teaching and learning styles, for example, result from or are associated with secondary cultural differences. For involuntary minorities, school learning may be equated with learning the culture and language of White Americans—the enemy or oppressor. Accordingly, schools may be viewed as a systematic attempt to displace their social or racial identity and values, as well as feelings of self-worth. Because of persistent racism and other social injustices, Black students may not support the achievement ideology; they see no incentives to give up their differences or to play the game (Mickelson, 1984). The American Dream is a mirage to some of these students.

Black students, mainly those identified as gifted, motivated, or high achieving, who are encouraged to and then choose to support the achievement ideology risk facing social pressures from peers and the Black community (e.g., Ford et al., 2008b; Fordham, 1986, 1988; Fordham & Ogbu,

1986). Peers may perceive them as "acting White" and being disloyal to the Black community. This social pressure can result in psychological pressures, loss of peer affiliations, and personal conflict for gifted and/or achieving Black students.

Several survival strategies can be adopted by involuntary minority students. First, Black students can choose to emulate the values associated with White Americans (i.e., act White) and risk psychological ramifications. Second, they can accommodate without assimilating, as is characteristic of voluntary minority groups. The result is biculturality—adopting two frames of references that are often oppositional. Third, Black students can camouflage their abilities by becoming jesters, class clowns, and/or athletes. According to Ogbu (1993, 2004, 2008), when these students do well in school, they can attribute success to natural talent or smartness. Finally, Black students can choose cultural encapsulation, characterized by a strong, unwavering support to values embraced by peers, even an anti-achievement ethic.

SUPPORT FOR THE ACHIEVEMENT IDEOLOGY

Albeit indirectly, Ogbu's (1993) theory demonstrates and articulates how belief in the achievement ideology plays an important role in achievement among Black students. The extent to which gifted Black students support the achievement ideology cannot be overlooked by educators. Individuals who support the achievement ideology often increase their opportunities of succeeding both in school and life. Such students support the values of middle-class Whites whereby they believe that one's chances for success and upward mobility increase with effort and hard work. However, such support may not necessarily be found among gifted Black students who underachieve.

Most theories describe achievement motivation using the expectancy-value paradigm (e.g., Dweck, 1975, 1999). Achievement motivation increases when one hopes for *and* expects success, and when one *values* the task and goal. However, the major shortcoming of the aforementioned theories is their inattention to the social and cultural contexts that affect achievement, motivation, and performance. Instead, it is too readily concluded that certain racial groups lack achievement motivation. All children are born with the motivation to achieve. Certainly, the more Black students (or any students) support the American achievement ideology, the greater their chances for achievement motivation and academic success (MacLeod, 1987, 1995; New America Media, 2007).

LEARNING AND CULTURAL STYLE DIFFERENCES

As noted earlier, school achievement is influenced significantly by one's learning style (Griggs & Dunn, 1984, 1989; Shade & Edwards, 1987) and cultural styles (e.g., Boykin, Albury, et al., 2005; Boykin et al., 2005; Boykin et al., 2006; Hale, 2001); hence, what contributes to school disengagement and failure is not solely what is taught, but also how it is taught, learned, and experienced.

In terms of instruction, three African proverbs illustrate the significance of learning styles to Black students: "Seeing is better than hearing"; "Seeing is different from being told"; and "Sitting is being crippled." These proverbs reflect preferences for visual, tactile, and kinesthetic learning experiences among Black youth. Hale's (2001) book titled *Learning While Black* speaks volumes on this issue.

Dunn, Beaudry, and Klavas (1989) defined learning styles as a biologically and developmentally imposed set of personal characteristics that make the same teaching method effective for some students and ineffective for others. In other words, all students are products of family and community settings that have predisposed them to patterns of behaviors that are more or less functional in school settings (Sinclair & Ghory, 1992). Dunn, DeBello, Brennan, Krimsky, and Murrain (1981) defined learning styles as the way individuals concentrate on, absorb, and retain new or difficult information or skills. Style, they added, comprises a combination of environmental, emotional, sociological, physical, and psychological elements that permit individuals to receive, store, and use knowledge or abilities. Saracho (1989) described learning styles as a distinctive pattern of apprehending, storing, and employing information, or more simply, as individual variations in methods of perceiving, remembering, and thinking. All of these definitions reflect a belief that learning is based on the way children manipulate and process information in the material that is being taught. In essence, they reflect each learner's mode of selecting, encoding, organizing, storing, retrieving, decoding, and generating information, all of which influence learning and performance (Frederico & Landis, 1980). Most researchers agree that every person has a preferred learning style, which is highly resistant to change, particularly after elementary school.

Learning styles are significantly influenced by culturally induced cognitive styles related to communicating, interacting, perceiving, and acquiring knowledge (Hale, 2001; Saracho & Gerstl, 1992; Shade, 1994, 1997; Shade et al., 1997). Failure may result when there is an incompatibility between Black students' learning styles and the instructional preferences of schools (i.e., teaching styles), which generally favor field-independent, abstract, and analytical styles of learning. Schools also favor students who have long attention spans, who can adhere to time constraints, who can spend extended periods of time doing seatwork, and who learn individually, independently, and competitively.

Research suggests that the culturally influenced learning styles of gifted, Black, and underachieving students are rather dissimilar. In general, gifted students prefer formal learning classroom designs, less structure in learning materials, and auditory modes of presentation, and they are reflective, tactile, kinesthetic, and field-independent learners. They are responsible for their own learning, and are persistent, motivated, and task-oriented. Black students, however, are likely to be field-dependent, holistic, relational, and visual learners; they learn best in social and cooperative settings, are socially or other oriented, and they prefer tactile and kinesthetic learning/teaching experiences. Underachievers tend to be impulsive, low task-oriented, nonconforming, creative, visual, and tactile and kinesthetic learners.

Boykin's model of Afrocentric styles, discussed in Chapter 3, is germane to this discussion, but will not be reiterated here. When teachers understand and use verve, movement, harmony, affect, communalism, oral tradition, spirituality, social time perspective, and expressive individualism when teaching, underachieving Black students are more likely to be engaged and to achieve at higher levels. Table 5.2 aligns these cultural styles with teaching styles and strategies so that they are compatible (see Ford & Kea, 2009).

In essence, the learning style preferences of gifted students and Black students appear oppositional in more than one way, whereas the styles of Black students and underachievers appear more similar. This certainly poses a dilemma for teachers as well as gifted Black students, whose school performance may be hindered. Stated differently, Black students do not necessarily fail in school because of learning style differences, but because schools fail to accommodate these differences with their teaching/instructional styles (Ford & Kea, 2009).

Table 5.2
Culturally Responsive Instruction: Aligning Afrocentric
Learning Styles With Teaching Styles and Strategies

Afrocentric learning style (Boykin)	Sample teaching styles and strategies
Verve, movement, harmony	Goal: Support tactile and kinesthetic learners Field trips, manipulatives, graphic organizers, creative movement
Oral traditional	Goal: Support verbal skills and provide other means of communicating learning Speeches, debates, oral reports, oral exams, projects and presentations, role-plays, simulations, poetry, skits/drama, word games, lectures, Socratic questioning method, storytelling
Expressive individualism	Goal: Support and nurture creativity and self-expression Creative writing, journaling, essays, poetry, drama, artwork, music, songs, projects, storytelling
Spirituality	Goal: Provide a optimistic, positive learning environment Encouragement, praise, compliments, affirmations
Communalism, affect, harmony	Goal: Establish family environment/climate, a sense of community and belonging, decrease individual competition Group work, collaborative learning, peer buddies, peer tutoring, study groups, class mascot and name, constructive feedback
Social time perspective, affect	Goal: Provide strategies that add to students' sense of time; monochromic and polychromic supported; increase engagement and interest Time management strategies, organizational strategies, due date reminders, assignments divided into smaller tasks, culturally relevant curriculum (materials, topics, current events grounded in the lives of students)

IDENTIFICATION AND ASSESSMENT

Predicting underachievement is as difficult as predicting the weather. The burden of proof for designating students as underachievers is on educators and researchers. They must have confidence in the instruments chosen, and be cautious in interpreting the results.

Intelligence, aptitude, and achievement tests have been used to operationalize the various conceptual definitions of underachievement described earlier. The same instruments that are used to identify and label gifted students are used to identify and label underachieving students (e.g., Wechsler Intelligence Scale for Children, Stanford-Binet IV, Comprehensive Tests of Basic Skills, Iowa Tests of Basic Skills, Cognitive Abilities Test, Otis-Lennon School Ability Test). Yet, the legitimacy of the concept of underachievement based on both psychometric and statistical bases is questionable, particularly as measurement criteria are less than perfect. Further, underachievement, like giftedness and intelligence, is not a unidimensional construct and should not be evaluated solely with one measure or with unidimensional instruments. Because of its complex and multidimensional nature, underachievement may be better understood by including nonverbal measures with noncognitive and qualitative information.

NONCOGNITIVE MEASURES

Measures of noncognitive variables provide more educationally relevant data than standardized tests scores of intelligence and achievement. Psychological, affective, motivational, attitudinal, and social factors play important roles in students' achievement and test performance. Assessments of motivation and test anxiety increase our understanding of: (a) the reasons gifted Black students may underachieve, (b) the difficulties of identifying gifted Black students, and (c) the reasons for poor test scores. As described below, assessing and understanding Black students' achievement depends upon the extent to which educators use both quantitative and qualitative indices.

Motivation. Student motivation can be assessed with a variety of measures, including the Achievement Motivation Inventory (Schuler, Thornton, Frintrup, & Mueller-Hanson, 2002), Achievement Motivation Profile (Mandel, Friedland, & Marcus, 1996), Low Achievement Scale (Biggs & Felton, 1977), The Underachievement Scale (McQuary &

Truax, 1955), the Bell Adjustment Inventory (Dana & Baker, 1961), and the Scale of Intrinsic Versus Extrinsic Motivation in the Classroom (Harter, 1982).

Self-concept. Students' self-image has a powerful effect on their achievement (Haynes, Hamilton-Lee, & Comer, 1988). Students' self-concept can be assessed using measures by Harter (1982; The Perceived Competence Scale for Children); Piers, Harris, and Herzberg (2002; Piers-Harris Children's Self-Concept Scale, Second Edition); Marsh (1990; Self-Description Questionnaire II); and others who have developed measures of self-concept.

Racial identity. Racial identity must also be assessed, particularly as it represents an important component of self-concept and self-esteem. Marks, Settles, Cooke, Morgan, and Sellers (2004) and Ponterotto, Casas, Suzuki, and Alexander (2001) provided comprehensive lists of measures.

Test anxiety. For far too many students, tests are academic electric chairs. Variables such as test anxiety, particularly chronic test anxiety, can have debilitating effects on students' performance. When students are too nervous, too tense, and/or too worried about the outcomes of the results, they have difficulty performing at even minimal levels on the tests. Similarly, fear of failure, fear of success, low self-confidence, a lack of motivation and persistence, a lack of commitment to the task (i.e., test), and preoccupation with other issues not germane to the test can negatively affect students' performance.

Educators must observe gifted Black students, particularly underachievers, during test-taking situations to look for undue stress and anxiety and to follow-up by talking with students about their concerns and making appropriate referrals. By teaching students relaxation, time management, and test-taking and study skills, as well as positive self-talk or affirmations, teachers and counselors can help gifted Black underachieving students to increase their comfort level, as well as their test outcomes. It may also prove invaluable to provide students with alternative assessment tasks (e.g., written report, project) from which teachers can evaluate learning and alternative study environments (e.g., group) to promote self-confidence.

Several test anxiety instruments are available for use by teachers, including the Achievement Anxiety Test (Alpert & Haber, 1960); the Test Anxiety Scale for Children (Sarason, Davidson, Lighthall, & Waite, 1958); the Test Anxiety Scale (Sarason & Ganzer, 1962; Sarason, Pederson, & Nyman, 1968); Test Anxiety Questionnaire (Mandler &

Sarason, 1952); and School Anxiety Test (Phillips, Pitcher, Worsham, & Miller, 1980).

Learning and cognitive styles. Any discussion of poor achievement would be incomplete without addressing how students learn, as well as how educators teach. Although there is certainly debate and disagreement about how students learn, especially Black students, I am convinced that any teacher recognizes that students learn differently—they have different learning styles. Helpful instruments for identifying learning and cognitive styles include: Learning Style Inventory (Dunn & Dunn, 1992); Kolb Learning Style Inventory (Kolb & Kolb, 2005); Gregorc Style Delineator (Gregorc, 1984); Myers-Briggs Type Indicator (Briggs & Myers, 1980); Group Embedded Figures Test (Witkin, Oltman, Raskin, & Karp, 1971); and Edmonds Learning Style Identification Exercise (see Shade, 1994).

School attitudes. Several instruments are available to assess Black students' attitudes toward school, including the Estes Attitudes Scales (Estes, Estes, Richards, & Roettger, 1981) and the Self-Perceptions of School Achievement Survey (Ford, 1991). The Self-Perceptions of School Achievement Survey (Ford, 1991) assesses Black students' perceptions regarding social, cultural, and psychological factors affecting their achievement. Students are also surveyed regarding their level of support for the achievement ideology and variables related to home, peers, and teachers that significantly influence their achievement motivation and orientation.

Figure 5.2 presents a checklist designed to assist teachers with identifying factors that contribute to or exacerbate school problems for gifted Black students. Teachers are encouraged to examine school factors, peer relations, familial factors, personality factors, and academic factors. All of these issues are given greater attention in later chapters.

Classroom climate. The classroom climate sets the emotional and motivational tone for learning and is influenced by a number of variables, including Black students' perception of teacher expectations, parent-teacher relations, peer relations, gifted program demographics, and curriculum and instruction. The underlying concern is the degree to which students feels a sense of membership and belonging, as well as some sense of connection to what is being taught (see Haynes, Comer, & Hamilton-Lee, 1989; Haynes & Hamilton-Lee, 1986).

As with any test, checklist, or assessment instrument, validity and reliability issues must be given considerable attention. Identification and assessment should be comprehensive and dynamic, including traditional,

Social Factors

____ Student's primary social group is outside of the school, AP class, or gifted program.
____ Student participates in little or no extracurricular activities.
____ Student socializes with gang members/leaders, drug users, and/or delinquents.
____ Student's need for affiliation (peer acceptance and relations) outweighs his or her need for achievement.

Family Factors

____ Student has one parent/caregiver in the home.
____ Student has relatives who have dropped out of school.
____ Student has little parental/family supervision; poor family relations.
____ Parental/caregiver expectations for student are too low or unrealistic.
____ Low-income and/or socioeconomic status.
____ Communication between home and school is poor (weak, inconsistent).
____ Student's home life is stressful.
____ Student lives in a home where there is a low parental/caregiver educational level.

School Culture/Climate Factors

____ Teachers and school personnel hold low expectations for Black students.
____ Gifted program/AP class is racially homogeneous; it lacks cultural and racial diversity relative to students.
____ Gifted program/AP class is racially homogeneous; it lacks cultural and racial diversity relative to teachers.
____ Little attention is given to multicultural or culturally responsive education (curriculum, instruction, assessment).
____ Teachers and other school personnel lack substantive training in gifted and AP education.
____ Teachers and other school personnel lack substantive training in multicultural or culturally responsive education (curriculum, instruction assessment).
____ Black students are underrepresented in gifted program and activities and AP classes.
____ Black student feels alienated and isolated from teacher(s) and/or school personnel.
____ Black student feels alienated and isolated from classmates.

Psychological/Individual Factors

____ Student's academic motivation is consistently low.
____ Student has low tolerance for structured and/or passive activities.
____ Student relates poorly to authority or adult figures (e.g., teachers, parents/caregivers, school administrators).
____ Student has experienced emotional trauma on more than one occasion.
____ Student has poor self-concept and/or poor racial identity (e.g., pre-encounter or immersion-emersion identities).
____ Student has health or medical problems.
____ Student attributes failure to lack of ability; attributes success to low intelligence, luck or easy task.
____ Student has low self-esteem.
____ Student has low/poor academic self-confidence.
____ Student has low/poor/negative social self-concept.
____ Student has negative attitude toward school.
____ Student consistently seeks immediate, short-term gratification.
____ Student's learning style preferences are inconsistent with teaching styles.

Student Achievement Behaviors

____ Student has low standardized test scores.
____ Student exerts little effort, has poor work ethic.
____ Student avoids challenging work.
____ Student has low grades or grade point average.
____ Students gets bored or disinterested easily; dislikes drill work and rote practices.
____ Student disrupts the class.
____ Student procrastinates on school assignments.
____ Student resists/refuses participation in AP classes or gifted program services (e.g., resource room).

Figure 5.2. Checklist for identifying indices of underachievement among gifted Black students. Rate on a scale of 1 to 5 (1 = *Strongly disagree*; 5 = *Strongly agree*).

nontraditional, and noncognitive measures of underachievement (Ford & Whiting, 2009).

STRATEGIES FOR REVERSING UNDERACHIEVEMENT

In general, strategies for reversing underachievement must address students' academic skills deficit (e.g., test-taking and study skills), include curricular changes (e.g., multicultural education) and instructional changes (e.g., accommodations to learning styles).

ACADEMIC UNDERACHIEVEMENT

Whitmore (1980) recommended three classifications of strategies that empower students to become more self-sufficient learners: supportive strategies, intrinsic strategies, and remedial strategies, as presented in Table 5.3. I've added a fourth set of strategies: challenging strategies. Supportive strategies are facilitative; they affirm students' sense of worth (self-esteem) and convey the message that success is both possible and a positive experience. Intrinsic strategies help students to develop self-initiation and internal motivation. These strategies communicate the importance of an internal locus of control, that is, internal more than external motivation. Remedial strategies are designed to improve students' academic performance in the specific area(s) of difficulty. Challenging strategies focus on rigor and expectations; here, Black students are thought to be and expected to be capable of high performance.

BEYOND INTELLIGENCE AND ACADEMICS: OTHER AREAS OF UNDERACHIEVEMENT

Creative underachievement. Creative underachievers may need to be taught critical thinking, convergent thinking, and test-taking skills and strategies. They should be given opportunities to learn independently and to take risks. Time management skills may also help these students cope with multiple problems, ideas, and products. These students need opportunities to demonstrate their abilities and master learning material in alternative formats.

Leadership underachievement. Students who use their leadership

Table 5.3
Strategies to Enhance Academic Achievement
Among Gifted Black Students

Strategy	Goal/Objective	Recommendations
Supportive strategies	To affirm the worth of students and convey the promise of greater potential and success	• Consistent opportunities to meet with teachers and other educators to discuss, recognize, problem solve, and resolve concerns • Collaborative, reciprocal partnerships with primary caregivers and families • Accommodate learning styles (e.g., provide options for students to demonstrate mastery of material; teach students to be bicognitive) • Mastery learning • Cooperative learning • Positive reinforcement • Authoritative learning climate • Multicultural counseling
Intrinsic strategies	To help students develop self-initiation and internal motivation	• Mentorships and role models • Positive reinforcement and constructive feedback • Independent study projects • Accommodation of learning styles • Multicultural education; culturally responsive education
Remedial strategies	To improve students' academic performance in the specific area or areas or difficulty	• Academic counseling (tutoring, study skills, organizational skills, test-taking skills) • Small-group instruction; cooperative learning and flexible grouping practices • Learning contracts; daily, written contracts
Challenging strategies	To improve rigor by challenging and engaging students; to communicate high expectations	• High expectations • Challenging and rigorous assignments • Placement in challenging courses with emotional and academic support • Constructive feedback

skills in socially unacceptable and harmful ways should be provided opportunities for introspection—looking inward so that they can see how their behaviors affect others. Counseling, mentoring, and other opportunities to interact with successful Black peers are three common recommendations, but students can also be exposed to theories of moral development and given opportunities to study topics such as politics in depth. For example, older students can take courses in philosophy, social psychology, child development, and law. As Silverman (1993) noted,

> leadership ability without ethics leads to manipulation and corruption; leadership with ethics leads to service to humanity. . . . Moral leaders choose ethical rather than expedient alternatives when faced with a dilemma; they are willing to go against the group rather than to compromise their values; are committed to principles and causes; identify with humanity, not just their own group; feel compassion and forgiveness; admit to their shortcomings; and hold their own personal ideals, transcending societal norms. (p. 312)

These characteristics are somewhat analogous to Dabrowski's (1972) multilevel individuals (Levels III–V) and Maslow's (1968) level of self-actualization.

Visual and performing arts. Underachieving students gifted in the visual and performing arts may need access to scholarships, internships, and mentorships to develop their abilities, particularly low-SES students. Shy, introverted students may also need to work with counselors to increase their self-concept for assertiveness training and public speaking.

SUMMARY

Motivation is not synonymous with achievement, and student motivation cannot be inferred by examining achievement test scores. Test scores are determined by a variety of factors. By evaluating the success of students by how well they achieve in school and on standardized tests, we lose sight of other factors affecting their achievement and test outcomes. Teachers must develop an understanding of why student motivation is lacking. Motivation and school performance are affected by students' self-worth, attributions for success and failure, and sense of hopefulness or helplessness, all of which are influenced significantly by parents/caregivers, peers, and teachers/educators.

Perceptions about gifted students in general have been shaped by stereotypes and myths about these students that describe them as motivated learners, with outstanding school performance and leadership. Gifted students are seldom perceived as unmotivated, lazy, procrastinators, or emotionally immature. Although the idea of gifted underachievers seems contradictory, it is a logical concept based on the reality that gifted students are represented among school dropouts. The concept is further supported by the fact that numerous definitions and several theories of gifted underachievement have been advanced.

Underachievement is a ubiquitous term, and little consensus exists regarding the definition that promises to capture the greatest number of youths who fail to reach their potential in school. Whereas many definitions support a behavioral, qualitative perspective of achievement (and underachievement), studies of gifted underachievers have traditionally supported a psychometric or quantitative definition. That is, educators have often used psychometric and quantitative definitions to identify gifted underachievers. These definitions tend to describe gifted underachievers as having a discrepancy or gap between some standardized test score and school performance, or a discrepancy between two standardized test scores (such as intelligence and achievement).

These psychometric definitions, however, have several shortcomings. First, they may encourage or cause educators to overlook learners who do not score well on standardized intelligence, achievement, and ability tests. Second, they ignore the fact that "a valid ability-reference requires evidence of optimum effort" (Nicholls, 1984, p. 41). As Glasser (1965, 1986) asserted, we are mistaken if we believe that discipline, dropout rates, and drugs are what's wrong with today's schools. As serious as these problems are, they represent symptoms of a much larger underlying problem: Far too many capable students make little or no effort to learn. Third, the overreliance on tests to assess underachievement, or the use of tests as the sole criteria for determining underachievement, is antithetical to what many researchers in education have argued: Tests do not always measure adequately and reliably the potentials and abilities of many students. Moreover, they are often biased against racially and culturally diverse groups. Essentially, tests fail to consider students' level of test anxiety, test-taking skills, level of motivation or task commitment, interest, learning styles, and the many risk factors impacting performance. Further, tests fail to explore students' self-concept, fear of failure, fear of success, perfectionism, locus of control, lack of skills, and rebellion against authority figures. They fail to consider the cultural, personal, and family backgrounds of individual students and fail to consider the reality that ability does not always determine performance.

Educators must be cautious when interpreting and defining achievement and its antithesis, underachievement, in narrow and exclusive terms. For example, how logical is it to assume that IQ scores are immune to or exempt from the effects of nonacademic factors that are frequently associated with poor school performance (e.g., motivation, task commitment, interest, test anxiety, self-concept, self-esteem, racial identity)? To what extent do total battery scores obscure the presence of specific types and areas of underachievement? How valid and reliable are results in which a single measure of intelligence is used to predict school performance? How are grades/evaluations affected by teacher stereotypes, prejudices, and biases, along with experience, special interests, and/or students' attitudes, behavior, and work habits? These same questions were raised by Thorndike (1963) several decades ago. Assuming that students come to school with well-developed self-systems, including self-esteem and motivation, future research must examine the nature and etiology of underachievement.

Increased attention to and research on underachievers with different gifts and talents and interests are needed. This research should explore definitions and correlates of underachievement among gifted students whose strengths are in creativity, leadership, and visual and performing arts—and who fail to develop to (or fall short of developing) their potential.

Underachievement can be a dangerous, downward spiral resulting from many factors, and it seldom occurs in a simple, unidirectional fashion. Lack of achievement motivation and underachievement involve a broad range of persons, groups, and settings. Because all children are born with the motivation to achieve, these issues are by no means solely problems of racial or cultural groups. Yet, they are problems for those whose racial and cultural background are different from that which is represented, espoused, or understood by the majority of society and the status quo.

Although underachievement is a complex, multifaceted concept that remains elusive to definition and identification, we cannot and ought not abandon the concept. Instead, we can define it in more specific, culturally responsive, and comprehensive ways. Future research must focus on the etiology of underachievement among gifted Black students, including its nature, scope, duration, and intensity. When definitions of underachievement are psychometrically driven to the exclusion of other factors such as motivation, many (perhaps most) underachievers will go underidentified, misunderstood, and undersupported.

Many major factors and correlates contribute to the inaccurate and prejudicial prediction of Black students' skills, potential, and ability. This chapter has attempted to demonstrate that factors and correlates other than psychometric ones are involved in the achievement gap and under-achievement—and all of its faces. Unmodifiable factors include students' race, gender, and, at times, income and socioeconomic status. Factors amenable to intervention include anxiety, study and test-taking skills, and motivation. As such, identification and reversal of underachievement have to include comprehensive and multidimensional assessment practices that are also culturally responsive. Instruments should, for example, assess students' ability and potential, learning style preference, self-concept, personality, anxiety, motivation, and perceptions of achievement, as well as those of teachers, parents/caregivers, and peers. For results to be impactful, meaningful, and prescriptive, assessments should be culturally sensitive, valid, and reliable. With this climate of holistic and culturally responsive assessment, the probability of gifted Black students' being misdiagnosed decreases considerably.

Important philosophies to keep in mind include "no excuses" (Carter, 2000) and "failure is not an option" (Blankenstein, 2004). More often than not, we (educators and families) can and do make a difference. When we set goals and develop appropriate attitudes, strategies, and resources, Black students will perform at higher levels, including levels commensurate with their White classmates.

SOCIAL FACTORS AS CORRELATES OF UNDERACHIEVEMENT AND ACHIEVEMENT

Because of societal underachievement, an individual does not necessarily have to choose to underachieve. He/she may have no choice.

—Fine (1967, p. 233)

No child is inherently at risk for underachievement. Rather, he or she is put at risk because of various external disadvantages. Perhaps the greatest challenge facing educators is assuring student achievement and positive student outcomes in terms of excellence and equity. The unfortunate and unnecessary reality that many Black students withdraw from school mentally, emotionally, and physically highlights the need for increased attention to factors (both internal and external to schools and home) at work to undermine the academic success of and opportunities for these students to reach their potential.

The social ring of influence, illustrated in Figure 6.1, is the focus of this chapter. Social or environmental factors are broad and encompass a number of variables that cannot all be addressed in this book and chapter. Social factors are defined as the largest context that affects students'

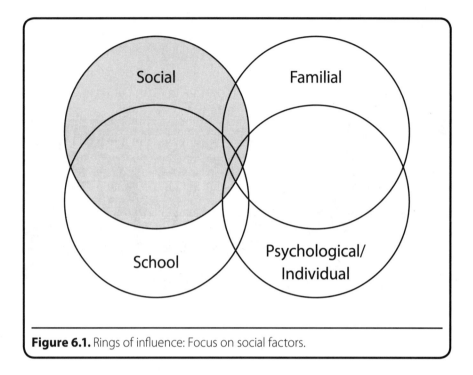

Figure 6.1. Rings of influence: Focus on social factors.

quality of life. Specifically, social factors such as low expectations on the one hand, and racism, discrimination, and prejudice on the other hand, all play substantive roles in underachievement among gifted Black students, as well as their lack of participation in gifted education programs and AP classes. This chapter focuses on the many environmental factors that place Black students at risk for underachievement and underrepresentation in gifted education programs.

QUESTIONS TO CONSIDER:

❖ What are some fundamental social or societal issues that contribute to and/or exacerbate underachievement among gifted Black students, or those who could otherwise be identified as advanced learners and benefit from gifted education?

❖ What are some key indicators of social outcomes, especially negative outcomes, about Black students?

❖ What social factors (e.g., risk factors) outside of school settings influence (hinder or promote) Black students' achievement?

❖ Which social factors, including real and potential risk factors, outside of family settings influence (hinder or promote) Black students' achievement?

❖ How do social factors affect Black students' view of themselves as learners?

SOCIAL/ENVIRONMENTAL FORCES

Numerous social factors influence and confound the underrepresentation of Black students in gifted education and AP classes, and contribute to their lower than expected achievement. A litany of scholars, including Bowles and Gintis (1976), Bourdieu (1977), Giroux (1983), Hart and Risley (1995), and Lee and Burkham (2002), have described how social class inequality passes from one generation to the next. They highlighted the reality that social capital—and lack of it—matters. For example, Giroux observed that social inequality persists because society values the social capital (educational and cultural capital) of the dominant/predominant culture and devalues that of economically and racially and culturally different groups. That is to say, the beliefs, attitudes, values, norms, customs, and traditions of the status quo are what is often valued and deemed valid and valuable. Those who do not advocate, adhere to, or demonstrate what is "normal" to the status quo are relegated to second-class status and otherwise devalued.

One theory in particular holds much promise for shedding light on how social and even cultural capital is experienced in the United States. Specifically, Ogbu (1983, 1988) attributed the poorer school performance of Blacks to structural inequality: racism, discrimination, and other social injustices. He postulated that injustices, including job ceilings and unequal power relations, reproduce class and social inequality such that those at the bottom of the socioeconomic ladder remain at the bottom. These forces often undermine the achievement of gifted Black students. Educators who hold a cultural deficit hypothesis reinforce this cycle of low representation of Black students in gifted education and AP classes. This paradigm was commonplace during the 1960s, à la Moynihan (1965) and Coleman et al. (1966), to name but two views, when the poor or relatively poorer school achievement among Black students was explained by their "culture of poverty" and presumed inadequate or inferior socialization practices. Similarly, Jensen (1969) and Herrnstein and Murray (1994) believed that race and inherited intellectual inferiority explained the poorer school performance of Black students. All of these scholars are guilty of deficit thinking in which Black students are viewed as culturally and/or genetically inferior to White students.

As noted in previous discussions about the achievement gap (e.g., Barton & Coley, 2009; Coley, 2003; Lubienski, 2001, 2007, 2008; Lubienski & Gutiérrez, 2008), several social or environmental factors place Black students at risk for educational disadvantage on a consistent basis: poverty, residing in a single-parent family, mother's level of education, and language skills and differences. It would be inaccurate and misleading to deny or minimize social ills, such as stereotypes and racial discrimination (Dovidio & Gaertner, 1986; Dovidio, Glick, & Rudman, 2005; Sue, 2003; Sue et al. 2007).

RISK FACTORS

All the men of genius that we have ever heard of have triumphed over adverse circumstances, but that is no reason for supposing that there were not innumerable others who succumbed in youth.

—Bertrand Russell

Although definitions of what it means to be at risk vary, there is consensus that many students lack the home and community resources to benefit from schooling. That is, differences in learning outcomes result from the two-sided interaction or conflict between Black students and the environment (Sinclair & Ghory, 1992). Although poverty, cultural differences and conflicts, and linguistic differences, for example, contribute to many Black students having low academic achievement and high dropout rates, the reasons for these outcomes cannot and must not be attributed mainly or solely to cultural and/or internal variables.

Poverty is slavery, to say the least, because it limits and hinders potential. Singly or in unison, poverty and the various other risk factors effectively wreak havoc on *any* student's achievement and motivation. They threaten, in particular, to undermine the school achievement and motivation of Black and other culturally different students who are disproportionately represented in at-risk conditions (Garcia & Walker de Felix, 1992; Hart & Risley, 1995; Hodgkinson, 2007; Lee & Burkham, 2002; Levin, 1990; Walker de Felix, 1992). In essence, for some low-income or low-SES gifted Black students, survival takes a strong precedence over educational achievement and developing gifts and talents.

Race. For numerous reasons, Black students are less likely to complete high school, more likely to have lower standardized test scores, more likely to be retained, less likely to be placed in upper tracks and ability groups (including gifted programs and AP classes), and more likely to be placed in special education than are White students. A core reason that appears to influence the above outcomes is deficit thinking, which is fueled by low expectations for and negative stereotypes about Black students, even when they do not live in poverty.

Poverty or low-income status. Poverty is a circumstance, not a measure of inherent worth. Twenty-one percent of all children under the age of 18 live in poverty; they represent 40% of the total population of people in poverty, and children in poverty represent the largest and fastest growing group of the poor in the U.S. (Bempechat & Ginsburg, 1989; Davis & McCaul, 1990; Hodgkinson, 2007; U.S. Census Bureau, 2006). Blacks have the highest rate of poverty in the U.S., with a large percentage receiving free and reduced lunch, and many living on welfare. The poverty rate for Black families and children has been high in both historical and contemporary America (U.S. Census Bureau, 1982, 1983, 1984, 1986, 1990, 1992, 2006). For example, in 1967, 50% of Black families were poor compared to 20% of the general populations; in 1980, 70% of Black families lived in a family with an income less than two times the poverty level (U.S. Census Bureau, 1982, 2006); and in 1982, 51% of Black children under the age of 3 and 48% of those between 3 and 13 lived in poverty (U.S. Census Bureau, 1982, 2006). Equally troubling is that the median income of Black families is about half that of White families (Planty et al., 2009).

Edelman (1985), Kozol (2005), and Barton and Coley (2009) reported, as have other researchers and social justice advocates, that Black children face staggering obstacles to achieving decency, dignity, and success in American society and its schools. These children suffer disproportionately from the downward trends in the economy and from a kind of "bystander effect" shown by the lack of commitment toward alleviating problems in health, education, housing, and employment. Ladson-Billing's (2006) notion of America's educational debt is also timely. Much work is needed to eliminate years of benign neglect.

Regardless of their race and culture, students in economically impoverished conditions have fewer resources and less access to formal learning opportunities; more and greater health problems and psychological difficulties; and more handicapping conditions that affect educational outcomes (U.S. Department of Education, 2009). A report by the Council for Exceptional Children (1994) indicated that Black students comprised

24.2% of youth with disabilities. Students with disabilities have poor graduation rates: 36.1% of students with learning disabilities did not complete high school in 1991, compared to 24.4% of students in general (Wagner, 1991).

Single-parent family. Twenty-six percent of children under the age of 18 live in single-parent families; of these, 13 million live with their mother, and 1.6 million live with their father (Bempechat & Ginsburg, 1989; Davis & McCaul, 1990). In 1982, more than half (53%) of all Black children were born to single mothers, and 60% overall did not live with both parents/caregivers (National Center for Health Statistics, 1983). Single-parent/caregiver families are often characterized by poverty, and a disproportionate percent are racially and culturally different students. Data indicate that approximately half of Black single-parent families are poor (U.S. Census Bureau, 1986, 2006).

Mother's educational level. A little more than 20% of all students nationwide have mothers who have not graduated from high school (Bempechat & Ginsburg, 1989; Davis & McCaul, 1990). A little more than one third (36%) of Black students attended college in 1982, a significant decrease from the 50% that was reported in 1977 (Bureau of Labor Statistics, 1983). Relative to the 43% of Black mothers who have not graduated from high school, 44% were never married, 27% were separated, 6.9% were widowed, 20.3% were divorced, and other reasons were given for the remaining 1.8% (U.S. Census Bureau, 1983, 2006). Students of parents/caregivers who have low educational levels tend to have low achievement levels and high dropout rates. Major educational issues for parents/caregivers include less personal contact with and lower expectations from school personnel, coupled with caregivers having less knowledge about schooling and having less social and cultural capital.

English as a second language. English represents the second language for an increasing number of students. Language barriers contribute to social isolation from peers and teachers, due to lack of communication, lack of understanding, and lack of appreciation for languages other than English. Other educational issues include inappropriate assessment tools that do not accommodate language differences in U.S. schools.

Few educators understand that Black English is the primary language of some Black students, and they seem not to appreciate the history or origins of Black English, which dates back to slavery. Rather, Black English is often considered inferior to standard English. Similar to bilingualism, when teachers hold this assumption, students who speak Black English may be at risk for educational problems. Allington (1980), Ladson-

Billings (2009), Delpit (2006), and Good and Brophy (1987) revealed that teachers' negative attitudes regarding Black English contribute to and exacerbate underachievement among Black students. Specifically, students who speak Black English are likely to be seated farthest away from the teacher, to be called on less frequently, to be given less time to respond to questions, to receive more negative criticism, to get less praise for correct answers, and to have their responses interrupted more frequently. Taylor (1983) also found a significant relationship between negative attitudes toward Black English and lowered teacher evaluations of the reading comprehension of students.

Black English or Ebonics is considered by many linguistics to be a legitimate, rule-governed, and fully developed dialect (Delpit, 2006; Dillard, 1972, 1992; Labov, 1969, 1985; McDavid, 1964; Shuy, 1969; Smitherman, 1983). Black English speakers are highly competent language users when speaking their vernacular (Labov, 1972, 1976, 1985; Smitherman, 1977, 1983, 1999). Most language educators agree that modification of teachers' attitudes toward the dialect of their students and development of a greater understanding of diverse or different linguistic backgrounds should be a primary concern of the education profession (American Speech and Hearing Association, 1983; Bowie & Bond, 1994; Dandy, 1988; Delpit, 1995). Black English does not represent a speech disability or impairment, as noted by a position paper of the American Association of Speech and Hearing (1983).

The risk factors just described cannot be viewed independently or in isolation. To do so is naïve and an oversimplification. For example, almost half of Black students live in one or two risk categories: 43% live in poverty and 67% in single-parent homes (Waxman, 1992). The various risk factors take their toll on students, as reflected in the fact that Black students drop out at a 40% rate or higher than White students (Bridgeland et al., 2006; Garcia & Walker de Felix, 1992; Planty et al., 2009). Logically and statistically, gifted and AP students must be present in situations and environments that place them at risk for underachieving, exhibiting low motivation, dropping out, and otherwise not reaching their potential as students and adults.

SOCIAL INJUSTICES— RACISM AND PREJUDICE

With respect to prejudice, the worst contemporary blood, if one regards the IQ as a mirror held up to the genotype, is Black blood.

—Anonymous

At least three reasons help to explain and understand the negative or poor school experiences of Black students in education: chance or random occurrence, deficit theories, and racist believes and behaviors. Chance explanations assume that there are no compelling forces that cause or contribute to the negative educational outcomes experienced by Black students. These outcomes are believed to occur as natural phenomenon relatively free of outside influences. Within this perspective is the assumption that the underrepresentation and underachievement of gifted Black students has little to do with the student or the school setting. This argument is analogous to being at the wrong place at the wrong time. Tannenbaum's (1983) theory of giftedness is the only one to include the notion of such chance variables. Statistically speaking, the persistent underrepresentation of Black students in gifted education programs and services cannot be a function of chance alone. It is virtually impossible, which calls into question other explanations.

Deficit hypotheses and theories, explained in other chapters as well, have also been advanced to explain the social, educational, or achievement outcomes of Black students. These hypotheses maintain that there are predetermined deficiencies among Black students (and other racially and culturally diverse students) that relegate them to an inferior status. One aspect of the deficit hypotheses claims that Blacks are genetically intellectually inferior (e.g., Gould, 1991, 1995; Valencia, 1997; Valencia & Solórzano, 1997). It is contended, therefore, that biology or genetics plays the primary role in the determination of intelligence and potential. Another perspective holds that Blacks have personality deficits in which they are "abnormal" in character and behavior, a perspective that is more likely to be openly discussed and debated in the psychological or mental health profession (Ridley, 1989; Sue, 2003; Sue et al., 2007) than in education.

The third explanation holds that racism, prejudice, and stereotypes affect significantly the educational outcomes of Black students. Prejudice is a set of negative generalized beliefs or stereotypes about a group, a feeling of dislike for that group, and a predisposition to behave in a negative way about a group, directly as well as vicariously. Prejudice is an attitude that grows out of stereotypes or generalizations about a group of people (Allport, 1954; Dovidio et al., 2005). They are overgeneralizations that are both inaccurate and resistant to new information and change (Ford, Moore, & Whiting, 2006; Ford & Trotman Scott, 2010).

Racial attitudes and preferences are learned early in life. Bronson and Merryman (2009) reported that infants as young as 6 months judge others based on skin color. Certainly then, as early as 3 or 4 years of age, children become aware of their racial background. From this age until about 7 or 8, children demonstrate increasing competence in perceiving similarity to their own group. Specially, children at this age can accurately categorize different groups based on perceptual cues (race, language), and they understand the notion that race and ethnicity are unchangeable (Comer, 1989; Katz, 1976; Ponterotto & Pedersen, 1993, 2006). For gifted students, as a function of their advanced cognitive development, the onset of prejudice may appear earlier; they may note social injustices much earlier than other students.

Undeniably, parents and caregivers contribute to prejudice attitudes and preferences among their children by: (a) not discussing racial issues like stereotypes, prejudice, and discrimination in the home (e.g., a belief that the subject is too touchy or sensitive to talk about, or too developmentally inappropriate); (b) not having a culturally different group of friends visit the house with regularity; (c) not confronting prejudicial remarks when heard in the company of their children (e.g., remarks in the media or those made by other children); (d) allowing their children to remain in segregated environments (e.g., attending all-White schools or all-White gifted programs) or not making attempts to compensate for such isolation (e.g., interracial social groups); and (e) not pointing out the positive aspects and strengths of diverse cultures, including their own (Ponterotto & Pedersen, 1993).

Schools have been criticized for fostering the status quo that caters to middle-class White students. Aspects of schools that promote the development of racial prejudice include: (a) an administration and faculty that is primarily White and high income (who are not racially and culturally different); (b) a student body that is low in racial and cultural differences; (c) a curriculum that emphasizes and prizes European history and the experiences, values, and customs of the dominant culture; (d) a school culture that fails or refuses to incorporate training in race relations as an integral part of the curriculum and professional development; and

(e) a learning environment that caters to only one value system, specifically middle-class White value biases (Ponterotto & Pedersen, 1993). Ponterotto and Pedersen (2006) added that the media, employers, politicians, and government also "teach" prejudicial attitudes and preferences.

Allport's (1979) seminal work indicated that prejudice takes various forms and expressions, which range from mild and overt to harsh and covert. His five-phase model of acting out prejudice ranged on a continuum from least to most energetic: antilocution, avoidance, discrimination, physical attack, and extermination. *Antilocution* is the "mildest" form of prejudice. It is characterized by prejudicial talk among persons who hold similar beliefs. It is a rather controlled expression of antagonism that is limited to small circles (Ponterotto & Pedersen, 1993). For instance, White parents or caregivers may express concern that gifted or AP classes are becoming too integrated and that, as a result, the quality of their child's schooling will decrease and their children will more likely be exposed to aggressive classmates. In a second example, White students might express concerns about sitting next to a Black student in class.

Avoidance occurs when individuals move beyond lip service or talking about Black students to deliberate efforts to avoid them. In an attempt to avoid contact with gifted Black students, parents/caregivers may withdraw or transfer their children to another school. According to Ponterotto and Pedersen (1993), such inconvenience is self-directed; for the most part, no overt harm is directed against the group being avoided. The students are not being denied services; rather, the main effect is little to no interaction between Black and White students and families.

Discrimination occurs when individuals take active steps to exclude or deny Black students entrance or participation in an activity such as a gifted program or AP class. Discrimination practices range from segregated educational programs, employment practices, and social privileges, to recreational opportunities (Ponterotto & Pedersen, 1993, 2006; U.S. Department of Education, 2008). By way of illustration, a member of the identification and placement panel votes against, without justification, the admittance of a Black student seeking entrance into the program. In a second example, the identification and placement committee may indicate that efforts should not be focused on affirmative action because "we've already admitted two Black students into AP classes." In a third example, a teacher refuses to refer any Black students for identification and assessment, or for placement in gifted or AP classes, even when their grades and test scores meet screening or placement criteria.

Physical attack represents one of the more extreme forms of prejudice. The notion of physical attack is self-explanatory; it goes beyond mental/psychological abuse and stereotypes to acts and behaviors that express/communicate one's beliefs, attitudes, views, and values. It is most likely to occur during tense or emotionally laden conditions, and during economically stressful times.

Extermination represents the highest degree of prejudice, according to Allport (1979). Extermination involves the systematic and deliberate destruction of Blacks and other groups based on their race. Lynchings and massacres are two forms of extermination that have been aimed specifically at Blacks. Other forms include sterilization and procedures that stop procreation.

Racism, whatever its form, systematically denies access to opportunities or privilege to one group while perpetuating privilege to members of another group (McIntosh, 1988, 1992; Ridley, 1989; Sue et al., 2007). Racism is the ubiquitous social problem—its cause is often hidden, but the result is known. As Howard and Hammond (1985) stated, Blacks continue to suffer racism, discrimination, and oppression, which are the root of many of today's social problems. More specifically, these authors suggested that the high dropout rate and poorer performance of Black students on intelligence measures are two of the most pernicious effects of racism. The expressed racial attitudes of White Americans have changed over the years (Condran, 1979; Federal Bureau of Investigation [FBI], 2008; Hochschild, 1984; Hyman & Sheatsley, 1956, 1964; Kinder, 1986; Myrdal, 1944; National Opinion Research Center, 1980–1987). The collective findings indicate that prejudice is evident among some Whites who unabashedly dislike Blacks. By way of illustration, in 1942, approximately 70% of White respondents did not believe Black and White students should attend the same school. In 1985, approximately 90% believed that it was acceptable. FBI (2008) data indicated that most race-based hate crimes are against Blacks.

Although most White respondents in various studies agree that it is acceptable for White and Black students to attend the same schools, they are less accepting of more intimate forms of contact and interaction (e.g., dancing with a Black person, interracial marriages, living in the same neighborhood, and bringing a Black friend home to dinner; Dovidio et al., 2005; Pettigrew, 1981). Pettigrew (1981) also found that 15% of White adults surveyed were extremely prejudiced, approximately 60% are conforming bigots, and about 25% are anti-racist in behavior and ideology. Devine (1989) reported that people who considered themselves unprejudiced were aware of cultural stereotypes, but they consciously suppress their prejudicial thoughts and feelings; 3 in 4 persons supported racial prejudice to some degree. Merton's (1936, 1968) classic 2 x 2 model of prejudice and discrimination described the relationship between prejudicial attitudes and behaviors or decisions. His typology showed that even individuals who are not prejudiced often act in bigoted and discriminatory ways. The "all-weather liberal" is not prejudiced and does not discriminate, whereas the "all-weather bigot" is prejudiced and does discriminate. The other two combinations, however, are inconsistent. The "fair-weather liberal" discriminates without holding prejudiced attitudes, whereas the "timid bigot" is prejudiced but does not discriminate. These inconsistencies between attitudes and behavior are not uncommon and may be caused by a variety of social pressures, including the desire to conform to the expectations of others. They illustrate the fact that prejudice (attitude) and discrimination (behavior) can be somewhat independent of each other. Essentially, racial prejudice is accepted in principle but not in practice. Pettigrew reported that White Americans are reluctant to accept and act on measures necessary to eliminate prejudice and discrimination. Ongoing race-based or race-related discrimination cases brought to the attention of the Office for Civil Rights reinforce this reality (U.S. Department of Education, 2008).

Manifestations of racism appear at either the individual or institutional level (Jones, 1981), and are overt, covert, or unintentional. In contemporary America, most racism is subtle and aversive rather than blatant (Dovidio & Gaertner, 1986; Dovidio et al., 2005; Kinder, 1986); it is camouflaged by a more indirect or covert exterior, yet few people are immune to subtle prejudice.

According to Ridley (1989), institutional racism includes the intentional and unintentional manipulation or toleration of institutional policies that unfairly restrict the opportunities of targeted groups. Table 6.1 presents examples of individual and institutional racism in schools offering gifted programs and AP classes. Individual racism represents a person's race prejudice based on biological considerations. It also involves behaviors that are discriminatory, as already noted by Allport (1954) and others.

Ponterotto and Pedersen (1993, 2006) discussed the concept of cultural racism, defined as individual and/or institutional expressions of superiority of one racial group's cultural heritage over others. In such instances, one racial group's values and behaviors are considered the

---

Table 6.1
Possible Manifestations of Racism in Gifted Educational Settings

	Individual racism	**Institutional racism**
Overt/intentional	A teacher believes that Black students lack motivation and on this basis, he or she requests that Black students be assigned to low-ability groups or tracks without assessment information.	School personnel openly deny admittance of Black students into the gifted program for fear of flight by White parents/caregivers to other schools.[1]
Covert/intentional	A school psychologist interprets high test scores received by Black students as a fluke, and requests that they be retested.	School personnel deliberately set test scores above the range scored by the majority of Black students nationally or in the school district. This practice excludes them from the gifted program and AP classes and otherwise limits the number of identified and served Black students.
Unintentional	A school counselor misinterprets Black dialect as an inability to understand standard English. The student is referred to speech therapy or placed in remedial language classes.	Admission to the gifted program and services is based on standardized tests without consideration of group differences and biases in the test construction and interpretation.

Note. Adapted from Ridley (1989).
[1] This practice is now illegal.

model or normative and normal system, and those individuals with different cultural orientations are considered deficient in some way.

Whether it is overt or covert, or at the individual or institutional level, racism interrupts the normal and potential development of those persons subjected to it. It hinders their ability to function at their full potential as both children and adults and increases their levels of stress. Comer (1989) maintained that racism contributes to children's greater involvement in social problems such as poor school learning, juvenile delinquency, teenage pregnancy, and substance abuse. Further, children who are victims of racism or racial discrimination have no way to understand the inequities as anything but deficits within their own group, which can lead to unhealthy or insecure racial identities (Locke, 1989).

Leveled aspirations are all too common in low-income and Black communities where their efforts, hard work, and support for the achievement ideology do not always reap positive outcomes. Ford (1991, 1992, 1993a) found that gifted Black underachievers represented a paradox of underachievement; while supporting *ideals* undergirding the achievement ideology, they were also troubled about the *reality* of social injustices, For instance, while believing that Blacks could and should become successful if they worked hard, spoke standard English, and so forth, gifted Black underachievers feared that such success would also be tempered with racism and other social barriers; thus, only those Blacks who were "lucky" would succeed. Gifted Black underachievers, therefore, question the integrity of the achievement ideology, as noted by Mickelson (1984, 1990).

SOCIAL SELF-CONCEPT—NEED FOR ACHIEVEMENT VERSUS NEED FOR AFFILIATION

Children's social, emotional, and educational problems often relate to an inability to fulfill their basic needs (Maslow, 1954). One of our basic needs is the desire to belong and to feel loved (Glasser, 1986). Perhaps the needs that our society and schools have the most trouble fulfilling for gifted Black students are the need for self-esteem (e.g., racial pride and identity, academic identity) and the need to belong, both of which relate to our social self-concept. Although educators and counselors acknowledge the interrelation of the emotional, social, and cognitive domains of development, programs for gifted students appear to have largely neglected their emotional and social needs and development (Barnette, 1989; Ford, 1996; Ford & Harris, 1995a).

Janos (1983), Janos and Robinson (1985), and Li (1988) have shown that many studies purporting gifted students to have higher self-concepts investigated only the general domain, rather than specific domains such as social self-concept in which gifted students frequently score poorly. Winne, Woodlands, and Wong (1982) and Whitmore (1980, 1986) noted the feelings of difference and isolation gifted students experience due to their unique gifts and talents. Ford (1996), for example, reported that gifted elementary students expressed embarrassment, guilt, and even confusion about their academic success, which had negative effects on their peer relationships. Gifted children surveyed by Galbraith (1985) had numerous concerns, including that they feel different and alienated and that they are often teased by peers.

Educators must understand that being placed into programs with students (and teachers) who look, speak, and behave differently can negatively influence one's social self-concept. This phenomenon is best explained by the *social comparison theory*, first posited by Festinger (1954) and expounded upon by Coleman and Fults (1985):

> in the absence of objective standards of comparison, people will employ significant others in their environments as bases for forming estimates of self-worth and, given the choice of relatively similar or dissimilar others, they are more likely to select similar others as the bases for social comparison. (p. 8)

As a cultural group, Black students are socially oriented, as reflected in strong fictive kinship networks and large, extended families (Boyd-Franklin, 2003; Boykin, Albury, et al., 2005; Boykin et al., 2005; Boykin et al., 2006; Bradley, Rock, Caldwell, Harris, & Hamrick, 1987; Clark, 1983; Dilworth-Anderson & McAdoo, 1988; Harry, 1992; Hill, 1971; McAdoo, 1988, 1993; McAdoo & Younge, 2009). There is a strong need to belong and for affiliation, and also a need to bond with others who share similar concerns and interests. In many ways, groups represent a mechanism for self-preservation. This need for group affiliation, however, can have unfortunate ramifications when an anti-achievement ethic is espoused by the peer group.

Specifically, social identity can be an important source of vulnerability for Black youths. Black students confronted with racism and who respond with anger and rebelliousness may develop an *oppositional social identity* (Ogbu, 1988, 2003, 2004, 2008). They may deliberately perform poorly in school, rebel against authority figures (e.g., teachers and school administrators) who are perceived as agents of oppression, and rebel against any behavior associated with mainstream society. To protect their self-esteem, Black students may develop ineffective coping styles that alienate them from school and are harmful to academic achievement. For instance, in a predominantly White gifted program, Black students may limit or avoid completely any contact with their White peers, and they may deliberately exert little effort in school because it is associated with the White culture. One widely held supposition is that many Black children hide their academic abilities by becoming class clowns (Comer, 1989, 1990), dropping out, and suppressing effort (Ford, 1991, 1996). The possibility that Black students may sabotage any chance of academic success is a disturbing prospect in urban and gifted education.

Secondly, other Black youth may have a *diffused identity*, characterized by low self-esteem and alienation from both the Black culture and the mainstream culture. Their poor academic and social competencies result in educational, social, and psychological adjustment problems (Ford, 1996). This identity is most likely to develop when the values, attitudes, and behaviors espoused in the home and school are incongruent; this incompatibility or contextual dissonance between the home and school can cause considerable stress for Black students, particularly if the schools attempt to acculturate them by eliminating their cultural differences (Boykin, 1983; Boykin, Albury, et al., 2005; Boykin et al., 2006). Clark (1983) added that although schools require a high degree of mainstream socialization from students, they do not always provide the environments necessary for Black students to gain mainstream skills while remaining connected to their home and community environment. The result is increased intense barriers to gifted Black students' academic success.

Happily, some teachers working with gifted Black students have reported successes in their identification and placement of these students. They appear more concerned, however, about the high rate of flight of Black students from gifted education and AP classes and their determination to camouflage their gifts and talents and to avoid behaviors that might reveal or call attention to their accomplishments/achievements and abilities. Much of this flight has been attributed to poor social relations, specifically negative peer pressures and low teacher expectation (Burton, Burgess Whitman, Yepes-Baraya, Cline, & Kim, 2002; Clewell, Anderson, Bruschi, Joy, & Meltzer, 1994; Coley & Casserly, 1992). That is, once identified and placed in gifted and AP classes Black students make numerous sacrifices and take many risks. They risk, for example, rejecting peers in their home school or community who may perceive gifted Black students as untrue to their cultural and racial group, they risk isolation and alienation from White peers in the gifted program or AP class who do not understand Black students, and they also risk poor relationships with teachers. Burton et al. (2002) ended their study with the following: "We were not able to find a group of teachers who are enthusiastic recruiters of minority students. . . . Finding out how to bring minority students into the AP classroom is a crucial issue that needs to be understood" (p. 29).

These feelings of isolation and alienation may result in a forced-choice dilemma between friendships and school. In this emotional tug-of-war, the school (gifted program, AP class) too often loses. Fortunately, the College Board (2002), in its report *Opening Classrooms Doors: Strategies for Expanding Access to AP*, showed that some schools are making strides, when they are proactive and equity conscious. Subsequent reports are not as optimistic, showing that teachers and counselors continue to be gatekeepers, closing doors to AP classes for many African American students. There is, in other words, large equity gaps in AP classes for this student population (College Board, 2008, 2009).

RECOMMENDATIONS

Prejudice reduction in the schools is essential given the increasing heterogeneity of students. Ultimately, we cannot place the responsibility for change directly on the shoulders of students. Educators and other school personnel must seek training in multicultural or culturally responsive education that is extensive and ongoing. To reach their potential, gifted Black students must feel empowered and have a sense of belonging both within and outside school. Teachers are in an ideal position to empower all students to be culturally competent, sensitive, and aware, as described by Ford and Whiting (2008).

ACTIVITIES

Ponterotto and Pedersen (1993) present six activities, two of them described below, designed to enhance race relations in the schools. Other exercises described by Ponterotto and Pedersen (1993, 2006) focus on stereotypes, history, being normal and abnormal, and patterns of differences. Gabelko (1988) offered activities for secondary school students.

Exercise 1: The Label Game. The objective of this exercise is to generalize feedback by others to discover the labeled identity that they perceive the individual to have. Follow the procedure below:

1. Prepare a variety of *positive* adjectives (e.g., friendly, generous, caring, empathetic) on sticky labels.
2. Attach one label to the back of each student as he or she comes into the classroom. The student should not be able to read the label.
3. Allow students to mingle and interact on a topic of interest.

4. Instruct students to treat every other student as though the label the individual is wearing is true—to say and do things one would with that kind of person.

5. After 10 minutes, students are given one guess at the label, after which they can remove it.

During debriefing, students are asked to disclose how they decoded the feedback from others, and to discuss how they felt about being both labeled and treated as if the label were accurate. The ultimate learning principle is that we all wear labels as though they were true. By increasing awareness, we can become more aware of the labels that others perceive about each of us.

Exercise 2: Symbols of Our Culture. The objective of this exercise is to get students to get in touch with the emotional symbols of our cultures. Students are asked to draw the symbols of their culture without including words. In this manner, students are encouraged to explore the less articulate aspects of their racial identity.

First, students are assembled in a room with sufficient table space so that each one can spread out a large sheet of paper. Supply students with different colored crayons or markers. Second, students are instructed to draw symbols, a picture, lines, designs, or scribbles on the paper that symbolizes their own personal ethnic, racial, or cultural identity. Instruct students not to draw or write words on the paper. After 10 or 20 minutes of drawing the symbols of their culture, students are divided into small groups. Each student explains his or her drawing and how it symbolizes significant parts of his or her identity.

During debriefing, students can find similarities between the drawings, and well as note the frequency of recurring symbols, and which symbols are negative and which are positive. With this exercise, students learn about the difficulty of discussing in words their identity. It is important for students to accept themselves, even if they are different from the majority of students.

ANGER MANAGEMENT AND CONFLICT RESOLUTION: COPING AND OVERCOMING

Children are frequently punished for exhibiting aggressive or destructive behaviors, yet they are seldom taught how to cope with anger (Ford & Harris, 1995a, 1995b; Harper, Terry, & Twiggs, 2009; Heuchert, 1989;

Johnson, 2006; Omizo, 1981; Omizo, Hershberger, & Omizo, 1988). On a daily basis, many students, especially gifted Black students, deal with the realities and ramifications of stress, anxiety, frustration, and anger that interrupt the learning process (Harmon, 2002). For gifted Black youth, prejudice may be a daily reality, a persistent reminder of their marginal status. Consequently, they may come to school angry, enraged, and estranged. When students are unable to cope with their angry feelings, the result may be violence, crime, substance abuse, depression, suicide, and self-destructive behaviors (Omizo, 1981; Omizo et al., 1988). Thus, students choose their teachers and classmates as targets for venting their emotions. Problematic behaviors, however, are not an individual's total personality and behavioral repertoire; they are responses to how a student perceives his or her environment and to how he or she is being treated (Sinclair & Ghory, 1992).

Relaxation training and stress management are recommended for helping gifted Black students cope with their feelings. It is important to teach them to understand stress, how the body responds to stress, and that stress is inevitable or unavoidable. Exercises to release stress include breathing, muscular relaxation, mental imagery, and biofeedback (Angus, 1989; Oldfield, 1986; Roome & Romney, 1985). Encouraging gifted Black students to ask for time out and providing a safe environment where they can go to vent their frustrations are also important (e.g., time out or venting room). Other outlets include group counseling where students can discuss their concerns and experiences with relevant others, as well as share effective coping behaviors. For example, Peterson (1990) developed a noon-hour discussion group for gifted students to share their concerns. Topics included stress, personality styles, testing, recognizing strengths and weaknesses, family conflicts, career concerns, and relationships.

Omizo and colleagues (1988) conducted 10 group counseling sessions in three phases. The major goal of the first phase was to have students develop an understanding of anger and differentiate between its positive and negative aspects. Students were also taught that anger is a normal feeling that is experienced by most people. Phase 2 focused on helping students identify factors that precipitated their angry feelings. Students were taught alternative strategies for responding to stressors, explored constructive versus destructive responses, and learned how to make choices. Phase 3 focused on opportunities and situations to practice appropriate behaviors. Modeling, role-playing, and giving feedback were used. Stress management can help gifted Black students feel empowered and in control of their anger (and other emotions). It can also turn acting out and self-defeating behaviors into more adaptive behaviors.

Several principles are suggested to facilitate the teachers' and counselors' work with gifted Black students who are coping with feelings of anger, frustration, and anxiety:

- ❖ *Teach gifted Black students that anxiety and anger are healthy responses.* Equally important is that gifted Black students understand the difference between healthy and excessive/unnecessary emotional responses (e.g., violence, substance abuse, passive aggressiveness).

- ❖ *Provide gifted Black students with coping strategies for releasing excessive emotions.* Strategies include walking, singing, writing, and talking. Unfortunately, society expects males to maintain a macho image that negates emotions. It is, therefore, especially important that (Black) males be allowed to *feel* and to *accept* their emotions; that they learn to express their emotions by talking as well as crying. However, schools have not always encouraged the expression of feelings, including the role of feelings in the learning process (Wittmer & Myrick, 1989). Also see the extensive works of Tatum, listed in the references, whose work focuses on teaching reading to Black males as a way of self-expression, self-understanding, and communication with others.

DEALING EFFECTIVELY WITH
POOR PEER RELATIONS

One in six Americans does not have a friend with whom he or she can confide (Matter & Matter, 1985). Byrnes (1984) reported that 19% of school children may be considered social isolates. Loneliness and isolation are of special concern to educators for various reasons. Specifically, good interpersonal relationships and feelings of relatedness and belonging are considered essential to mental health (Maslow, 1954, 1968; Murray, 1938). Persistent feelings of isolation make students vulnerable to depression, juvenile delinquency, physical illness, and suicide (Matter & Matter, 1985).

The need to belong and have friends is important for all children, but it may be especially important for Black students, as they are severely underrepresented in gifted programs. As one of a few Black students in the program, it is likely that a student will experience feelings of alienation and isolation. Imagine the damaging impact of eating lunch alone, of having no date for parties or the prom, of being the last to be chosen for a team. Achievement and social-emotional well-being are a function of student and the context. Thus, the problems of socially isolated students do not stem solely from children's personal characteristics, but from how they fit into the overall classroom dynamics. Counselors, in collaboration with teachers, can positively influence the classroom dynamics and increase its sense of community such that schools truly become sanctuaries for learning—a welcoming rather than alienating place (Sinclair & Ghory, 1992)—for gifted Black students.

Groups have a powerful emotional influence on their members, and classrooms, as the longest lasting academic groups, represent an important arena for fostering cohesion and belonging (Whiting, 2006a; Wynne & Walberg, 1994). Group work, particularly cooperative activities, is essential in promoting social contact among gifted Black and gifted White students. Competition tends to bring out the best in products and the worst in people (Grantham, 1994; Wittmer & Myrick, 1989). That is, the amount of time spent in interdependent, cooperative, and noncompetitive activities can encourage friendships and decrease feelings of social isolation, fears, and stereotypes. Teachers and counselors can help gifted Black students discover interests similar to other students; they can persuade them to join clubs and organizations, for instance, based on these interests.

Teachers can also work with counselors to create more opportunities for interaction and building positive and trusting relationships. For instance, Fantuzzo, Polite, and Grayson (1990) found peer tutoring to be effective in maximizing positive classroom interactions, friendships, prosocial behaviors, as well as self-esteem and achievement among economically disadvantaged students considered at risk for academic failure. Cooper and Robinson (1987) found that structured academic support groups improved underachieving students' achievement and academic self-concept. Students were taught how to set academic goals and commitments, time management and study skills, test anxiety management, stress reduction, career and life planning, and ways to increase motivation. Ultimately, exposing *all* students to multicultural curricula has a positive influence on promoting understanding, increased awareness, and heightened sensitivity to individual and cultural differences.

Social skills training can also help gifted Black students explore self-defeating thought processes that contribute to loneliness and inappropriate behaviors (such as attention seeking, becoming the class clown, or putting sports before academics). Social skills training includes focusing on conversational skills, asking questions, initiating conversations, giving constructive feedback and comments, and accepting feedback. The most effective way to prepare students for a satisfying life is to give them a wide repertoire of techniques for lifelong learning (Walker de Felix, 1992; Whiting, 2006a, 2006b).

Wittmer and Myrick (1989) described group activities that can facilitate healthy and productive social relationships among students. In one activity, students are asked to pick a corner of the room. The corners are labeled "strongly agree," "agree," "disagree," and "strongly disagree." The center of the classroom is labeled "neutral." Students are presented with a timely and relevant statement in which they express their level of agreement or disagreement (e.g., "In my school, all students are treated fairly or equally"; "Peer pressure does not exist in my school"). Students are given a few minutes to select their corner; once chosen, they take time to discuss their perspectives. Next, students are paired with one of the other groups (corners) in order to convince that group to see their point of view. For instance, the strongly agree group could be paired with the neutral group.

In another exercise, students can be assigned the task of critiquing their favorite television shows or books for instances of bias. After writing a brief description of the biases found, students can discuss how they felt about the discovery, and how the individual or group being discriminated against probably felt. In a third exercise, students can be placed in dyads where one member is given a card containing emotions. This student attempts to communicate nonverbally the emotion(s) on the card. The purpose of this activity is to increase students' awareness of nonverbal behaviors and messages: Were the nonverbal and verbal messages consistent? Were some students more effective than others at communicating nonverbally? Which parts of the body did students use most often? In what ways might other cultural groups be more effective or skilled at nonverbal communication? Which communication style are they most comfortable with? Why?

In a different activity, students are asked to wander about the room without talking. They must join a group of exactly four students (or some other designated number). Once all students have joined a group with the designated number, they are asked to make observations about each group (e.g., What do they have in common? How are they different? Do the groups contain all girls or boys?). Ultimately, students are asked to share and discuss the reason(s) they join a particular group. These exercises and others described by Wittmer and Myrick (1989) offer much promise for discussing social and controversial issues in a nonthreatening, cooperative way.

The following principles may help teachers, counselors, and other school personnel to promote social and emotional well-being among gifted Black students and their peers:

- ❖ *Determine the causes underlying poor or negative peer relations.* Use writing exercises (diaries, journals), incomplete sentence exercises, sociograms, and other techniques to gain a comprehensive assessment. In many cases, information may be better gained from nonverbal cues and observations than from verbal data. These methods also utilize the strengths or preferences of Black students who feel uncomfortable expressing their feelings verbally (e.g., because they are not ready or they express themselves better nonverbally).

- ❖ *Advocate for cooperative rather than competitive group activities.* It may be more productive to begin with small groups (four or five students). Rather than let students choose group members, teachers and counselors should randomly select students (e.g., Group 1 contains all students with blue shirts or those born in November).

- ❖ *Teach gifted Black students how to cope with rejection using strategies that are specific to the problem.* If appropriate, discussions about prejudice should be addressed, particularly as Black students learn early that racial prejudice is a reality. Bibliotherapy and cinematherapy (Newton, 1994) can also provide gifted Black students with effective strategies to handle adverse situations. See the works of Tatum (e.g., 2007a, 2007b, 2009), Hébert (1998, 2009); and Hébert, Long, and Speirs Neumeister (2005) for more information on these strategies.

- ❖ *Explore the nature of trust.* To facilitate positive social interactions, counselors can work with gifted Black students to understand the nature of trust, particularly the difference between naïve trust and overgeneralized distrust (Grantham, 1994; Harmon, 2002). Naïve trust leaves one vulnerable to hurt and betrayal; overgeneralized distrust leaves one cautious, guarded, self-protecting, lonely, needy, and depressed (Eisenberg & O'Dell, 1988).

Summary

Social and environmental factors can hinder the successful identification of gifted Black students, and contribute to academic difficulties, including academic burnout. Maslach and Jackson (1981) described burnout as emotional exhaustion, depersonalization, and feelings of low personal accomplishment. (Also see Maslach, Jackson, & Leiter, 1996.) Low societal expectations, racism, job ceilings, and other forms of discrimination call into question the social justice quotient for Black students.

Educators must consider the influence of peer pressure on achievement and effort. Pressures from peers to forego achievement can undermine the academic success of bright Black students. The fear associated with losing friendships and being isolated from peers because of outstanding achievement can undermine the motivation and effort of gifted Black students (Ford, 1993a, 1993b, 1996; Ford et al., 2008a, 2008b; U.S. Department of Education, 1993). As Tomlinson (1992) reported,

> Peer pressure profoundly influences the academic behavior of students. . . . Typically, peer pressure motivates students to stay in school and graduate, but even as they frown on failure, peers also restrain high achievement. . . . Some student cultures actively reject academic aspirations. In this case, high grades can be a source of peer ridicule; and when effort is hostage to peer pressure, those high achievers who persist may face strong social sanctions. (p. 2)

It is also necessary to explore underachievement relative to social forces, including: (a) the influences of overt discrimination and low teacher expectations; (b) psychological or affective issues, such as fears and anxieties; and (c) cultural barriers to achievement, such as home and community values, that differ from values espoused in the schools by teachers and administrators. Because all students need to feel a sense of competence and social belonging, we must direct more attention to affective and social needs and issues. And we cannot ignore the extent to which underachievement is shaped by social factors, particularly racial and economic injustices.

CHAPTER SEVEN

SCHOOL FACTORS AS CORRELATES OF UNDERACHIEVEMENT AND ACHIEVEMENT

There is no such thing as a neutral educational process.
—Friere (1970)

On a daily basis, one can expect educators, researchers, and social scientists to expound on the problems of schools. Numerous reformers and their reports highlight the concerns of educators, parents, and sometimes children. More often than not, these reports and critiques examine pedagogy and the content of the curriculum rather than the environment in which children learn and achieve, despite the abundance of discussion and data indicating that learning environments have a significant impact on students' achievement (Ford & Harris, 1999; Ford & Kea, 2009; Fraser, 1994; Stockard & Mayberry, 1992). The school and classroom environment—climate, atmosphere, ethos, and ambience—sets the socioemotional and relational tone for learning. Figure 7.1 highlights the focus of this chapter.

Critical features or characteristics of learning environments in

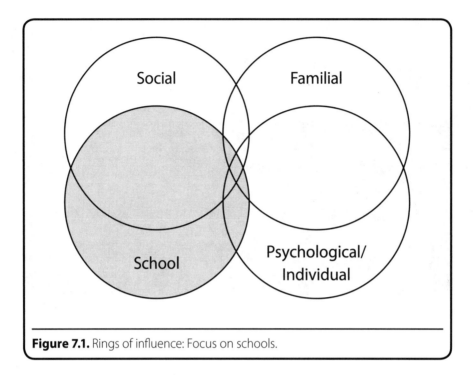

Figure 7.1. Rings of influence: Focus on schools.

schools, classrooms, and, by extension, gifted programs, include not only the physical facilities, but also their size. Equally important are the school and classroom climates (e.g., prevailing norms and values, sense of community and cohesion, student-teacher and peer relations, student and teacher morale). School and classroom climates themselves are influenced by demographic variables, teacher expectations of students, attention to individual student needs, and curriculum and instruction (e.g., quality and quantity, student learning styles, teaching styles).

This chapter focuses on literature and research addressing learning environments—the quality of life in classrooms. Schools and classrooms in general serve as the primary unit of analysis for this chapter, with implications for gifted programs and AP classes. Why study learning environments? The most obvious answer is that students spend a significant amount of time in schools. Csikszentmihalyi and McCormack (1986) argued that the time students spend with teachers is the *single most important opportunity* for them to learn from adults.

A second reason for studying learning environments is that the quality of schools varies considerably, as does their impact on students' achievement, which was already noted in discussions of the achievement gap. The impact of high- and poor-quality schools and educators on students' educational outcomes cannot be ignored, trivialized, or denied.

Students in low-income and low-SES schools, for example, have different and fewer learning opportunities than those in high-income and high-SES schools.

A third reason is that school climates vary considerably from teacher to teacher; some classrooms are warm, nurturing, supportive, and orderly, while those at the other extreme are chaotic, disorganized, hostile, and unfriendly. Still others fall in the middle of these two. In the latter instance, low teacher morale, expectations, and relationships with students can frustrate and inhibit students' achievement or motivation to achieve. In numerous studies of urban and Black high school dropouts, a common theme is that students believed that school was boring, unchallenging, or a hostile place (Bridgeland et al., 2006; Fine, 1986; Ford, 1991, 1996; Ford et al., 2008b; Rumberger, 1983, 1987).

The primary purpose of school is to educate students, to provide them with the fundamental knowledge and skills deemed necessary to survive and thrive. Thus, it is essential to explore how the learning environment of schools and classrooms impede or facilitate this goal. To more fully understand how learning environments affect gifted Black students' achievement, it is necessary to examine aspects of classrooms and gifted programs such as demographic variables, peer relations, teacher-student relations, teacher expectations and morale, and curricular and instructional issues.

QUESTIONS TO CONSIDER

❖ Why do we need to study learning environments, and how do learning environments and climates influence student achievement?

❖ What specific school and classroom variables negatively affect the decision of Black students to remain in gifted programs and AP classes? What are some of the determinants of classroom environments?

❖ How can these variables and practices be altered to enhance the achievement of gifted and underachieving Black students?

❖ Do students and teachers hold similar perceptions about the quality of the learning environment? What are the similarities and differences?

INTRODUCTION

Schools are social organizations that, like individuals, have their own personality (Moos, 1979) and psychosocial characteristics. Schools and classrooms that improve student achievement are often characterized by high academic expectations, effective leadership, a respect for individual differences, and warmth, concern, and appreciation for each other. Thus, measures of learning environments are like measures of motivation and achievement (Fraser, 1994). Seventy-five years ago, we learned from Lewin (1936) that students' behaviors are a function of their personality characteristics and the learning environment. Perceptions are the primary method for measuring the quality of learning environments. Such perceptions vary from student to student, and between teachers and students. For example, Fisher and Fraser (1993) found that teachers tend to perceive the classroom or learning environment more positively than students; further, students often prefer to have a more positive climate than is actually present.

Learning environments can be described by the school and/or classroom climate and culture. School climate is the relatively enduring quality of the school environment that is explained by participants' affect and behavior, and is based on their collective behaviors and perceptions (Hoy, Tarter, & Kottkamp, 1991). According to Tagiuri and Litwin (1968), organizational climates are defined by their: (a) ecology—the physical environment in which groups interact; (b) milieu—the social characteristics of individual and group participants in the organization; (c) social system—the patterned relationships of persons and groups; and (d) culture—the collectively accepted beliefs, attitudes, values, customs, and meanings of the group. The classroom culture gives both schools and classrooms their distinctive identity.

Edmonds (1979) wrote extensively on the characteristics of effective urban schools that distinguish them from their less effective counterparts. Edmonds perceived such schools as having more than high test scores. At the very least, effective schools generate higher achievement among students, hold high expectations for students, strive for excellence, and have high student and teacher morale. The high-performing schools profiled by Carter (2000) share this philosophy, as do the schools founded by James Comer (http://medicine.yale.edu/childstudy/comer), by Geoffrey Canada in the Harvard Children's Zone (http://www.hcz.

org), and by the founders of the SEED School of Washington, DC (http://www.seedfoundation.com), to name a few.

Lightfoot's (1983) ethnographic research found that high-achieving secondary schools have staff members who are concerned about the academic and overall well-being of students and the integrity of the curriculum, and are committed to academic pursuits. In others words, among educators, this is a sense of responsibility toward and co-destiny with students. As Lightfoot (1983), Brophy and Good (1986), Rosenthal and Jacobson (1979), and others have noted, high teacher expectations for students lowers or eliminates students' sense of futility, indicates that teachers care, and communicates that students can and will succeed. Furthermore, teachers' satisfaction with their work is positively related to students' achievement. Teachers who express, directly or indirectly, high morale are more supportive of students, and students who perceive their teachers as satisfied with their jobs are more likely to exhibit high levels of attendance and achievement (Brookover & Lezotte, 1979; Peske & Haycock, 2006), high morale about their school and learning environment, and stronger academic self-efficacy and confidence (Edmonds, 1979). Stated differently, high morale among teachers, other educators, and students maximizes students' chances of developing and nurturing positive attitudes about their own abilities, which promotes achievement and motivation.

In terms of Black culturally different students, Carter and Chatfield (1986) described effective schools as well-functioning, total systems that produce a school climate that promotes positive outcomes. Specific characteristics crucial to this effectiveness and positive school climate include: (a) a safe and orderly school environment; (b) positive leadership; (c) common agreement on a strong academic orientation, including academic goals, objectives, and plans; and (d) well-functioning methods to monitor school inputs and student outputs. A positive school social climate was characterized by: (a) high staff expectations for students and the instructional program; (b) strong demands for academic performance; (c) denials of the cultural-deprivation argument and the stereotypes that support it; and (d) high staff morale, including strong internal support, job satisfaction, sense of personal efficacy, sense of multicultural self-efficacy, a sense that the system works, and the belief that resources are best expended on people (i.e., students and school personnel) rather than on educational hardware.

Certainly, working with underachievers can test morale and professional efficacy, even for veteran teachers and/or teachers who have a strong sense of occupational pride and efficacy. When teacher and student morale is high, a circle of positive causation (Stockard & Mayberry, 1992), as presented in Table 7.1, is established in the classroom—high student achievement affects teacher morale, efficacy, and expectations which, in turn, influence students' achievement (Ashton & Webb, 1986; Newmann, Rutter, & Smith, 1989; Rosenholtz, 1985).

OTHER CONDITIONS IN SCHOOLS THAT CONTRIBUTE TO UNDERACHIEVEMENT AMONG GIFTED BLACK STUDENTS

Data indicate that the majority of teachers are White (85%) and White females (75%; see Planty et al., 2009). The number of racially and culturally different teachers in general education is dismally small—some 15% for all culturally different groups combined, and 6% for African American teachers (including only 1.2% for African American males). Reasoning by analogy, one can assume that racially and culturally different teachers are almost invisible in gifted education (Ford, 1999; Ford, Grantham, & Harris, 1997). Is it little wonder that Black students may enter schools (and gifted programs and AP classes) with "healthy suspicions" (Sue, 2003; Sue, Arrendondo, & McDavis, 1992) about the conscious and unconscious motives of teachers and other educators?

Education is not a neutral process or profession. Teachers are human beings; as such, they are not immune to racial and cultural biases. Teaching and expectations are influenced by the status of race relations in the larger society. Issues of democracy, equal access and opportunity, and liberty and justice for all may be unrealistically reflected in educational philosophy but not practice. Yet, more than 55 years after *Brown v. Board of Education* (1954), we still see de facto segregation in general education and, more frankly, in gifted education and AP courses. As noted earlier, Black students are underrepresented by almost 50% nationally in gifted education programs. Some school districts are effective in recruiting (identifying and placing) students into gifted education and AP classes; others are not and may even resist doing so. Similarly, some schools are more effective at retention efforts than others.

It is unrealistic and perhaps fruitless to assume that teaching occurs in isolation from social and political forces, which influence both our per-

Table 7.1
Independent and Interacting Factors Affecting
Teacher Expectations of Students

Factor	Teacher expectations
Income and/or SES	Lower expectations for lower income and/or SES students (including free and reduced lunch, parents' level of education, types of jobs, place of residence).
Gender	Lower expectations for elementary boys and for older girls. Lower expectations for Black males than any other group at all educational/age levels.
Race	Lower expectations for racially and culturally diverse students, especially Black students.
Test scores; permanent records	Belief in "fixed ability" keeps one from recognizing progress, especially small successes.
Negative comments about student	Lounge talk, other teachers or principal's evaluation results in lower teacher expectations.
Type of school	Lower expectations for students in rural and inner city (urban); higher for suburban.
Oral language patterns	Lower expectations for anyone who speaks nonstandard English or English as a second language.
Neatness; appearance	Lower expectations associated with general disorganization; poor handwriting, dress, etc.
Halo effect	Tendency to label a child's overall ability based on one characteristic.
Teacher training institutions	Perpetuation of myths and ideologies of limitations of certain groups.

Note. Teachers are influenced by these variables both individually and collectively. For example, Black males face low expectations related to race and gender.

sonal and professional lives. Monocultural values and ideologies permeate educational practices. Several perspectives have, in both the past and present, affected our perceptions of Black and other culturally different students:

❖ *Pathological model*: The notion of inferiority guides this perspective. The overriding belief is that culturally different groups are genetically inferior and on the lower evolutionary scale than Whites. Because Blacks and some other culturally different groups are perceived as more primitive, they are considered more pathological. Supporters of this view, therefore, blame genes and biology for the educational problems of culturally different groups, for lower standardized test scores, and for poor representation in gifted education and AP classes.

❖ *Culturally deficient model*: This perspective assumes that Black and other culturally different groups are culturally deprived or inferior. Rather than blaming genes or heredity, proponents of this perspective blame the negative educational outcomes of culturally different groups on their culture.

These two perspectives have had at least three longstanding effects on educational practice. First, they perpetuated myths and stereotypes that Black students were inherently pathological; second, they perpetuated racist research and educational practices; and, third, the perspectives provided excuses for educators not to take action to rectify social inequities in schools (see Ford, 2004; Gould, 1991, 1995).

During the 1980s, other models emerged to replace genetic inferiority and cultural deprivation models (Ford, 2004). Accusations or assumptions about pathology, inferiority, and deprivation were no longer equated with differences. Further, newer models (cultural difference and cultural conflict models) both acknowledged the differences and supported the notion of biculturality among Blacks and other racially and culturally different groups as a desired goal. Accommodation rather than assimilation was and is valued.

Many persistent school practices contribute to, increase, or cause underachievement among Black students. Schools that are consistently unsuccessful with Black students tend to be mired in a slough of attitudes and counterproductive practices that defy efforts by underachieving students, parents, and educators to break the cycle of failure (Sinclair & Ghory, 1992). Colangelo et al. (1993) reported that gifted underachievers were less likely to be satisfied with high school class instruction and guidance services than gifted achievers. Most gifted achievers rated their high school education as "excellent," while most gifted underachievers rated their education as "good." Three interesting findings are that: (a) 61% of gifted underachievers and 15% of gifted achievers expressed a need to improve study skills; (b) 64% of gifted underachievers and 19% of gifted achievers did not have an interest in taking freshman honor courses; and (c) 49% of gifted underachievers and 31% of gifted achievers expressed an interest in independent study (Colangelo et al., 1993).

MORE ON CLASSROOM CLIMATES

School climate is often as palpable as the weather. Some schools have a warm, friendly ambience, while others have a cold, foreboding environment that permeates classrooms and offices.

— Montgomery and Rossi (1994, p. 9)

School and classroom climates influence students' sense of belonging and performance, with positive and supportive environments more likely to facilitate achievement and social and emotional well-being than others. For instance, Schlosser (1992) reported that the ultimate act of disengagement—school dropout—is influenced significantly by:

- low teacher expectations,
- lack of teacher understanding,
- teacher distance and impersonalized classroom environment,
- teacher-directed and lecture-based instruction,
- poor achievement,
- feeling isolated from classmates,
- cultural dissonance and conflicts,
- little opportunity for success,
- irrelevant curriculum, and
- an inability to identify with school.

These assertions were strongly reinforced by the study of dropouts among high-achieving culturally different students (Bridgeland et al., 2006). Likewise, some years ago, Fantini and Weinstein (1968) interviewed a large number of students in urban schools to identify their perception of school-related problems and needs. The majority of problems related to identity, connectedness, and powerlessness. Fantini and Weinstein found that schools reinforce disconnectedness by depriving students of meaningful discourse with their peers at the affective or socioemotional level, and it is reinforced by the formal business-like relationships between teachers and students.

Teachers and administrators often complain about counterproductive groups and negative peer pressure. The need for connectedness and social belonging (Maslow, 1954) can be so strong that groups will form in spite of the system (Bonner, 2010; Grantham, 1994; Noguera, 2008; Whiting, 2006a). In some respects, the educational system motivates students to join counterdependent groups—groups whose values, standards, and goals are in defiance of the system. For example, educators allow little time for students to talk with each other about feelings, needs, desires, concerns, dislikes, problems, and so forth. Schools oftentimes foster disconnection competition. Although competitive environments can be motivating and invigorating for some students, they are unmotivating and disempowering for others. Through individualistic competition, students are encouraged not to be cooperative, not to help or show compassion, and not to trust. The sense of community that is so important for learning and socioemotional well-being is disrupted.

Feelings of disconnection also increase because schools foster conformity and assimilation somewhat akin to the proverbial (and unrealistic) melting pot phenomenon. As described later, the hidden curriculum promotes assimilation, to which many Black students may object. The combination of academic frustration and disengagement and the desire not to conform creates problems for some gifted Black students, particularly creatively gifted Black students who are radical and spirited in disagreement, uninhibited in expressing their opinions, and concerned about social injustices. This tenaciousness and other attributes, for instance, may be seen by teachers as negative rather than positive.

Educators are encouraged to examine the classroom climate relative to its (a) ecology (physical and material aspects of climate that are external to individuals, such as school and classroom size), (b) milieu (characteristics of people and groups), (c) social system (relationships of people and groups), and (d) culture (belief systems and values; Tagiuri & Litwin, 1968). Several recent educational and social reports (e.g., Boyer, 1983; Bridgeland et al., 2006; Goodlad, 1984; Kirsch, Braun, Yamamoto, & Sum 2007; Schott Foundation for Public Education, 2008, 2009; Search Institute, 2010; Sizer, 1984) stressed that students' social and psychological development is more critically important today than ever before. The reports emphasized what ought to be apparent to all educators—that students need to have opportunities to develop their talent and potential, to learn about and understand their potential, to increase their self-esteem, to set personal goals, to make informed decisions, to persevere, and to see differences as good and desirable. These recommendations indicate that schools cannot be places where only academics are taught. Humanistic/affective education recognizes the cause-and-effect relationship between students and their social environment, and the importance of educating the whole child (Boy & Pine, 1988). Stated differently, gifted young minds also have inner feelings, emotions, and perceptions that influence when and how the mind functions. According to Childers and Fairman (1986),

> schools have an obligation to provide a healthy organizational climate that is conducive to optimal personal-social and academic learning. Environments that provide individuals with a feeling of significance, a sense of competence, and a belief that they have some control over important aspects of their environment will enable these individuals to feel more comfortable, feel greater self-worth and, consequently, take more risks. The lack of these elements in public school is a predominant cause of student failure. (p. 332)

Affective/humanistic and culturally responsive educators place students at the center of learning. They recognize that: (a) students have individual psychological, emotional, and social needs; (b) schools can help students to identify, integrate, and balance their emotional, social, and psychosocial needs; and (c) students gain more from an academic curriculum when these various needs are concurrently met (Boy & Pine, 1988).

Clearly, gifted Black students must be exposed to teachers who hold high expectations; who are empathetic, accepting, child-oriented, interested, understanding, and genuine (Guggenheim, 1969; Solomon, Houlihan, & Parelius, 1969; St. John, 1969); and who foster a "curriculum of caring" (Bronfenbrenner, 1986) that is culturally responsive. With this responsive, supportive, and nurturing environment, teachers can expect gains in Black students' academic achievement, self-concept, self-esteem, racial identity, intrinsic motivation, and attendance and class participation, and decreased feelings of alienation, isolation, and rejection. Boy and Pine (1988) lamented: "We may never know the untold number of boys and girls who could have achieved optimum benefits from their educational experience, but did not because their emotional problems prevented them from doing so" (p. 223).

In other words, classroom climates for gifted Black students must be characterized by empathetic understanding, acceptance, sensitive listening, authenticity, presence, immediacy, and equality. In this environment, teachers acknowledge that students' hearts are as important as their heads.

LACK OF RACIALLY AND CULTURALLY DIFFERENT TEACHERS

A disproportionate number of Black and other culturally different teachers is commonplace throughout schools, even in urban areas. As mentioned above, nationally, only 6% of teachers are Black, and little more than 1% are Black males (Planty et al., 2009). Only one study could be found that reported the percentage of Black teachers in gifted education programs (Ford, 1999). It seems reasonable to assume, that just as Black students are underrepresented in gifted education and AP classes, and Black teachers are underrepresented in education at large, so too are Black teachers underrepresented in gifted education and AP classes.

Serwatka, Deering, and Stoddard (1989) found the percentage of Black teachers to be a significant predictor of underrepresentation among Black students in gifted classes: As the percentage of Black teachers increases, the underrepresentation of Black students in gifted programs decreases. Accordingly, more Black teachers may increase the aspirations, expectations, motivation, and, ultimately, achievement of gifted Black students for both gifted education and AP classes. Although not focused specifically on gifted education, Delpit (1995), Hale (2001), Ladson-Billings (1994, 2006), and Irvine (2002) have effectively described many of the critical characteristics of teachers who are cultural brokers and advocates (i.e., successful and effective) with Black students.

LACK OF TRAINING AMONG SCHOOL SUPPORT PERSONNEL IN GIFTED EDUCATION AND AP CLASSES

Many programs designed to assist Black students center around career or vocational counseling (Ford, 1995). Less often are the psychological, affective, and social needs of gifted Black students addressed in educational programs; less often are services comprehensive so that students' needs are addressed through full consideration of internal and external variables: social, cultural, psychological, and academic.

Most states lack certification laws for teachers of the gifted (NAGC, 2009), and most general education teachers have received no formal training or professional development in gifted education (Council for Exceptional Children & National Association for Gifted Children, 2006). Similarly, more than half of the states require no certification or endorsement in gifted education. According to Karnes and Whorton (1991), only three states make this training optional; only five states have statements of competencies, only 14 require practicum experiences, and only eight require teaching experience in the regular classroom prior to teaching gifted students.

The impact of inadequate preparation to work with gifted students contributes in meaningful ways to teachers and other educators who are ill-qualified to refer, screen, teach, counsel, and assess gifted students, especially if they are African American and/or low income. This paucity of preparation feeds underidentification, underachievement, and underrepresentation.

MISUSE AND ABUSES OF IDENTIFICATION AND ASSESSMENT INSTRUMENTS

The majority of schools rely upon standardized tests as the ultimate arbiter of educational value and achievement or performance. Too often, the well-documented biases and disparate impact of these tests in predicting academic success among Black culturally different students has had little effect on educational policy and decision making. Many educators rely indiscriminately on intelligence tests and unidimensional instruments, particularly intelligence tests, to define, label, and identify giftedness.

Seemingly, educators have not heeded Binet and Simon's (1905) warning more than a century ago that the IQ test was primarily a measure of school-related proficiency and was not to be used outside of that framework. A multitude of measurement strategies should be used when judging intelligence in order to increase or ensure validity and reliability for gifted Black students (Ford, 2004, 2007b, 2010). Therefore, educators who rely solely on standardized tests to identify giftedness among Black students ignore that tests can and do misinterpret intelligence, ability, and potential. They ignore the potential and real harm of testing in general and high-stakes testing in particular. Using designated score ranges on an intelligence or achievement test as the only qualification for giftedness can and does significantly hinder Black students' chances for inclusion in gifted programs and AP classes. It may also contribute to underachievement among Black students who are excluded from such classes, programs, and services, given that their needs are not being met.

Gifted Black students have always been a puzzle to educators because

of their unresponsiveness to standard measures of intellectual performance, yet educators know these students have substantial ability, talent,
and potential. We all know of at least one person who has passed standardized tests, yet "flunked" life—and someone who flunked tests, but
succeeded in life. In essence, student performance on standardized tests
measures neither innate aptitudes nor an individual's ability and potential. To interpret IQ scores and test results in this manner is dangerous,
unproductive, and indefensible.

LACK OF TRAINING AMONG SCHOOL PERSONNEL IN MULTICULTURAL OR CULTURALLY RESPONSIVE EDUCATION

Few teachers are trained in gifted and multicultural education. Yet,
meaningful multicultural education—education that is culturally responsive—begins with teacher self-awareness, an ingredient that is often
absent from debates about multicultural education (Banks & Banks,
2010). Misconceptions, naïve thinking, hidden assumptions, and prejudices that teachers hold cannot surface without formal, ongoing, and
substantive multicultural education preparation. It is inconceivable, given
the nation's changing demography, that educators of the gifted would not
be required to take coursework and practica in multicultural education.
An important factor in improving Black students' access to gifted education and achievement rests in improving teachers' decisions and attitudes;
multicultural preparation promises to increase teachers' effectiveness or
efficacy in this regard. With this training, teaches are less likely: (a) to
hold negative expectations of Black students, (b) to abuse identification
practices, and (c) to abuse tracking and ability grouping.

Currently, several states (e.g., California, Pennsylvania, North
Carolina, Minnesota, and New York) require multicultural training for
the recertification of school personnel. In 1973, Minnesota was one of
the forerunners of states requiring training in human relations to develop
intercultural skills. According to Filla and Clark (1973), teachers were
trained to: (a) understand the contributions and lifestyles of various racial,
cultural, and economic groups; (b) create learning environments that
contribute to the self-esteem of all persons and to positive interpersonal
relations; (c) recognize and deal with dehumanizing biases, discrimination, and prejudices; and (d) respect human diversity and personal rights.

Ladson-Billings (1990a, 1990b, 2006) distinguished between teach-

Table 7.2

Assimilationist Versus Pluralist Perspectives on
Racially and Culturally Diverse Students

	Assimilationist	**Pluralist**
Source of underachievement	Cultural deficit perspective: within the child based on culture and experience; need for intervention directed at deficits	Social deficit perspective: within system or within interactions between system and child; need for empowerment of child; seeks to change the system
Purpose of schooling	Assimilation: transmission of mainstream values toward maintenance of core or predominant culture; melting pot philosophy	Accommodation: understanding many cultural perspectives toward creation of a society that values diversity
Identification	Standardized assessment practices, instruments, and procedures; unidimensional	Alternative, dynamic, multidimensional assessment; nonbiased and comprehensive
Instructional practices	Focus on individual achievement; competitive; helping child fit the school	Focus on democratic structures; cooperative; changing the school to fit the child
Curriculum	Academically responsive: problem solving and critical thinking applies to mainstream culture and history; monocultural	Socially and academically responsive: problem solving and critical thinking applies to culture and history of many and diverse groups; building skills to transform society; multicultural

Note. Adapted from Kitano (1991).

ers who hold assimilationist as opposed to pluralistic conceptions of teaching relative to themselves as teachers, their social relationships with Black students, and their views about knowledge (see Tables 7.2 and 7.3).

ETHNOCENTRIC/MONOCULTURAL CURRICULUM

Students learn more in school than is included in their formal curriculum. The hidden curriculum exacerbates achievement problems among gifted Black students. It conveys different messages to students of different income, socioeconomic status, gender, and racial backgrounds.

Table 7.3
Assimilationist Versus Culturally Responsive Philosophies of Teaching

Assimilationist	Pluralist
Conceptions of Self/Other	
Teacher sees self as technician; teaching is a technical task	Teacher sees self as artist; teaching is an art
Teacher sees self as an individual who may or may not be a part of the community; encourages achievement as a means of students escaping community	Teacher sees self as part of community and teaching is giving back to the community; teacher encourages students to do the same
Teacher believes failure is inevitable for some students	Teachers believes all students can achieve
Teacher homogenizes students into one "American" identity	Teachers helps students make connections among their community, racial, ethnic, and national origins
Teachers sees teaching as putting in knowledge—like banking	Teacher sees teaching as pulling out knowledge—like mining.
Social Relations	
Teacher/student relationship is fixed, tends to be hierarchical, and limited to formal classroom roles	Teacher/student relationship is fluid, humanely equitable, extends in interaction beyond the classroom into the community
Teacher demonstrates idiosyncratic connection with individual students	Teacher demonstrates a connectedness with all students (oneness)
Teacher encourages competitive individual achievement as a priority	Teacher encourages a community of learners as a priority
Teacher encourages students to learn individually, in isolation	Teacher encourages students to learn collaboratively; students are expected to teach each other and be responsible for each other
Conceptions of Knowledge	
Knowledge is static, passed in one direction—from teacher to student	Knowledge is continuously recreated, recycled, and shared by teachers and students; it is not static or unchanging
Knowledge (content) is infallible	Knowledge (content) is viewed critically
Teacher is detached, neutral about content	Teacher is passionate about content
Teacher expects students to demonstrate prerequisite knowledge and skills (students build their own bridges)	Teacher helps students develop prerequisite knowledge and skills (build bridges or scaffolding)
Teacher sees excellence as a postulate that exists independent of student diversity or individual differences	Teacher sees excellence as a complex standard that may involve some postulates but takes student diversity and individual differences into consideration

Note. Adapted from Ladson-Billings (1990a, 1990b) and Kitano (1991).

That is, schools magnify or reinforce racial, gender, income, language, and SES differences (Bowles & Gintis, 1976). White students, and in particular, middle-class White students, are privileged in school and social settings (see McIntosh, 1992, on the notion of White privilege). Jackson (1968) described the hidden curriculum as the implicit messages in school that convey "appropriate" or "normal" values, behaviors, and beliefs to students. These messages are transmitted to students through the underlying rules that guide the routines and social relations in school and classroom life (Bourdieu, 1977; Giroux, 1983).

When Black children come to school, they are expected to adopt styles, values, and beliefs that may be incongruent with the styles, values, and beliefs of their indigenous culture. To be successful in school and life, gifted Black students have been required to be bicultural, bicognitive, and bidialectic. This is not a choice, but a prerequisite. Seldom are teachers required to straddle two cultures; yet, they must learn to do so for the sake of their students and for their own sake. Adhering to monocultural models of teaching, learning, and assessment in the face of our diverse schools and societies is a recipe for disaster in which teachers and gifted Black students experience (unnecessary) cultural disharmony or conflict. Simply put, being culturally competent is a survival skill that educators must have.

Current forecasts project that by the end of the 21st century, half the student population will be comprised of Black and other racially different students (Hodgkinson, 1988, 2007; Planty et al., 2009). Hence, the recruitment and retention of Black students in gifted programs and AP classes may also be influenced by the nature and extent of multicultural education training among teachers and other school personnel. This preparation—which focuses on nonstereotypical individual differences attributable to race, gender, income, socioeconomic status, and geographic locale—is necessary to narrow any cultural gaps and clashes that may exist among teachers, other educators, and Black students and their families.

Gay (1990, 2002) argued that segregation of the curriculum and instructional inequities exist in a wide array of schools (and, by inference, gifted programs and AP classes) where Black and other culturally different students are denied equal access to high-status knowledge and learning opportunities because of biases about their race, gender, nationality, cultural background, and/or socioeconomic class.

"Curriculum segregation" occurs when different course assignments, instructional styles, and teaching materials are routinely employed for different groups of students; it constitutes a form of discrimination that mirrors the prejudices and inequities in the larger educational system and in society. In the books and content that are regularly taught, the role models that are commonly presented, the way students are treated in classroom interactions, and the assignment of certain students to instructional programs all convey subtle—but powerful—messages about just how separate and unequal education is. (Gay, 1990, p. 56)

The curriculum consists, therefore, of implicit and explicit messages to all students about differential power and social structures—students learn how to work in schools, what kinds of knowledge is valued and devalued, and by whom, and how students are valued in their own right. Giroux (1983) stated that these messages are learned informally and sometimes unintentionally as a result of formal structure and curriculum. That is to say, students learn through acts of omission and commission; they learn from what is presented and omitted from the curriculum. Due to a keen awareness of inconsistencies, gifted Black students in particular may note these discrepancies.

Monocultural curriculum and instruction in general education, AP, and gifted education classes predestine all Black students to disengagement; diminished self-esteem, self-concepts, and racial identities; feelings of inferiority; and, subsequently, underachievement (Ford & Harris, 1999). Clearly, success begets success—and failure fosters failure. Failure at school, even with success at home, may contribute to or cause Black children to develop poor identities and take on the unsatisfactory, painful role of a failure.

It is my belief that *all* students (and, ultimately, the larger society) benefit when the curriculum is multicultural or culturally responsive. In their model, J. Banks (2006, 2010) and Banks and Banks (1993, 2010) focused on levels of integration of multicultural content into the curriculum (see Figure 7.2). In Level 1, the Contributions Approach, educators focus on heroes, holidays, and discrete elements, or the four Fs (food, fashion, fun, and folklore) at the expense of more substantive topics and events. This is the most frequently adopted and extensively used approach to multiculturalism in the schools. An important characteristic of this approach is that the traditional ethnocentric or monocultural curriculum remains unchanged in its basic structure, goals, and salient characteris-

---

Level 4
The Social Action Approach

Students make decisions on important social issues and take actions to help solve them. Students become empowered to make meaningful contributions to the resolution of social issues and problems.

Level 3
The Transformation Approach

The structure of the curriculum is changed to enable students to view concepts, issues, events, and themes from the perspectives of diverse racial and cultural groups. Educators are active and proactive in seeking training and experience with racially and culturally diverse groups.

Level 2
The Additive Approach

Content, concepts, themes, and perspectives are added to the curriculum without changing its structure. Students fail to understand how the predominant culture interacts with and is related to racially and culturally diverse groups.

Level 1
The Contributions Approach

Focuses on heroes, holidays, and discrete cultural elements. Students acquire a superficial understanding of racially and culturally diverse groups.

Figure 7.2. Levels of integration of multicultural content into curriculum. Adapted from Banks and Banks (1993).

---

tics. Students are introduced to racially and culturally diverse heroes and artifacts, such as Crispus Attucks, Martin Luther King, Jr., Booker T. Washington, Harriet Tubman, and Benjamin Banneker. These individuals, however, are usually discussed in relation to White heroes, such as Abraham Lincoln, George Washington, and Thomas Jefferson. Further, individuals who challenged the predominant cultures' ideologies, values, and conceptions, and who advocated radical social, political, and economic reform are often ignored in this approach. As a result, Martin Luther King, Jr. is more likely to be discussed than Malcolm X; Booker T. Washington is more likely to be discussed than W. E. B. DuBois. The result is that the heroes and events found acceptable to White Americans, rather than those also valued by racial and cultural groups, are discussed with students.

Another characteristic of this basic approach is that cultural traditions, foods, music, and dance may be discussed, but little (if any) attention is given to their meanings and significance to racially and culturally diverse groups. Also, within this level is the heroes and holidays approach in which ethnic content is limited primarily to a special day, weeks, or months related to racial and cultural groups (e.g., Black History week or month, Martin Luther King, Jr.'s birthday). Students, regardless of their race, learn little to nothing about the occasion, group, or individual being celebrated.

The contributions approach is quite superficial; it provides teachers with a quick, safe, nonthreatening way to "integrate" the curriculum, and teachers themselves can adopt this approach without knowing much about racial and cultural diverse groups. It can also reinforce stereotypes and misconceptions about Black and other culturally different groups, especially by using safe, nonthreatening heroes found acceptable to the predominant culture for inclusion in the curriculum (while excluding others).

In Level 2, the Additive Approach, the content, concepts, themes, and perspectives of racially and culturally diverse groups are added to the curriculum without changing its structure. For instance, teachers may add a book, unit, or course to the curriculum that focuses on diverse groups or topics. Again, however, although the content changes slightly, there is little restructuring of the curriculum relative to purposes and characteristics. This approach requires little time, effort, training, and rethinking of the curriculum (its purpose, nature, and goals). For instance, Black students learn little of their own history, and White students learn little of the true history and contributions of other racial and cultural groups to American society in the past and present. Students reading *The Autobiography of Malcolm X*, for example, lack the concepts, content background, and emotional maturity to understand, appreciate, respect, and deal effectively with the issues and problems discussed in the book. The Additive Approach fails to help all students view society from diverse perspectives and to understand the ways that the histories and cultures of the nation's diverse racial, cultural, ethnic, and religious groups are interconnected (Banks & Banks, 1993).

In Level 3, the Transformational Approach, the structure of the curriculum is changed to enable students to view concepts, issues, events, and themes from the perspectives of diverse ethnic and cultural groups. This is a fundamental change from the previous levels; one now sees changes in the basic assumptions, goals, nature, and structure of the curriculum.

A primary goal is to help *all* students feel empowered. According to Banks and Banks (1993), the curriculum should not focus on the ways that various racial and cultural groups have contributed to mainstream society and culture; instead, it focuses on how the common U.S. culture and society emerged from a complex synthesis and interaction of the diverse cultural elements that make up the United States. This approach requires extensive curriculum revision, teacher training, time, and effort.

In Level 4, the Social Action Approach, students make decisions on important social issues and take action to help solve them. Students are not socialized to accept unquestionably the existing ideologies, institutions, and practices of the predominant group. At this level, students not only feel empowered, but they are proactive. Students are provided with the knowledge, values, and skills necessary to participate in social change. Student self-examination becomes central in this approach through value analysis, decision-making, problem-solving, and social action skills. For example, students examine issues surrounding prejudice and discrimination, and develop ways to improve race relations. This approach is least likely to be adopted by educators, primarily because teachers often lack training, experience, understanding, and personal knowledge of racially and culturally different groups (e.g., histories, values, beliefs, customs). Equally important, few teachers adopt proactive strategies and philosophies themselves, and the majority come from monocultural or ethnocentrically oriented educational programs. Even at institutions of higher education, curriculum and instruction are at the Contributions and Additive levels.

Gifted Black learners are hungry for curriculum that is enriched with content reflecting diversity and the inadequacy of racism, sexism, and discrimination. Because the infusion of multicultural education into the content is empowering for Black students, multiculturalism must continually permeate the curriculum for gifted students. For instance, a Black History month each February provides insufficient time to infuse gifted Black students with pride in their racial and cultural heritage and the contributions of their ancestors to American history. All children, regardless of race, benefit both from multiethnic education (which focuses on race and ethnicity) and from multicultural education (which focuses on human diversity and individual differences in gender, race, socioeconomic status, and geographic origins). A lack of racial and cultural diversity in a school or community, and in a gifted program or AP class, cannot be used as a rationale for the absence of multicultural education. Clearly, Black students benefit when their education is culturally responsive; so do other culturally different students and White students.

INSTRUCTIONAL/PEDAGOGICAL ISSUES

Kitano (1991), Harmon (2002), and Ford and Harris (1999) have each written one of the few articles or books specifically on promoting pluralism and multicultural education in gifted programs. They cogently argued that gifted programs continue to espouse assimilationist rather than pluralistic approaches to cultural diversity. Assimilationists favor the relinquishment of diverse students' original culture. These students are expected to adapt to the values, attitudes, and behaviors of the predominant culture—the child is responsible for changing. On the other hand, pluralists support the retention of students' original culture. When accommodation of schooling to diverse gifted students' experiences occurs, the school bears the responsibility for changing. Certainly, when the culture of children is valued, educators are more likely to witness fundamental and essential changes in those students' achievement, motivation, and behavior.

Much of the focus on multicultural education has centered on curriculum. However, because of cultural differences in learning styles, as discussed in other chapters, changes are also essential relative to instruction if Black students are to succeed (see Figure 7.3). In a thoughtful and informative book, Milgrim, Dunn, and Price (1993) shared how gifted students from different cultural backgrounds have similar and different learning styles.

As presented in Figure 7.3, in Level 1, Assimilation of Learning Styles, Black (and other culturally different) students are often required to assimilate—to give up their learning style preferences in order to succeed in school. For instance, most schools cater to students who prefer lecture-based instruction, and who are passive, abstract, and auditory learners. Yet, many Black students tend to be prefer didactive learning experiences; they are often visual, concrete, tactile, and kinesthetic learners. In terms of instruction or pedagogy, teachers seem to bear little responsibility for modifying their instructional practices; students bear the greatest responsibility for adapting to how they are taught and expected to learn. This "sink or swim" approach is reminiscent of the cultural melting pot philosophy.

In Level 2, Assimilation of Teaching Styles, teachers modify the

Figure 7.3. Levels of accommodation and assimilation of instruction.

process—how the material is presented and taught—to students' learning styles. Teachers are the active participants, while students are passive. Either through intuition or formal training, teachers attempt to adapt their teaching styles to learning styles. In this sense, teachers adopt the siphon philosophy. At the individual student level, teachers may modify assignments for students. As shown in Figure 7.3, at the class level, they may use both visual and auditory modes of instruction. With this approach, students can become dependent on teachers who are willing to make modifications in their instruction. When students encounter teachers who adopt the assimilationist approach, they are more likely to experience stylistic conflicts, frustration, and failure. These students are academically incompetent in that they lack the skills necessary to achieve with different teachers and in diverse academic settings or contexts.

In Level 3, Accommodation of Learning Styles, students (and teachers) are bistylistic. Students depend less upon teachers to modify instruction (Level 2), and there is less need for students to bear the responsibility for change (Level 1). At this level, students are more academically competent such that they can adapt their learning styles to the learning context (e.g., teaching style, instruction, curriculum). For example, visual learners know how to reorganize notes presented in lecture format to depict models and diagrams; others use tape recorders, borrow notes from classmates, work with other students to capture themes and concepts, and so forth. Without teacher support, however, in-school modifications or accommodations (e.g., use of tape recorders) may not be possible.

In Level 4, Accommodation of Learning and Teaching Styles, both students and teachers are active participants and partners. Teachers are aware of students' learning styles and related needs; similarly, students are aware of and respectful of teachers' instructional preferences. Teachers support is essential for many of the in-class modifications that students may wish to make. There is mutual understanding, respect, and accommodation to differences and preferences.

Essentially, the model asks three central questions: (a) Are racially and culturally diverse students required to assimilate or accommodate their learning styles? (b) To what extent do teachers accommodate their teaching styles to diverse learning styles? and (c) To what extent are students taught and do teachers seek to be bistylistic?

TEACHER EXPECTATIONS

Teacher expectancy theory (Brophy & Good, 1974; Rosenthal & Jacobson, 1968) holds that teachers communicate their expectations of students through both subtle and overt behavioral cues. For instance, a teacher who believes that Black students are not as competent as White students might communicate this belief by assigning easy tasks to the Black students, and assigning more difficult and challenging tasks to White students. The teacher's behavior is likely to indicate to Black students that they are not capable of mastering challenging work, and that White students are more competent. When such behaviors are consistent, Black students begin to internalize these beliefs. Other behaviors include giving Black students less opportunity to speak in class, seating them at the back of the class, ignoring their questions or raised hands, and offering less praise or feedback to them. This example also applies to low-income/SES and high-income and/or low-SES students, or to males and females (particularly in the areas of computers, mathematics, and science; Lubienski, 2007, 2008).

Negative attitudes and expectations of educators who do not believe that Black students (and other racially and culturally different students) are capable of high levels of intelligence and/or giftedness persist. Academicians have created a cult of failure, a cult whose doctrine holds that variations in school resources have limited effects on learning; that schools themselves really have little to do with who learns what and how much they learn; that the children's background has the greatest influence on educational outcomes; and that reform is meaningless for such students (Bitting et al., 1992).

Proponents of this cultural deficit perspective believe that Black students are intellectually inferior, that race itself explains their intellectual inferiority, and that this deficiency is therefore biologically determined or inherited (Burt, 1972; Goddard, 1912; Herrnstein & Murray, 1994; Jensen, 1969, 1979; Spearman, 1927). The cognitive or performance gap between Black and White children is biased further by researchers' lack of understanding of the Black culture and by research conducted without ethnic-relevant content.

ABUSES OF TRACKING PRACTICES

Tracking and ability grouping[1] placements often inhibit the school achievement of Black students. Tracking, the widespread use of grouping by ability, appears to contribute to or cause underachievement among and the "miseducation" (Woodson, 1933/2000) of gifted Black children. Although tracking and ability grouping are commonplace in many American school systems, both rank high among the most controversial and debated school practices. On one side, proponents argue that tracking and ability grouping help teachers to better target individual

---

1   I prefer the term *skills grouping* to *ability grouping*; the former has an academic focus; the latter smacks of genetics. No one knows what any individual is capable of, but one can tell the specific skill level at which a student is performing.

needs and, subsequently, students learn more and more effectively. On the other side, opponents argue that tracking and ability grouping stereotypes students by labeling them as "unable" or "less able." The latter concern carries significant implications for Black, culturally different, poor, and urban students, many of whom are found disproportionately in the lower ability groups and tracks.

In general, the majority of the literature, as well as considerable empirical evidence, court decisions, and reform proposals, suggests that ability grouping and tracking have no overall positive effects because lower track students, the majority of whom are economically disadvantaged and Black, achieve less than their higher track counterparts (Oakes, 1988, 2005, 2008; Orfield, 2001; Orfield & Frankenberg, 2007; Orfield & Lee, 2007). The placement of students into groups or tracks based upon academic "ability" (as measured by standardized instruments that are normed or validated on middle-class Whites) or teachers' perceptions of students' abilities, affects lower track students in several ways: Lower track students typically have lower self-concepts than higher ability/track students. The placement in lower tracks and groups contributes to low self-concept. Decreased levels of motivation to achieve have been found among lower track students. These students have higher dropout rates, more school misconduct, and higher delinquency than students in higher groups and tracks. In other words, tracking and grouping creates biases more than grades and aptitudes. Lower track students become inattentive more frequently than those in higher tracks. This inattentiveness is primarily characterized by easy distractibility by peers and general disinterest in learning or school. Tracking and ability grouping contribute to stereotyped and stratified roles that inhibit the social development of lower track students. This inhibition is characterized by poor relationships with peers, parents, and teachers as well as immaturity and disruptiveness.

Both practices also affect teachers' expectations, level of encouragement, and assumptions regarding lower track students and their abilities or potential: Teachers generally expect less from lower level students. The underlying belief is that these students can accomplish very little academically. Teachers of lower track students tend to be more punitive and less encouraging than those of higher track students. Consequently, students become less motivated. Teachers often equate low placement with low ability, low potential, and low competence. This is quite disconcerting considering that some standardized tests that are biased against Blacks and low-income and/or low-SES students are the primary methods of assessing intelligence and deciding group placement. Because of the high representation of Black students in lower tracks, Irvine (1991) called tracking "educational ghettos" for Black students.

RECOMMENDATIONS

If both the field of gifted education and educators of gifted students take proactive, strong stances in adopting multiculturalism and responsiveness as a model of curriculum and instruction, for example, then positive educational outcomes will increase for Black and other culturally different students. Multiculturalism promises to redress many of the current inadequacies in gifted education—the underrepresentation of racially and culturally different students, the lack of diversity among teachers, monocultural curriculum and instruction, biased and standardized identification and assessment practices, inadequately prepared teachers in cultural diversity, and policies that reinforce (directly or indirectly) these problems.

Today's schools are ill-designed to accommodate today's culturally different students. Although almost every aspect of U.S. society has entered into the technological age, the U.S. school system remains in the industrial age. The programs, curriculum, and even buildings are essentially the same as they were 100 years ago. Probably the only thing that has changed is the learner (Bitting et al., 1992). But as Korman (1974) stated decades ago, professionals have an ethical responsibility to seek training and preparation in working with racially and culturally diverse persons: The provision of professional services to persons of culturally diverse backgrounds by those not competent in understanding and providing professional services to such groups shall be considered unethical.

Although speaking specifically to the counseling profession, Korman's (1974) statement seems equally appropriate for the education profession. Professionals without training or competence in working with racially and culturally different persons are unethical and potentially harmful, which borders on a violation of human rights (Sue et al., 1992), and possibly malpractice.

In essence, we cannot give lip service to multicultural concerns in education. There must be a commitment to translate ethical principles and standards into practice. Given the nation's changing demographics, monocultural and ethnocentric practices are increasingly becoming a form of maladjustment. Monoculturalism acts as an invisible veil that prevents people from seeing education as a potentially biased system (Sue, 2003; Sue et al., 1992; Sue et al., 2007). Accordingly, educators need to become culturally aware and competent; education needs to become culturally responsive and responsible to its constituents.

Multicultural education is an effective means of addressing attendant issues of diversity (Ford & Harris, 1999). The lack of multicultural education in schools and other practices has been attributed to ineffective curricular and instructional practices, as well as poor educational outcomes for racially and culturally diverse students (e.g., Banks, 1993, 2006, 2010; Banks & Banks, 2010; Dilworth, 1992; Gollnick & Chinn, 1988). In gifted education, similar issues have been raised (Ford, 1995; Ford & Harris, 1999; Frasier, 1992; Kitano, 1991). To what extent is the underrepresentation and underachievement of Black and other culturally different students a function of monocultural and ethnocentric education and related practices?

Locke (1989) recommended several strategies to enhance the relationship between racially and culturally diverse students and school personnel:

- ❖ Be open to the existence of culturally sensitive values and attitudes among students; be honest in relationships with culturally different students.
- ❖ Avoid stereotyping racially and culturally different groups (retain the uniqueness of each student); strive to keep a reasonable balance between your views of students as human beings and cultural group members; teach students how to recognize stereotypes and how to challenge biases.
- ❖ Ask questions about culturally and racially diverse students. Encourage gifted Black students to discuss and be open about their concerns, beliefs, and cultural values; talk positively with Black students about their physical and cultural heritage; make sure that all students understand that one's race and ethnicity are never acceptable reasons for being rejected.
- ❖ Hold high, positive, and realistic expectations for all students.
- ❖ Participate in the cultural communities of culturally and racially diverse students; learn their customs and values; and share this information with students, teachers, and other colleagues.
- ❖ Encourage school personnel to acknowledge the strengths and contributions of racial and ethnic groups.
- ❖ Learn about one's own culture and cultural values (p. 254).

Some of the most promising strategies for helping Black students succeed in gifted programs focus on: racial identity (or identity as being both gifted and Black), peer pressure and relations, feelings of isolation from both classmates and teachers, and sensitivity about feeling different or misunderstood (Ford, 1996; Ford, Harris, & Schuerger, 1993), especially if they are one of a few Black students in the gifted program. Ultimately, we must teach gifted Black students how to be bicultural—how to cope with cultural conflicts and differences, and how to live and learn in two cultures that may be different and conflicting.

B. Ford (1992) proposed a multicultural framework entailing the following six essential components: (a) engaging teachers in self-awareness activities to explore their attitudes and perceptions concerning cultural groups and beliefs, and the influence of their attitudes on students' achievement and educational opportunities; (b) exposing teachers to accurate information about various cultural and ethnic groups, including their historical and contemporary contributions, lifestyles, interpersonal communication patterns, and parental attitudes about education; (c) helping educators explore the diversity that exists within and between cultural and ethnic groups; (d) showing teachers how to apply and incorporate multicultural perspectives into the teaching-learning process to maximize the academic, cognitive, personal, and social development of learners; (e) demonstrating effective interactions among teachers, students, and families; and (f) providing opportunities for teachers to manifest an appropriate application of cultural information to create a healthy learning climate.

INTEGRATING MULTICULTURALISM INTO GIFTED EDUCATION CURRICULUM AND INSTRUCTION

Attention to multicultural issues and concerns is not new, but it has increased as the nation becomes more racially and culturally diverse. Multicultural education gained momentum in the 1980s, with the works of Banks, Gay, Ladson-Billings, Irvine, Chinn and Gollnick, Bennett, Heid, Sleeter and Grant, and others. These authors focused on the need: (a) to development multicultural curriculum and instruction, and for multiculturalism to permeate educational practices and programs; (b) for commitment by educators, policy makers, and decision makers to the cause; (c) for a more racially and culturally diverse teaching force; (d) to view multicultural education as a legitimate enterprise; and (e) to study the quality of multicultural education so as to ensure that it is substantive and integral rather than superficial and ancillary. Their collective works indicate that most teachers, the vast majority of whom are White females, have little (if any) formal training in multicultural education; similarly, they have little daily or practical experience with racially and culturally diverse students because most teachers do not live in the same neighborhoods in which they teach (Dilworth, 1992).

It is gratifying to see an increase in both literature and research on the issue at hand; however, we have not witnessed a similar movement in gifted education. With the Jacob K. Javits Gifted and Talented Students Act, hope was on the horizon in gifted education. Ideally, this act would be followed by efforts to not only diversify gifted education relative to student representation, but also be proactive and aggressive in: (a) implementing hiring practices to recruit a more diverse teaching corps; (b) changes in curriculum and instruction; (b) teaching gifted and multicultural competencies; and (d) substantive revisions of policies. However, changes were temporary, and often things went back to the status quo once the funding was gone.

There are pockets of progress in gifted education; the majority of which are spearheaded by The National Research Center on the Gifted and Talented (NRC/GT). Impressive efforts to reach educational consumers—students—are underway at the NRC sites. Those efforts are aimed at equitable identification and assessment practices, curriculum and instruction, and teacher preparation. Such energy and commitment, however, are needed on a larger and more consistent basis.

This section addresses what is needed in gifted education if it is to truly become multicultural. As described below, educators in gifted education must explore the need and rationale for curriculum, instruction, and learning; for teacher preparation; for identification and assessment; and for research that is multicultural. Suggestions for realizing these goals are presented, along with characteristics of culturally competent educators and culturally responsive education. The recommended multicultural competencies described herein refer to groups that have historically been underrepresented in gifted education and/or who have been subjected to discrimination: Blacks, Hispanic Americans, Native Americans, and Asian Americans. Although this section focuses more specifically on Blacks, readers are encouraged to relate appropriate information to other oppressed groups. This discussion begins by presenting philosophies, rationales, and definitions of multicultural education (see Table 7.4).

MULTICULTURAL EDUCATION: PHILOSOPHIES AND RATIONALE

Although all of us are racial, ethnic, and cultural beings, belonging to a particular group does not automatically endow a person with multicultural competence, or with the skills necessary to be a culturally competent and responsive educator. As Sue and colleagues (1992) stated, being born and raised in a family does not mean that one will be a competent family educator.

What is multicultural education? The American Association of Colleges for Teacher Education (AACTE, 1973) defined it in the following way:

> Multicultural education is education that values cultural pluralism. Multicultural education rejects the view that schools should seek to melt away cultural differences or the view that schools should merely tolerate cultural pluralism. . . . It affirms that major education institutions should strive to preserve and enhance cultural pluralism. To endorse cultural pluralism is to endorse the principle that there is no one model American. (p. 264)

In accordance with the AACTE definition of multicultural education, effective implementation of multicultural education should have four major objectives: It (a) teaches values that support cultural diversity and individual uniqueness; (b) encourages the qualitative expansion of existing ethnic cultures and their incorporation into the mainstream of American socioeconomic and political life; (c) explores alternative and emerging lifestyles; and (d) encourages multiculturalism (AACTE, 1973). Banks and Banks (1993) and Banks (2006) defined multicultural education as:

> an educational reform movement designed to change the total educational environment so that students from diverse racial and ethnic groups, both gender groups, exceptional students, and students from each social-class group will experience equal educational opportunities in schools, colleges and universities. (p. 359)

Table 7.4
Characteristics and Dimensions of Culturally Competent Educators

Characteristics	Dimensions		
	Attitudes and beliefs	Knowledge	Skills
Self-awareness	• Aware of self as a cultural being; seek to understand own cultural heritage • Aware of own biases, attitudes, and values, and how they influence the educational process • Recognizes limits of their competence and experience • Comfortable with differences between self and students relative to race, ethnicity, and culture	• Has knowledge about own cultural heritage and how it affects them both personally and professionally • Understand the social and cultural privileges of being White (i.e., understands how racism, prejudice, and discrimination and subsequent oppression also affects them personally and professionally)	• Seek educational training experiences to enrich their understanding of and effectiveness in teaching and working with culturally different students • Seek consultation to enhance their effectiveness • Seek to understand themselves as racial and cultural beings, and actively work for a nonracist identity
Cultural awareness	• Aware of their negative reactions toward culturally different students; seek to be nonjudgmental • Aware of stereotypes and preconceived notions held toward culturally different students • Familiar with research and latest findings regarding education and culturally different students (e.g., understand that traditional identification and assessment practices tend to be ineffective in identifying gifted characteristics among culturally different students)	• Understand how cultural differences influence and may conflict with their teaching and students' learning (including learning styles, communication, and behaviors) • Are aware of culturally sensitive identification and assessment practices, including appropriate tests and other instruments	• Seek to redress equities in education relative to curriculum and instruction, and identification and assessment (e.g., inform colleagues and others of pitfalls and promises in these areas) • Advocate for culturally different students; confront injustices at all levels—classroom, school, community, and social—on their behalf • Actively involved with culturally different students outside of school setting (e.g., family and community events, social and political functions, celebrations); their relationship with culturally different students is more than an academic exercise • Work with families to enhance the educational process for culturally different students (including extended family members)

Table 7.4, continued

Characteristics	Dimensions		
	Attitudes and beliefs	Knowledge	Skills
Techniques and strategies	• Have a clear and explicit knowledge and understanding of the generic characteristics of teaching and learning, and how they may conflict with cultural values of culturally different students	• Aware of social and institutional barriers that prevent culturally different students from truly having equitable and equal education • Can interpret test results and school performance in a culturally sensitive manner	• Able to engage in variety of helping responses; eclectic in teaching; willing to adapt teaching styles to learning styles and teach students how to be bistylistic in learning • Recognize when students' problems stem from racial injustices • Take responsibility for modifying curriculum and instruction so that they are culturally sensitive • Take some of the responsibility for teaching culturally different students to be bicultural, to understand their educational rights, and to hold realistic and high expectations and aspirations
Socially responsive	• Seek to increase racial harmony within classroom; seek to decrease negative beliefs and attitudes of White students toward culturally different students through awareness and understanding of human diversity and individual differences • Address issues of social injustices in both heterogeneous and homogeneous classrooms; lack of cultural diversity is not used as an excuse for ignoring social and cultural problems	• Aware of problems associated with monocultural and ethnocentric educational practices relative to White students • Seek to acquire facilitative skills for working with students' affective and cognitive needs	• Practice multiculturalism and substantive multicultural education on a consistent basis • Able to address inequities as they arise in the classroom and school • Seek to empower all students to be proactive, culturally aware, and respectful of individual differences

To be culturally competent in working with these students, educators must take a proactive stance in incorporating standards and practices that reflect the diversity of the U.S.

CULTURALLY COMPETENT EDUCATORS: CHARACTERISTICS AND DIMENSIONS

The need for multicultural education is urgent and long overdue, as is the requirement for educators to become culturally competent. This section presents an overview of characteristics of culturally competent educators. I have adopted models proposed by Mason (1996), Storti (1999), Sue and Sue (1990) and Sue et al. (1992)[2], which individually and collectively hold that culturally competent professionals have the following core characteristics:

- *Self-awareness and self-understanding*: Culturally competent educators seek greater self-awareness and understanding regarding their biases, assumptions, and stereotypes. This self-awareness is reflected in their worldviews and an understanding of how they are a product of their cultural conditioning. They recognize that their assumptions and biases influence their teaching, expectations of, and relationships with racially and culturally different students (and their families).

- *Cultural awareness and understanding*: Culturally competent educators seek to understand the worldviews of racially and culturally different students, without holding negative judgments. They do not have to adopt these different views, but they respect them as legitimate rather than inferior or otherwise substandard.

- *Techniques and strategies*: Culturally competent educators seek to deliver more effective education to racially and culturally different students. Education is relevant, appropriate, and sensitive to students' diverse or different needs, including attention to teaching and learning styles (see Chapter 3). In general, such educators work proactively and assertively to adopt principles of learning that are necessary to meet the academic, as well as social, emotional, and psychological needs of students.

- *Socially responsive*: Culturally competent educators seek to increase multicultural awareness and understanding among *all*

---

2   The work of Sue and colleagues is aimed specifically at counseling professionals. In this article, their recommendations have been adapted for educators; however, a fourth characteristic of culturally competent educators (socially responsive) has been added.

students. Included in this statement is the assertion that educators practice multiculturalism, even in homogenous settings where there is little racial and cultural difference. The shortage (or absence) of Black and other culturally different students in the gifted program, AP class, school, community, or state is not used as an excuse for the lack of attention to multiculturalism and related educational practices.

DIMENSIONS OF CULTURAL COMPETENCE

Sue and Sue (1990) and Sue et al. (1992) have also proposed that cultural competence falls into at least three areas: attitudes and beliefs (e.g., disposition), knowledge, and skills.

❖ *Attitudes and beliefs*: This dimension refers to the need to check biases and stereotypes, to develop positive orientations toward multiculturalism, and to understand the ways in which beliefs and attitudes interrupt the educational process, as well as the academic, socioemotional, and psychological development of students.

❖ *Knowledge*: Educators understand their own worldviews, as well as those of other racial and cultural groups. Moreover, they understand social and political influences on educational practices and student outcomes.

❖ *Skills*: Culturally competent educators acquire skills and strategies to work more effectively with culturally different students. These competencies include social, communication, affective, and educational skills and strategies.

Table 7.5 presents a more in-depth look at the relationship between the four characteristics and the three dimensions that promise to increase the cultural competence and responsiveness of educators. Relative to this discussion, Storti's (1999) model of cultural competence is also noteworthy. Storti's model acknowledges that cultural competence cannot and must not be painted with broad strokes. Instead, educators can perceive themselves to be (or actually be) culturally competent with one culturally different group but not another.

Table 7.5
Storti's (1999) Levels of Cultural Competence and Descriptors

	Incompetence	Competence
Conscious	Blissful Ignorance	Spontaneous Sensitivity
	You are not aware that cultural differences exist between you and another person. It does not occur to you that you may be making cultural mistakes or that you may be misinterpreting much of the behavior going on around you.	You no longer have to think about what you are doing in order to be culturally sensitive (in a culture you know well). Culturally appropriate behavior comes naturally to you, and you trust your intuition because it has been reconditioned by what you know about cross-cultural interactions.
Unconscious	Spontaneous Sensitivity	Deliberate Sensitivity
	You no longer have to think about what you are doing in order to be culturally sensitive (in a culture you know well). Culturally appropriate behavior comes naturally to you, and you trust your intuition because it has been reconditioned by what you know about cross-cultural interactions.	You know there are cultural differences between people, you know some of the differences, and you try to modify your own behavior to be sensitive to these differences. This does not come naturally, but you make a conscious effort to behave in culturally sensitive ways. You are in the process of replacing old intuitions with new ones.

SUMMARY

Dewey (1963) noted it is the role of the educator to change conditions until opportunities for action and reflection are created that promote student learning. It is frustrating and sad to say that schools often permit a significant degree of marginality—that is, disconnection between students and the conditions designed for learning. In other words, schools allow individuals or subgroups to develop and sustain faulty or incomplete relationships with other school members and programs. Most schools tolerate the existence of a fringe population that is not fully wanted, welcome, and/or involved in mainstream school life. These marginal students learn and contribute only a fraction of what they can and, thus, use only a portion of their potential in school and the larger society (Sinclair & Ghory, 1987, 1992).

Far too many Black students, even when identified as gifted, have difficulty relating and connecting to school settings. This is not to say that schoolwork is difficult for these students or that it is beyond their ability. Rather, the point is that the quality of the relationships between Black students and teachers, for example, is less than adequate. Such poor relationships and subsequent lack of mutual understanding make it difficult for students to appreciate school tasks and objectives—and for educators to appreciate Black students (and their families).

The primary issue of underachievement in school is the responsiveness of schools to differences among students. As such, school and classroom environments contribute to underachievement among Black students, including those identified as gifted. Clearly, schools also represent an important mechanism for preventing and reversing underachievement among students. Just as the school environment is alterable, so too is underachievement.

Underachieving students balance a fine line between academic success and mediocrity or failure. If students lean (or are pushed by the school environment) toward underachievement or failure in school, they risk becoming marginal or marginalized. For the considerable number of students who do cross the line and become marginal, the opportunities for learning and for receiving quality education are less than for successful learners. Marginal students, then, have unequal access to knowledge and are, in many ways, limited to educational experiences that do not expect or encourage them to learn and achieve. Over time, this unproductive relationship with the curriculum of the school limits their life and educational expectations and options (Sinclair & Ghory, 1987, 1992).

There is too little research on how gifted Black students perceive the process of schooling. Some Black students question the merits of formal education, even though education has provided a means of social improvement, especially for the poor and racially different. These students and groups learn to become distrustful of the educational process, viewing it less as an opportunity for social advancement and more as an instrument of the dominant culture designed to rob them of their unique cultural values, beliefs, attitudes, and norms.

Black students may experience cultural conflict and shock relative to supporting the beliefs, values, behaviors, and norms of the dominant or predominant culture as opposed to their indigenous culture. For gifted Black students, the problems are compounded. Some gifted Black students feel guilty, alienated, and unsure of how, where, and if they fit in. A sense of social isolation may leave many gifted Black children with a social or racial identity crisis—a confusion about who they are and who they should become. Consequently, they show ambivalence about their intellectual and academic abilities. This quandary may result in a lack of academic motivation to achievement, and efforts to sabotage being formally identified as gifted (e.g., Ford, Grantham, & Whiting, 2008a, 2008b).

Unidimensional instruction and monocultural curriculum contribute to and may exacerbate stereotypes about Black students and other racially and culturally different groups. All students, including White students, are miseducated when schools and programs adopt curricular and instructional practices that are void of diversity and responsiveness. All students benefit from education that is pluralistic.

When gifted Black students underachieve, it is important to understand how schools may force a disconnect between learning and achievement. A crucial priority of educators is to find meaningful ways to serve (and identify) gifted Black students and to get in touch with their needs, interests, and values. This is particularly important for gifted underachieving Black students who have yet to find sufficient reasons or means for success in school. Genuine concern for these students promises to produce constructive changes in their lives and school performance. When children enter classrooms, teachers have 6 hours each day to use their creativity, resources, and determination to help resolve problems facing Black students in education.

The school doors and teachers' arms must be open to Black (and all) students. Schools are social institutions, but they are also communities. Schools without a sense of community contribute to underachievement or poor student motivation and engagement. Schools should provide a supportive and nurturing environment for all students. This requires embracing Black students as individuals *and* cultural beings, and helping them to feel connected to and valued and affirmed by educators. It is liberating and empowering for Black students to know that educators care about them and have their best interests at heart. Learning outcomes appear to be related, in major part, to the ability of teachers and other school personnel to balance successfully the expressive or social and emotional dimensions of schools and classrooms (Stockard & Mayberry, 1992). Teaching is an art and science; it requires great sensitivity to the needs and demands of students. There is no magic or "teacher-proof" curriculum (Brophy, 1986, p. 107) patterned to benefit all students. Thus, the dispositions, knowledge, and skills of teachers play a significant role in optimizing Black students' academic achievement.

The preparation of teachers and other school personnel to work with Black students is never-ending. School personnel must be trained or retrained to work more effectively with the gifted student population. A significant portion of this preparation should also be in multicultural education. Gifted Black students need a place to turn emotionally, social, psychologically, and educationally in order to express their concerns and needs. This support is especially meaningful and effective if imparted by a professional (e.g., teacher or school counselor) who is trained to work with both gifted and culturally different students.

Although there are different ideas on promising practices for educating Black students, few schools systematically operationalize the findings. More often than not, in practice, schools fail to reflect promising practices and recommendations. For instance, schools often fail to celebrate multiculturalism other than the perfunctory Black History month in February. In this respect, curricular and other educational practices are not pluralistic or multicultural or responsive.

A philosophy of multiculturalism and responsiveness must be infused throughout education, including gifted education and AP classes. Comprehensive preparation should (re)educate teachers and other school personnel so that inaccurate perceptions and uninformed beliefs do not restrict students' learning. Too many Black students fail in school because the culture of the school ignores, minimizes, or degrades their family, community, and cultural backgrounds. Teachers who reflect, support, and advance ethnocentric values are likely to devalue and single out for criticism the attitudes, interests, values, and behaviors of Black and culturally different students. They can crush the well-being of gifted Black students and neglect the strengths that these students bring to the educational setting.

A FINAL WORD

Current forecasts project that, by the end of the 21st century, half of the student population will be comprised of non-White students (Aud et al., 2010; Hodgkinson, 1988; Planty et al., 2009). Hence, the recruitment and retention of Black and other culturally different students in gifted programs and AP classes may also be influenced by the nature and extent of multicultural or culturally responsive education training among both current and future teachers. This preparation—which focuses on nonstereotypical individual differences attributable to race, gender, poverty, socioeconomic status, and geographic locale—is necessary to narrow any cultural gap(s) that may exist between educators and Blacks and other racially and culturally different students.

The U.S. is a multicultural society, as are our schools. However, gifted programs and AP classes are more monocultural—less racially and culturally different—than general education programs. The impact of social injustices in attitude and practice on the educational well-being of gifted Black students cannot be denied, for schools are not devoid of racist practices, and educators are, after all, human beings. As teachers, administrators, and adults charged with taking care of students, we can do much to interrupt or decrease social injustices in both principle and practice. If, indeed, schools are the greatest equalizer (see Horace Mann), educators must be culturally competent and (gifted) education must be culturally responsive. To accept and practice anything short of this is and has been a travesty, an act of benign neglect.

CHAPTER EIGHT

FAMILIAL FACTORS AS CORRELATES OF UNDERACHIEVEMENT AND ACHIEVEMENT

The familial ring of influence is the focus of this chapter (see Figure 8.1). As already mentioned elsewhere in this book, terminology is important. I believe that the term *parent* is passé, too narrow or delimiting, and fails to capture the richness and diversity (and reality) of family structures in the United States and the world. Many Black students live in extended family structures, often with one or more grandparents, aunts and uncles, cousins, or close friends, all of whom play a meaningful role in child-drearing. A grandparent or aunt, in particular, may be the main contact with school matters. Thus, the term *family* is more appropriate than parent. Related, some children do not live with their parent(s); instead, they may be raised by grandparent(s), aunts(s), or older sibling(s). And in some cases, they are in foster homes and other settings. In these cases, the term *caregiver* is likely to be more appropriate. Thus, I prefer the terms families

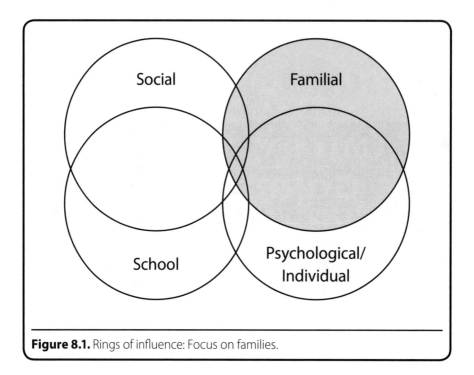

Figure 8.1. Rings of influence: Focus on families.

and caregivers to just parents. These terms are a deliberate and necessary effort to be inclusive, contemporary, accurate, and culturally responsive. No family structure is relegated to second-class or inferior status, so to speak, when these two terms are used.

No discussion of gifted Black underachievers is useful and complete when parents/families are left out of the discussion. As noted in previous chapters, the achievement gap is complex, stubborn, and pervasive, and parents/families play a significant role in this problem—and the solution. In presenting the major achievement gap correlates, six home correlates were reported by Barton and Coley (2009), and although all are not reiterated throughout this chapter, there is no intent to imply that each correlate is tangential to the parents/families of gifted Black children who are underachieving and underrepresented in gifted and AP classes.

The parents/families of gifted students have received attention in the gifted education literature. The focus of this research has varied, but common issues include attention to family dynamics, sibling rivalry and relations, social-emotional issues with peers, parenting styles, sources of intelligence, effects of labeling, preventing underachievement, and concerns regarding how best to understand, cope with, and meet gifted children's academic, social, affective, and psychological needs. A resounding finding is that the presence of a gifted child in the family can be a stressful event, one that changes in many ways the dynamics of the family (as is the case with other children with special or exceptional needs).

As indicated later in this chapter, much of this work on families of gifted children has limited generalizability or validity to families of gifted Black children. This limited generalizability exists for at least three reasons: (a) differential family structures or composition between Black and White families; (b) differential childrearing practices between the two groups; and (c) differential life experiences that have quantitatively and qualitatively varied implications for gifted Black children and those responsible for them. The noticeable absence of research and literature on the parents/families of gifted Black students raises several important questions:

- ❖ How do Black families/caregivers differ from White families in structure or composition, and what are the educational implications for gifted Black children?
- ❖ What are the primary concerns of parents/families relative to meeting the specific educational, cultural, social, and psychological needs and development of gifted Black children?
- ❖ What do we know, or how much do we know, about the concerns and needs of Black families with gifted children?
- ❖ What dynamics in Black families influence the achievement of gifted Black students (e.g., childrearing practices, achievement orientation, school and school involvement, identity development)?
- ❖ What factors inside schools pose barriers to Black parent/family involvement? What are some strategies for culturally responsive involvement?

I know of no educator who does not believe that parent/family involvement has a positive effect on their children's achievement and school success. However, Black parent/family involvement is a thorny, contentious issue. Educators seem to want such involvement, but mainly on their own terms and on their turf. They often set the agenda, dates, times, and activities for "involvement" (e.g., meetings, conferences, events, due dates), and appear to rarely seek input about what is desired, needed, and possible from caregivers with less social, cultural, and economic privilege and capital.

This chapter presents an overview of timely scholarship on the achievement gap relative to Black caregivers. This discussion is followed by a focus on families of gifted children, highlighting major issues, themes, concerns, and recommendations. No attempt is made to present an exhaustive review of the literature on either gifted children and their families, or on Black students and their families, as space is limited. This discussion continues with research and literature on Black families with gifted children. Given the paucity of empirical and theoretical work on Black families who have formally identified gifted children, the next part of the chapter draws implications from gifted education and urban education to highlight some of the major concerns and needs of Black families with gifted children. Finally, recommendations for families, educators, and researchers are offered. Several premises guide this chapter, many of which are discussed by C. Banks (2010), who shares a notion of family involvement that I espouse:

> Many of these concerns derive from a limited view of the possibilities for parent involvement. Frequently, when parents and teachers think of parent involvement, they think it pertains to doing something for the school generally at the school or having the school teach parents how to become better parents. In today's ever-changing society, a traditional view of parent involvement inhibits rather than encourages parents and teachers to work together. Traditional ideas about parent involvement have a built in gender and social-class bias and can be a barrier to men and low-income parents. (p. 425)

The next premise is that it is dangerous, erroneous, and unproductive to assume or presume that many or most low-income, low-SES, and Black parents/families do not have a vested interest in their children and education. Although the adage "misery loves company" may have merit—depending on the circumstance—few, if any, caregivers want their children to be failures in school and life. And should caregivers (from any group) not want the best for their children, it is likely that there are extenuating circumstances—that they are mentally unstable or otherwise unfit to be parents/families. This is *not* the traditional low-income, low-SES, or Black family.

The third premise is that parent/family involvement is influenced by the attitudes and beliefs held by school personnel, not just about involvement but about those who come from backgrounds different from their own. When Blacks sense they are not welcome or feel unappreciated, they are less likely to be involved (C. Banks, 2010; Boutte, 1992).

A fourth premise is that traditional views and models of parent/family involvement are exclusionary and riddled with negative stereotypes about Black, low-income, and/or low-SES families; they rarely include a focus on nontraditional family structures, and their values and needs. Such inaccuracy and negativity is counterproductive to the educational enterprise; no one (students, parents/families, or educators) benefits with such a mindset and attendant learning environment *and* school climate.

A fifth premise is that school personnel can and must work proactively to ensure both family involvement and engagement. Excuses aside, I am convinced that educators are more than capable of creating schools that are welcoming to, supportive of, and collaborative with those who are legally responsible for taking care of children when they have not just the desire and commitment, but also the *opportunity*, to do so.

QUESTIONS TO CONSIDER

❖ What terms are more inclusive at capturing the range of family structures?

❖ How diverse are Black families?

❖ What are the strengths of Black families, even when low income?

❖ What practices in families contribute to or exacerbate underachievement?

❖ What practices in families promote achievement?

❖ Why must families and schools collaborate to prevent underachievement and to increase achievement among capable Black students?

FAMILIES AND THE ACHIEVEMENT GAP: AN OVERVIEW

Low-income parents are often among the strongest supporters of education because they often see it as a means to a better life for their children. However, their definition and understanding of "support for education" may be different from that of the school staff.

—C. Banks (2010, p. 425)

As discussed in the introductory chapter, Barton and Coley (2009) identified the top 16 correlates of the achievement gap that were placed into three categories or clusters. To reiterate, the family correlates were as follows.

PARENT-STUDENT RATIO

The extent to which parents or primary caregivers are available to and spend quality time with their children varies by family structure and composition. A larger percentage of Black students compared to White students live in single-parent homes, and many of these are low income and/or low SES. When parent/caregiver presence is low, students are left to make choices for themselves. This lack of supervision results in less structure and discipline for students; they may not spend their unsupervised time studying and/or participating in school-related activities, causing them to fall further behind White students.

PARENT PARTICIPATION

The extent to which parents/families are involved in their children's education affects students' achievement and behavior. Reports indicate that Black parents/families tend to participate less in their children's education at school than others. As with findings regarding lack of parent/family availability, student achievement suffers.[1]

STUDENT MOBILITY

There are many negative consequences to changing schools. Black students, especially those who live in poverty, have the highest rates of changing schools. Data indicate that almost half of students who change schools frequently are below grade level in reading and one-third are below grade level in math. The many studies and discussions by Lubienski (e.g., 2001, 2007; Lubienski & Bowen, 2000) shed substantive insight on this problem in math and related areas.

---

1   C. Banks (2010) noted that "perhaps the most important way schools can work with low-income parents is to recognize that they can contribute a great deal to their children's education. Even though their contribution may not be in the manner traditionally associated with parent involvement, they can be very beneficial to teachers and students" (p. 438).

SPEAKING, WRITING, AND READING

I am of the belief that literacy is the key to all other learning—math, science, social studies, history, art, and music. Reading positively correlates with language acquisition, literacy development, test scores, and achievement. It is an unfortunate reality that Black caregivers tend to read to and talk to their children less often than caregivers from White and other racial groups. This ongoing reality has historical roots dating back to American slavery on the one hand and culture on the other. It cannot be denied or trivialized that slaves were denied during slavery and after, the right to an education, including reading. Even with *Brown v. Board of Education* in 1954 and the Civil Rights Act of 1964, Blacks were denied a free, equal, and appropriate education, including the right to literacy. Legally, in practice and in philosophy, Blacks were prohibited from having access to this key developmental and lifelong asset. Thus, if and when Black caregivers desired to read to their children, they themselves may not have had the resources and skills to do so. And for those Black families (often higher income and educated) who knew (and know) the power of literacy, there was, has been, and is now rightful anger, frustration, and resentment.

The consequences of poor reading, writing, and speaking skills are serious and long term, with gifted Black students subsequently performing poorer on intelligence and achievement tests, and having difficulty keeping up in other subject areas.

EXCESSIVE TV WATCHING

Excessive and unsupervised TV watching negatively affects students' achievement, with students doing less homework and reading, and participating in fewer afterschool and intellectually stimulating activities.

SUMMER ACHIEVEMENT GAINS/LOSS

Students who do not continue their learning over the summer are likely to fall behind those who do. Much of what was learned in school can be lost during these 3 months. Unfortunately, low-income and low-SES families are less likely to have the resources and skills to provide educational opportunities for their children, which contributes to academic attrition and underrepresentation. Caregivers who have sought out summer programs know the expenses and costs involved.

FAMILIES WITH GIFTED CHILDREN: AN OVERVIEW

Coleman (1987) noted that mass formal schooling has a short history in that it barely existed until the 20th century. Until this time, children grew up in the context of the household and the immediate community. All of the activities and training of children were confined to on-the-job training, which was closely linked to household activities. For many children, then, the family and community constituted their "school," as continues to be the case in Third World or underdeveloped countries. With this in mind, it is little wonder that families, both then and now, represent a significant factor in the educational, cultural, social, and psychological well-being of their children.

Families are critical variables in the translation of talent, ability, and promise into achievement. They provide the context for the transmission of values through direct and indirect behaviors and modeling, including the importance of hard work, success, effort, independence, and self-sufficiency (Boutte, 1999; Franklin, 1988; Kulieke & Olszewski-Kubilius, 1989; McAdoo & Younge, 2009; Olszewski, Kulieke, & Buescher, 1987). Parents/families also play a major role in talent development by selecting and providing opportunities for children; by monitoring, organizing, and prioritizing children's time; and setting, communicating, and reinforcing standards for performance and achievement.

Bloom (1985) emphasized that parents who hold high expectations and achievement standards for their gifted children exert pressures for them to achieve by stressing a strong and positive work ethic and by valuing intellectual endeavors, success, ambition, and diligence. As Sanborn (1979) contended, it goes without saying that parents/families play a powerful role in the development of children. For better or worse, the capacities and proclivities of children reflect the impact and resources of parents/families. In essence, parents/families provide the initial and basic climate for learning in the home and school. But learning does not stop here.

A reading of the gifted education literature reveals that the concerns of parents/families of gifted children are numerous (Morawska & Sanders, 2009). General concerns include feelings of personal inadequacy, frustration, and helplessness in meeting the various needs of their children (e.g., lack of financial resources and support; lack of understanding and experience); feeling threatened by their children's abilities; feeling guilty when their children experience social and psychological concerns or are not readily accepted by their peers; being fearful of what giftedness means and its long-term implications; and holding unrealistic expectations for their children. These various issues, described below, have one common denominator: preventing underachievement among gifted students, regardless of its severity and manifestation. And should underachievement be a problem, the concern is on reversing it.

Labeling Issues

Notions of what is gifted or not varies across cultures, and Black parents/families generally feel ambivalent about labeling their children as gifted. Contrary to some beliefs, most parents/families do not pray to have gifted children (Silverman, 1993). Parents/families' feelings and reactions may vacillate from denial to overidentification (Sebring, 1983). In this latter situation, parents/families may live vicariously through their gifted children, seeing giftedness as a status symbol, or even exploiting their talents, ability, and skills. The children's abilities and accomplishments become the family's primary concern; family members forget that gifted children are "children with gifted abilities." This narcissism or overinvestment (Cornell, 1989) can have a debilitating influence on students' achievement and identity, resulting in perfectionism and underachievement, for example.

Giftedness is a family affair (Morawska & Sanders, 2009; Silverman, 1993), thus, having a gifted child can also negatively affect marital relations, particularly when parents/families hold oppositional perceptions of giftedness (e.g., one parent perceives the child's giftedness as a burden and the other sees it as an asset). Cornell (1989) noted such problems when one parent perceives giftedness as achievement and the other perceives it as developmental differences (i.e., inheritance).

When only one child in the family is formally identified as gifted, siblings not identified as gifted may feel neglected and may have lowered self-esteem and/or academic self-concept. If the nongifted[2] child is older than the gifted child, he or she may feel resentful; when both are gifted, competition, resentment, and anxiety may occur (Keirouz, 1990).

2   I prefer to not use the term *nongifted* as it can be viewed as elitist and otherwise communicates that giftedness can be dichotomized—gifted or not. This simplifies the notion of gifted.

Having a child identified as gifted also impacts the family's adaptability and cohesion (Morawska & Sanders, 2009; West, Hosie, & Mathews, 1989). Adaptability, which ranges from rigid to chaotic, represents the family's ability or skills to be flexible to changes in its power structure, role relationships, and family rules in response to the context or situation. Cohesion, which ranges from disengaged to enmeshed, represents the degree to which members of the family are separated from or connected to each other. It is generally assumed that balanced families are more effective at nurturing and sustaining their children's achievement. Findings by West and colleagues (1989) indicated that most (86%) of the parents/families of gifted children sampled were balanced (in the midrange on the variables) in terms of family functioning. The findings are generalizable, however, only to intact families—the focus of the study—and the extent to which these findings hold external validity to Black families is questionable.

EDUCATIONAL NEEDS

In a review of the literature, Colangelo (1988) identified common questions and concerns of parents/families of gifted students. Many of these concerns related to meeting students' educational needs, understanding and addressing their social and psychological adjustment, determining appropriate placement (e.g., the benefits of gifted education versus regular education curricula), working effectively with school personnel, and providing appropriate stimulation at home.

Kaufmann and Sexton (1983) surveyed parents of gifted students regarding their primary concerns. The responses of parents/families of students at three school levels (preschool, grades 1–6, and grades 7–12) were summarized. Noteworthy is that one third of parents/families with children at all of the levels expressed dissatisfaction regarding their children's needs being met in school. In terms of specific academic needs, parents of children in formal schooling (grades 1–6 and 7–12) did not believe that their students were challenged intellectually in school (61% for parents of elementary students; 39.9% for parents/families of children in junior high and high school, respectively); 46.4% and 27.4%, respectively, did not believe that their children's social needs were being met; 51% and 33.1% did not believe that material was covered in depth; 48.3% and 31.2% did not consider learning opportunities were being adequately met; 52.1% and 34.2% were not satisfied with enrichment experiences;

and 58.1% and 36.5% did not believe their children's higher level needs were being met in school. The concerns of parents/families with pre-school children were distributed somewhat evenly across the variables. Racial differences, while worthy of investigation, were not reported.

UNDERACHIEVEMENT

Green, Fine, and Tollefson (1988) studied the families of 45 under-achieving gifted males. Gifted students were identified as those scoring in the top 2% on the WISC-R or Stanford-Binet; underachievers were identified using one of three criteria: (a) earning a C or below in one or more major academic subjects; (b) having at least a one-year difference between expected and actual performance on a standardized achieve-ment tests; or (c) failing to complete work or submitting incomplete work at least 25% of the time as indicated by teacher records. The authors con-cluded that family relations and other adjustment issues play a central role in underachievement. Specifically, family stress and conflict, poor communication, overemphasis on dependence, and low parent achieve-ment orientations were identified by gifted underachieving males as major adjustment issues. Thus, the majority of the families were con-sidered dysfunctional as perceived by their underachieving gifted male children. The findings of Green and colleagues, however, lack generaliz-ability because of the homogeneous nature of the sample—participants included only male students in nuclear and middle- and high-SES fami-lies. Further, the definition of giftedness in particular was exclusive and narrow (based on unidimensional definition and one criterion—often a cutoff score from one test).

Rimm and Lowe (1988) studied the family environments of 22 underachieving gifted students. As with other studies (Bloom, 1985; Kerr, Colangelo, Maxey, & Christensen, 1992), male underachiev-ers considerably outnumbered females. Rimm and Lowe reported that underachieving gifted students often had families characterized by inconsistent expectations, organization, and structure. Parent relations were oppositional, sibling rivalry was extreme, and relationships were negative. The children tended to view their parents as inconsistent, weak, and manipulable. Further, although parents/families of underachievers showed concern about their children's achievement, they did not promote intrinsic and independent learning, nor did they model positive com-mitment to a career or respect for school to the same extent as parents/

families of achieving gifted students. Qualitative differences in enrichment activities were also noted, with underachievers having a plethora of activities and lessons that were so time-consuming as to leave little room for independent projects and intrinsic home learning. Other barriers to achievement included the direct opposition of parents/families to teachers and school policies.

FAMILY STRUCTURE

Families are more diverse and different in structure/composition than ever before. All families, whether or not they have children identified as gifted, are experiencing major changes in family structure due to divorce, widowhood, separation, teen pregnancy, and other variables. There is limited research on gifted children in single-parent families, even though at least 1 in 4 children under the age of 18 live with only one parent. Data indicate that some 50% of all children will live in a single-parent family for at least some part of their childhood (Demo & Acock, 1991; U.S. Census Bureau, 2006). Parents raising grandchildren are on the rise, mainly in Black families (see Pearson, Hunter, Ensminger, & Kellam, 1990; Strom, Collinsworth, Strom, Griswold, & Strom, 1992).

It seems to be a common assumption that children in nuclear families and middle- and high-income and high-SES families have more academically successful students than those from low-income and/or low-SES levels. Little is known about children who are gifted and poor (VanTassel-Baska & Stambaugh, 2007) relative to their concerns, needs, and desires, but we do know that higher income and higher SES students are well-represented in gifted education and their caregivers tend to be assertive, well-resourced advocates for them. For example, the U.S. Department of Education (1993) reported that higher SES students represent 44% of students in gifted programs nationally, compared to 25% of lower SES students. Some studies reveal even lower percentages. Specifically, VanTassel-Baska and Willis (1987) reported that 15% of gifted students in their study were low SES; in a different study, VanTassel-Baska (1989) reported a figure of 20% for the representation of low-SES gifted students. The underrepresentation of low-income and low-SES students is significant given that at least 50% of students live in poverty, namely Black and Hispanic students (VanTassel-Baska, 2010; VanTassel-Baska & Stambaugh, 2007).

DeVaul and Davis (1988) also reported that children in single-parent families are less likely than students in nuclear families to be identified as gifted. A study of children who attended the University of Oregon's Summer Enrichment Program for Talented and Gifted Students suggested that the school achievement of gifted students is negatively affected if they come from a single-parent household (Gelbrich & Hare, 1989). One explanation for these two findings is that single-parent status and poverty often (not always) go hand-in-hand; the terms are almost synonymous to some scholars and laypersons. Although there is an inverse but meaningful correlation between poverty and achievement, caution is necessary to avoid causation and deficit thinking or any form of blaming the victim and denying social injustices (see Chapter 6). Black students in either or both circumstances are often discriminated against by educators in terms of lowered teacher expectations, neglect, and humiliation (Zill, 1983). Low-income and low-SES students and students in single-parent families are referred less often by teachers to gifted education for identification, which contributes to their poor representation in gifted and AP classes (see Ford et al., 2008a; McBee, 2006).

Albeit dated, Gelbrich and Hare (1989) conducted one of few studies on gifted students in single-parent families. They surveyed the parents of 10- to 16-year-old students in a summer enrichment program. Parents rated their feelings of agreement or disagreement to 32 items that focused on school achievement, peer relations, and characteristics associated with achievement. The authors concluded that a negative relationship existed between school achievement and single parenthood. For instance, single parents rated their children lower in achievement than their peers. They also found that males were more negatively affected by single parenthood than females, primarily due to single-parent families being headed most often by females. This lack of a father figure may translate into fewer role models for gifted Black males. However, the external validity of this study is questionable for several reasons: (a) comparisons by income and SES were ignored; (b) no mention of the sample demographics relative to race was provided; (c) no family demographic data were provided (e.g., race, gender, educational level, composition); (d) exclusive attention was given to family structure rather than family dynamics and processes; and (e) the likelihood of students in a summer enrichment program underachieving is rather slim given the often stringent admissions criteria.

Rogers and Nielson (1993) conducted a review of the literature on the incidence of divorce in families of gifted children. They found a noticeable paucity of attention to this issue in both theoretical and data-based work. Only five articles could be located using the descriptors of "gifted and divorced" in their search; a couple of articles were peripheral to the topic. Only by broadening their search to children of divorce in general, teacher expectations, and teacher and peer perceptions of divorce were Rogers and Nielson able to find additional sources.

In Terman's (1925) seminal longitudinal research on gifted students, conducted at a time when issues regarding Black students and equity were of little interest and commitment, only 10.8% of the parents/families had divorced, separated, or widowed at some point in the study. Barbe (1956) conducted a retrospective study of gifted students in the Major Work Program in Cleveland and found that almost 7% reported that their parents/families were divorced, and 5% of single-parent status was due to widowhood. One of the 12 students in Hollingworth's (1942) longitudinal study lived in a single-parent family due to parental separation, and in Sheldon's (1954) study, three of 28 students had lived in a divorced family at some point in their life.

Despite the inevitable differences in family structure, these researchers did not specifically focus on this variable. In addition, only one article (Gelbrich & Hare, 1989) specifically addressed gifted students in single-parent families. Thus, research on the family structures of gifted students has not kept pace with realities and the times—the increase in diverse family structures has not been accompanied by an increase in research on these families. Thus, our knowledge base about gifted children living in single-parent families, whether a function of choice, divorce, widowhood, or separation, is virtually nonexistent. Based on this limited data, inaccurate conclusions have been drawn, as witnessed by Keirouz (1990) who stated that "overall, the percentage of parents/families of the gifted who have stable marriages is at least as good (if not better) than the national average" (p. 57), based on roughly five studies (discussed above), several with as few as 12 gifted students. This is not to say that gifted children who live in single-parent families are not gifted; only that their family structures have not been studied.

Researchers have taken a piecemeal approach to studying gifted children and their families. They have focused almost exclusively on: (a) issues (e.g., concerns, fears) in isolation of processes (e.g., child-rearing practices, achievement orientations, socialization); (b) parents/caregivers rather than families; and (c) homogenous families rather than heterogeneous families relative to composition and structure, race, and socioeconomic status. Zuccone and Amerikaner's (1986) review of the literature concluded that the level of family functioning may be more relevant to the treatment of underachieving behaviors than income, SES, family size, and other characteristics. That is, the difficulties of gifted under-achievers may be understood best as a part of the larger family context, for this is the context within which the most significant transactions occur. However, only with a comprehensive study of family processes and functioning, as well as demographic variables, can we gain a thorough understanding of gifted students and their families.

Conspicuously absent from the literature just cited on families of gifted children is attention to Black and other minority families. Although gender differences were discussed in some of the studies, none of those cited above (and few in gifted education at large) address the concerns of Black families and their gifted children. The following sec-tion addresses these shortcomings. It is contended that Black families are quantitatively and qualitatively different from White families. These dif-ferences are evident not only in their experiences, but also family struc-ture and composition, child-rearing practices, educational involvement, achievement orientations, and demographic variables.

BLACK FAMILIES: AN OVERVIEW

Black families are like any other family institution in that it wants the best that life has to offer educationally, financially, spiritually, politically and socially for its members. Simultaneously, it is unlike any other family due to its unique status imposed by the deep structure (warf and woof of racism) of the American social system. Black families have not been entirely free to manipulate the essen-tial components of life to the same degree as have their White counterparts.
—Jenkins (1989, p. 139)

Unfortunately, the blame game is common in schools and families—and the larger community. Too few caregivers own up to their role in stu-dents not doing well; too few educators acknowledge that they may have miseducated and marginalized gifted Black students and their families. Underachievement among Black students has frequently been attributed to or blamed on their culture, families, and communities. Calabrese (1990) stated:

Public school officials refuse to identify the American educational process itself as discriminatory. Instead, armed with research findings, they continue to blame the victims of discrimination, suggesting that poor environmental circumstances produce disadvantaged students who are thus predisposed to second-class status and failure. (p. 148)

Given the high rates of school failure, underachievement, illiteracy, and dropout rates among Blacks, social and behavioral scientists have begun to explore more diligently and responsibly the role that families play in children's school success or failure. One goal of this work has been to demythesize misperceptions or negative perceptions of Black families, including:

- ❖ Black parents/families are homogeneous; regardless of income, SES, and structure, they hold the same beliefs, attitudes, and values, and display the same behaviors.
- ❖ Black parents/families have little to no interest in their children's education.
- ❖ Parents/families who do not become involved in the schools are not interested in their children's educational well-being.
- ❖ The matriarchical structure of Black families is dysfunctional.
- ❖ Grandparents/families and other extended family members are ancillary to the educational process; they provide economical rather than educational or academic support.

Renzulli, Reis, Hébert, and Diaz (1994) noted that the priority many Black students place on their family relations and responsibilities may negatively affect the development of talent among this group. The importance of families to the social and psychological health of Black students has been explored by Billingsley (1968), Boyd-Franklin (2003), Clark (1983), Goodwin and King (2002), Hill (1971), McAdoo and McAdoo (1985), McAdoo and Younge (2009), Staples and Johnson (1993), Wilson (1986, 1989), and others. Extended families and fictive kinships, in particular, represent an important and consistent source of support in these students' lives—they provide financial independence, psychological support, and educational encouragement to its members (e.g., Manning & Baruth, 2010). As such, extended families help blunt social and socioeconomic injustices and hardships; in the process, they promote self-efficacy, self-esteem, racial identity and pride, and self-reliance among Blacks (Ford, 1993b, 1993c, 1996; Ford, Harris, & Turner, 1990/1991).

A considerable portion of research on the "pathology" of Black families appeared in the 1960s, but has by no means decreased or disappeared. These studies primarily compared Black families with White families using data gathered on the latter group. Holding the nuclear family as the norm and as healthy, even though it represents only 30% of all U.S. families (McAdoo & Younge, 2009), researchers proceeded to label extended families as pathological and otherwise abnormal. Not surprisingly, a cultural deficit perspective emerged from this era. Low-income, low-SES, extended, and/or matriarchical families were equated with low achievement orientations rather than viewed as strengths and sources of support for members. Too often, a negative stereotype is that poverty is analogous to lacking ambition and motivation (Manning & Baruth, 2010). Essentially, Black families became both the victims of and accountable for the circumstances of their children—with educators being exonerated for their negative roles and impact. For example, the famous but controversial Moynihan Report (Moynihan, 1965) blamed the "pathology" of the Black family on the "inability" of Black fathers to find steady employment and to achieve at higher levels academically. The report, however, failed to probe the many past and current factors associated with social injustices, like racism and discrimination, that have played (and still play) a significant role in chronic unemployment and underemployment; it also failed to examine the social circumstances and realities of life for Blacks in the United States: racism, stereotypes, discrimination, and prejudice. In summary, in issuing a general or umbrella indictment of Black families, Moynihan (1965) indicted all Blacks; the family replaced IQ in determining the children's learning potential (Slaughter & Epps, 1987). This has had multiple influences: (a) it invited a general denial of social injustices that persists and prevails in the U.S. and our schools, (b) it invited and fueled a denial of the heterogeneity of Blacks and their culture, and (c) it encouraged and promoted an almost total disregard for individual and within-group differences among Blacks and their family structures. Clark (1983) maintained:

> Practically all of the empirical research done to date has reported statistically significant relationships between "family background" and American children's achievement levels. Unfortunately, none of these studies analyze the total form and substance of family life. Rather they tend to focus on surface characteristics (such as parents' occupation, education, family size, and material possessions) . . . while virtually ignoring the framework of psychological orientation and activity patterns that more closely represent the life blood of the family interpersonal experience. (p. 7)

In a more recent report, the New America Media (2007) surveyed White Americans as well as racially and culturally different groups about race relations in the U.S. More than any other group, Black respondents were less likely to believe that the American Dream is applicable to them. Blacks also feel more segregated than do other groups and express stronger feelings about isolation and facing barriers to their success. Sadly, but not necessarily surprising, the report revealed that other groups have negative stereotypes about Blacks.

The nuclear family—traditionally comprised of a married mother and father and their children—has represented the "ideal," "normal," or "typical" family pattern in the United States, until recently (see McAdoo, 1988, 1993; McAdoo & Younge, 2009; U.S. Census Bureau, 2006; Wilson, 1986). That is, the general notion of "family" is associated most frequently with two parents/families and their dependent children. This is not necessarily the typical model today, as indicated by McAdoo and Younge (2009). However, this value in the nuclear families persists, so that those in different family structures are often stereotyped or devalued. On this note, Ford (1994a) surveyed almost 500 college students majoring in education or family studies regarding their definitions and perceptions of different family structures (e.g., nuclear, extended, single parent). Results indicated that the vast majority of the students, most of whom were White, higher income females from nuclear families, held traditional notions of families that included a husband, wife, and offspring. Students were less likely to perceive extended, cohabiting, and single parents as legitimate family types/structures.

Many societies and cultures eschew the nuclear family as the family arrangement to be emulated, imitated, or idealized. There are, indeed, benefits to growing up with two caregivers. Yet, among Blacks, extended families are quite common. Anderson and Allen (1984) reported that Blacks are twice as likely as Whites to have grandmothers in residence, and the majority of grandmother-headed households are Black (Donenberg, 2004). Yet, as Wilson (1989) observed, the importance of the extended family in influencing child development has been largely ignored because the normative nuclear family definition of family necessarily implied that the extended family was not a legitimate phenomenon of American family life.

It cannot be emphasized enough that our nation's changing demographics require professionals, especially family scientists and educators, to be ever more mindful of the family arrangement in which Black and other children are reared. One cannot, for example, view the relationship between grandmothers and their grandchildren, or cohabiting couples and their children, in isolation and as substandard.

Based on demographic projections, society can expect to see even greater numbers of diverse families in the future. The major demographic shifts underway suggest that, as a society, we should question our notions of the ideal family when such a family is on its way toward extinction. For Blacks, the nuclear family tends to offer an inadequate survival or pragmatic nurturing strategy. Rather, extended families increase the chances for improving gifted Black and underachieving students' situations. Black families have been increasingly called upon to use available family members as resources to minimize the effects of environmental stress such as poverty, racism, and discrimination. Needless to say, for Blacks, the family system is, as it must be, quite fluid or adaptive. As described in the following sections, extended families serve as an important coping and survival mechanism for children and family members.

SINGLE-PARENT FAMILIES

Data indicate that Blacks have the highest percentage of teenage pregnancy of any racial group and that approximately half of all Black children are born to single mothers (Waxman, 1992; U.S. Census Bureau, 2006). Moreover, many Black children under the age of 3 do not live with both parents. Other data indicate that at least half of all Black children live with female heads of household (U.S. Census Bureau, 2006). More specifically, McAdoo and Younge (2009) reported, using Census data, that: 34% of African Americans are married; 22% are widowed, divorced, or separated; and approximately 4 out of every 10 African American men and women have never been married, the highest proportion of any racial category.

Despite the increasing numbers of single parents, Crawley (1988) contended that this family composition is severely threatened because of the problems attendant to being single, being a parent, and belonging to a racial minority group. For teenage mothers, a grandmother's presence tends to buffer or partially ameliorate the negative consequences of child rearing (García Coll, Sepkoski, & Lester, 1981; McAdoo & Younge, 2009; Nobles, 1985; Strom et al., 1992; Strom, Strom, Collinsworth, & Griwsold, 1993; Tinsley & Parke, 1984). Grandmothers, in many instances, become the primary caregivers. These grandparents, therefore, provide gifted Black and/or underachieving students with social and psychological support, as well as academic support.

POVERTY

Despite what many allege to be the positive gains of the 1960s and 1970s, the problems of poverty and racial oppression continue to plague large numbers or percentages of Blacks (Staples, 1986, 1987). Studying the dimensions of poverty, Duncan found that between 1979 and 1985, the poverty rate for Blacks increased from 30% to 41% (as cited in McLoyd, 1990). In 2006, the U.S. Census Bureau reported that approximately half of all Black children were poor. Regardless of the specific numbers and percentages, poverty comprises an immediate reality of life for Black children, many of whom, statistically speaking, must be gifted.

Poverty represents one of the most pernicious effects of a society stratified by income and socioeconomic status. Undeniably, the impact of poverty is destructive, and these effects manifest themselves earnestly in educational and social milieus. The correlation between income and SES with IQ has been established, but more work is needed relative to race and gender. That is to say, data and speculation need to be disaggregated by the combination of poverty, race, and gender (e.g., poor Black males vs. poor Black females vs. poor White males vs. poor White females).

For a myriad of reasons, students in poverty are severely underrepresented in gifted education programs, representing only 11% of those being served (U.S. Department of Education, 1993; also see VanTassel-Baska & Stambaugh, 2007), not only due to problems that permeate the screening and identification process (e.g., referral and testing), but also due to lack of learning opportunities that money, education, and social and cultural capital provide. For the sake of argument, placing race temporarily aside, students in poverty, specifically, are likely to have nutritional, neurological, and other health problems that contribute to mental retardation, physical disabilities, and developmental delays, for example (see Barton, 2003; Barton & Coley, 2009). They also have less access to enrichment opportunities and learning experiences at home, at school, during the academic year, and during the summer than higher income and higher SES students. Even when such learning experiences exist among low-income and/or low-SES families, they tend to be quantitatively and qualitatively different from high-income and/or high-SES families. For example, high-income and high-SES parents/families tend to have higher educational levels, which translate into more academic know-how regarding what to teach their children, the learning experiences necessary for their children's school success, and increased contact with school personnel (e.g., parent-teacher organizations, school boards). Research on gifted children and their families highlight the extent to which higher income and higher SES parents/families, particularly those who are White, ensure, by any means necessary, that their children's gifts are found, valued, developed, and nurtured:

❖ Parents/families seek special instruction and effective teachers for their children. For example, they work with role models, mentors, and tutors for training, advice, and guidance; parents/families themselves serve as role models.

❖ Parents/families encourage participation in events and activities that display and otherwise showcase their children's abilities (e.g., competitions, recitals, contests, concerts).

❖ Parents/families provide encouragement for children to explore interests; small signs of interest and capability are encouraged, rewarded, and nurtured.

❖ Parents/families use both formal and informal opportunities to develop children's abilities and interests; they endeavor to make learning interesting, engaging, and fun.

❖ Parents/families hold high expectations for children; they expect children to have a talent area(s) and to excel in the area(s). This expectation is accompanied by specific opportunities for students' abilities to develop (e.g., clear schedules for practice, as well as guidelines and timelines for achieving objectives and goals).

In a seminal study dating several decades ago, Clark (1983) studied low-income Black students' achievement and underachievement in the context of their family. Achieving Black children had parents who: (a) were assertive in their parent involvement efforts; (b) kept abreast of their child's school progress; (c) were optimistic and tended to perceive themselves as having effective coping mechanisms and strategies; (d) set high and realistic expectations for their children; (e) held positive achievement orientations and supported tenets of the achievement ideology; (f) set clear, explicit achievement-oriented norms; (g) established clear, specific role boundaries; (h) deliberately engaged in experiences and behaviors designed to promote achievement; and (i) had positive parent-child relations characterized by nurturance, support, respect, trust, and open communication. Conversely, underachieving Black children had parents who: (a) were less optimistic and expressed feelings of helplessness and hopelessness; (b) were less assertive and involved in their children's education; (c) set unrealistic and unclear expectations for their children; and (d) were less confident in terms of parenting/caregiving skills.

Around this same time, Lee's (1984) research with rural Black adolescents and their families also revealed eight psychosocial variables that contributed to students' academic success: (a) close family relations and structure, (b) high degree of parental control, (c) moderate to high degrees of family openness, (d) strong family values, (e) high level of educational encouragement and achievement orientation, (f) good relations with siblings, (f) extended family networks, and (g) a sense of responsibility fostered through required chores. Similarly, MacLeod's (1995) research on low-income Black males indicated that achievement-oriented students had parents who set clear, high, and realistic expectations for their sons. They encouraged their sons to achieve and to support the achievement ideology of hard work and effort.

In essence, whereas all parents, regardless of income and SES levels, want to provide stimulating, directive, supportive, and rewarding environments for their children, higher income and higher SES parents/families have more capital—they have the fiscal and social means to provide their children with such opportunities. In general, it is valid to assume that many Black families may be more survival-oriented than child-centered due to economic and social hardships; the need to survive may mitigate against a child-centered approach to childrearing and to family involvement, yet children are the most precious resources of Black families (Slaughter & Kuehne, 1988). In essence, too often we view Black parents/families as being "good" or "not so good," without fully considering the circumstances of their lives and the social injustices that they face and must cope with in past and contemporary America: "Black children have always borne a disproportionate share of the burden of poverty and economic decline in America and they are at substantially higher risk than White children for experiencing an array of social-psychological problems" (McLoyd, 1990, p. 311).

Clark (1983) concluded that the form and substance of the family psychosocial patterns are the most significant components for understanding the educational effects of high achievers' families and low achievers' families, not their race or social class background per se. That is, family processes and culture rather than structural and demographic variables determine the achievement orientation of Black children (Clark, 1983). Quality of life is not always determined by family composition, marital status, income, and the educational level of parents. Neither are educational outcomes necessarily determined by these social and demographic variables.

BLACK FAMILIES AND GIFTED CHILDREN

As stated earlier, formally identified gifted students tend to have high-income or high-SES family backgrounds and live in nuclear families. Does this mean that giftedness resides most in high-income, high-SES, and nuclear families, or that higher income and higher SES levels and nonminority status increase one's chances of being identified and placed in gifted programs? Tannenbaum (1983) proposed that chance variables (environmental support and luck) play an important role in the identification of gifted students. Bowles and Gintis (1976) noted that the cultural capital—the many unearned and taken for granted privileges—of higher income and higher SES groups, and White students and families specifically, are more valued and revered in education (and society at large) than those of low-income, low-SES, Black, and racially and culturally different students. White and higher income and higher SES students are most likely to receive (unearned) optimal educational experiences due to wealth, power, and privilege (McIntosh, 1988, 1992), and a disproportionate number will be referred for and/or identified as in need of gifted education services or AP classes.

Black parents/families often experience crises regarding their children's education. Said another way, for a larger number of Black parents/caregivers, there is a crisis of confidence in the schools and their children's ability to benefit from them (Calabrese, 1990; McAdoo & McAdoo, 1985; Slaughter & Kuehne, 1988). Although Black families favor schooling as a means for upward mobility and success, they often worry about the commitment and efficacy of schools to meet the social, cultural, psychological, and educational needs of their children. Many of them are alienated from schools (Calabrese, 1990), but not always by choice.

VanTassel-Baska (1989; VanTassel-Baska & Willis, 1987), Marion (1980, 1981), Davis (2009), Ford (1993b), Exum (1983), and Prom-Jackson, Johnson, and Wallace (1987) have provided basically the only work specifically on gifted Black students and their families—and this work is need of updating. Exum (1983) identified key issues of families of gifted Black children. Although written for counselors, the concerns he identified carry important implications for educators. Exum (1983) cautioned counselors against understanding gifted Black children in isolation of their family context and encouraged them to work with extended family members. Four major parental/familial concerns were described by Exum (1983): (a) the family's loss of authority and control of the gifted child; (b) the child's loss of respect for the family; (c) the child's loss of respect for the community and/or culture; and (d) the child's psychological stability and ability to interact with other people. More specifically, issues surrounding elitism and assimilation may prevail among Black parents/families, which makes placing their children in gifted and AP classes a dilemma. Black parents/families may be concerned (and rightfully so) that school curricula will be monocultural and ethnocentric—devoid of culturally relevant material needed to promote self-esteem, identity, and pride in their children. On a similar note, Black parents/families may be concerned about the schools promoting individual rather than group affiliation, and otherwise contradicting the values often characteristic of Black families. Marion (1980, 1981) noted that Black parents of gifted children may cling to the belief that children are gifted to the extent that they embody the values and beliefs highly prized by their culture. Gardner (1985), Sternberg (2007), and Sternberg and Davidson (1986) also recognized the significance of cultural and contextual definitions of giftedness.

Exum (1983) described a cycle in which Black parents may become more authoritarian in child-rearing practices as they seek to prevent forced assimilation by their children; children react by underachieving and attempting to disprove their giftedness in an effort to return the family to homeostasis. However, because the family knows that the child is gifted, it applies even more pressure to promote achievement. Ultimately, the gifted Black child may seek refuge in his or her peer group, all of which results in frustration, disappointment, and puzzlement by both the gifted child and the family.

To reiterate, other concerns of Black parents/families include student-teacher-family relations, especially the effects of teacher expectations on their children's achievement. Again, McBee (2006), Pegnato and Birch (1959), and High and Udall (1983) found that teachers underrefer Black students for gifted screening, identification, and assessment. That is, low teacher expectations for these students must certainly influence these low rates of referral. Low teacher expectations can result from inadequate training and formal experiences in gifted education and multicultural

Social Awareness and Knowledge
- Information on changing social and familial demographics

Self-Awareness
- Knowledge, attitudes, and misperceptions regarding diverse families and family involvement

Communication and Social Skills
- Modes of communication (e.g., nonverbal, verbal), including one's own style
- Effective interpersonal communication strategies/skills
- Power issues
- The art of compromise

Parents/Families' Rights
- Improving home-school relations and communication
- Types of parent/family involvement
- Personal perceptions about the types and preferences
- Strategies for increasing parent/family involvement

Figure 8.2. Professional development for involving Black parents/families in the educational process. Training should be consistent, ongoing, and based on a needs assessment from the home.

and urban education, in addition to misperceptions and preconceived notions about Black families and their children. Only when there is a marriage between nature and nurture theories of giftedness can Black parents/families hope that their children might be equitably included in gifted and AP classes (Marion, 1980). Figure 8.2 illustrates professional development for involving Black families in the educational process.

VanTassel-Baska (1989) focused on the role of families in the lives of 15 economically challenged (low income and/or low SES) gifted students, eight of whom were Black, and many who were living in single-parent families. Her findings revealed that low-income Black families held high expectations, aspirations, and standards for their children, as well as positive achievement orientations. Along with extended family members, the Black parents/families sought to promote self-competence and independence in their children. Parents/families were described as watchful of their children, hyperaware of children's accomplishments, and actively involved in developing their abilities.

The Black students studied by VanTassel-Baska (1989) most often attributed their accomplishments to maternal figures, namely mothers and grandmothers, who represented sources of social and psychological support. These maternal figures also instilled positive achievement orientations, work ethic, independence, and self-sufficiency in children. VanTassel-Baska's (1989) findings underscore the reality that children in economically impoverished families have parents/families who are more similar than different from economically advantaged families in their values; that the high and positive achievement orientations of Black, low-income, and low-SES parents/families can and do promote academic, social, and psychological resilience in children; and that family structure may play a secondary rather than primary role in gifted Black students' achievement behaviors and motivation to achieve. I have proposed this point throughout my career (e.g., Ford, 1993b, 1996, 2010; Ford et al., 2008a, 2008b; Ford, Wright, Grantham, & Harris, 1998). Strong Black families do exist and they are (and have been) quite adept at fostering resilience in their children.

Educators and researchers must study more systematically home environmental variables and their effect on Black students' achievement, a line of research that promises to explain why some Black children do well academically and others do not. I concur with Prom-Jackson and colleagues (1987) who argued for less research on family structure and configuration (e.g., single versus nuclear family), and more research on parental values and beliefs. They conducted a study of 767 minority graduates of A Better Chance, Inc. (ABC), a nonprofit educational organization that identifies academically gifted, low-SES minority students as possible candidates for college preparatory secondary schools. A little more than one fourth of the students (28%) lived with their mothers only, and 13% lived in extended families. The authors surveyed the ABC graduates regarding school experiences, academic performance, career choice and progress, perceived academic ability, leadership and athletic skills, and personality and attitudes. Information was also gathered on parents/families' educational level, occupational status, self-aspirations, family size and structure, expectations for their children, attitudes toward achievement, and encouragement for education.

Prom-Jackson and colleagues (1987) concluded that low-SES gifted minority students had parents/families of all educational levels. Parental educational level was not a good predictor of minority students' academic performance. Further, living in single-parent families did not negate the development of academic excellence and success; contrary to what might be expected based on previous research, the ABC students in single-parent families had slightly higher achievement scores than students in two-parent families. Mothers in both single- and two-parent families had the greatest impact on gifted Black students' educational achievement and self-identity. In summary,

> the evidence on parental beliefs and values suggests that in spite of social hardships and barriers, which often tend to limit achievement and social advancement, this group of parents/families must have had high aspirations for and high expectations of their children in order to have encouraged them to pursue high levels of education and to pursue challenging careers. (Prom-Jackson et al., 1987, p. 119)

This finding is consistent with the research of Clark (1983), Ford (1993b, 1993c), Lee (1984), and VanTassel-Baska (1989). For instance, Ford (1993c) reported that 18% of the Black students in her study lived in extended families with many configurations. Regardless of family structure and whether they had been identified as gifted or not, most of the students believed that their families valued achievement and gifted education.

Research on gifted Black children and their families, although limited in number, suggests the need to consider student achievement in the total context in which beliefs, aspirations, and expectations are developed and nurtured. It is through the enactment of parental ideology that the external world is buffered and filtered for children. Children's self-images and perceptions—self-esteem, self-concept, and racial identity—are formed under the auspices of the family and primary caregivers (Billingsley, 1968; Exum, 1983; Ford, 1993a, 1993b, 1993c, 1996; Hill, 1971). The significance of Black parents/families on the social, psychological, and academic health of their children carries equally important implications for their identification and assessment.

FAMILIES AND THE IDENTIFICATION OF GIFTED BLACK STUDENTS

Families—be they headed by one parent or caregiver, two parents, or extended family members—offer the greatest potential or hope for cultural cohesion, and they continue to perform the most complex, subtle, and difficult tasks associated with socialization. In addition to transmitting roles, rules, and values, families can and do assist gifted and AP program personnel in understanding the abilities and potentials of their

Black children. Few people would disagree that parents/families know their children better than anyone else, especially young children. There are more parents/families who have gifted children and do not know it than there are parents who do not have gifted children and think they do (Ginsberg & Harrison, 1977). Louis and Lewis (1992) found that 61% of parents who thought their children were gifted were correct—their children had IQ scores of 132 or higher when tested. Stated differently, parents represent one of the most potent identifiers of giftedness and creativity (Colangelo & Dettman, 1983; Davis, 2009; Feldhusen & Kroll, 1985; Ford, 1993b, 1996; Ford et al., 1998; Ford et al., 2008a; Scott, Perou, Urbano, Hogan, & Gold, 1992).

The effectiveness of parents/families in the identification of gifted students has been investigated by several researchers (e.g., Scott et al., 1992). Because testing can contribute to the most friction between schools and Black families (Marion, 1980), parents/families can provide feedback on instruments (tests, checklists, and nomination forms) for bias relative to language, questions, and illustrations. Parents/families can help to make tests, nominations, checklists, and forms more sensitive to cultural differences. Many parents/families (including middle-class White parents/families) have complained to me that some of the parent gifted education checklists and nomination forms take a Ph.D. to understand and complete.

Information on assessing noncognitive (e.g., social and psychological) variables can also be gathered from an interview with or survey from parents/families and extended family members. Exum (1983) found that issues surrounding racial identity represented an important concern of racially and culturally different parents/families. Other social and psychological issues include families' understanding of peer relations and pressures, student-teacher relations, teacher expectations, and the classroom climate.

Black parents/families (and their children) should be encouraged to visit gifted and AP classes to make a placement decision. Parental/family questions regarding the classroom climate and demographics can be addressed more fully once they have met the teacher and other students.

How might Black parents/families define a good education for their gifted children? Certainly, a good education consists of high academic standards, where students are exposed to a great deal of enriching, challenging, and relevant content. A good education also includes cultural responsiveness regarding the curriculum, instruction, and assessment. Further, parents/caregivers of Black students may define quality education from an affective and culture-centered perspective. Thus, a quality education recognizes, first and foremost, the worth of Black children as individuals, human beings, and culturally similar and different. This means that schools recognize and affirm Black children and their families. This need for affirmation and affective relations with teachers/educators has been supported by the research of Hale (2001), Hale-Benson (1986), and others who describe Black students and families as having an affective orientation characterized by social and interpersonal relations. Black families are very psychologically charged and people-oriented—a characteristic that Black children look for, expect, and desire in teachers and school/classroom environments.

When deciding upon placing their children in gifted programs or AP classes, racial composition is an important consideration for Black parents/families (Boutte, 1992). Is diversity or difference celebrated in the school, AP class, and gifted program? The answer to this question requires that parents/families visit the school and gifted program, and talk with staff, administrators, and other school personnel. Beyond such discussions, visits to the gifted program allow parents/families to see whether school personnel are racially and culturally diverse, and to see how school personnel interact with students. Do students come from more than one race and culture? Where are Black students seated? Do Black students appear comfortable and uninhibited? Are they interacting with other students, namely students from other racial and cultural groups? Do Black and other students segregate themselves racially? Do they socialize outside of the school? Are there social and educational activities that focus positively and proactively on the Black experience? Similarly, to what extent do curriculum and instruction respect diversity? To what extent are Black parents/families involved (and encouraged to be) in school decisions and committees? What efforts have been made to secure their involvement?

Parents/families who visit gifted programs also have the opportunity to listen for cultural competence. What do school personnel say about differences? Does a colorblind philosophy permeate the school? Do school personnel, particularly teachers, hold high and realistic expectations for racially and culturally different students? Do teachers welcome parents/families? Do school personnel, particularly administrators, feel comfortable with questions regarding the lack of diversity, for example, in the gifted program and AP classes? What efforts have been initiated to increase the representation of Black students in these programs or classes? How diverse or representative are teachers of gifted students, and what are their experiences in working with gifted Black students?

The significance of parents/families in nurturing the abilities and potential of their children is well established. The role of parents/families in this respect does not cease when children enter formal school, thus parents/families must become partners with teachers in the educational process. This partnership begins with parent/family empowerment, asking parents/families for their guidance and knowledge, and then using this information to ensure the successful recruitment and retention of Black students in gifted education. Without this partnership, identification, placement, and programming for gifted Black students cannot be optimal. Equally important, if gifted Black students are not identified and served, their right to appropriate education is violated. Possible outcomes may be underachievement in its many forms (e.g., poor grades, dropping out, lack of motivation, refusal to participate in AP or gifted classes).

Well-informed and empowered parents/families are intellectual consumers of information. There should be agreement or consensus that parents/families and teachers have one common denominator—their concern for the education and welfare of children (Marion, 1980). All families can benefit from information on nurturing giftedness, understanding their child's specific area of giftedness, understanding the achievement gap, recognizing underachievement and how can it be prevented or reversed, learning how to meet children's social and psychological needs, understanding developmental issues specific to gifted students (e.g., asynchronous development), and learning how to set realistic and appropriate expectations for their children relative to strengths and potential. Figure 8.3 presents an outline of parent/family education for empowerment—for understanding and working effectively with their children.

RECOMMENDATIONS

This chapter examined the topic of Black parents/families and other caregivers as adaptive, coping mechanisms for gifted and underachieving Black students. Much of the data pointed to the extended family as a problem-solving and coping system that adapts to and focuses the family resources on both normal and transitional situations and crises. In addition and more generally, it helps family members beat the odds in

- Remember that parents/families have the ultimate authority over their children for decisions. Work with rather than against parents/families to meet students' various needs.

- Be receptive to the diversity of families (e.g., single parents/families, cohabiting, nuclear). Seek to develop substantive and active parent/family involvement.

- Establish a good rapport with families; try to put family members at ease using kindness, friendliness, humor, and informality (if appropriate). Initially, communicate with parents/families when feedback is positive (as opposed to constant negative feedback). If working with underachieving gifted Black students, contact parents/families even when progress is small.

- Use clear language and avoid jargon. Avoid being overly complicated; only when both parties understand each other and issues can ideas be exchanged.

- Be genuine and sincere with parents/families. A sincere and authentic interest in Black parents/families and their children will increase their trust and self-disclosure about feelings, fears, and concerns.

- Try to empathize and avoid sympathy/pity. Try to put yourself, to the extent possible, in the place of Black parents/families.

- Understand and be aware of all means of communication, particularly your own verbal and nonverbal messages; seek consistency between the two. Nonverbal communication (e.g., facial expressions, gestures, distance, body posture, intonation) can often be more of a barrier to establishing a healthy relationship with Black parents/families than verbal messages.

- Gather as much information on the child's family as possible before talking with them. Collect data regarding demographics, educational status, occupation, and the like, so that you will understand the family's circumstances. Do not use this information to stereotype or categorize, but rather to set a tentative framework for understanding.

- Be familiar with cross-cultural child development principles; be aware of the multiplicity of factors affecting these children's behaviors and achievement.

- Identify community leaders and how they can work with parents/families on behalf of Black students and their caregivers.

- Identify resources for parents/families to help them meet students' needs (e.g., mentors, educational organizations, literature).

- Avoid being judgmental; try not to show surprise or disapproval of what parents/families say and do. Due to potential cultural differences, teachers and parents/families may have differential (and perhaps oppositional) values, beliefs, and behaviors. Make compromises with families that result in win-win situations for children.

- Be proactive and optimistic—operate from the assumption that Black parents/families have their children's best interest at heart.

- Remember that the ultimate goal of family involvement is to enhance the academic, social, and psychological well-being of children.

Figure 8.3. Suggestions for working with Black parents/families.

a nation still plagued by racial and economic injustices. Franklin (1988) persuasively stated that: "The strong family tradition among Blacks thus survived the slave system, then legal segregation, discrimination, and enforced poverty, and finally, they had to contend with racially hostile governmental and societal practices, policies, and attitudes" (p. 25).

The time is long overdue for studying more thoroughly the critical importance of Black parents/families as positive socialization agents, and examining the influences of extended family members on students' achievement. For many gifted Black students, a grandmother's or aunt's presence may make the difference between stagnation and growth, between success and failure, in a society that clings to the status quo relative to its traditional, inflexible, subjective, and narrow notions of family structure—notions often inadequate when applied to Black family arrangements.

Educators and counselors must pay closer attention to cultural family patterns, and to the reality that grandparents and other relatives often represent persons of significance for gifted Black children. Subsequently, researchers should begin to study more carefully the effects parents/families exert on the achievement of children. Along with researchers, school personnel must expand their definition of the family to include those persons of significance one typically finds in extended families. Because the family is a primary socialization agent, family processes should be examined in education and teaching preparation programs. Educators and researchers must look beyond nuclear families when examining the social, affective, psychological, and academic development of gifted Black students. Figure 8.4 presents some guidelines for working effectively with Black parents/families of gifted children (see also Banks, 2010; Goodwin & King, 2002, Manning & Baruth, 2010; Weiss, Kreider, Lopez, & Chatman-Nelson, 2010). More specifically and by implication, researchers should study the consequences of the more or less continual presence of parents/families, stepparents/families, cohabiting adults, and same-gender relationships on gifted and underachieving Black students' developmental outcomes. This broadened perspective highlights the dynamic nature of families and the culturally influenced, contextual nature of achievement.

Substantive or meaningful family involvement is a prerequisite to successful educational outcomes for gifted underachieving Black students. Parents/families—a child's first and forever teacher—play a vital, necessary role in Black students' orientation toward achievement, not simply because they have the right to be, but because they do, in their priorities,

What Is Giftedness?
- Overview of local, federal, and contemporary definitions of giftedness
- Overview of contemporary theories of giftedness

Characteristics of Culturally and Racially Different Gifted Students
- Scholars such as Frasier, Torrance, Baldwin, Ford, and Sternberg

Identification and Assessment of Giftedness
- Local practices and instruments, along with their implications for gifted Black students

Programming Options and Features
- Purposes, types, pros and cons of each option
- How gifted education differs from regular education teacher training

Information on Specific Areas and Characteristics of Giftedness for Their Children
- Intellectual, academic, creative, visual and performing arts, and leadership in general and through a cultural lens

Developmental Issues of Gifted Students
- Academic needs (including curriculum and instruction)
- Social and psychological needs (including peer relations, teacher relations)
- Psychological needs (racial identity, self-esteem, self-concept)

Underachievement
- Definitions, types, contributing factors; strategies for prevention and reversal

Concerns of Family Members
- Social needs, emotional needs, psychological needs, academic needs

How to Be an Advocate for Gifted Children
- Parent/family/community involvement
- School and community organizations
- Professional associations and organizations

Figure 8.4. Parent/family education for engagement and empowerment: A model for homes with gifted children. Parent/family and educator training personnel should include a minimum of the following four personnel: teacher, counselor, psychologist, and consultant (or someone competent in family education and involvement training). The specific topics and their order should be generated based on a parent/family needs assessment survey.

expectancies, and behaviors, influence the course of the child's achievement development (McAdoo, 2001, 2006; Slaughter & Epps, 1987).

Educators are urged to become more proactive at increasing family engagement, which consists of their physical involvement and presence in schools, and their beliefs and attitudes about being in school settings.

Black caregivers must feel welcomed, needed, valued, and appreciated. Educators can begin to establish such a tone or environment when they engage in honest self-reflection with questions such as those below (see Manning & Baruth, 2010, for additional questions, and Weiss et al., 2010, for case studies and activities):

❖ Are my opinions of parents/families based on stereotypes and prejudgments or are they based on accurate and objective views? Am I willing to change negative views?

❖ Have my experiences included positive, firsthand contact with caregivers from racially and culturally different backgrounds? How can I gain such experience?

❖ Do I understand and appreciate the role of extended family members in the lives of students? How can I learn about these members and encourage their involvement in my classroom/school?

❖ Do I have the interest, motivation, attitudes, and skills to develop close, respectful, and cooperative relationships with Black families/caregivers? Am I willing to become (more) culturally competent?

❖ How have I either encouraged or discouraged Black families from feeling welcome and being involved in my classroom/school? What strategies have I used to welcome them?

Respect, understanding, and effective communication are key factors to active and proactive Black family involvement—to family involvement that is meaningful and effective. Harry (1992) recommended that substantive Black family involvement should be manifested in several roles: (a) parents/families who join official assessment teams can alter or even eradicate the assumptions held by parents/families that educators have a monopoly on knowledge; (b) parents/families can form policy as members of advisory committees and local educational agencies, on school site-based management teams, and teachers' aides; and (c) parents/families can serve as advocates and peer supports where they offer advice and input in the assessment and placement of their children. These same recommendations are appropriate for other family members of gifted Black students—grandmothers and grandfathers, aunts and uncles, cousins, and significant others in students' lives and homes. Families can make a difference in the lives of their children, but only when their role in schooling is meaningful, empowered, and sustained (Langdon, 1991). Empowered and engaged families/caregivers of gifted Black students are aware of: (a) the nature and needs of their gifted children; (b) definitions and theories of giftedness and underachievement; (c) their role in decreasing the achievement gap; (d) their responsibility in enrolling their children in gifted and AP classes, and ensuring that they persist once enrolled; (e) social and psychological needs, including peer relations and pressures, racial identity and pride, and access to resources for meeting their children's specific needs; and (f) how to recognize and reverse or prevent underachievement, including the importance of collaborating with educators and demanding excellence and equity from teachers.

When teachers and school personnel make family/caregiver involvement part of their philosophy of teaching, families increase their interactions with children at school, feel more positive about their abilities to help their children, and rate teachers more positively. Just as important, Black student achievement increases (C. Banks, 2010; Bronfenbrenner, 1979; Comer, 1990; Epstein & Dauber, 1991; Haynes et al., 1989; Hochschild, 1984). Levels of family involvement have been identified; the more substantive the involvement, the more positive students' achievement and attitudes toward school.

Parents/families of gifted Black students have the same needs of parents/families in general, but their concerns are also shared with those of Black families who do not have children identified as gifted. Teachers and school personnel must understand that parents/families of gifted Black students may be frustrated at not being able to facilitate their child's development to the fullest extent (Boutte, 1992). Limitations may result from a lack of financial security, as well as a lack of feeling empowered when communicating with school personnel. They may also experience frustration and anxiety trying to meet daily and fiscal demands, while still providing a responsive environment for their gifted child(ren). Black parents/families in low-income and/or low-SES environments may experience despair over their inability to provide special services (e.g., music lessons, art supplies, special equipment, tutoring) for their child to develop his or her gifts and talents.

Clearly, not all Black parents/families are from low-income or low-SES backgrounds. Beyond economics, other concerns relate to racial discrimination in attitudes and behaviors. Black caregivers need evidence and assurance that their children will be treated in fair, judicious, nondiscriminatory ways by students and educators. They need evidence that their children will be held to high, rigorous standards, and that their educational experiences will be culturally responsive. Black families need assurance that they are valued as an educational partner.

High-income and high-SES Black families also may be overwhelmed by being viewed as a credit to their race (Sue et al., 2007; Witty, 1978). When their children are formally identified as gifted, some Black parents/families may fear isolation and alienation from Black and White peers, and be concerned with elitism often associated with gifted and AP classes. Finally, depending on past experiences, Black parents/families may perceive that gifted and/or AP classes lack credibility in that they can rob Black children of their unique cultural values and beliefs. Teachers can effectively allay these concerns by encouraging active and substantive family involvement.

Several recommendations are offered for educators to keep in mind as they work with Black parents/caregivers. These recommendations fall under the notion of being culturally responsive in both philosophy and practice.

CULTURALLY RESPONSIVE PHILOSOPHY

- ❖ Recognize and accept that parents/families matter. Parents/families know their children best; they are in the best position to inform schools about their children's needs.
- ❖ Educators who are cognizant of social injustices faced by Blacks in social settings and schools are more likely to have effective relationships with them. Educators must work diligently to examine their biases, prejudices, and stereotypes, and then rid themselves of deficit thinking about Black families and children.
- ❖ Schools and classrooms that operate under the assumption that Black parents/families care about their children are more likely to work with families to promote student achievement.
- ❖ Educators must be mindful of the many realities associated with White privilege or social and cultural capital. Not all families have access to such privileges, especially Black and low-income and/or low-SES families.
- ❖ Black families must not be viewed as a homogeneous group; when some Black families are not involved, they must not be viewed as representing the views and needs of other or all Black families.
- ❖ Communication must be ongoing and aggressive. Every effort must be made to ensure that Black families are kept informed and abreast of school activities, programs, and the like.
- ❖ Families must be viewed as an equal partner in the educational process.

❖ There is no one ideal model of family involvement. Models need to be flexible and responsive to the needs and lives of Black families and their children.

CULTURALLY RESPONSIVE PRACTICE

❖ Proactively and clearly communicate commitment to family involvement by writing a mission statement, setting goals, and measuring achievement of goals.

❖ Survey Black parents/families about their concerns and needs, along with recommendations for helping their children to achieve at higher levels.

❖ As with teacher professional development, it is necessary to hold workshops aimed at informing and empowering Black families.

❖ Hire a family liaison who is a member of the Black community, who has key insights, and is respected to serve as a cultural broker and advocate for Black families.

❖ Take steps to ensure that the climate is welcoming to families when they visit schools. Avoid jargon, communicate that families are equal partners with educators, and listen to families. (Also see C. Banks, 2010; Goodwin & King, 2002; Manning & Baruth, 2010; Weiss et al., 2010.)

SUMMARY

Blacks have struggled for generations to provide educational opportunities for their children, usually against difficult odds and often in the face of severe threats to their own safety. In a climate of even overt and violent racism, Black parents doggedly persisted in providing sound educational experiences for their children.

—Corder and Quisenberry (1987, p. 154)

The primary premise of this chapter is that our notions about traditional, nuclear families and caregiver involvement must be broadened and updated. This more inclusive and contemporary notion of families includes greater attention to the reality that mothers and/or fathers are not the not the only caregivers in Black families; it includes going from the notion of *parent* involvement to *family* involvement in the educational process at home and at school.

There is unanimous acceptance that parents/families make a significant contribution to the education of their children; just as important, they play fundamental roles in the recruitment and retention of students in gifted and AP classes. Parents/families play an essential role in the development and nurturance of children's abilities. They represent a microcosmic social system that transmits roles, rules, and values to children. In essence, parents/families bear a great deal of responsibility for socialization and enculturation, and the educational process is incomplete without them.

Unfortunately, research and writing on Black parents/families with gifted children can be counted on two hands. The need to conduct more research on gifted children in different or alternative family structures; to conduct more research on gifted Black students; to focus on the strengths of Black and other racially and culturally different families; and to increase the role of families (particularly extended family members) in the educational process is critical to the academic, social, and psychological well-being of gifted Black students in general, but especially underachieving students. It is an unfortunate fact that educators working with gifted Black underachieving students have little by way of strategies, theory, and research to inform and guide their beliefs and practice.

With regard to economically challenged and Black parents/families, all educators must recognize that poverty and limited formal education do not equate to limited motivated, limited intelligence, and/or poor social competence, even if the media project a view of low-income and low-SES Black families as entrenched in destructive forms of urban life. Modern folklore and urban legends like this give school personnel an excuse to avoid interactions with families from urban neighborhoods. Many mainstream teachers reflect society's pervasive fears of Black neighborhoods and culture, yet most Black students have safe and loving homes and families. Parents/families from all income and SES levels bring to schools valuable insights and unique perspectives from which to enhance home-school relationships, student behaviors, academic achievement, and participation in gifted education and AP classes. It is better for students and educators to have families as allies than adversaries.

Society's outdated but longstanding belief in the ubiquity of the nuclear family is frequently inconsistent with the family experiences of the millions who do not live in a household or family comprised of mother, father, and children. But the quickly increasing number of single and never-married mothers, teenage parents/families, and divorcees; the persistence of poverty among Blacks; and the vicious cycle of racism and discrimination against Blacks and other racial minorities guarantee the proliferation of extended families. Given these conditions, the larger society can ill-afford to ignore the contributions that extended families make to the financial, social, and psychological well-being of Black children. In fact, extended Black families deserve much credit and respect for helping children to achieve and, thereby, escape the more debilitating repercussions of poverty, classism, and racism. Consequently, school professionals need additional theory and research on the significance of culturally different child-rearing practices on the children's social and psychological lives. No longer, then, can we speak of the singular influence of mother or father, or both, on Black students' achievement or underachievement. Black family structures have always been diverse in composition, consisting of fictive kinship networks and extended family members (Billingsley, 1968). Again, as in the past, the concept of parent involvement is passé and exclusionary.

To the degree that educators place the nuclear family on a pedestal, they will view the extended family of Blacks as pathological or culturally deficient. But this perception is unwarranted, and educators and researchers must consider more closely the contributions of the Black family, in all of its manifestations, to the culture and stability of Black students in our nation's schools and gifted programs and AP classes. Despite popular, polemic, myopic, and misguided beliefs, Blacks readily acknowledge that the spirit—indeed the soul—of the Black community rests with those who excel academically and economically (Ford, 1993b).

CHAPTER NINE

PSYCHOLOGICAL FACTORS AS CORRELATES OF UNDERACHIEVEMENT AND ACHIEVEMENT

The psychological ring of influence (see Figure 9.1) is the focus of this chapter. The purpose of this chapter is to help bridge the fields of education, psychology, and counseling, focusing in particular on the academic, social, emotional, and psychological concerns and needs of gifted Black students. A key proposition of what is presented here is that whereas Black and White students share many problems and concerns associated with being gifted, Black students also have differential issues to contend with as they endeavor to achieve and thrive in school and the larger society. These meaningful differences are both quantitative and qualitative. The literature on gifted students most often ignores or discounts, perhaps more unconsciously than consciously, these differential needs. Teachers, administrators, and school counselors and psychologists must be cognizant of and sensitive to these concerns and needs, and to the spe-

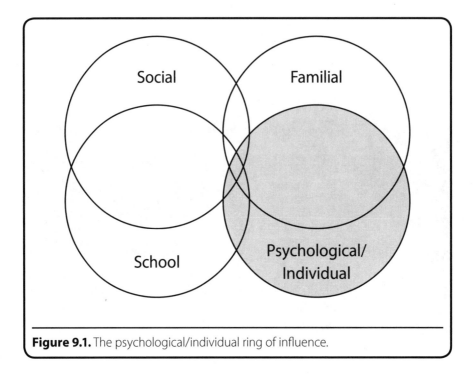

Figure 9.1. The psychological/individual ring of influence.

cific, unique, and individual problems that gifted Black students confront and present to them. As reflected throughout this chapter and book, like teachers and administrators, counselors and psychologists are in an ideal position to ensure that Black students remain in gifted programs and AP classes once identified and placed; counselors and psychologists represent an important component of both the recruitment and retention of Black students in gifted programs and AP classes.

QUESTIONS TO CONSIDER

- ❖ What are the shortcomings in scholarship relative to understanding and meeting the psychological needs of gifted Black students?
- ❖ What are some of the key psychological issues affecting the academic well-being of Black students in general and gifted Black students in particular?
- ❖ What role does racial identity play in the academic achievement of gifted Black students?
- ❖ What formal preparation is needed by counselors and psychologists to work effectively and in culturally responsive ways with gifted Black students?

❖ What are some culturally responsive recommended prevention and intervention strategies and resources for guiding gifted Black students in their area of their development?

INTRODUCTION

It has almost become a cliché to state that some gifted students are in psychological jeopardy (Manaster & Powell, 1983) for not reaching their potential in school and life, particularly if their academic, psychological, and socioemotional (also referred to as social and emotional) needs are not understood or not adequately addressed. It is unfair and indefensible to propose that gifted students will make it or "have it made" *because* they are gifted. Being gifted does not immunize or inoculate one from hardships, trials, and tribulations. This belief is irrational, elitist, and outdated. Historically, however, little attention has been given in both education and mental health professions to counseling and guiding gifted students (Ford, 1996; Wood, 2010). Rather, the primary focus has been on educating gifted learners—meeting their academic and vocational interests and needs—rather than their socioemotional and psychological needs. Yet, as Silverman (1993) noted some time ago, giftedness has both cognitive and emotional components: Not only do gifted students *think* differently from their peers, they also *feel* differently.

This chapter is based on the proposition that counseling and psychological variables are linked directly to the academic achievement and social success of gifted Black students. An historical overview of the counseling movement in gifted education is presented. Also presented is information on the counseling and psychological concerns and needs of gifted students in general and Black students in particular. Within this discussion is an examination of variables such as social rejection, anxiety, self-esteem, self-concept, and racial identity, within the context of a "paradox of underachievement" (Ford, 1991; Mickelson, 1990).

HISTORICAL OVERVIEW OF THE COUNSELING MOVEMENT IN GIFTED EDUCATION

The movement in counseling gifted students has often been attributed to Lewis Terman (1925) and Leta Hollingworth (1926). Terman's longitudinal study of middle-class White students helped to dispel many myths and stereotypes about gifted learners. One myth was that gifted children were inherently well adjusted and, consequently, did not need counseling services. Hollingworth (1926) also found that gifted students are not immune from psychological and social and emotional difficulties. Perhaps her greatest contribution was calling attention to the gap or dyssynchrony between a gifted student's intellectual and socioemotional development, often referred to as "old heads on young shoulders." That is, cognitively or intellectually, the student may be beyond his or her chronological age, but socially and emotionally, the child is at his or her developmental age.

Colangelo (1991) noted that it was not until the 1950s that increased attention was devoted to counseling gifted students. Over the course of the latter half of the 20th century, labs and guidance programs were established at several universities, with the leadership of researchers such as John Rothney, Charles Pulvino, Nicholas Colangelo, Philip Perrone, Barbara Kerr, John Gowan, James Webb, Linda Silverman, and James Delisle. These scholars highlighted the heretofore ignored issues related to suicide, depression, perfectionism, self-concept, self-esteem, anxiety, and poor peer relations among some gifted students.

The history of counseling gifted students regarding their psychological and social and emotional concerns, while not new, remains in its infancy. In particular, few counselors and psychologists have addressed the psychological, social, and emotional needs of gifted students (Barnette, 1989; Mendaglio & Peterson, 2007; Peterson, 2009; Wood, 2010), and the term "emotion" is conspicuously absent in the indexes of most books on the gifted, indicating how too little attention has been addressed concerning this important issue (Silverman, 1993). A search of ERIC and PsychLit abstracts indicated a dismally small number of articles on counseling gifted students. Specifically, between 1966 and 1994, 64 articles appeared in ERIC; only four appeared in PsychLit between 1987 and 1994. This paucity of information is even greater relative to gifted Black students. Less than a handful of articles referenced in the above databases focused exclusively or specifically on counseling gifted Black students from a psychological and socioemotional perspective (see Ford et al., 1993). Similarly, there are a limited number of books specifically on counseling gifted students (e.g., Kerr, 1991; Mendaglio & Peterson, 2007; Milgrim, 1993; Milgrim et al., 1993; Silverman, 1993) and meeting their psychological and social and emotional needs (e.g., Cross, 2004; Delisle, 1992; Delisle & Galbraith, 2002; Neihart, Reis, Robinson, & Moon, 2002; Peterson, 2009; Peterson, Duncan, & Canady, 2009; Schmitz & Galbraith, 1985). Books often contain a perfunctory chapter on "special populations," a term that has become synonymous with minority and low-income (most often Black) students. It is unfortunate that the issues confronting gifted Black and culturally different students are not interwoven throughout the texts, as such an approach would highlight the heterogeneity and differential issues and needs that exist within the gifted population.

A few studies have explored public school counselors' awareness of issues confronting gifted students, as well as their preparation to work with this population. As Peterson and Morris (2010) reported, few counselors have formal training to work with gifted students, much less gifted students who are from low-income and/or from minority backgrounds. For example, Klausmeier et al. (1987) found that most school counselors considered their preparation in recognizing gifted students to be less than average, and their training with minorities, low-income, and low socioeconomic groups to be below average or completely lacking. In their study of state certification endorsement for school counselors in special education, Frantz and Prillaman (1993) found that 11 states required at least one course in special education for certification as school counselors, 17 were in the process of changing certification requirements for counselors and considering including a course in special education, and another 17 states neither required any courses nor were they in the process of considering changes in certification.

In a recent study, Wood (2010) surveyed gifted adolescents about their experiences with the counseling techniques, strategies, and approaches advocated for counseling gifted students in order to determine if these best practices were taking place. Findings indicated that few of the best practices were occurring. Wood recommended that school counseling programs develop coursework that addresses the specific and unique needs of gifted students.

In a national study of university counselors, Ford and Harris (1995a) found that only 10% reported training in working with gifted learners. The findings also indicated that the majority of the counselors were unaware of or indecisive about the issues hindering the achievement of both gifted Black and gifted White students.

In essence, counselors, psychologists, and other mental health professionals have not been an integral part of gifted education (Barnette, 1989; Ford & Harris, 1995b; Kerr, 1991; Silverman, 1993; Webb,

Meckstroth, & Tolan, 1982), and their roles have been limited primarily to academic counseling and assessment and placement issues (Ford & Harris, 1999; Milsom & Peterson, 2006; Wood, 2010). Unfortunately, as Gerler, Kinney, and Anderson (1985) noted, educators and policymakers frequently do not recognize the contributions of counselors to students' success in school. Because more children are entering school with serious personal problems, the roles and responsibilities of counselors are changing (Lee & Workman, 1992; Milsom & Peterson, 2006; Peterson, 2009; Sears, 1993; Welch & McCarroll, 1993; Wood, 2010), expanding to meet the needs of all students who need and/or seek their guidance and assistance.

Because a major goal of counseling is to promote healthy self-images and to ensure psychological growth, counselors must have an awareness and understanding of the many issues that hinder students' psychological, social, and emotional well-being. Along these lines, the National Association for Gifted Children (2000) developed a position paper on the importance of addressing and meeting the socioemotional needs of gifted students and the importance of counselor training in order to do so. Likewise, the American School Counselor Association (ASCA) recognized that school counselors are poorly prepared to work with gifted students. In its 2007 position paper, the organization stated that the school counselor "assists in providing technical assistance and an organized support system within the developmental comprehensive school counseling programs for gifted and talented students to meet their extensive and diverse needs as well as the needs of all students" (p. 1). In general, the assistance and support provided to gifted students by counselors ought to include: participating in identification; providing group and individual counseling; recommending resources; engaging in gifted education professional development; and promoting an understanding and awareness of gifted students' needs. Just as important, ASCA's position paper referred to these areas: (a) underachievement, (b) perfectionism, (c) dropping out, (d) depression, (e) delinquency, (f) stress management, (g) difficulty in peer relationships, (h) meeting expectations, (i) goal setting, and (j) career development.

Relative to gifted Black students, counselors and other helping professionals also must understand and provide guidance on: (a) classroom behaviors (e.g., attention, cooperation, time on task, assertiveness, communication modalities); (b) affective factors (e.g., feelings and thoughts about self, interests, and anxiety); (c) sensory factors (e.g., auditory and visual functioning); (d) imagery factors (e.g., beliefs, ideas, and perceptions); (e) interpersonal factors (e.g., teacher-student relations, teacher expectations of students, peer relations, family-child relations); and (f) physical factors (e.g., health; see Gerler et al., 1985; Lazarus, 1985). They must also be familiar with intrapersonal factors (e.g., learning styles, motivation, achievement attitudes) and other cultural factors (e.g., racial identity, behavioral styles, communication styles, family values and structures).

A perusal of the literature indicates that much of the contact between school counselors and gifted students centers on academic and vocational or career issues. One reason may be that students in general are less likely to seek the assistance of school counselors for personal problems; this underuse of counseling is common among Black students. According to Hutchinson and Reagan (1989), the more personal the problem, the less likely gifted students are to seek out school counselors. In their study, approximately 40% of students would seek assistance with peer conflicts, 46% for assistance in exploring feelings and values, 37% on how to get along in life, and 27% for relieving tension. Viewed through a cultural lens, given their importance of spirituality in their lives, Black students are more likely to seek the guidance and support of their pastor or spiritual leader than a counselor in the traditional sense (Harper et al., 2009; Parham & Brown, 2003; Vontress & Epp, 1997; Whaley, 2001). Yet, a Citizens Policy Center for Oakland (1984) study found that perhaps the most important component of student success is meeting their psychological need for human contact—finding someone to care about them. Students may require the assistance of counselors to fulfill that important need.

As noted in other chapters, Bridgeland et al. (2006) conducted focus groups with almost 500 Black and other culturally different high school students who dropped out of school. Although several findings are disturbing, four in particular are worth mentioning here. First, some 88% of these dropouts had *passing* grades; second, the majority believed they would have graduated had they persisted; third, most reported that teachers held low expectations of them; and, fourth, the primary reason they dropped out of school was poor relationships with school personnel.

All students can benefit from counseling and support that is culturally responsive, but Black students may be less likely than White students to seek guidance and counseling, particularly those who hold negative images of Whites in general (and by extension, White counselors/psychologists; Ford et al., 1993; Sue, 2003). The race of the counselor or psychologist may be the only factor that causes some (or perhaps many)

Black students to avoid counseling or to prematurely terminate counseling and/or psychological services. However, race is often ignored in the helping process because too few counselors and psychologists are aware of how race and culture interfere with the process of growing, achieving, and living fully (Sue, 2003). These issues are discussed in the sections that follow.

PSYCHOLOGICAL FACTORS AND UNDERACHIEVEMENT

The personality of an individual plays an important role in his or her achievement. Personality epitomizes the integration of all of the other factors into an interactional response to the environment (Shade, 1978). Black students who do well academically appear to have numerous personal characteristics in common that foster resilience, including a willingness to conform to adult demands, and a greater need for conformity than independence (Epps, 1969; Ford, 1996).

Educators, counselors, and psychologists have associated various psychological and socioemotional problems with gifted students. Issues related to locus of control, anxiety, isolation and alienation, self-esteem and self-concept, and racial identity needs and development are discussed in this chapter as these factors have been found to have a significant impact on students' educational well-being.

LOCUS OF CONTROL

Dirkes (1985) reported that some gifted students do indeed have an external locus of control, a low sense of adequacy, feelings of isolation, and self-contempt. Gross (1989) suggested that gifted students often face the dilemma of choosing to satisfy their drive for excellence at the risk of sacrificing relationships with peers, as did Whiting (2006a, 2006b) with Black males who focused on the need for achievement versus the need for affiliation among this group. If the choice for friendship is more important, gifted students might choose to underachieve to avoid feelings of isolation, which suggests perhaps that gifted students who are forced to choose between psychosocial needs and achievement tend to sacrifice their "gift."

Several studies have found an external locus of control among poorly achieving Black students, particular those who feel that they have little control over their educational outcomes due to social injustices such as discrimination and other barriers to social mobility and academic success. For example, too many Black students see other Black adults in educational and occupational positions that hold little power and prestige (Metropolitan Life Insurance Company, 2009; Mickelson, 1990). One has only to look at the positions held by Black and White employees in schools—teachers, counselors, psychologists, and administrators. Those in positions of power are most often White; custodial and cafeteria workers and those not directly involved in educating students are most often Black. Some of these children have mothers and fathers with college degrees who are unemployed or underemployed. These discrepancies can contribute to an external locus of control among low-income and/or low-SES Black students: Why bother to work hard in school when there are differential rewards for doing so across racial lines? The payoffs appear to be limited, and gifted Black students, with their keen sense of logic, recognize and grapple with this injustice.

Coleman and colleagues (1966), Mackler (1970), Mech (1972), and Shade (1978) reported that high-achieving Black students perceive themselves as being internally controlled and in command of their academic and social destiny; accordingly, they hold high aspirations and expectations regarding success. This is what we must strive for with all students, especially those who are disenfranchised and marginalized.

ANXIETY

Anxiety comes in many guises—insecurity, test anxiety, perfectionism, fear of failure, fear of success, and other forms of stress. Anxiety is a state marked by heightened self-awareness, awareness of others, and perceived helplessness or hopelessness. Oftentimes, anxious individuals are unable to cope with task demands, are unable to understand the situation and related demands, are uncertain about consequences, feel inadequate in coping with the demands, have unrealistic self- and other expectations, and are self-preoccupied. All of these factors have physiological and behavioral consequences, and they interfere with, jeopardize, or compromise effective and successful task performance. Ineffective performance includes focusing on irrelevant information, misinterpreting test questions and directions, attention blocks or deficits, and self-preoccupation. Maladaptive coping strategies also accompany test anxiety. For instance,

the test taker may cope through avoidance, procrastination, defensiveness, blaming, and anger.

Test anxiety is the most widely studied of anxieties (Sarason,
Davidson, Lighthall, Waite, & Ruebush, 1960). Tests are noxious experiences for many students: Some 5 million children suffer from mild test
anxiety; another 5 million suffer from chronic, debilitating test anxiety. Test anxiety is learned. It is associated with previous experiences
that were evaluative and high stakes. Further, for educators, parents, and
students, test results carry high salience and face validity. Contrary to
popular opinion, test anxiety, especially when chronic, does not motivate
or stimulate the individual into action.

Dusek (1980) reported a negative correlation between test anxiety
and achievement and IQ scores. Low test anxious individuals tend to
do well on such tests, while those with high anxiety perform poorly.
Essentially, when tests have high salience and are perceived as evaluative,
test anxiety increases. Level of test anxiety can inhibit students' identification as gifted, which highlights the importance of understanding the
phenomenon of stereotype threat by Steele and colleagues (e.g., Steele,
1997, 1999; Steele & Aronson, 1995).

An increasing body of work focuses on a type of text anxiety rather
specific to Black students. In a number of studies, Steele (1997) and
Aronson, Fried, and Good (2005) reported that Black adolescents and
college students may suffer from stereotype threat, a phenomenon that
occurs when an individual who is subject to inauspicious stereotypes is
negatively affected in testing situations by the salience of his or her category membership. That is, stereotype threat is a type of confirmation
bias that can be either positive or negative, and seems to be most often
negative for Black students. Frequently, stereotype threat manifests when
a categorical group is told or shown that the group's performance is worse
than another group before giving them a test. The test results are often
lower than for control groups. An important finding is that "When capable Black college students fail to perform as well as their White counterparts, the explanation often has less to do with ability than with the
threat of stereotypes about their capacity to succeed" (Steele, 1999, p. 50).
These researchers report that making race salient when taking a test of
cognitive ability negatively affects high-ability Black students.

ISOLATION AND ALIENATION

Generally, gifted students, particularly those identified as highly gifted, tend to feel alienated from, unaccepted by, and unconnected to others not formally identified as gifted. They may become introverted as a result of the comparatively small quantity and reduced quality of their social and emotional relationships. The sense of not belonging has been viewed as the basis of most gifted students' psychological and emotional maladjustments. Issues surrounding isolation and social rejection are especially important for Black students and other culturally different students in predominantly White schools, gifted programs, and AP classes. They may have difficulty forming friendships or building social networks with White classmates in such racially different settings.

As discussed in Chapter 6, Allport's (1954) model of prejudice relative to gifted Black students is apropos here. His model illustrates that prejudice comes in different degrees, from verbal attacks to extermination. Antilocution refers to the verbal expression of negative attitudes against a targeted group and its members. Avoidance refers to taking steps or going through the pains of ensuring that there is no contact with another group or individual from that group. Discrimination refers to acting upon one's dislike or disdain for a group or its members by denying them opportunities; this exclusion of the target groups includes systemic segregation and providing lower quality resources, for example. Physical attack refers to violence against the target group and/or members. Extermination is the highest degree of prejudice, according to Allport (1954). This refers to acts that seek to extinguish the life of a group or its members, including murder and/or sterilization.

With gifted Black students, prejudice can come in all degrees, but the first four are most relevant. They may face negative remarks from educators and classmates (see Harmon, 2004). White caregivers and students may not want Black and White students to be in the same classes, especially gifted and AP classes, which are types of avoidance and discrimination. Avoidance can take the form of parents placing their students in private schools or moving to suburban areas to decrease their chances of being in contact with Black students; discrimination can take the form of educators having policies, procedures, and instruments that keep Black students from meeting gifted education and AP criteria, thus, hindering placement. Annually, the Office for Civil Rights, as discussed in Chapter 2, continues to address violations based on race in gifted education and AP classes. In addition to negative words being said about and/

or exchanged, fights and other physical confrontations can and do take place between students from different racial and cultural backgrounds. Regardless of its form, the American Psychological Association (2006) recognized that racism and racial discrimination adversely affect mental health by diminishing the victim's self-image, confidence, and optimal mental functioning. Further, in *Racism's Hidden Toll* (Blistein, 2009), Caldwell, Kohn-Wood, Schmeelk-Cone, Chavous, and Zimmerman (2004), Sandhu and Aspy (1997), Vontress and Epp (1997), Vontress, Johnson, and Epp (1999), and Whitley and Kite (2006) reviewed studies showing that racism and discrimination, not surprisingly, play a major role in hindering the mental and psychological health and well-being of Blacks, including their self-perception.

SELF-ESTEEM AND SELF-CONCEPT

The terms *self-esteem* and *self-concept* are often used interchangeably. However, a careful reading of the literature reveals important and significant distinctions between the two. Self-esteem represents the affective component of one's self-perception; it represents the value we place on our worth as a person, as a human being. Self-concept represents the cognitive view we hold of ourselves, namely, what we think about our abilities in various areas. Self-concept is often described or referred to as if it is a unidimensional, global construct. However, Harter (1982) and others argued that individuals have self-concepts. The general self-concept is comprised of academic and nonacademic self-concept. Academic self-concept refers to a student's self-perception in specific subject matters, such as English, math, science, and history. Nonacademic self-concept includes social (self-perception with peers and significant others), emotional (particular emotional states), and physical areas (ability and appearance). Shavelson and colleagues (1980) also maintained that one must examine self-concept in specific situations or contexts rather than in isolation (e.g., school, sports, visual and performing arts).

Although there are studies about gifted students' self-esteem and self-concept(s), few empirical studies have been conducted using gifted Black students as the primary subject group. The paucity of research in this area prevents one from drawing definitive conclusions about their roles in the underachievement of gifted Black students. However, by examining the research conducted on the self-concept and self-esteem of both White gifted students and of Black students in general, implications can be made.

Cooley, Cornell, and Lee (1991) compared the self-concept domains of gifted Black and White students in grades 5–11, but found no significant difference between the measures of academic self-concept and peer acceptance of the two groups. Bartley (1980) examined self-concept scores of Black and White secondary students, including gifted students. They found not only an equivalence in academic self-concepts for the two groups, but also that Black students had slightly higher general self-concepts than White students.

Haynes et al. (1988) compared the self-concept scores of high-, average-, and low-achieving Black students. They found that high achievers scored highest in the academic, physical appearance, and overall happiness self-concept domains. The authors asserted that a positive relationship exists between academic achievement and self-concept domains in Black students. This assertion is supported by Turner and McGann (1980), who found that high-achieving Black students have greater self-confidence and self-concept than low-achieving Black students.

None of the studies just described have examined the relationship of self-esteem and self-concept among Black students by considering feelings about their racial identity. How does racial identity influence the achievement and social relations of gifted Black students? This question and others are described below.

RACIAL IDENTITY

An often ignored but critically important variable related to self-concept among Black students is racial identity. Racial identity development plays an important role in their psychological adjustment, academic motivation, and achievement (Cross & Vandiver, 2001; Ford et al., 1993; Ford, Harris, Webb, & Jones, 1994; Helms, 1994). Attention to racial identity among Black students dates back to the early work of Clark and Clark (1940), who used Black and White dolls to examine the extent to which Black children recognized themselves as racial or ethnic beings, and how they felt about being Black or different from Whites.

Figure 9.2 presents a model depicting racial identity as an integral component of a Black student's self-concept. This model expands upon the model presented by Shavelson and others (1980) by including psy-

.

.

.

.

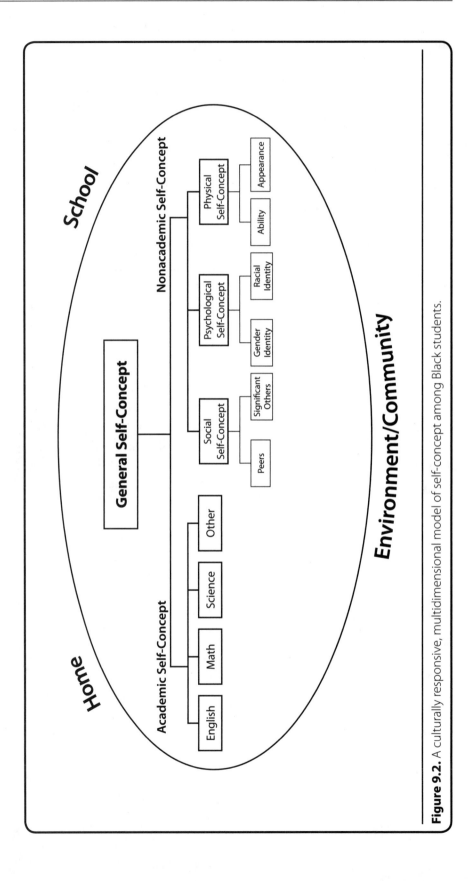

Figure 9.2. A culturally responsive, multidimensional model of self-concept among Black students.

chological self-concept as an integral component of nonacademic self-concept. Psychological self-concept includes racial and gender identities.

Black students encounter more barriers to racial identity development than do White students (Helms, 1989, 1994; Parham & Helms, 1985; Smith, 1989; Spencer & Markstrom-Adams, 1990). Moreover, gifted Black students may experience more psychological and emotional problems than Black students not identified as gifted. For example, Lindstrom and Van Sant (1986) argued that gifted culturally different students find themselves "between a rock and a hard place" (p. 584) when the cultural expectations of their indigenous groups are in conflict with those of the dominant group. They quoted one gifted Black student who said, "I had to fight to be gifted and then I had to fight because I am gifted" (Lindstrom & Van Sant, 1986, p. 584). Another student stated, "I'm not White and I'm not Black. I'm a freak" (Lindstrom & Van Sant, 1986, p. 584).

What cultural factors contribute to such difficulties among gifted Black students? Maslow (1962) highlighted the significance of peoplehood and belonging when he suggested that the sense of belonging is essential for mental health. An unhealthy sense of belonging works in opposition to the sense of peoplehood. Peoplehood, which is based on more than just skin color, represents a cultural symbol of collective identity, ethnic consolidation (Green, 1981), and mutual interdependence among Blacks. The terms imply the particular mindset, or worldview, of those persons who are considered to be Black, and it is used to denote the moral judgment the group makes on its members.

Smith (1989) argued that race serves to create a common referent of peoplehood such that individuals tend to define themselves in terms of membership in a particular group. In other words, the collective identity, which manifests itself in the form of peoplehood, represents the sense of ethnic belonging that is psychologically important for people. For Black students, this sense of peoplehood is challenged primarily in school, when school and community compete for the Black students' loyalty. As stated by Weis (1985) and MacLeod (1987), for some gifted Black students, the mere act of attending school is evidence of a semiconscious—or even conscious—rejection of the Black culture. School is seen by some Black students and their families as a symbol of the dominant culture, which communicates both directly and indirectly that to succeed Blacks must become "un-Black" (Fordham, 1988, p. 58).

To reinforce the belief that they are still legitimate members of the Black community, gifted Black students may sabotage any chance they have of succeeding outside of it. With this "anti-achievement ethic" (Granat, Hathaway, Saleton, & Sansing, 1986, p. 166), gifted Black students may underachieve, drop out, camouflage their abilities, and otherwise fail to reach their academic potential in school. This under-achievement may be especially evident when gifted Black students attend predominantly White schools and programs. During this time, they may become confused about which cultural orientations to support. Because of the myriad of difficulties that can and do influence the psychological well-being of gifted Black students, an analysis of at least one theory of racial identity is necessary.

Nigrescence theory: One theory of racial identity development. Nigrescence or racial identity development is a nondiaphanous concept (Cross, 1989). Cross (1989) has proposed that an understanding of the term lends itself well to how the process that binds people together can also tear them apart. Further, knowledge of Nigrescence is akin to per-sonality development. Smith (1989) asserted that racial identity develop-ment is a process of coming to terms with one's racial group membership as a salient reference group. Phinney and Rotherham (1987) defined self-identification as the accurate and consistent use of an ethnic label, based on the perception and conception of belonging to an ethnic group. Just as important, Nobles (1989) has contended that the fundamental and only substantive justification for the study of Black psychology is that Blacks are culturally, philosophically, and spiritually distinct from other socio-cultural groups.

It is becoming increasingly clear that race and culture affect psycho-logical health. That is to say, the complexity of racial identity formation may increase as a function of color and physical features. Spencer and Markstrom-Adams (1990) indicated that the issue of color may be more salient for Blacks (and Native Americans) than any other minority group. Essentially, White students are less likely to experience the chronic stress and problems associated with racial identity because the color of their skin is not a barrier. Perhaps Edwards (2006) stated it best when he said that Blackness can be a liability because of attendant racism and dis-crimination. In short, race is the most onerous obstacle in the lives of some Black students.

Cross (1971) developed a theory entitled the Negro-to-Black con-version in an attempt to explain racial identity among Blacks. The most studied theory of racial identity was introduced by Cross in 1971, in which he outlined the stages of individual Black consciousness devel-opment associated with involvement in the Black Power Movement of

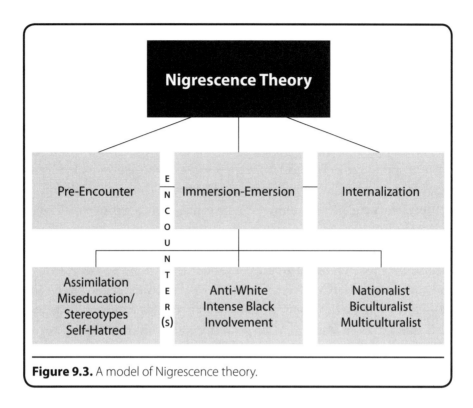

Figure 9.3. A model of Nigrescence theory.

the late 1960s (Cross & Vandiver, 2001). Since 1971, the theory has undergone two revisions based on much research, representing changes every two decades (1991 and 2001). In the most recently revised model of Nigrescence theory, Cross and Vandiver (2001) distinguished between personal identity (PI) and social identity, also called reference group orientation (RGO), and clarified when to use the model developmentally and, thus, distinguish between stages versus types of racial identities.

Nigrescence theory (also referred to as Nigrescence expanded theory and illustrated in Figure 9.3; Cross & Vandiver, 2001) rests on the assumption that the self-concept has two components: a general personality or personal identity component and a reference group orientation or social identity component. In the expanded theory, personal identity plays a minor role in the definition of Black identity, with social identity (RGO) playing the key role. PI refers to one's personality (e.g., shy, quiet, aggressive, outgoing, mathematically inclined), while RGO refers to an individual's sense of him- or herself as a social being.

When Nigrescence theory focuses on the outcomes of differing socialization experiences, the identity outcomes are called racial-reference group orientations or identity statuses rather than stages (Cross & Vandiver, 2001). However, when the focus is on social identity change in the context of an adult identity conversion, the identity types are called stages. As described below, the theory presents three major exemplars (i.e., pre-encounter; immersion-emersion, and internalization) that are subdivided into eight identity types.

Pre-encounter exemplar. There are three pre-encounter racial identity types; all types share the belief that "White is right" and hold pro-American attitudes. Further, they share some level of disengagement (i.e., low salience and negative valence) from their social or racial group identity as Black individuals. Thus, when accused of "acting White," those identities that personify the pre-encounter exemplar may feel complimented rather than offended.

Assimilation. The assimilation type describes a Black person whose social identity is organized around his or her sense of being an American and an individual (Cross & Vandiver, 2001). This person places little salience on racial group affiliation and, consequently, is detached or distanced from the Black community and culture, even showing some disdain for Black culture. His or her primary identity is being an American—without qualification and without apology. One belief is that "We are in America, so get over the past."

Miseducation. Related to the work of Woodson (1933) on "the miseducation of the Negro," this identity type is representative of a Black individual who accepts, unquestionably, the negative images, stereotypes, and historical misinformation about Blacks (Cross & Vandiver, 2001). This person sees little strength and few positives in the Black community, hesitates to engage in solving or resolving issue social injustices, and psychologically and physically distances him- or herself from the Black community. According to the theory, this individual tends to compartmentalize stereotypes so that such negative group images do not affect his or her personal self-image. Thus, this person often is likely to hold the attitude, "That's the way *they* act, but *I* am different" (Cross & Vandiver, 2001, p. 376).

Self-hatred. In this third pre-encounter type, the individual experiences profoundly negative feelings and severe self-loathing about being Black. This dislike is internal, unhealthy, and the individual may resort to all sorts of tactics (including surgery) to modify physical features. Being Black may even be viewed as being cursed. Cross and Vandiver (2001) asserted that race has low salience and high negative valence in this identity type.

Movement from any one of the pre-encounter types comes from experiencing encounters, called conversion experiences. Sue and colleagues

(2007) also termed these experiences as microaggressions—racial insults and offenses. They provided nine cogent examples of microaggressions that potently remind Blacks that they may be viewed by other groups as inferior. These insults can be direct or indirect, and small (so to speak) or large. Examples include being told that "you speak well," having your academic credentials questioned, being questioned about your ability to purchase an expensive item, watching a Black individual on television being abused and/or beaten by police, being told by a teacher that you cheated on an assignment because it was so well done, being punished for an incident in which a White student was not, and so much more.

Immersion-emersion exemplar. This identity exemplar is characterized by two identity types, associated with a form of anti-White sentiment or extreme/militant pro-Blackness. There is a high degree of racial engagement. This is the antithesis of the pre-encounter exemplar. Thus, when accused of "acting White," both types may have responses that range from feeling slighted to angry to enraged. To stop being accused of "acting White," an individual may stop displaying the characteristic(s) associated with the accusation (e.g., dress or talk differently, disengage from academics, downplay intelligence).

Anti-White. The Black individual who holds anti-White sentiments is nearly consumed by a hatred of White people, and all that whiteness represents, such as privilege, power, and prestige. This person is frequently full of fury and pent-up rage associated with social injustices (Cross & Vandiver, 2001); rather than take on the role of victim, he or she may victimize those viewed as the oppressor. Within the school/educational context, there is a dislike of having White teachers and administrators, a disdain for learning about White Americans, and a refusal to take directions from Whites, especially those in positions of authority.

Intense Black involvement. With this identity type, the individual often holds a simplistic, romanticized, and obsessive dedication to all things Black. There is unbridled enthusiasm to acquire information on Blacks, along with their history and accomplishments (Cross & Vandiver, 2001). He or she engages in "Blackness" in a hyper-vigilant and/or cult-like fashion. This person, for a myriad of reasons, may exaggerate or distort his or her sense of what is means to be "Black." Those who personify intense Black involvement are in the first step toward moving to an internalized Black identity, according to Vandiver, Fhagen-Smith, Cokley, Cross, and Worrell (2001). A noteworthy, distinguishing feature among the three exemplars is not only Black self-acceptance but mental health (Vandiver et al., 2001).

Internalization exemplar. The internalization exemplar is comprised of three identity types. The underlying characteristic among them is high racial salience or engagement (i.e., Black pride and acceptance), and a sense of wholeness or peace. There is also a keen sense of social justice, equality, and equity. This individual is not likely to succumb to accusations of "acting White" or "selling out"; it has little to no effect on the person's psyche and performance.

Nationalist. This identity type emphasizes an Afrocentric perspective about him- or herself, other Blacks, and the world. This individual proactively and assertively engages in and contributes to the Black community, endeavoring to decrease social injustices facing Blacks.

Biculturalist. This identity type represents a Black individual who gives equal importance and salience to being a Black *and* an American. He or she celebrates being both, and engages positively in both cultures—without identity conflicts, doubt, and self-questioning.

Multiculturalist. This type represents the prototype of a Black individual whose identity merges three or more social categories or frames of reference. This person is interested in resolving issues that address multiple oppressions, and is confident and comfortable in multiple groups and settings. Racial salience and pride as a Black person are positive in all settings.

Albeit rather confusing, when Nigrescence theory is applied to the study of Black identity change, the three major exemplars or orientations (pre-encounter, immersion-emersion, and internalization) are viewed as stages. However, when the focus is on the socialization experiences, covering infancy through early adulthood, the exemplars are viewed as bounded and fairly stable identity or reference group orientations (Cross & Vandiver, 2001). From a developmental perspective, a final point is that individuals will periodically pass in and out of certain Nigrescence types, which is not to be interpreted as confusion or being unstable. Rather, such individuals are experiencing "recycling" to lifespan challenges that, ideally, will result in a deeper understanding and appreciation of one's Blackness. Recycling strengthens and enriches whatever identity type is in question.

This theory helps to explain some of the psychological and social dilemmas confronting gifted Black students. Realizing the usefulness of the theory, several researchers have applied or modified it to understand more fully the psychological needs of gifted Black students. For example, Banks (1979) and Exum (1979) stated that gifted Black students experience cultural conflict relative to supporting the beliefs, values, and norms of the dominant culture as opposed to their parent culture. Consequently, they show some degree of ambivalence about their abilities, considering them as envied by others—yet personally undesirable.

Several qualifications require attention at this point. First, as just noted, one must consider that Blacks in predominantly White settings (like gifted education and AP classes) may experience more negative racial encounters than those in predominantly Black settings (Ford, 1992; Smith, 1989). Secondly, Blacks in predominantly White settings also may experience such encounters at an earlier age than Blacks in predominantly Black settings. A third consideration is that, because of characteristics often associated with giftedness (e.g., insightfulness, intuitiveness, sensitivity, keen sense of justice), gifted Black students may be particularly aware of and sensitive to racial injustices (encounters and microaggressions). Finally, one's type or stage of racial identity may be related to achievement (Ford, 1996; Ford et al., 2008b; Ford et al., 1993). Specifically, there may be a curvilinear relationship between racial identity and achievement, with those in the earliest type (pre-encounter) and those in the last type (internalization) having the highest achievement orientation and being less vulnerable to peer pressures. Achievement orientations and academic performance may be similar between those in the different types (earliest vs. latest), but the extent to which the individual is perceived as "acting White" or "selling out" is different. Pre-encounter individuals, because of their low-salience or anti-Black attitudes, are likely to be rejected by some members of the Black community; conversely, immersion-emersion and internalization individuals, because of their strong and positive racial identity and salience, bicultural stance, and pluralistic perspectives, seem more likely to be accepted by members of the Black community. Individuals with the middle type of racial identity (i.e., immersion-emersion) appear so subsumed with finding and validating their identity that academic achievement may have low significance in their lives—the need for affiliation may be stronger than the need for achievement.

Ford, Harris, and Winborne (1991), Fordham (1988), and others have devoted much attention to the issues gifted Black students confront about assimilating and otherwise adopting characteristics, values, and beliefs of the predominant culture. Findings indicate the racial identity is affected and determined by social and environmental pressures and circumstances. Blackwell (1975) stated that:

Two kinds of forces have always been at work in the Black community: (1) centripetal forces—elements that draw members of a minority toward their group, and (2) centrifugal forces—those elements that magnetize minority group members in the direction of the dominant group's cultural values, societal norms, and institutional arrangements. (p. 282)

Essentially, gifted Black students often confront conflicting values from which they must choose when forming a racial identity. Exum (1979, 1983) focused on the ramifications of racial issues to the detriment of achievement among this group. He stated that gifted Black students are especially vulnerable to problems because they are (or feel) less accepted by peers and parents. Jenkins (1950) noted that these students will become more sensitive to and preoccupied with racial problems than other Black students.

In her compelling work, Fordham (1986, 1988) applied this confusion over racial identity to high-achieving and gifted Black students and stated that such students sometimes make the conscious decision to underachieve academically so as not to be perceived as "acting White" or "selling out." Fordham (1986, 1988) argued that high-achieving Black students must assume a "raceless" persona if they wish to succeed academically. This racelessness occurs when gifted Black students empty themselves, so to speak, of their culture, believing that the door of opportunity will open to them if they stand raceless before it. That is, raceless students adopt characteristics of the dominant culture (e.g., speaking standard English, straightening their hair, wearing blue or green contact lenses), and in other ways subscribe to the White American achievement ideology of hard work, educational attainment, and equality of opportunity. Relative to gifted or high-achieving Black students, Fordham (1988) argued that

Out of their desire to secure jobs and positions that are above the employment ceiling typically placed on Blacks, they have adopted personae that indicate a lack of identification with, or a strong relationship to, the Black community in response to an implicit institutional mandate: Become "un-Black." (p. 58)

To reiterate, Cross and Vandiver (2001) suggested that individuals with the pre-encounter type of racial identity view the world from a White frame of reference and develop attitudes that are pro-White and thereby anti-Black. Two penalties accompany a rejection of the Black culture: (a) the Black community rejects the gifted Black student, and (b) the gifted Black student suffers psychologically, emotionally, and socially. All of this is to say that racelessness threatens the survival of the Black community and its culture; it creates suspicion among Blacks about members' loyalty. Hence, the Black community may reject gifted or high-achieving Blacks not because they achieve academically, but rather because they appear removed and detached from their indigenous community. The Black community tends to reject high-achieving Black students who identify with the dominant culture, desire to join it, and accept its behaviors as paradigms worth copying. Two high-achieving Black students who made the following statements might be considered raceless and in the pre-encounter stage of racial identity development:

> I'm trying very hard to get away from Black people. . . . I've tried to maintain an image of myself in the school—getting away from those people [other Black students]. (Student, as cited in Petroni & Hirsch, 1970, pp. 12, 20)

> To Whites, I tried to appear perfect—I earned good grades, was well-mannered and well-groomed. . . . I behaved, hoping that no one would associate me with them [other Black students]. (Student, as cited in Gray, 1985, pp. E1, E5)

Which culture, then, should gifted Black students support when trying to fulfill their potential? Which belief and value system should they incorporate? Black students may vacillate between allegiance to their racial group and the dominant group. For some Black students, racelessness is a pragmatic strategy, but for others it represents only a pyrrhic victory (Fordham, 1988).

Meanwhile, gifted Black students contend not only with concerns that resemble the distresses of the dominant culture but also with misfortunes that inhere in being Black and culturally different from the dominant culture—and more importantly, from other Blacks. These problems suggest the need for support services to help gifted Black students understand, cope with, and appreciate their abilities.

PARADOX OF UNDERACHIEVEMENT

Black students, especially adolescents, may have an attitude-achievement paradox, which Mickelson (1984, 1990)[1] defined as a discrepancy between Black students' beliefs regarding the relationship between education and hard work, and their effort and achievement or performance in school. The paradox results from a discrepancy between the positive attitudes Black students hold about education and their low achievement in school.

Compared to the general population, African Americans, Hispanics, and Asians are less likely to say they have achieved the American Dream than their Caucasian counterparts. Although 34% of Americans overall—and 38% of Caucasians—believe that they have achieved the dream, the percentage falls to 30% for Asians, 29% for Hispanics, and just 19% for African Americans (Metropolitan Life Insurance Company, 2009). However, the report goes on to say that despite conventional wisdom, minority populations are more optimistic than Caucasian Americans that the dream is still possible. Nearly 9 in 10 (89%) Hispanic Americans believe that they will achieve the American Dream in their lifetime, as do 82% of African Americans and 83% of Asian Americans. Only two thirds (66%) of Caucasians concur (Metropolitan Life Insurance Company, 2009).

Mickelson (1984) found that Black adolescents who underachieve represent an attitude-achievement paradox, as illustrated by "the paradoxical faith in education held by Black students who nevertheless fail to perform in school at levels expected of people who believe that education is important" (p. 44). According to Mickelson (1984), Black adolescents hold dual and opposing beliefs regarding achievement. First, there are abstract or idealistic attitudes characterized by an unrelenting faith in the achievement ideology, the Protestant work ethic, and the promise of schooling, hard work, and effort as vehicles for success and upward mobility. There are also concrete or realistic attitudes that reflect the empirical realities that culturally different groups experience relative to returns on education from the opportunity structure.

These dual belief systems are often in conflict. On one hand, Black students have been taught by teachers and/or parents that hard work and effort reap rewards relative to achievement, employment, and upward mobility—that the American Dream can become reality for any person,

---

1   Mickelson (1984) first coined this phrase, which perhaps describes, more than other terms in contemporary education, the problems of identifying and understanding achievement among Blacks.

regardless of his or her race, gender, or social circumstance. On the other hand, for too many Black students, the rewards for education have not proved tangible in terms of good paying jobs or upward mobility. Instead, they see other Blacks who are underemployed and unemployed and subjective to negative stereotypes, prejudice, and discrimination. They learn that schooling does not reap the rewards promised by the nation's democratic principles, by the achievement ideology. When Black students learn that the rewards and promises of educational attainment do not pay off, it is not long before they realize that acquiring an education carries little guarantee. Ultimately, Black students conclude that the American dream is a mirage, and Blacks and other culturally different students are less likely than White students to achieve in school and life. The result is a credibility gap between schools and gifted Black students. These dual beliefs between the ideal and the real are extremely confusing and can drain the motivation of Black students, especially gifted Black students who are attuned to social injustices and inequities and Black adolescents dealing with identity and vocational issues.

BARRIERS TO MEETING THE PSYCHOLOGICAL NEEDS GIFTED BLACK STUDENTS

The major challenge facing gifted Black students is to integrate both their identity as Black individuals and their identity as gifted individuals into their various self-concept domains. This can be an especially difficult task, considering that these two identities often elicit conflicting societal messages. Giftedness and achievement are associated largely with White culture and, thus, for Black students to acknowledge their talents and to pursue them in educational settings (especially in gifted education programs) may impede these students' attempts to acknowledge and accept their racial identities.

Fishman (2001) found that Black students in racially segregated schools had higher self-concepts than Black students in racially integrated settings. Because many gifted programs consist of disproportionate numbers of Whites, racially different students can expect not only to be surrounded by students who challenge them academically, but also by students who exhibit majority culture values and norms. Separation from racially and culturally similar peers may be extremely detrimental to the general and social self-concepts of some gifted Black students. Thus, whereas any Black student who pursues academic achievement risks ostracism from peers, those placed in segregated gifted programs are likely to experience both social *and* physical separation from significant others.

The types of learning experiences found in most gifted programs (e.g., independent study) encourage traits such as autonomy, initiative, and risk-taking. Such traits may be in conflict with the academic self-concepts of many Black students, who possess a strong self-image of being unable to perform the wide range of tasks needed to pursue a problem and solve it on their own (Swicord, 1988). Also, although the Black culture traditionally has valued creative traits such as fluency and divergent thought (Boykin, 1986; Boykin et al., 2006; Gay, 1978; Shade et al., 1997; Torrance, 1978)—qualities also valued in most gifted programs— Black students may have had these traits stifled by previous teachers and curricula that perceive any form of creative expression as nonconforming and otherwise threatening to majority culture values.

These concerns are not raised to deter the placement of bright Black students into segregated gifted programs, but rather to make teachers, program coordinators, counselors, and other school personnel aware of the special needs minority students may have. In fact, experiences in gifted programs may ultimately strengthen the various self-concept domains in Black students. Activities that allow students to explore topics and projects of interest may be one place where Black students can conduct meaningful study of their own culture. Also, once they become comfortable with creative expression, minority students can exhibit and celebrate their traditional cultural traits in an enlightening and productive manner.

Researchers and counselors have found that Blacks and other racial minority groups underutilize counseling services and have higher attrition rates from counseling, especially after the first session (Sue, 2003; Sue & Sue, 1990). In their study of the reasons minority students do not seek counseling, Atkinson, Jennings, and Liongson (1990) found the counselor's race to be a significant factor. Specifically, the availability of culturally similar and culturally sensitive counselors is an important determinant of whether or not Black students will seek counseling services. The issue of race may be particularly important for gifted Blacks in the immersion-emersion stage of racial identity development, where Black students avoid interaction with and any behaviors associated with White students (Ford et al., 2008b).

A similar explanation for this underutilization of counseling services is that Black students may not believe that White counselors have the skills necessary to be culturally sensitive. The expectation is that the counseling experience will be negative or inappropriate (Sanchez & King, 1986) not because of lack of understanding, awareness, and empathy, but rather pity, apathy, distrust, and prejudices on the part of the counselor, for example. Hence, many Black students seek support from significant others, such as their family, friends, and religious leaders. The following list represents other variables likely to contribute to the underutilization of Black students (and by implication, gifted Black students) in counseling (See Sue, 2003; Sue & Sue, 1990, Sue et al., 2007 for more detailed information):

- Counseling centers often consist of predominantly White staff, even in predominantly Black school settings. This lack of diversity presents gifted Black students with few mentors and role models and few cultural translators, which makes it difficult to seek out counseling services.

- The services offered by counseling centers are usually traditional and individual (on a one-to-one basis) and take place in the counselor's office. This type of approach may be less appropriate than meeting with Black students in a different context. Black students may find the one-to-one format too formal, removed, or alien. A nontraditional, multicultural approach would be to meet with Black students in their environment (on their "turf") or at a neutral setting, as well as in a group format.

- The primary vehicle for communication in counseling is verbal; one's ability to verbalize is the primary condition for counseling. A person who is relatively nonverbal, who is learning English as a second language, or who uses nonstandard English may be placed at a disadvantage. Counselors (and teachers) want students to be articulate and clear in expressing their feelings and thoughts. When students don't, we may perceive them as inarticulate and less intelligent. Yet, much data indicate that Black students: (a) prefer and are quite capable of expressing their ideas in nonverbal ways (with eyes, hands, posture, proximity), and (b) express ideas and feelings with fewer words than their White counterparts (Gay, 1978; Hale-Benson, 1986; Sue, 2003; Sue & Sue, 1990; Sue et al., 2007).

- Characteristics of counseling can hinder working with gifted Black students. As indicated below, many of the values and characteristics seen in both the goals and process of counseling are not always shared by Blacks and other racially and culturally different groups:

◇ *Insight*: Most theories of counseling place a premium on the attainment of insight, which is usually the ultimate goal for "curing" clients. However, insight is not necessarily valued in some minority cultures, and there are income and/or SES differences relative to learning styles. In other words, insight assumes that one has time to sit back, to reflect, and to contemplate about motivations and behavior. To be able to sit back and reflect, and to relate to the future is a luxury of middle- and upper income groups. Individuals from low-income and/or low-SES groups tend to perceive insight as inappropriate for their life circumstances and situations. Their major concerns may be: How can I afford to take care of my sick mother? How do I feed my family? Where do I find a job and dependable income and support? This orientation toward insight in the counseling session may, therefore, prove counterproductive to the effectiveness of counseling.

◇ *Affect*: Some cultural groups (e.g., Asian and Hispanic populations) refrain from expressing strong feelings; instead, maturity is seen as the ability to control emotions and feelings. Counselors who are unfamiliar with these cultural values may perceive their clients negatively, assuming they are lacking in spontaneity, depressed, and repressed.

◇ *Self-exploration*: Black and Asian groups, for instance, tend to believe that thinking too much about something can cause problems—negative Karma. Focusing on one's own problems is, therefore, considered selfish and egocentric because one's family should be the center of attention.

◇ *Self-disclosure (openness)*: Counseling and psychological theories often hold that the more one discloses, the healthier the individual. Yet, for many, going to a counselor or psychologist is a sign of weakness and a bad reflection on the family. When students are not open, counselors may erroneously conclude that they are shy, withdrawn, inhibited, repressed, or passive. Counselors must remember that self-disclosure implies that there is a trusting relationship between the counselor and student. As indicated earlier, Black students may not perceive (White) helping professionals as persons of goodwill, which virtually halts self-disclosure. Rogers' (1961) client-centered theory proposed that effective counseling is virtually impossible unless a trusting relationship has been built. Successful counseling is mediated by a relationship between the counselor and the student that is characterized by trust, warmth, empathic understanding, and acceptance. If counselors are to facilitate the academic and social and emotional well-being of gifted students, they must be willing to enter their lives, to share their triumphs and successes, as well as their failures and disappointments, and hurt and pride (Wittmer & Myrick, 1989).

◇ *Individual orientation*: Counseling is often a one-to-one activity that encourages students to talk about or discuss the most intimate aspect of their lives. This individual orientation is not necessarily valued by Black students, who tend to prefer group settings and situations.

◇ *Lack of structure*: The counseling situation is often an ambiguous one, with students discussing their problems and counselors responding. This unstructured situation forces minority students to be the primary and active agent. Although an active stance to learning and communicating is preferred by Black students, they may be more passive if trust, empathy, and respect are not present in the counseling relationship.

◇ *Monolingual orientation*: Counselors/psychologists may not be accustomed to the phrases and words used by many Black students. Failure to understand imagery, analogies, nuances, and sayings may render the counselor ineffective in establishing relationships with Black students, and in gaining some level of insight into their concerns.

◇ *Long-range goals*: Short-term and immediate needs outweigh long-term needs or goals for some minority groups. Meeting basic needs may supersede those of insight, behavioral change, and increased achievement, for example.

◇ *Cause-effect relationships*: The lives of students in at-risk situations and environments are so complex as to make cause and effect conclusions (a logical interpretation of their issues) almost impossible. It is more practical and realistic to help gifted Black students to isolate and examine one or two major issues in their overall situation.

◇ *Less attention to nonverbal communication and behaviors*: Culturally different students, especially Black students, often master the art of reading nonverbal cues/behaviors, such as knowing when an individual says one thing but means another (e.g., Boykin, 1986; Boykin, Albury, et al., 2005; Boykin et al., 2005; Ford & Kea, 2009; Hale, 2001; Shade, 1997; Shade & Edwards, 1987). This art or skill is a physical and psychological survival strategy. When gifted Black students note discrepancies, counselors/psychologists will have difficulty establishing a productive counseling relationship.

Essentially, Sue (2003) and Sue and Sue (1990) have maintained that counseling is: (a) culture-bound—centered on the individual in which verbal, emotional, and behavioral expressiveness and communication patterns are unidirectional (from client/student to counselor), linear, verbal, and analytical (emphasizes cause and effect); (b) class-bound—a strict adherence to time schedules, ambiguous or unstructured approach to problems, and focus on long-range goals or solutions; and (c) language-bound—a heavy reliance (or overreliance) on using standard English; a strong emphasis on verbal communication.

RECOMMENDATIONS

Counselors and educators must adopt many roles—advocate, mentor, role model, teacher, and collaborator with teachers and families—to meet the academic and nonacademic needs of gifted Black students. Few counselors would disagree with Carl Rogers' (1951, 1961) sage advice that the first step toward helping individuals is to build a trusting, respectful relationship. Erikson (1968) viewed trust versus mistrust as a critical issue of his first developmental stage, and Maslow (1954, 1968) maintained that children who do not feel safe cannot trust; they are stuck at the level of trying to keep safe, and energy is directed toward trying to maintain security, which results in views about themselves filled with self-doubt rather than self-certainty. Students who develop a stance of trust have developed a base for reaching out to the world and making contact (Eisenberg & O'Dell, 1988). Thus, the underlying principle of many counseling/psychological theories and orientations is that healthy development cannot occur when respect, safety, and trust are absent.

This trust and support may be especially important when counselors and psychologists work with students from racial and cultural groups different from themselves. Care and empathy from a school counselor, psychologist, and/or teacher can help restore safety and trust in gifted Black students, particularly those who feel disenfranchised from the educational system and school personnel. Hence, when working with gifted Black students, counselors must draw upon Rogers' (1951, 1961) notion of unconditional positive regard, in which students are looked upon as individuals with unique concerns regardless of the color of their skin, income, socioeconomic status, gender, achievement, and intelligence. Stated differently, acceptance and approval are of the utmost importance in all students' developmental sequence; yet, feelings and emotions are seldom recognized in the classroom (Wittmer & Myrick, 1989).

Casas, Ponterotto, and Gutierrez (1986) asserted that the counseling of culturally different persons by those untrained for or incompetent to work with such clients should be regarded as unethical. Hence the need for standards and guidelines in this area. Gifted Black students need a place to turn emotionally in order to express their concerns, fears, and difficulties. This support is especially meaningful and effective if imparted by a professional (e.g., teacher, psychologist, or school counselor) who is effectively trained to work with both gifted students and culturally different students. Such preparation can be acquired from educational institutions, human service organizations, and professional associations. Locke (1989) recommended several strategies to enhance counselors' multicultural competence:

❖ Be open to the existence of culturally sensitive values and attitudes among students; be honest in relationships with minority students.

❖ Avoid stereotyping racial minority groups (retain the uniqueness of each student); strive to keep a reasonable balance between the views of students as human beings and cultural group members; teach students how to recognize stereotypes and how to challenge biases.

❖ Ask questions about culturally and racially diverse students. Encourage gifted Black students to discuss and be open about their concerns, beliefs, and cultural values; talk positively with students about their physical and cultural heritage; and make sure that students understand that one's race and ethnicity are never acceptable reasons for being rejected.

❖ Hold high expectations for all students.

❖ Participate in the cultural communities of culturally and racially diverse students; learn their customs and values; and share this information with students, teachers, and other colleagues.

❖ Encourage school personnel to acknowledge the strengths and contributions of racial and ethnic groups.

❖ Learn about one's own culture and cultural values.

With these guidelines, tolerance and acceptance for differences can become commonplace in schools. The initiatives used by counselors to promote intragroup cohesion and support should be multifaceted (eclectic, with varied activities and services); inclusionary (engages teachers, students, family members, administrators, and other school staff and personnel); developmental (holistic and proactive rather than reactive; prevention- and intervention-oriented); continuous (ongoing, consistent); and substantive (detailed, relevant, responsive).

To work effectively with gifted Black students, counselors must enhance their own knowledge, awareness, and skills. By increasing their knowledge of other cultures, broadening their perspectives of personal values, and learning new skills, counselors will be better prepared to work with racially and culturally diverse students. Gaining an awareness of cultures empowers counselors with more appropriate counseling skills and increased respect for individual and group differences. The challenge before counselors is to become sensitive to cultural pluralism, and to become aware of how their values can hinder the counseling relationship. This introspection requires courage and time, especially when one risks looking inward at how his or her *own* behavior can be unhealthy. Once knowledge, skills, and awareness are enhanced, counseling issues can be addressed and intervention can begin. According to an African proverb, "before healing others, heal thyself."

The philosophy of existentialism is also helpful when working with gifted Black students. Given the myriad issues facing these students, they may experience an existential crisis: Who am I? Why do I exist? Where am I going? Most adults know what it is like to lack meaning or a sense of purpose. Black students have the added concern of their identity as a Black person in a predominantly White nation, school, or gifted program, which means dealing with racial prejudice and all that it encompasses.

Individual psychology (Adler, 1964) emphasizes that human nature is fundamentally social and we are constantly striving to meet our needs for power/control, success, and belonging. Counselors can work with gifted Black students to enhance their interpersonal relationships with teachers, parents, and peers. For example, counselors can teach them: (a) how to respect the rights of others; (b) how to be tolerant of and interested in others; (c) how to encourage others; (d) how to exert genuine effort; (e) how to share—to hold a "we" versus "I" perspective; and (f) how to feel as if they belong. In short, counselors are encouraged to empower gifted Black students.

Reality therapy is also valuable for addressing issues surrounding self-direction and independence, and can teach gifted Black students to take responsibility for their behaviors. Reality therapy asserts that all behavior is internally motivated, and that individuals must learn to take responsibility for their choices and behaviors. Reality therapy, therefore, re-educates and empowers students to identify their needs, wants, and goals; to establish realistic behaviors necessary to attain these goals; and to explore negative school experiences (Hart-Hester, Heuchert, & Whittier, 1989). Reality therapy helps gifted Black students explore the need to belong, the need for power and control, and the need for freedom. When needs are met, gifted Black students are more likely to have an increased self-esteem and positive racial identity. Counselors and psychologists can help gifted Black students to establish and evaluate their present behaviors, to develop a plan of action to cope effectively with specific situations and immediate concerns, and to make a commitment to take action. Equally important, these students should be encouraged to not make excuses for their behaviors or to give up, and to realize that change or growth is a slow process.

Rational Emotive Therapy (RET; Ellis, 1962; Ellis & Harper, 1975) is an active-directive approach that is effective in helping students cope with high frustration levels, impulsivity, academic underachievement, anxieties and fears, and social isolation. It is especially suited for social, emotional, and academic problems because it acknowledges the wide variety of individual differences in the way students react to school and problems—unfair treatment, failure, criticism, and frustration, for example (Bernard, 1990). RET has the expressed goals of decreasing negative emotions (e.g., anxiety, anger) and inappropriate behaviors that cause or contribute to school problems. Gifted Black students may need assistance with identifying these problems and the causes, interpreting their thoughts, and setting goals to best overcome or cope with their concerns.

Behavioral counseling also has much promise for increasing the school achievement and coping skills of gifted Black students. Its primary philosophy is that all behavior represents our best attempts to satisfy our most pressing need(s): the need for love and to belong; the need for power; the need for freedom and fun; and the need for safety, food, and shelter (Glasser, 1986; Maslow, 1954, 1962). Whether the issue is teasing, academic failure, criticism, unfair treatment, or frustrating and difficult tasks, children and adolescents experience different degrees of adaptive and maladaptive behaviors and emotions (Bernard, 1990). Twenty percent of children are affected by stress on a continuous or chronic basis (Eisen, 1978), particularly students living in at-risk environments. In 2010, researchers from the C. S. Mott Children's Hospital National Poll on Children's Health asked adults to rate 20 different health concerns for children living in their communities (e.g., obesity, drug abuse, smoking and tobacco use, bullying, Internet safety). Stress ranked among the top 10 child health problems, with 25% of respondents indicating it was a "big problem," and was especially of concern for children in lower income communities. Levels of stress among children may relate to economic stresses faced by their families in the current economic downturn. Using this approach, counselors can help gifted Black students to understand what stress is, to explore their feelings and reactions to various stressors, and to develop ways to cope with specific stressors.

Multimodal therapy was developed by Lazarus (1985) to delineate the psychological makeup of students. Lazarus argued that human concerns can be categorized as Behavior, Affect, Sensation, Imagery, Cognition, Interpersonal relationships, and Drug/biology (BASIC I.D.). This model has proven effective for use with students experiencing academic problems, including procrastination, underachievement, and classroom misbehavior (Gerler, Drew, & Mohr, 1990). Using this approach with high school students, Gerler and colleagues (1990) focused on helping students to (a) identify with successful people, (b) feel more comfortable in school, (c) become more responsible for their decisions and behaviors, (d) become better listeners, (e) feel comfortable asking for help, (f) improve school achievement and attitudes toward school, (g) increase their self-acceptance and self-esteem, and (h) improve relationships with peers and teachers.

Morse (1987) found a multimodal approach to be effective with procrastinators. Utilizing Keat's (1979) HELPING acronym (Health, Emotions, Learning/school, People/personal relationships, Imagery/ interests, Need to know, and Guidance of actions), Morse focused on the following: perfectionism, locus of control, fear of failure, fear of success, self-concept, rebellion against authority figures, and lack of academic skills. Students participated in relaxation training (Health); discussed feelings, frustrations, and fears (Emotions); shared feelings about school, favorite subjects, and performance, as well as problems related to completing assignments (Learning/school); shared feelings about family and friends, discussed relationships with classmates, practiced communication skills (People/personal relationships); discussed strengths and weaknesses, shared likes and dislikes, discussed self put-downs, and participated in guided imagery to develop positive self-images (Imagery/interests); discussed the difference between thoughts and feelings, identified and categorized positive and negative self-thoughts, practiced positive self-talk, and discussed how choices are made (Need to know); identified putting off behaviors, discussed how time is wasted, listed daily accomplishments, wrote short-term goals and strategies to meet them and, ultimately, discussed long-term goals and strategies (Guidance of actions).

Essentially, an eclectic and developmental approach to counseling is recommended in which counselors consider the uniqueness and individuality of gifted Black students relative to their needs and concerns. Counselors must be willing to redefine the counseling situation so that communication, change, and growth are possible. Regardless of one's counseling orientation, counselors must be ever mindful of: (a) the worth and dignity of gifted Black students and their right to be respected; (b) their capacity and right to self-direction; (c) their ability to learn responsibility; (d) their capacity for growth, for dealing with feelings, thoughts, and behaviors; (e) their potential for change and personal development; and (f) their individuality relative to values, lifestyles, and aspirations.

COUNSELING INTERVENTIONS: TECHNIQUES, STRATEGIES, PHILOSOPHIES

Counseling interventions must help Black students cope with the following difficulties inherent in being part of gifted programs: identity of being both gifted and Black, peer pressures and relations, feelings of isolation from both classmates and teachers, and sensitivity about feeling different as one of a few Black students in the gifted program. As Shade (1978) noted, gifted Black achievers find ways to manage dual and conflicting situations. Counselors must teach gifted Black students how to be bicultural—how to live and learn in two cultures that may be different and how to function effectively in multiple social and cultural environments. This social competence represents a survival strategy. The interventions discussed in the following paragraphs relate to (a) self-concept and racial identity, (b) underachievement, (c) peer relations, and (d) learning styles.

Students' negative self-perceptions are formed from evaluations placed on them by others; these evaluations promote the belief that they are worthless, stupid, and unlovable persons. Once formed, negative self-concepts are difficult to reverse (Omizo, 1981; Thompson & Rudolph, 1992). A more positive self-concept and identity can help gifted Black students deal more effectively with barriers to school achievement and social and emotional well-being. To develop a positive self-concept in gifted Black students, counselors must deal with all areas of their life. Keat's (1979) HELPING model can be an effective multimodal intervention. Each session should focus on improving the self-concept and racial identity of gifted Black students in one of these areas.

Gifted Black students need opportunities to explore their feelings about being gifted, being a member of a minority group, as well as their feelings about peer relations. It is important, therefore, that they interact with older Black males and females who are confident and academically and professionally successful. High school and college students, community leaders, and teachers can be recruited to serve as mentors and role models throughout the school year.

Cinematherapy (Newton, 1994), multicultural bibliotherapy (Ford, Howard, & Harris, 1999; Ford, Tyson, Howard, & Harris, 2000; Hébert, 2009), journal writing, visualizations, self-affirmations, and mentorships can be used to promote self-awareness and racial identity. These techniques are described throughout the following sections relative to specific issues and concerns of gifted Black students. Rather than having a grab bag or hodgepodge of interventions, counselors and psychologists need to adopt techniques and strategies that are unique to gifted Black students and their concerns and context, as well as techniques that respond to the individuality of gifted Black students. In addition to the techniques and strategies adopted by counselors and psychologists, the following set of guidelines is recommended for working with gifted Black students to promote healthier or positive self-concepts and racial identities:

❖ *Focus on the strengths of gifted Black students.* Use activities and exercises based on these strengths. Formal and informal assessments of learning style preferences (e.g., visual, social, tactile, kinesthetic, relational) and area(s) of giftedness (e.g., creativity, specific academic, leadership, music, spatial) can provide valuable information for counseling gifted Black students. Role-playing and other tactile and kinesthetic experiences capitalize on learning style preferences through active involvement. Include gifted Black students in the assessment process so that they, too, are aware of their strengths and preferences. On a consistent basis, ask gifted Black students to focus on their strengths and positive attributes. What do they do best inside and outside of school? A focus on the positive increases racial identity, self-esteem, and self-concept.

❖ *Provide opportunities for success.* Use praise and reinforce gifted Black students' behaviors whenever possible. Because both gifted and Black students are often adept at reading nonverbal behaviors (and seeing discrepancies between verbal and nonverbal cues), counselors and psychologists must be genuine in their praise and positive feedback. Praise that lacks authenticity falls on deaf ears; it also raises barriers to trust and self-disclosure from Black students.

❖ *Work with gifted Black students to develop realistic and attainable goals that are personally meaningful to them.* This person-centered approach makes counseling more valuable, promotes responsibility, and helps to ensure success among gifted students. Help gifted Black students to understand the difference between and importance of both short- and long-term goals, including the importance of delayed gratification.

❖ *Establish more opportunities for group interaction.* Gifted Black students who have poor, negative, or unrealistic self-concepts should be involved in more group activities (e.g., tutoring, mentorships, group counseling) and cooperative activities. Working with other students is likely to help gifted Black students to feel better about themselves. Group affiliations can promote a sense of identification, a sense of belonging, pride, respect, and recognition, as well as direction. They provide opportunities for gifted Black students to learn from other students, which is often less threatening than learning from adults. Recommend that gifted Black students participate in community events and organizations where they are likely to experience success and acceptance. Explore the social context of students. Who can gifted Black students turn to at home and school for advice, guidance, and understanding?

❖ *Provide a safe, nonthreatening, and nurturing environment.* Ask gifted Black students to share their concerns about both the counseling and the counselor; this is especially important when they have been referred (as opposed to volunteered) for counseling services. Involve peers and family members (e.g., parents, grandparents, aunts, uncles) whenever necessary and possible. When attempting to build a trusting relationship, meet gifted Black students at a neutral setting.

❖ *Encourage and support positive moral values.* Gifted students are often concerned about world and community issues such as death, crime, poverty, famine, and war. Capitalize on these positive moral values by helping gifted Black students to reframe negative thoughts by encouraging positive thinking. Establish an Optimist Club in the school where *all* students have the opportunity to develop proactive attitudes and behaviors. Introduce gifted Black students to inspiring and motivating poems, books, and movies produced by successful Black role models. Books on African proverbs, for example, are especially uplifting.

❖ *Focus on the cognitive strengths of gifted Black students.* It is important that educators and counselors do not equate low standardized intelligence test scores with low cognitive ability. As indicated in this book and elsewhere, many factors contribute to low test scores for Black students. We must work to increase students' awareness of the relationship between thoughts, feelings, and behaviors or actions. Reading, writing, and researching this topic represent important learning opportunities. Introduce gifted Black students to books on counseling and psychology written specifically for their age group; recommend that older gifted Black students enroll in an introductory course in psychology, philosophy, Black studies/history, or sociology.

SUGGESTIONS FOR WORKING WITH UNDERACHIEVING BLACK STUDENTS

Students who fail on the margins are as deserving as those who thrive on the mainstream. Too many students have become separated from constructive learning.

—Sinclair and Ghory (1992, pp. 33–34)

This section discusses techniques, strategies, and principles that counselors can use when working with gifted Black students who are underachieving because of lack of basic skills, lack of motivation, lack of empowerment, high stress, and negative or self-defeating thoughts.

Perhaps the most common recommendation for improving students' achievement is to enhance their learning skills: study habits, time management, and stress reduction (Mallett, Kirschenbaum, & Humphrey, 1983), as well as listening skills, goal setting, and self-concept (Gerler, Bland, Meland, & Miller, 1986; Grantham, 1994; Whiting, 2006a, 2006b). Rathvon (1991) found that enhancing underachievers' study habits (at home and school), test-taking habits, and attitudes facilitated achievement. In Session 1 of Rathvon's study, students' test-taking and study habits and attitudes toward school were assessed. In Session 2, underachieving students were given "prescriptions for improvement" handouts containing suggestions for their specific concerns (e.g., procrastination, test anxiety, poor motivation or task commitment, poor school attitudes). In Session 3, they were given one of five "emergency exam" vignettes that illustrated problems frequently encountered by middle school students when preparing for and taking exams. Discussions revolved around the problems and solutions to the emergencies. In the fourth and final session, students reviewed their study and test-taking profiles; they were also administered "action plans for exams." Counselors can modify and tailor this type of program to the specific needs of gifted Black students to help teachers ensure that basic skills are addressed.

Other strategies and techniques offer promise for promoting gifted Black students' achievement and motivation. Campbell (1991) used group guidance with academically unmotivated students, and Ruben (1989) found group guidance helpful with students at risk of dropping out of school. Guidance techniques used by Campbell (such as guided fantasy, positive affirmations, and visualizations) increased students' self-concept, and provided them with new, alternative behaviors. Guided fantasy exercises that focus on successful experiences such as making friends, getting along with teachers, and being successful on a test or in a class are important topics to explore with gifted Black students. After such exercises, counselors can invite gifted Black students to debrief—to explore their feelings, attitudes, and behaviors: How did it feel to . . .? How important is working toward your goal of . . .? What did you like best about taking the test? How did it feel to approach John? Homework assignments in which gifted Black students practice role-playing and/or relaxation exercises can help reinforce the desired and agreed upon behaviors.

Positive affirmations help eliminate self-defeating thoughts and behaviors. Help gifted Black students identify specific goals, recognize negative self-messages, and rephrase/reframe the messages into positive thoughts and realistic goals. Use visualizations to capitalize upon gifted Black students' imagination and to foster feelings of empowerment. Invite such statements as:

> I see myself taking the test. I am smiling and feeling confident. I understand the materials, and I am prepared. I complete the test, I feel satisfied and proud of myself as I turn it in. I leave the room refreshed, humming to my favorite tune. (Campbell, 1991, p. 306)

Bernard (1990) recommended the use of a catastrophe scale to help students put stressors into perspective. For example, ask gifted Black students to rate on a scale of 1 to 100 the worst things that could happen to them (e.g., being teased, car accident, failing a test, being discriminated against, being sick, parents dying, earthquake). Ultimately, they will come to understand that teasing, for instance, is not the worst thing that could happen. Further, counselors can encourage them to reframe self-statements ("Teasing is not so bad. I can take it"; "Mark may tease me, but I am friends with Kareem"; "Just because I'm teased doesn't mean *all* kids don't like me").

Counselors and psychologists are advised to have many concrete educational teaching aids on hand—visual aids to depict important ideas. It is recommended that one behavior at a time be targeted, even though gifted Black students may be experiencing multiple problems. Work with gifted Black students to identify and then prioritize their concerns. Counselors need to model the behaviors they wish students to adopt; similarly, using diagrams, pictures, and other visual teaching aids can facilitate the counseling process, which focuses on learning style preferences and strengths.

Counselors and psychologists should explain/clarify the relationship between thinking and feelings; they should help gifted Black students to realize that their intense feelings are not (necessarily) caused by negative events, but by the manner in which they personalize, perceive, and interpret those events (see Bernard, 1990; Zionts, 1983). That is, the negative event (stimulus) generates thoughts (perceptions and beliefs) that lead to negative emotions (response). It is, therefore, important to focus on gifted

Black students' cognitive strengths by teaching them how positive thinking can reduce their emotional upsets. Focus on current events and relate them to how gifted Black students could cope with similar or related events in the future. Important techniques include role-playing, role modeling, and homework assignments, which give gifted Black students an opportunity to practice newly discussed or acquired behaviors and thinking skills. The following principles are also recommended, regardless of the particular technique or strategy counselors choose to adopt.

❖ *Adopt broader and more comprehensive definitions of underachievement.* Underachievement is often defined as a discrepancy between the student's ability and expected or predicted achievement. These definitions rely heavily on standardized tests, which often fail to capture the strengths of Black and other minority students. Use observations and formal and informal assessment strategies to understand the individual nature of underachievement for each student.

Perhaps one of the better tests for assessing underachievement among gifted Black students is the "cardiac test." Too often the standardized test score supersedes our own inclination that a student has potential; yet, many supportive and caring teachers often lament, "The test says he is not gifted; but in my heart, I know he is." In other words, the discrepancy definition must not be the sin qua non definition of underachievement; it overlooks many students who do not test well due to test anxiety, lack of task commitment or interest in the test, bias within the test, and a host of other issues.

❖ *Determine the nature, scope, intensity, and duration of underachievement.* Is underachievement mild, severe, or chronic? It is subject specific? Teacher specific (e.g., all gifted Black students seem to have similar concerns relative to one teacher)? Is there is a learning disability (e.g., dyslexia)? Physical disability or problem (e.g., poor eye-hand coordination, needs eyeglasses)? Learning style differences? A lack of motivation? More extrinsic than intrinsic motivation? A lack of effort? Test anxiety? Poor study skills? Poor test taking skills? Poor testing conditions (e.g., test directions poorly explained, too noisy, too quiet, poor lighting, uncomfortable chairs, too much or too little structure)? Poor timing (e.g., headache, sleepy, hungry, forgot eyeglasses, uncooperative mood)?

❖ *Explore factors that contribute to or exacerbate underachievement.*

Too many Black students see schools as "academic prisons" where they have been sentenced for 12 years; the only hope for parole is by dropping out, either mentally or physically. Consequently, it is crucial that counselors determine the factors that contribute to and/or exacerbate underachievement as perceived by the gifted Black student. Use active listening and observations to gather additional information. Talk with and involve parents and teachers. Explore peer relations. What is the student like when not in school? What does he or she like or dislike about school? Use this information in prescriptive ways, to develop a holistic perspective of underachievement.

❖ *Involve peers in the learning process whenever possible.* Peers (same age or older) can serve as tutors, role models, and mentors. Recruit college students, particularly those from Black service organizations (e.g., fraternities and sororities) and sports teams to participate, for example, by serving as big brothers and sisters. Establish internships with Black business organizations or companies.

❖ *Integrate multicultural curricula throughout the learning process.* This will increase the relevance of the learning experience for gifted Black students. Whereas gifted underachievers may be bored and disinterested in school because it is unchallenging, gifted Black underachievers may also be detached because the curriculum is irrelevant and lacks purpose and meaning. Gay (1990, 2000, 2002) highlighted the importance of desegregating the curriculum to increase the significance of school for Black students. We must bring the gifted Black students' reality into the classroom and counseling process.

SUMMARY

In the literature, one finds some useful discussion and analyses of the psychological, emotional, and social needs of gifted students. However, the database regarding the specific psychological needs of gifted minority students is not as full; even more specifically, one finds less information on their cultural needs. This chapter examined the psychological and related social and emotional challenges or issues confronting gifted Black students. In addition, several perspectives and theories of racial identity development, including the significance of culture on achievement and psychological well-being, were discussed. Counseling and psychological issues and theories were described, recommendations were set forth, and counseling interventions appropriate for use with Black students in general and gifted Black students in particular were proposed.

The chapter focused on some of the primary issues facing gifted Black students, specifically underachievement, racial identity, and psychological, social, and emotional issues. It was emphasized that, like teachers and administrators, counselors and psychologists have many roles and responsibilities that call for increased attention to recognizing, understanding, and addressing barriers to gifted Black students' achievement and motivation. It was also stressed that learning styles, lack of motivation, poor peer relations, low/poor self-concepts, weak racial identities, and environmental risk factors can and do work to the detriment of too many gifted Black students. Finally, it was emphasized that school personnel should recognize both individual and group differences among *all* students.

The most promising strategies for helping Black students succeed in gifted programs focus on: (a) racial identity (or identity as being both gifted and Black); (b) peer pressures and relations; (c) feelings of isolation from both classmates and teachers; and (d) sensitivity about feeling different or misunderstood, especially if they are one of few Black students in the gifted or AP class. Ultimately, we must teach gifted Black students how to be resilient and bicultural—how to cope with cultural conflicts and differences and how to live and learn in two cultures that may be different.

The primary message of this chapter is that gifted Black students are first and foremost human beings in need of understanding, caring, respect, and empathy. With this basic awareness and appreciation, school psychologists and counselors can begin the process of effective servicing. It is incumbent upon school counselors and psychologists to help gifted Black students to manage and appreciate their gifts and talents, to manage negative peer pressures, to make appropriate educational choices, to learn effective coping strategies, to accept failure, and to set realistic goals and expectations. These efforts should be prevention and intervention focused. Given the nation's changing demographics, counselors and other school personnel are experiencing increased contact with Black and other racially and culturally different students. With an understanding of their needs, counselors, psychologists, and all helping professionals can better serve this student population by celebrating diversity and advocating for the human rights of all students.

The strategies, interventions, and philosophies espoused through-out this chapter and book emphasize the importance of developing the whole child. This includes focusing on the needs and concerns of gifted students in general (e.g., high anxiety and stress, low self-concept, poor peer relations) and Black students in particular (e.g., racism, low teacher expectations, disproportionate dropout rates, learning style differences, poor racial identity). There are no easy solutions to the many problems facing gifted Black students. It is clear, however, that with counselors, psychologists, and teachers as advocates, gifted Black students will be better prepared to achieve in school and life.

Counseling and psychological experiences and programs for gifted Black students should be based on the premise of valuing cultural dif-ferences, and should guard against teaching gifted Black students that they are "different" from their cultural group, thereby encouraging gifted Black students to abandon their culture and heritage. Instead, gifted Black students should be helped to understand giftedness in general and the compassion and competence needed by gifted people. These students should be free to be themselves as they develop their gifts and talents.

CHAPTER TEN

Gender Issues and Considerations in Underachievement and Achievement

Students' identity and school experiences are shaped by their memberships in sociodemographic groups. Educators and other professionals concerned with equity and excellence in education frequently direct their efforts toward issues of race, income, and/or SES, often ignoring how gender affects and is affected by school experiences. Also neglected is attention to student outcomes by the combination of race and gender.

A chapter on gender differences among Black males and females is warranted in this book on giftedness and underachievement for a number of reasons. First, Black males and females experience schooling and gifted education in drastically different ways, with Black males consistently experiencing the most negative and detrimental social, economic, and academic outcomes of any race-gender group, regardless of income or SES. Black males comprise the largest portion of underachievers. Secondly, as noted in Chapter 1, although both groups are underrepresented in gifted education, Black males are the most underrepresented of any gender-racial group. They by no means experience the same success in school and society as White males. Jenkins (1936, 1950) was perhaps the first scholar to study gender differences between gifted Black males and females. He also conducted one of the most extensive studies of intellectually gifted Black students, and reported that Black females outnumber Black males in gifted programs by a ratio of 2 to 1. Gallagher and Gallagher (1994) reported similar results. The authors attributed this finding less to test performance and more to teacher perceptions; teachers were more willing to accept Black females as gifted due to their greater tendency toward conformity and greater responsibility for learning. To reiterate, in 2006, Black students were underrepresented by 47% in gifted education; Black females were underrepresented by 35% and Black males by 55%. This 47% equates to almost 250,000 Black students (101,000 Black females and 153,000 Black males) who were not identified as gifted (U.S. Department of Education, 2006b)!

Highlighting the more negative experiences of Black males is by no means meant to trivialize or relegate to second-class status the experiences of Black females. Compared to White females, for example, Black females are underperforming. We certainly must be as vigilant in our passion and compassion for Black females as we are for Black males. Because females comprise 51% of the U.S. population, they do not fit traditional notions or definitions of minority group status. Yet, the attributes traditionally associated with minority group status are often applicable to females (e.g., discrimination; underrepresentation in positions of authority and power; lower teacher expectations in science, technology, engineering, and mathematics [STEM] fields; underemployment), but gender has been ignored historically as an equity issue in schooling (e.g., Sadker & Sadker, 1982). Just as problematic and underdiscussed is that within the movement to ensure equity for females, a color-blind approach is the norm, with the issues and needs of Black females mistakenly subsumed under those of White females. More than two decades ago, Tetreault and Schmuck (1985) indicated that gender was not considered a relevant category in the analysis of school excellence; that is, the goal of excellence did not have the female student in mind. At the time of that writing, this was certainly true, but this has changed with attention to STEM fields and *White* females. We have a long way to go with Black females and males in these fields. Essentially, this assertion rings loudly when the female is Black, for not only does she face sexism, she also faces racism.

Researchers, educators, and reformers frequently examine, in isolation and/or tangentially, the effects of race, gender, and income or SES on students' educational and vocational outcomes. This practice ignores the reality that every student comes to school as an endangered person due to his or her membership in a particular racial and social class group (DeMarrais & LeCompte, 1995). Thus, when we speak of equality of educational opportunity, it is in reference to providing *every* student the same educational opportunities, support, and expectations, regardless of gender, race, income, and SES—or a combination of these variables.

This chapter presents an overview of gender issues in gifted education and AP classes. Unlike most publications in the field of gifted education, which focus almost exclusively on underachievement among females, this chapter focuses on both Black males and females in gifted education. It also diverges from the norm by focusing on the combined effects of race and gender on social, psychological, and achievement or educational outcomes. There is more than one rationale for this chapter. Many shortcomings are evident in the research and literature on gender issues in gifted education and AP classes. First, the overwhelming majority of research on gender issues among gifted students focuses on White females, thereby ignoring not only gifted males, but also Black and other culturally different males and females. Second, scholars frequently write as if all females, regardless of race and culture, are homogeneous and experience life in the same way. Not only are there differences within each major racial category (e.g., Mexican vs. Puerto Rican vs. Cuban; Chinese vs. Vietnamese vs. Korean), we must be acutely aware that Hispanic American females differ from Native American females who differ from Asian American females. These differences carry important implications for both the students' and groups' educational, psychological, and social achievement and attainment. Third and similarly, gender differences in achievement and educational attainment are equally apparent across all income and SES levels (see Chapter 6). Low-income and low-SES females and males have different experiences than their higher income and SES counterparts. Fourth, conclusions based on predominantly White females and White males cannot and must not be automatically generalized to females and males from different racial and cultural backgrounds. This happens often because research and literature are seldom disaggregated by race and gender, or by income, SES, and gender. In 1992, the Wellesley College Center for Research on Women conducted an extensive review of the literature on the education of females. The center found that researchers seldom break down data by gender and race. Similarly, interactions between the two variables are rarely studied.

Lubienski's (2001) review of mathematics education research from 1982 to 1998 revealed that "only 3 of the 3,011 articles considered ethnicity, class and gender together" (p. 3).

Several premises guide this chapter. One premise is that gifted males and females face differential issues as they endeavor to achieve in school and life. A second premise is that, consequently, Black males and females have different academic, social, and emotional needs—not only from each other, but from White males and females as well. These two premises lead to the third premise: Issues facing gifted students cannot be examined without consideration of the interrelated and confounding effects of gender *and* race. More specifically, educators and scholars in gifted and AP education (or any discipline) cannot sufficiently or thoroughly describe the myriad of issues facing males and females without focusing on the impact of race in their analyses. Research and assumptions gathered from studies must examine the specific issues of gifted White males, gifted Black males, gifted White females, and gifted Black females, for example. As advanced throughout this book, neither gifted students nor Black students are a homogeneous group. Studies and discussions of giftedness, gender, class, race, and culture in education must reflect the heterogeneity of students.

This chapter begins with an overview of the research on gifted females in general, which is followed by a discussion of the triple quandary gifted Black females may find themselves in by virtue of being Black, female, and gifted. Also discussed are the various needs of gifted males in general and gifted Black males in particular. A discussion of gender bias in tests and curriculum and instruction are also briefly presented. Finally, recommendations are offered for educators and professionals interested in the broader nature of gender issues in gifted education and AP classes, particularly issues confronting Black males and females.

QUESTIONS TO CONSIDER

- ❖ What factors contribute to the paucity of research and literature on gifted Black males and females?
- ❖ What are some of the major gender biases in education?
- ❖ How applicable is the literature and research on gender issues in gifted education to Black males and females?
- ❖ How are the issues facing gifted White males and females similar to those of gifted Black males and females? How do they differ?
- ❖ What are some of the specific or unique concerns of gifted Black

males and females, and how can educators more effectively address their needs in gifted classes and AP classes?

GIFTED FEMALES

The surge of research on gifted females has been attributed to Leta Hollingworth. Silverman (1989), for example, considered Hollingworth not only one of the founders of gifted education, but also "the first champion of the cause of gifted girls and women" (p. 86). Research by Reis (1987, 1991), Hollinger and Fleming (1992), Callahan (1991), Noble (1987, 1989), Reis and Callahan (1989), and other scholars has raised the alarm that gifted females represent a population in need of special intervention to thwart failure or reverse underachievement in school and adulthood. The National Association for Gifted Children even has a special focus group on gifted females.

As early as 1926, Hollingworth observed that because the number of males and females is approximately equal at birth, the same proportion of females as males should be recognized for their achievements. Historically, however, remarkably fewer women have become eminent than their male counterparts (Read, 1991). They tend, for example, to be underrepresented in STEM fields, as well as in government, industry, and business (American Association of University Women, 1992, 2006; American Association of University Women Educational Foundation, 2004; Holahan & Stephan, 1981; Kerr, 1985, 1991; Rensberger, 1984; Reis, 2002, 2003, 2005, 2007), particularly when there is a leadership role or position or the person is in a position of authority. Fox and Zimmerman (as cited in Read, 1991) reported that many high school girls refuse to enroll in STEM classes, especially advanced mathematics, computer, or physics classes, and they often choose not to pursue graduate-level work, despite meeting admissions requirements. Albeit dated, one of the best examples comes from Kaufmann's (1981) follow-up studies of Presidential Scholars when she found that women were overrepresented among the unemployed and in clerical positions. Eccles (1985) concluded that:

> Gifted females do not achieve as highly as do gifted males either educationally or vocationally. They are less likely to seek advanced educational training, and even when they do, they do not enter

the same fields as do their male peers. They are over-represented in the fields of education and literature, and underrepresented in science, math, and engineering. Most importantly, they are, in fact, underrepresented in all advanced educational programs and in the vast majority of high-status occupations. (p. 261)

In a longitudinal study of high school valedictorians and salutatorians, Arnold (1993) found that the self-reported intelligence of females declined in their sophomore year of college. Females also chose less demanding careers than did males, even though female valedictorians outperformed males in college. Similarly, Benbow and Arjmand (1990) reported that, of the mathematically precocious youth they sampled and studied over time, the aspirations of females decreased significantly and fewer majored in the sciences. Further, during adolescence, some girls tended to find the gifted label to be unacceptable and stigmatizing; thus, they denied their gifts and talents, they wanted to be viewed as "normal" (Kerr, 1985), which meant underachieving and otherwise camouflaging their intelligence and skills but suppressing their aspiration.

It is also disturbing and perplexing that less than 2% of American patent recipients were female, and 36% of the 1987 National Merit semi-finalists were female (Banks & Banks, 1993; Ordovensky, 1988). Read (1991) studied the achievement and career choices of both gifted males and females in 142 school districts nationally. Under investigation was the extent to which males and females were enrolled in gifted programs, the ratio of boys to girls by grade level in gifted programs, the ratio of differences by school district, and the self-identified factors that discouraged students' participation in gifted programs. Results indicated that proportionately more girls than boys were in gifted programs. Moreover, at the elementary level, there were more girls; but, at the high school level, this trend reversed itself—in grades 10–12, males outnumbered females (Reis, 1987, 2005).

The literature on gender differences suggests that underachievement is often measured by enrollment in STEM areas, such as various science, technology, engineering, and mathematics classes, and by employment in such occupational positions as adults. Course enrollments alone, however, do not provide clear evidence that females have gained access to challenging or mainly male-dominated coursework. It is one thing to get equal access to the class, but another thing to get equal access to all resources, knowledge, and experiences once placed in the course. The irony is that Black and White females attain higher grade point averages, for example, at all grade levels than do their male counterparts, yet (White) females achieve less than White males as adults (Arnold, 1993; Davis & Rimm, 1994, 2004; Feingold, 1988; Reis, 1987, 2003, 2005; Schuster, 1990); conversely, Black females have more positive academic and social outcomes than Black males.

Fox and Turner (1981) asserted that females are at greater risk for underachievement than males for numerous reasons. First, compared to males, females tend to have less confidence in their intellectual abilities, particularly in STEM areas. Second, they are more likely than males to have social service than intellectual interests and values, which partly explains why females pursue fields such as teaching more than males, and are less likely to seek degrees in STEM fields. Third, depending on their stage of development, females are more likely than males to be concerned with peer or social acceptance than intellectual pursuits and development. Fourth, girls tend to experience more conflict and confusion than do gifted boys with respect to their life goals. The authors failed to consider and shed light on how these findings are similar to and different between females from different racial groups, for a look at virtually every study on low achievement or underachievement shows, as noted earlier, that Black males are the lowest performing group on a consistent basis. Thus, the assertions by Fox and Turner cannot be generalized to Black males and females.

Numerous social, psychological, environmental, and cultural influences affect the phenomenon of underachieving gifted females. Barriers include: rejection by family members, teachers, and peer groups when gifted females achieve at high levels; an underestimation of girls' abilities, skills, and potential by family members, teachers, vocational counselors, and others; receiving less encouragement and incentives than males to reach their potential as adults in certain disciplines; and reduced opportunities to develop their abilities and qualifications or skills because of a tendency among females to repudiate the label of gifted for themselves. For instance, Reis (1987, 2003, 2007) stated that some gifted females are unwilling to prepare for the future because they believe that someone else will take care of them, and they have unrealistic expectations about the future. Horner (1972) contended that females often fear success in general or may fear success more than they fear failure, and Clance and Imes (1978) introduced the idea of the imposter phenomenon whereby gifted females deny or hide their intelligence. For the most part, it seems reasonable to conclude that many gifted females have been and still are unaware of, ambivalent about, or frightened by their potential (Reis, 1991, 2007).

The avoidance syndrome regarding academic achievement (i.e., the motive to avoid success) among females, appears to be due, in part, to socialization at home, at school, with friends, and in other settings. Even in this new era and decade, too many parents/caregivers teach females to be subservient—yielding, selfless, accepting, and nurturing; whereas boys are taught to be assertive, self-reliant, leaders, and defensive of their masculine beliefs (Sadker, Sadker, & Klein, 1986; Sadker, Sadker, & Steindam, 1989; Whiting, 2006a). Females are also taught, in circuitous ways, to abandon risk-taking and independence. Consequently, a femininity-giftedness conflict develops.

Differential socialization patterns lead to differences in the goals of schooling for males and females. Males and females are expected to play different roles and are trained to fulfill these roles. By age 6 or 7, children have a clear idea about gender roles; they prefer segregated sex-play and strive to conform to stereotypic gender roles (DeMarrais & LeCompte, 1995). These perceptions continue into adolescence and adulthood. Kahle (1986) found that females and males hold different and stereotypical sex-role notions about STEM-related and social science fields. Engineering, physics, geology, chemistry, mathematics, and biochemistry are highly valued and represented by males, and considered masculine fields. Conversely, females have high enrollments in the liberal arts, social science, and nursing, all of which are stereotypically perceived as feminine occupations (or occupations with feminine characteristics). These various (mis)perceptions are a function of sociocultural influences that work to marginalize women in the scientific enterprise (Kahle & Meece, 1994).

Many variables have been attributed to the academic choices students, particularly females, make in the sciences and mathematics. It is common knowledge that expectations are powerful. According to Eccles (1989; see Figure 10.1), students' decisions to persist and to excel at a particular course of study are related to their expectations for success from self and others, and the subjective value of the achievement area (also see Hrabowski, 1998, 2001). These perceptions are shaped over time by their experiences with related activities, social and/or cultural norms, encouragement from others, and the opportunity structures (or lack thereof) that exist in society. The model is based on expectancy-value theories of achievement motivation.

Essentially, gifted females do not necessarily underachieve until adolescence but instead, later, as adults. Thus, equal ability, skill, potential, and/or achievement in school do not necessarily guarantee equal opportunity to achieve career success and satisfaction. Notwithstanding the legitimate problems facing gifted females in general, educators must also examine issues associated with being a member of a racial minority group or group that also faces racial discrimination. Underachievement

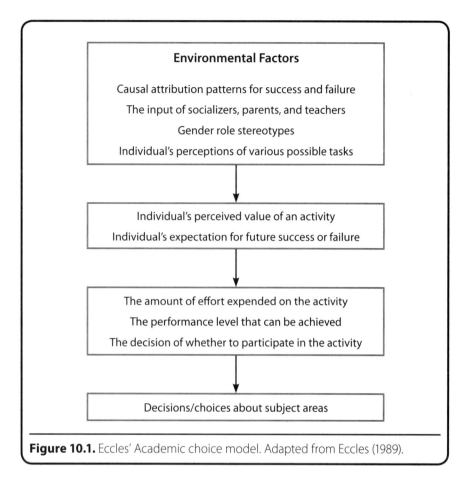

Environmental Factors

Causal attribution patterns for success and failure
The input of socializers, parents, and teachers
Gender role stereotypes
Individual's perceptions of various possible tasks

Individual's perceived value of an activity
Individual's expectation for future success or failure

The amount of effort expended on the activity
The performance level that can be achieved
The decision of whether to participate in the activity

Decisions/choices about subject areas

Figure 10.1. Eccles' Academic choice model. Adapted from Eccles (1989).

and lower than expected occupational attainment among gifted females is indeed a valid area of concern, yet there are other compelling reasons to address the specific concerns of gifted Black females—they are gifted and Black and female. As discussed below, when racial and cultural background is considered in relation to gender, gifted Black females are at greater risk for underachievement, dropping out, and school failure than White females, but not Black males.

Although it is undeniable that Black males are at the greatest risk of any group for failing to reach their potential, it is important not to trivialize the experiences of Black females. For a myriad of historical and contemporary reasons, Black females have been and are often denied a number of social and educational rights. They face stereotypes such as being the epitome of the single mother, superwoman, outspoken, over-independent, and aggressive. They are often encouraged and expected to pursue caregiving and social-oriented occupations, and are consistently put in the compromising position of having to compete with both White females and Black males in the affirmative action arena.

GIFTED BLACK FEMALES: A TRIPLE QUANDARY

Gifted Black females find themselves in a triple quandary by virtue of being gifted, Black, and female. That is, first, by virtue of being Black, they: (a) face racial discrimination; (b) are underrepresented in programs for the gifted and AP classes, (c) are overrepresented in special education classes, (d) are likely to confront social barriers to achievement and upward mobility, and (e) are more likely to experience cultural conflicts than are Whites. Essentially, Black females are whited out—almost ignored or discounted when compared to White females. Second, by virtue of being female, they face gender prejudice and discrimination in the form of low expectations, including barriers associated with tests, schooling, and employment opportunities. Specifically, Black females struggle with numerous social, cultural, and psychological barriers to achievement and success, despite legislative and legal efforts to provide quality and equity in education for females (Title VI of Civil Rights Act of 1964). Problems related to race, gender, and income and/or class persist in today's schools and society at large. Third, by virtue of being gifted, they share and face most or all of the challenges and needs specific to students identified as gifted (see Chapter 4).

Despite the aforementioned differences, the two groups are treated as one in the literature. A review of articles referenced in ERIC between 1982 and 1996 revealed that 131 focused on gifted females. Similarly, 43 articles on this topic were referenced in PsychLit since 1987. Noteworthy, however, is that none of the articles in the two database systems specifically addressed the issues of either gifted Black or other racially and culturally different females. To repeat, given that gifted females are not a monolithic group, we must examine the differential issues facing this student population.

Irvine's (1991, 2002, 2003) research has illustrated the powerful effect of teacher expectations on Black females. Along with several others, Irvine found that, compared to White females, Black females are often the recipient of low teacher expectations at all educational levels. In general, they receive less positive and constructive feedback and quality discourses from teachers, are often asked by teachers to take on caregiver roles for other students, are often ignored by teachers when they have questions and comments, and are more likely to be rebuffed by teachers when they seek attention. She also found that Black females are often expected by males and females to adopt service roles, they tend to be left out of friendship networks, and they learn to rarely attempt to interact with teachers (i.e., many Black females eventually choose to become invisible lest they lose their composure).

In gifted education, a few scholars, such as Sally Reis and Barbara Kerr, write consistently on gifted females, most of whom are White or their race is unidentified. I value their work; however, unfortunately, myself included, no particular scholar comes to mind who has devoted his or her professional career to addressing and redressing the issues and needs of either Black females or gifted Black females. This voiceless group has a story to tell and we must hear, listen, and respond to them.

Gender inequities toward females in education and society cannot be denied or disregarded. The following section concentrates on issues and needs facing gifted females and males in education by focusing specifically on problems in curriculum and instruction and testing.

BIAS IN CURRICULUM AND INSTRUCTION

The formal school curriculum serves as the core for the daily activities of teachers and students. Albeit painful to admit, a hidden curriculum operates in schools relative to gender. Hitchcock and Tompkins (1987) evaluated six editions of popular basal reading books to determine the gender of the main characteristics, and the range and frequency of occupations for female characters. Of the 1,121 stories reviewed, females were portrayed in 37 occupations (compared to five occupations in 1961–1963 readers and 23 occupations in 1969–1971 readers). The authors found that 18% of main characters were male and 17% were female. Most often, the main characters were neutral (e.g., talking trees or animals). Rather than accept the changes as proactive efforts, Hitchcock and Tompkins maintained that textbook publishers were avoiding issues of sexism by creating neutral characters. Further, Applebee's (1989) national study of book-length works used in high school English courses found only one woman author and no minority authors in the 10 most frequently assigned books. Applebee argued that little progress had been made in reading lists from 1907 and 1963; although I was not able to find more recent data on this issue by gender, I am sure that required books continue to be dominated by White, male authors. Relatedly, even a cursory look at basal or required readings in schools reveals that few are multicultural (Ford & Harris, 1999). This issue has not gone completely away; gender equity advocates (who, frankly, focus primarily on females), which I hope is every educator, must become or remain proactive for all female students.

As discussed in Chapter 6, bias is often out of our awareness and can be unintentional (Merton, 1968) and now more indirect or subtle (e.g., Dovidio et al., 2005). Sadker, Sadker, and Long (1993) identified six forms of bias in their work on gender equity and females, specifically, linguistic bias, stereotyping, invisibility, imbalance, unreality, and fragmentation, that educators must be mindful of personally and professionally:

❖ *Linguistic bias*: One of the most common forms of bias in education is the use of masculine terms and pronouns in curricular materials.

❖ *Stereotyping*: Many curricular materials contain stereotypes relative to gender and race. For example, White females are often portrayed in passive, docile, and dependent roles, while White males are characterized as ingenious, independent, athletic, and assertive. When one examines both racial and gender stereotypes, data (Britton & Lumpkin, 1983) indicated that White males tend to be portrayed as doctors, soldiers, and police officers; Black males are portrayed as workers, farmers, warriors, and hunters; White females are commonly depicted as mothers, teachers, authors, and princesses; and Black females are depicted primarily as mothers and teachers, followed by slaves, workers, porters, and artists.

❖ *Invisibility or omission*: Few curricular materials highlight the contributions females and racially and culturally different groups have made to the development of the U.S. In many subject areas (such as history, science, math, and language arts), minorities and females are underrepresented. Given that females represent a little more than half of the U.S. population, students are deprived of information about a significant number of females; monocultural curricular materials ignore the contributions of females to the historical and economic status of the U.S. and the world.

❖ *Imbalance*: Too often, curricular materials present one interpretation or perspective. For instance, the perspectives of both females

and minority groups are often given limited attention or completely ignored.

❖ *Unreality*: The U.S. is often portrayed in an unrealistic and idealistic manner. Not only is it portrayed as positively dominant,
superior, victorious, and powerful in most, if not all, circumstances, Americans are portrayed as humane, compassionate,
and equitable, regardless of whether they are wrong or guilty.
Curricular materials also ignore or minimize controversial issues
such as racism, classism, sexism, and other forms of prejudice and
discrimination.

❖ *Fragmentation*: Curricular materials discuss the contributions
of females and racially different groups in a piecemeal, disconnected, and isolated fashion. This fragmentation is evident in the
cursory or perfunctory book chapters (or sections of chapters) on
females and minority or disadvantaged students. There is little,
if any, integration of gender and/or racial issues throughout the
materials.

A checklist for examining gender and race bias appears in Figure
10.2.

TESTS AND GENDER BIAS

Issues surrounding gender bias in tests and testing practices also help
to explain underachievement among gifted females. Increased and long
overdue social conscience has led to movements in psychometrics and
gender issues that parallel movements in psychometrics for children of
color and those who are linguistically different. Thus, educational and
psychological tests have been examined for possible bias against females.
In 1989, for example, a federal court judge in New York ordered that colleges stop awarding scholarships based on SAT scores because of their
unfairness to females. It was found that the SAT scores of females were
significantly lower than the scores of males, even though females had
higher grade point averages (College Board, 2009; Worthen et al., 1993).

Generally, females (Black and White) perform as well or better than
males on educational tests. A major exception is that females tend to score
lower than males on mathematics and science tests (Jackson & Moore,
2006; Lubienski, 2007, 2008; Plake, Ansorge, Parker, & Lowry, 1982;
Waetgen, 1977). Tittle and Zytowski (1978) concluded that various tests

- What evidence is there of ethnocentricism?
- How will the materials affect students' self-image and esteem?
- Check illustrations for stereotypes and tokenism (e.g., minority families have many children; the father is noticeably absent; the family is poor; only one minority person appears in the entire book or material; females are depicted as nurses and teachers, males are doctors and administrators).
- Check storylines for standards of success and resolution of problems.
- Check lifestyle portrayals for inaccuracies and inappropriate depictions; how are families depicted?
- Examine the relations depicted between people. Who has power? Who solves the problems? How are problems resolved?
- Who are the heroes? Are they people from different racial and cultural backgrounds? Are they male and female? Are the heroes academicians? Entertainers and musicians? Athletes?
- What are the qualifications of the authors, illustrators, and other personnel?
- Are there loaded and offensive words?
- What is the copyright date and setting?
- What might a student interpret from the nonverbal messages in the material?
- What is the quality of the illustrations? Do females and Blacks have stereo-typical features, exaggerated features and appear unkempt?

Figure 10.2. Recommendations for analyzing curricular materials for sexism and racism.

(e.g., achievement, aptitude, vocational) are biased against females for several reasons; these biases are evident in both standardized and non-standardized tests:

❖ Achievement tests are selectively biased against females in language usage (as evidenced by an imbalanced ratio of male to female noun and pronoun referents).

❖ Achievement tests are selectively biased against females in content (male characters are mentioned more often).

❖ Achievement tests contain and reinforce numerous gender-role stereotypes (e.g., female characters are portrayed in more passive roles, while males are represented in more active roles).

❖ Vocational and career interest inventories often restrict individual choices for females because they have separate norms for males and females that result in differential and gender-specific counseling about career options.

❖ Aptitude tests are often written and interpreted according to gender-role stereotypes, including the GRE, SAT, MAT, and ACT.

Despite the reality of gender bias in instruments, and curriculum and instruction, the nature-nurture controversy often rears its ugly head in discussions of STEM achievement. Frighteningly, innate gender differences, cultural attitudes, and societal expectations and stereotypes have been advanced to better understand test score and achievement outcomes (Ford, 1996; Gould, 1995).

GIFTED MALES

A special issue of *Roeper Review* (1991) that focused on the social, emotional, and academic needs of gifted males was both timely and long overdue in education and gifted education. The authors noted that gifted males contend with issues about bonding, emotionality, and maintaining a macho image (Alvino, 1991; Hébert, 1991; Kline & Short, 1991; Wolfle, 1991), oftentimes by channeling their efforts into sports rather than academics. The authors also noted that gifted males are more likely than females to be labeled hyperactive, and they are less likely to be recommended for acceleration, namely early school entrance and grade skipping due, in part, to views that they are immature for their age, particularly compared to females. Kerr et al. (1992) found that 90% of the underachievers in their national study were White males. One shortcoming of the special issue, however, is that gifted males were addressed as if they are a monolithic group; little attention was devoted to issues confronting gifted Black males. As will be discussed below, although gifted Black and White males may share similar issues and barriers to achievement, gifted Black males have additional, distinct problems that can and do undermine their achievement and success.

BLACK MALES

Over the last 25 years, the social, educational and economic outcomes for Black males have been more systematically devastating than the outcomes for any other racial or ethnic and gender group. Black males have consistently low educational attainment levels, are *more* chronically unemployed and underemployed, are less healthy and have access to fewer health care resources, die *much* younger, and are *many times* more likely to be sent to jail for periods *significantly longer* than males of other racial/ethnic groups. On average, Back males are more likely to attend the most segregated and least resourced public schools. (Schott Foundation for Public Education, 2008, p. 3, italics in original)

National statistics help to explain what many are calling the "endangered Black male" (Bonner, 2001, 2003, 2010; Kunjufu, 2001; Schott Foundation for Public Education, 2008, 2009; Tatum, 2005, 2008a, 2008b, 2008c, 2008d, 2009; Whiting, 2006a, 2006b; Wright, 1991; Wynn, 1992). In a number of reports, the Carnegie Quarterly, National Urban League, and the College Board revealed the dismal educational status of Blacks in this nation. Most recently, the Schott Foundation for Public Education (2009) reported that Black students (42%) are more likely than any other group to attend poorly resourced, low-performing schools (35% for Latino students, 32% for Native American students, 21% for Asian American students, and 15% for White students). Further, Black males are three times as likely as White males to be in a class for the educable mentally retarded, but only half as likely to be placed in a class for the gifted (Donovan & Cross, 2002; U.S. Department of Education, 2006b). The U.S. Department of Education's Annual Reports to Congress (1978–2009) consistently and repeatedly reported that Black males continue to be referred and placed disproportionately more often in special education than any other racial and gender group of adolescents. Such disproportionate placement in special education results in separate and unequal circumstances and outcomes. This mislabeling as behavior disordered or seriously emotionally disabled increases one's probability of school failure, underachievement, and underidentification as gifted or potentially gifted.

Although Black males a comprise little over 8% of the total U.S. public school population, they are overrepresented among high school dropouts, school suspensions, the prison population, and students in special education classes; however, they are underrepresented in gifted programs and AP classes (Ford et al., 2008a, 2008b; Harper et al., 2009; Kunjufu, 1993; U.S. Department of Education, 2006b; Wynn, 1992; see Table 10.1). Equally disturbing, Black males score lower than any other group on standardized tests (e.g., Governors' Commission, 1989; Henry J.

Table 10.1
Educational and Social Indices of the Status of Black Males

Educational indices	Social indices
Lowest graduation rate	Highest unemployment rate
Highest dropout rate	Highest underemployment rate
Lowest test scores	Highest imprisonment rate
Lowest grade point average	Shortest lifespan
Lowest representation in gifted education and AP courses	Poorest healthcare
Highest representation in special education	Lowest societal expectations
Highest suspension rate	
Highest expulsion rate	
Lowest teacher/educator expectations	

Note. For more information, see Schott Foundation for Public Education (2008, 2009); U.S. Department of Education (2006b).

Kaiser Family Foundation, 2006; National Urban League, 2007; Schott Foundation for Public Education, 2008; Toldson, 2008). Although these data do not focus specifically on gifted Black males, one can reason by analogy that bright and highly capable Black males are represented in these alarming statistics.

In terms of teacher expectations, Irvine (1991) found that Black males at all educational levels are most likely to receive qualifying praise and controlling statements. Black males are most likely: (a) to be labeled deviant and described negatively, (b) to receive nonverbal criticism, (c) to be reprimanded and sent to the principal's office, and (d) to be judged inaccurately and negatively by teachers. They are most likely to be a victim of deficit thinking, as I have written about in many publications and in this book. On the other hand, they are least likely to receive positive teacher feedback and to interact with teachers, the majority of whom are White females (75%; Planty et al., 2009). In this case, it is impossible to rule out the interacting and powerful effects of racial and gender biases. Relative to student relations and interactions, Black males are most likely to interact with other Black males and to be socially isolated from White students; when interactions occur, they are not likely to be academic. Other distinctions by race and gender appear in Figure 10.3.

	Male	Female
White	• Probability of facing racial discrimination (4a) • Probability of facing gender discrimination (4a) • Unemployment and underemployment rates (4b) • Suspension rates (2b) • Dropout rates (4b) • Standardized test scores, particularly in math and science, and spatial ability tests and subscales (1b/2b) • Teacher expectations (1b) • Representation in gifted programs (1b/2b; varies with White females, depending on grade level)	• Probability of facing racial discrimination (4a) • Probability of facing gender discrimination (2a) • Unemployment and underemployment rates (3b) • Suspension rates (4b) • Dropout rates (3b) • Standardized test scores, particularly on reading, vocabulary, and comprehension tests and subscales (1b/2b) • Teacher expectations (2b) • Representation in gifted programs (1b/2b; varies with White males, depending on grade level)
Black	• Probability of facing racial discrimination (1a) • Probability of facing gender discrimination (4a) • Unemployment and underemployment rates (1b) • Suspension rates (1b) • Dropout rates (1b) • Standardized test scores (4b) • Teacher expectations (4b) • Representation in gifted programs (4b)	• Probability of facing racial discrimination (2a)* • Probability of facing gender discrimination (1a) • Unemployment and underemployment rates (2b) • Suspension rates (3b) • Dropout rates (2b) • Standardized test scores (3b) • Teacher expectations (3b) • Representation in gifted programs (3b)

Figure 10.3. Differential social and educational outcomes relative to gender and race. Ratings are on a 4-point Likert scale that range from 1 to 4; for clarity purposes, 1a = most likely; 1b = highest; 4a = least likely; 4b = lowest.
* Black and other culturally different females are the only group among the four to face both racial and sexual discrimination.

The Schott Foundation for Public Education's (2008) appropriately titled report, *Given Half a Chance*, focused on national and state-level reports of Black males in public education. It is quite revealing, leaving little room for states to hide behind national data and national averages; instead, it offers states opportunities to be more reflective and contextual in their issues, problems, and needs. For example:

❖ New York has three of the 10 districts with the lowest graduation rates for Black males.

❖ The one million Black male students enrolled in New York, Florida, and Georgia public schools are twice as likely not to graduate with their class.

❖ Delaware, Georgia, Illinois, Michigan, South Carolina, and

Wisconsin graduated fewer Black males than the national average.

❖ Nevada and Florida graduated less than a third of their Black male students on schedule.

❖ Illinois and Wisconsin have nearly 40-point gaps between how effectively they graduate their Black and White male students (Schott Foundation for Public Education, 2008).

Ford (1993a, 1996) examined gender differences in underachievement among gifted Black males and females in grades 5 and 6. Results indicated that Black males were more likely than Black females to be underachievers; they exerted considerably less effort in school and held more negative attitudes about school than females. They found school (e.g., topics, readings, discussions, activities) less relevant and personally meaningful than their female counterparts. Further, they were more pessimistic about social factors than were Black females. For example, several of the early adolescent Black males spoke with anger and disappointment about the injustices Blacks must wrestle with. These young Black males held concrete rather than abstract beliefs about the American Dream or achievement ideology. Thus, they supported the notion that hard work, effort, and persistence are part of the success equation, but they believed the American Dream benefitted White persons more than Black persons. The findings suggested that the Black males needed and desired more information on their racial heritage, more exposure to male and Black role models, increased affective educational experiences to feel connected to teachers, an increased sense of ownership of their schooling, and counseling experiences to cope more effectively with their anger and disappointment regarding social injustices (Bridgeland et al., 2006; Parham & Brown, 2003).

The Appendix includes profiles of Black males who hold promise for serving as vicarious role models who can motivate Black male students who find themselves in conflict socially and academically. The lives of a sample of Black males presented in the Appendix present a window into the lives of Black males that are both similar and different; richness offers Black males and readers a window into their individual and collective lives.

RECOMMENDATIONS

As this chapter indicates, educators and researchers must consider seriously the combined effects of race and gender on underachievement and other educational outcomes. The following recommendations focus on gender equity for both males and females. Due to the nature of the topic, some of the suggestions overlap with recommendations proposed throughout this book for racial equity.

GENDER EQUITY AND FEMALES

Educators must confront biases in curricular materials. Rather than ignore these issues, teachers should take the proactive stance of discussing them with students. Educators must also fill voids and omissions in curricular materials with supplementary materials. In addition, it is important to examine the classroom environment for segregation. By examining seating arrangements and sociograms, teachers can see if students are forming self-selected social networks relative to race and/or gender. Peer tutoring and cooperative learning can help increase positive social interactions among males and females.

The American Association of University Women (1992, 2006) proposed that gender-fair curriculum should adhere to the following six characteristics: (a) it must acknowledge and affirm diversity within and between groups of people; (b) it must be representative, having a balance of multiple and alternative perspectives; (c) it must be inclusive so that all students can identify positive messages about themselves; (d) it must be accurate, presenting verifiable and data-based information; (e) it must ensure that the experiences, interests, and needs of all students are integrated; and (f) it must be affirmative by valuing the worth of individuals and groups.

Because schools and their environment foster and nurture gender inequity, they must be explored. For instance, to what extent are all students encouraged to take leadership roles in the schools? Are all students exposed to a variety of professional and successful role models in the school? Are special guidance and counseling groups available relative to the specific issues facing groups by gender and/or race? Are all students encouraged to pursue traditionally male- and female-dominated careers, academic majors, and courses? Are school personnel (e.g., teachers, vocational guidance counselors) trained to recognize and eliminate subtle and overt biases relative to race, income, SES, and gender?

In terms of teacher biases, self-understanding and knowledge must be examined. For example, teachers must confront their own biases in instruction (e.g., questioning patterns, feedback, reinforcement, expectations), and choice of curricular materials (e.g., monocultural books, sexist books, noncontroversial topics). Males and females must be presented in a positive, yet realistic manner. This self-examination must focus on teachers' beliefs, stereotypes, fears, and behaviors, not just toward males and females in general, but minority males and minority females as well. School counselors and other personnel must explore their gender and racial stereotypes before they can work effectively with these students regarding their expectations and aspirations, sense of competence, achievement behaviors, and so forth.

Teachers can also use various strategies to identify positive, strong role models for gifted Black females. Bibliotherapy and cinematherapy are highly recommended for use with gifted students in general, as well as gifted Black students (e.g., Ford & Harris, 1999; Hébert, 2009; Tatum, 2007a, 2007b, 2008c). Gifted Black females may benefit academically, socially, emotionally, and psychologically from reading *Maizon at Blue Hill*, *Amazing Grace*, *Don't Say Ain't*, *Another Way to Dance*, and watching *Akeelah and the Bee*. Reading the biographies of resilient, high-achieving Black females also holds a great deal of promise. Contemporary Black female role models include Maya Angelou, Linda Darling-Hammond, Marian Wright Edelman, Michelle Obama, Angela Davis, Barbara Jordan, Oprah Winfrey, and Condoleezza Rice. (For a more comprehensive list, also see http://womenshistory.about.com/od/africanamerican/a/black_women.htm.)

Gender Equity and Males

Several educational implications and recommendations were suggested by Grantham (1994, 1997, 2004a, 2004b), Hrabowski (1998, 2001), Jackson and Moore (2006), Whiting (2006a, 2009), and Bonner (2010) on working with gifted Black males, the majority of which were directed at reforming schools and teacher professional development. First, it was urged that schools be reorganized into smaller schools, which are better structured to attend to students' social and emotional needs, and better able to match curriculum to learning styles. Second, schools should employ a talent development specialist to facilitate appropriate educational programs for gifted and potentially gifted Black males. Two responsibilities of the talent specialist include working with school personnel in program planning and implementation, and working with teachers to identify and reverse underachievement. It is also critical that teachers and school personnel receive ongoing and substantive preparation to acknowledge, own, and get rid of biases, stereotypes, and discriminatory behaviors against Black males.

Extensive staff development on underachievement for counselors and faculty was a third suggestion. Counseling must include honest and direct discussions about racism and discrimination (e.g., Caldwell et al., 2004; Harper et al., 2009; Johnson, 2006; Parham & Brown, 2003; Sandhu & Aspy, 1997; Vontress & Epp, 1997; Woodard, 1995). The fourth and fifth recommendations involved restructuring students' time for increased quality through substantive and meaningful extracurricular experiences (e.g., summer enrichment programs, mentoring programs like Upward Bound, 100 Black Men, Big Brothers Big Sisters, the Scholar Identity Institute, Young Warriors Program, Rites of Passage Programs) that focus on gender, racial, and academic pride; conflict resolution; anger management; and critical thinking and problem solving. These programs are aimed at the mind, body, and soul. Also needed is support with studying skills, organizational and time management skills, reading skills, math skills, and tutoring in other subjects. It seems important as well to replace study halls, for instance, with more productive options (e.g., tutoring, independent study, guest lectures, enrichment mini-courses and workshops). Exposing Black males to mentors and role models who have successfully balanced academics and athletics, and/or who encourage academics is also strongly recommended. Finally, there must be stronger family-school partnerships on behalf of underachieving, gifted, and potentially gifted Black males.

A developmental and holistic approach to helping gifted Black males is necessary for them to reach their potential in school and life (see Figure 10.4, applicable to both males and females). The model assumes that the needs of gifted elementary, middle, and high school students are quantitatively and qualitatively different. These issues can be categorized as affective (social and emotional), psychological, and academic, and they represent the primary means for prevention and intervention. Further, some issues are most germane to adolescent males, but irrelevant and inappropriate for younger children and females. Similarly, some issues are important to males, but may be more important or critical for females.

Affective Development (Social and Emotional)

- To increase intrapersonal skills and competencies (e.g., self-understanding, self-awareness, self-respect, and confidence), particularly healthy self-concepts and self-esteem [Eb, Mb, Hb]
- To improve interpersonal skills (e.g., social relations with peers, parents, teachers, and authority figures) [Eb, Mm, Hm]
- To appreciate similarities and differences between self and others [Eb, Mb, Hb]
- To understand and handle physical [Mb, Hb] and socioemotional [Eb, Mb, Hb] development and needs
- To accept self as an emotional being; to view compassion and empathy as humane rather than feminine [Em, Hb, Mb]
- To clarify values, set priorities, and resolve inner conflicts, particularly regarding school, achievement, and social relationships [Em, Mb, Hb]
- To promote biculturality—to enhance social and cultural competence [Em, Mb, Hb]
- To use abilities proactively and prosocially [Eb, Mm, Hm]
- To understand and cope effectively with frustration and anger, especially feelings of injustice regarding racial discrimination [Em, Mb, Hb] and sexual discrimination (Mf, Hf]

Psychological Development

- To increase understanding of racial identity and pride and its relationship to academic achievement, mental health, self-concept, and racism (Mb, Hb]
- To explore fears, anxieties, and stressors associated with success and achievement [Eb, Mb, Hb]
- To increase internal locus of control and self-efficacy [Eb, Mb, Hb]

Academic Development

- To develop positive attitudes toward school and achievement, including academic self-concepts and confidence [Eb, Mb, Hb]
- To improve academic and test performance [Eb, Mb, Hb]
- To improve basic skills, including test-taking and study skills [Eb, Mb, Hb]
- To strengthen critical thinking and problem-solving skills [Eb, Mb, Hb]
- To understand academic strengths and shortcomings, including learning style preferences and strategies for accommodating teaching styles [Eb, Mb, Hb]
- To explore options/experiences that nurture one's abilities [Eb, Mb, Hb]
- To set realistic and appropriate goals [Eb, Mb, Hb]
- To select challenging academic courses [Mb, Hb]
- To understand and resolve problems that hinder students' school performance (e.g., perfectionism, procrastination, fear of failure or success, test anxiety, poor motivation, negative peer pressures) [Eb, Mb, Hb]

Vocational/Career Development

- To explore aspirations and expectations [Eb, Mb, Hb]
- To develop an understanding of vocational/career options based on personal strengths and shortcomings [Eb, Mb, Hb]
- To explore (extensively) careers relative to educational requirements, salary, job requirements, and future demand/need [Eb, Mb, Hb]
- To visit postsecondary institutions and programs related to current career/vocational interests [Eb, Mb, Hb]
- To shadow professionals in the area of one's career/vocational interest [Eb,MB, Hb]

Figure 10.4. A goal-oriented, developmental intervention model for Black males and females. The suggestions are directed at students in all school levels (F = elementary students; M – middle school/junior high school students, H = high school students; m = males; f = females; b = both males and females). The model does not assume that the issues listed are equally important for males and females or for students at the three school levels. It recognizes, instead, that some issues are more urgent for one group than another from a developmental perspective.

For both groups, coping with racism and discrimination is essential. A preventive focus is vital—if all of the aforementioned issues are addressed at an early age (during preschool and elementary years), many of the issues may not be present in later years. Proactive efforts, therefore, seek prevention over intervention, and they are holistic because they address affective, psychological, and academic needs. The focus on prevention, intervention, affective development, and racial identity development is important for all Black students, particularly males.

In general, Black males need and want greater self-awareness, self-understanding, respect, and appreciation. They seek stronger and more positive social relations, and they need opportunities to express their emotions and feelings in positive and productive ways. They want fear to turn into reverence. These wants/desires and needs include dealing effectively with stress and anxiety, and understanding the use of defense and cognitive mechanisms. Defense mechanisms serve several purposes: They operate on an unconscious level, and they help individuals to cope with anxiety by denying and/or distorting reality. For gifted males, cognitive coping, the use of thoughts to diminish, eliminate, or help one feel better about negative events associated with stress, may represent an appropriate prevention (and intervention) strategy. Such coping includes:

- ❖ rational thinking (reasonable, realistic thinking that does not catastrophize);
- ❖ imagining or fantasizing (visualizing how things might have been done differently, how one would like it to be);
- ❖ denial (a conscious attempt to block out the source(s) of anxiety as if it had never happened);
- ❖ problem solving (mentally searching for alternative solutions, brainstorming);
- ❖ rationalization (justifying the stress);
- ❖ humor (coping with stress by confronting it directly, yet allowing for positive emotion/affect);
- ❖ prayer (appealing to a higher spiritual authority for some wish to be granted); and
- ❖ religious faith (comforting oneself with thoughts that whatever happened did so as a result of divine will).

Readings by Alfred W. Tatum (2005, 2007a, 2008a, 2008b, 2008c, 2008d, 2009) and Walter Dean Myers, and about President Obama, Dr. Martin Luther King, Jr., and Malcolm X are always important. But we cannot stop with these few Black heroes and role models. Other living, contemporary Black males who could be included in literature selections are Benjamin Carson, Sampson Davis, Rameck Hunt, George Jenkins, Farrah Gray, and Cedric Jennings.

Suggested strategies for prevention and intervention include exposing Black males (and females) to role models and mentors at an early age and throughout their lives; using counseling (peer, small group, individual) for affective development; using cinematherapy and bibliotherapy for increased understanding; employing relaxation training (e.g., journal writing, breathing, walking, exercising) as an emotional outlet; increasing their problem-solving skills; and helping students to examine their defense and coping mechanisms. Harper et al. (2009) recommended that Black males read and learn about the lives of such high-achieving Black males who faced and overcame many trials and tribulations, such as Frederick Douglass, Paul Robeson, Ralph J. Bunche, Ralph Ellison, Langston Hughes, Scott Joplin, Arthur Ashe, Jackie Robinson, Martin Luther King, Jr., Malcolm X, and Barack Obama. Figure 10.5 offers a list of high-achieving Black male role models. This list is by no means exhaustive.

A PROFILE OF ONE PROMISING PROGRAM: THE SCHOLAR IDENTITY MODEL FOR BLACK MALES

As already lamented, Black males represent two school populations that have been overlooked frequently for gifted education referral, screening, and placement. What can educators do to remedy the situation? Why do so many Black males find their identities on the athletic fields and in the entertainment industry? Why do so few Black males find their niche, their identities, and/or their self-efficacy in academic settings? What can educators do to develop or enhance a scholar identity among these male students? What is a scholar identity?

Whiting (2006a, 2006b, 2009) defined a scholar identity as one in which Black males view themselves as academicians, as studious, as competent and capable, and as intelligent or talented in school settings. Having worked with Black males for more than two decades, Whiting found several characteristics that contribute to a scholar identity. The model begins with a discussion of self-efficacy, which lays the foundation for other components of the model. For more than 4 years, the Scholar Identity Model has been used with Black males in the Scholar Identity

High-achieving Black male	Trials and tribulations
Arthur Ashe	Faced and overcame racism and discrimination to become the first to achieve in a number of areas, particularly tennis.
Ralph J. Bunche	Endured racism and discrimination to become a college scholar, United National Undersecretary, and Nobel Peace Prize Laureate.
Frederick Douglass	Born into slavery, self-educated; escaped slavery to become a world renowned slavery abolitionist, orator, statesman, and author.
Ralph Ellison	Faced racism and discrimination, often rejected on road to becoming a major literary writer.
Martin Luther King, Jr.	Was confronted often with racism and discrimination and was imprisoned, yet went on to become one of the most famous and influential civil rights leaders of all time. Earned/awarded the Nobel Peace Prize.
Barack Obama	Grew up in biracial, single-parent home. Despite facing racism and discrimination, became the first Black President of the United States.
Paul Robeson	Faced racism and discrimination, yet became a college scholar, all-American college athlete, Broadway theatrical actor and singer, professional football player, and lawyer.
Jackie Robinson	Faced racism and discrimination as the first Black professional Major League baseball player in the United States.
Malcolm X (El-Hajj Malik El-Shabazz)	Grew up in a low-income, unstable family; was imprisoned. Became an exceptional orator and civil rights advocate/leader.

Figure 10.5. A sample of positive role models of high-achieving Black males: Models of resilience. Adapted from Harper et al. (2009).

Institute, held at Vanderbilt University during the summer for 2 weeks (Whiting, 2009).

Self-efficacy. Black males who have a scholar identity believe in themselves; they are resilient, have self-confidence, self-control, and a sense of self-responsibility. They like who they are and believe they are stellar students. They are unwilling to succumb to negative stereotypes about Black males because they consider themselves to be intelligent and talented. Resilience is a noticeable characteristic of high-achieving or gifted Black students. They are not detracted by challenges or setbacks because they have personal faith and even seek out academic challenges.

Willing to make sacrifices. Many adults have learned through experiences and trials and tribulations that sacrifices are necessary for reaching both short- and long-term goals. Black males who have a scholar identity also understand how some sacrifices are necessary in order to reach many goals. Therefore, they are more likely to relinquish some aspects of a social life (e.g., parties, joining a fraternity, dating, popularity, and so forth) and other distractions (e.g., TV) in order to reach those goals that they desire.

Internal locus of control. Black males who have an internal locus of control are optimistic; these males believe they can do well because they work hard, study, and do school assignments. Just as important, when they fail or do poorly in school, they are willing to ask for help. Thus, these Black males are less likely to blame low achievement, failure, or mistakes on their teachers, families, and/or peers.

Aspirations. Motivation theories indicate that people who have aspirations tend to stay focused and to prepare for success. They think about both the present and the future, particularly regarding how one's current behaviors and decisions influence future achievements. Black males with aspirations are not overly concerned about immediate gratification and short-term interests and goals. These students set realistic goals; likewise, they recognize the importance of a high GPA, of excellent school attendance, and of participating in challenging courses to reach their dreams.

Self-awareness. Self-awareness is an honest appraisal and understanding of one's strengths and limitations. They do not let their weaknesses distract them from learning. Black males are able to adapt and find ways to compensate for their weaknesses (e.g., they seek a tutor in classes where they are not doing well; they study longer and more often).

Strong need for achievement. For Black males, the need for achievement must be stronger than the need for affiliation. Thus, their identity must not be determined by the number of friends they have or their popularity. Although they may be social and want to have friends, they are not troubled about being popular for the sake of popularity. Black males with a strong need for achievement understand that high academic achievement will take them far in life. Accordingly, school and learning come first—they do not sacrifice school achievement for friendships or a social life.

Academic self-confidence. Black males with academic self-confidence believe they are strong students. They feel comfortable and confident in academic settings, learning, and playing with ideas. Most importantly, they do not feel inferior in school, and they do not feel the need to negate, deny, or minimize their academic abilities and skills.

These males have a strong work ethic—they spend time doing school-work, they study, and they require little prodding from parents and teachers. Ultimately, those with a high academic self-concept understand that effort is just as important, or more important, than ability to be successful.

Racial identity and pride. Like self-esteem and self-concept, racial identity and pride affects students' achievement and motivation (Cross & Vandiver, 2001). For these males, race has high salience; they are comfortable being a person of color. They seek greater self-understanding as a racial being, but are also aware of the importance of adapting to their environment and being bicultural (Cross & Vandiver, 2001). Just as important, they do not equate achievement with "acting White" or selling out; that is to say, these young men refuse to be constrained by social injustices based on gender, socioeconomic status, and race or ethnicity.

Masculinity. Masculinity is a sensitive and controversial topic. Here, I refer only to the sense that Black males with a scholar identity do not equate being intelligent or studious or talented with being feminine or unmanly. Rather than take on these ideas, these diverse males believe that males are intelligent and that being gifted or intelligent does not subtract from one's sense of masculinity.

SUMMARY

Every student enters the classroom, gifted class, AP class, and other educational and social settings with differential characteristics, needs, and experiences. These differences are a function of their racial, gender, income, SES, and cultural membership. Research that focuses on gender and race in isolation provide insufficient data for educational practice and change. For example, the finding that females are underrepresented in math- and science-related classes and professions (STEM areas) obscures the reality that Black females are also sorely underrepresented in these areas. On this same note, when we find that males are overrepresented in math and the sciences, we must carefully interpret the findings because White males are overrepresented; conversely, Black males are underrepresented in these disciplines. Educators and researchers must use caution in generalizing findings from studies that focus exclusively on gender differences or racial differences.

Black students are a heterogeneous population. Black males and females have differential needs and concerns from each other and from

White males and female. For example, Black males tend to have lower test scores, higher dropout rates, and higher unemployment rates than Black females, despite the fact that Black females face both racial and gender inequities. Black males and females do not have the same chances for equal educational and employment opportunities; similarly their opportunities differ considerably from White males and females.

It cannot be denied that the U.S. is a male-dominated society; more accurately, however, is that the U.S. is a *White-male-dominated* society, with White females being second in command, rank, or status. Black males and females do not share the social and cultural capital as White males and females. Along with other racially and culturally different students, Black males and females confront racial discrimination in educational, employment, and social settings.

The literature is scarce regarding the interrelationship of race, class, and gender among gifted students, including those in AP classes. As the preceding chapters have indicated, gifted Black students, regardless of their gender, income level, and SES level, confront and contend with many and unnecessary psychological, social, and cultural barriers to achievement. These factors must be explored relative to the combined influence of race and gender on students' academic well-being. This neglect, this inattention to individual and group differences, must be rectified in future research and literature on gender and equity in access to challenging school programs and in academic achievement and educational attainment.

CHAPTER ELEVEN

ANOTHER LOOK AT THE ACHIEVEMENT GAP: LEARNING FROM THE EXPERIENCES OF GIFTED BLACK STUDENTS[1]

As noted in several parts of this book, many studies have been conducted on the achievement gap, with most findings pointing to how school and family variables affect Black students' achievement. Another body of work focuses on how social variables (i.e., peers) impact Black students' achievement, including how accusations of "acting White" affect the performance of Black students and contribute to the achievement gap. This chapter presents a descriptive and exploratory study that extends this work by examining peer pressure among Black students identified as gifted (n = 166). As part of a larger study, gifted Black students in grades 5–12 were surveyed regarding their achievement-related attitudes

1   Parts of this chapter originally appeared in Ford, D. Y., Grantham, T. C., & Whiting, G. W. (2008). Another look at the achievement gap: Learning from the experiences of gifted Black students. *Urban Education, 43,* 216–239.

and behaviors, and perceptions of "acting White" and "acting Black." Many of the gifted Black students demonstrated an attitude-behavior discrepancy, faced negative peer pressures, and attributed "acting White" to school achievement, intelligence, and positive school behaviors and attitudes; most attributed "acting Black" to negative school achievement, low intelligence, and poor behaviors and attitudes. Recommendations are provided.

We can learn much from listening to students. Perceptions are a powerful determinant of behaviors. As VanTassel-Baska, Feng, Quek, and Struck (2004) noted, it does not matter whether something is so or not; what is important is what people perceive the situation to be. What beliefs and concerns do Black students hold about school, learning, and achievement? What can they tell us about why Black students fail to achieve? What concerns do gifted Black students have about doing well in school? How much do they value learning and achievement? What barriers do gifted Black students face in academic settings?

The current study was designed with these questions in mind. Gifted Black students, an understudied group, were surveyed regarding different aspects of achievement. Building upon previous conceptual models by Fordham and Ogbu (1986), Fordham (1988), Ogbu (1987, 2004), Steele (1997), Mickelson (1990), Ford (1994b, 1996), and Ford and Harris (1996), this study focused on achievement attitudes and achievement behaviors, along with inconsistencies between attitudes and behaviors with a group of Black males and females who had been identified as gifted. It also explored their perceptions of social barriers to achievement, namely peer pressures associated with "acting White" and "acting Black."

QUESTIONS TO CONSIDER

- ❖ What similarities and differences exist relative to factors that influence achievement and underachievement among gifted and potentially gifted Black students? What, if any, differences exist between males and females?
- ❖ What differences exist in the perceptions of gifted and potentially gifted Black students regarding negative peer pressures? Are there gender differences?
- ❖ How do Black students identified as gifted and potentially gifted view barriers to their achievement, and what gender differences exist?

STUDY OVERVIEW

This study built upon the aforementioned theories and research by further describing and exploring some of the explanations for the achievement gap, as well as low achievement and underachievement among Black students who are gifted. It is unique in several ways. First, it focuses on gifted students who are African American. As has been consistently reported, Black students are sorely underrepresented in gifted programs. Further, Black males are less likely to be identified as gifted than are Black females. A paucity of studies on low achievement, underachievement and the achievement gap has been conducted with Black students identified as gifted (Ford, 1996, 2006). Second, the study goes beyond the focus on "acting White" to a focus on "acting Black"—a construct that has received virtually no attention in the literature. Finally, the study examines perceptions. Many studies have been conducted about students, with little information collected from them. In other words, researchers have surveyed educators (e.g., teachers, counselors, psychologists, administrators), theorists, and (less often) parents about why Black students underachieve or perform at low levels academically. Fewer studies have asked students questions regarding their own beliefs and behaviors. It is with students themselves that many of the answers and solutions to underachievement, low achievement, and the achievement gap may be found.

SAMPLING PROCEDURES AND SAMPLE

Several school districts were contacted about their willingness to participate in a study of high-achieving and gifted Black students' perceptions of factors that affect their achievement. School personnel with whom I had previously worked were asked to serve as the key contact person for the study. In return for participation, the districts received a report with recommendations to address the findings associated with their specific school. The findings from two districts are described in this study.

The school personnel were asked to administer the survey to gifted Black students and to other students with high grade point averages (A and B averages), resulting in a sample size of 372 students. This study focuses only on those students who were formally identified as gifted according to district criteria (n = 166). The two school districts are located in Ohio; they are similar in racial diversity (both have 70% Black students) but are different in other ways. One middle school from District A participated in the study. The district has more than 17,000 students; it is inner-city, low SES, and one of the lowest performing districts in the state. At the time of the study (2005), the district was in academic emergency, having passed only one of 18 state standards. Little more than half of the students (54%) graduate from high school. All of the middle school students from District A that participated in the study were Black and low SES, as indicated by free or reduced lunch status.

District B is suburban, with a student population of approximately 6,800 students. Students from five middle and high schools were surveyed. This district is higher performing, having passed six of the 18 state standards. According to its annual report (2002–2003 school year), the district has received several awards for student achievement, including almost 30 AP Scholars (17 national, 4 with distinction, and 8 with honors). The graduation rate is 88%.

In District A, 189 students completed the survey; there were 183 completed surveys from District B. Of these, there were 166 gifted Black students, with the majority attending District B (n = 142, 85.5%). In Ohio, students are identified as cognitively gifted with an IQ score of 127 or higher; academically gifted students are identified at the 98th percentile or higher on an achievement test. The students were in grades 5–12, with most being in grades 6 (n = 75, 45%), 7 (n = 34, 21%), and 8 (n = 36, 22%). There were 80 males (48%) and 86 females (52%).

RESEARCH QUESTIONS

This study was guided by several research questions: (a) What are their achievement-related behaviors? How do gifted Black students spend their time each week, and how much of their time is devoted to academic-related activities (e.g., studying, doing homework, reading)? (b) How consistent are students in terms of their academic-related attitudes and behaviors? (c) What peer pressures do gifted Black students face (i.e., How do gifted Black students characterize the notions of "acting White" and "acting Black"?)? (d) According to these gifted Black students, why do some capable students not perform well in school?

DATA COLLECTION INSTRUMENTS
AND PROCEDURES

Students were administered a survey whose items were based on a previous survey developed by Ford (1996) that looked at underachievement among gifted Black students. Based on literature reviews, items were developed that focused on social/peer pressures, interests and hobbies, time devoted to education (e.g., reading, homework) and other activities (e.g., sports), and work and study habits, as these variables have been found to affect student achievement and contribute to the achievement gap (Barton, 2003; Ferguson, 2002; Hart & Risley, 1995; Jencks & Phillips, 1998; Lee & Burkham, 2002; Peske & Haycock, 2006).

The survey was administered in groups by teachers in both schools, with oversight by the enrichment counselor in District B and school director in District A. Students were informed that the survey was designed to explore students' views about achievement. The survey took approximately one hour to complete.

In addition to demographic information, the survey consisted of 22 items, which contained multiple response formats: yes/no responses, Likert-type ratings, and open-ended responses. The survey was divided into seven major parts:

- ❖ *Demographic information*: Students were asked to indicate their age, grade level, gender, race/ethnicity, and indicate if they had been identified as gifted. Students were given the option of not writing their name on the survey.
- ❖ *Academic achievement*: Students were asked about the grades they received in school and overall GPA (school records were examined to corroborate self-reported achievement). They were also asked to rate, on a scale of 1 (*weak/poor*) to 3 (*excellent/strong*), academic-related skills (study skills, test-taking skills, reading skills, organizational skills, vocabulary/language skills).
- ❖ *Course enrollment*: This item asked students to check whether they participated in gifted education courses (e.g., honors, AP).
- ❖ *Academic resources and other resources at home*: Students were asked to indicate the number of books, CDs, DVDs, and games they have at home.
- ❖ *Interests and hobbies*: Students were asked about their favorite genre of literature, as well as the names of their favorite and least favorite books and authors. Also, students were asked: "What are your hobbies?"

❖ *School work habits.* Students were given a list of 10 activities (along with an "other" option) and asked: "Try to imagine a 'typical' week. During the week, approximately how may *hours* do you devote to the following (sample activities were studying, working/job, sports, watching television, being with friends, being with family)?" Students were also asked: "How would you describe your school work habits?" (Response options were *poor, good, very good,* and *excellent,* along with a prompt to explain their responses.) Also asked was: "Do you put forth your best effort in school?" (yes or no option, along with space for explaining their response).

❖ *Social or peer pressures related to achievement.* Seven questions addressed this area. For example, students were asked: "How popular are you at school?" with the option of checking *not popular, somewhat popular,* and *very popular.* Another question asked: "Have you ever been teased/ridiculed for doing well in school?" (yes or no response option). "If yes, by whom?" Students could select from seven options, including *classmates, friends,* and *family member.* Two items pertained to "acting White" and "acting Black." "Have you ever heard of the phrase 'acting White'?" Students were given the option of responding yes or no, and then asked to explain a "yes" response. The same question and response options related to "acting Black." Another question was open-ended: "Some capable (smart) students do not do well in school. Why do you think this happens?"

FINDINGS

ACADEMIC ACHIEVEMENT

One hundred and thirty-three students reported their GPA. The self-reported GPA (S-R GPA) had a mean of 3.4 and a median of 3.5. Due to missing names (providing their names was optional), the actual GPA was unavailable for most students. However, school personnel provided the GPAs of 53 students who listed their names on the survey; the actual mean GPA was 3.1 with a median of 3.0. The correlation between S-R GPA and actual GPA was 3.8 ($p < .05$).

ACADEMIC ACHIEVEMENT: ATTITUDES AND BEHAVIORS

Students were asked whether they put forth their best effort in school. More than one fourth of students responded "no" (n = 46, 28%). These students are considered underachievers given the strong possibility that they (most people) can perform at higher levels with greater effort; stated another way, even if earning A's and B's, if one does not apply him- or herself, this is a form of underachievement (see Ford, 1996).

Students were asked to indicate whether they study and do homework on weekends; 69% (n = 115) responded "no" to this item. Students reported spending an average of 7.2 hours per week studying and doing homework (mode = one hour), and 4.6 hours per week (mode = one hour) on readings assigned by teachers.

How do the gifted Black students spend their time when not in school? Students reported spending more time with their family (27.1 hours per week), followed by watching TV (13.7 hours), listening to music (10.4 hours), and being with friends (10.5 hours). Fewer than 10 hours were spent studying and doing homework (8.2), extracurricular activities (8.2), talking on the telephone (7.2), playing video games (6.5), doing reading assigned by teachers (4.6), and personal reading (4.1). In all cases, the modal hour was one or zero (see Table 11.1).

The gifted Black students were also asked about the number of books, CDs, DVDs, and video games in their homes[2]. The mean numbers were 212, 80, 45, and 21, respectively. Students were asked to indicate their hobbies by responding based on a predetermined list (e.g., reading, writing, sports, music, other). Thirty-five students (21%) indicated that reading is a hobby. Even fewer indicated that writing is a hobby (n = 14, 8%). More than one fourth of students (n = 46, 28%) reported that music is a hobby. However, the picture looks different relative to sports: Almost half of the students reported that sports is a hobby (n = 79, 48%).

PERCEPTIONS OF SOCIAL/PEER PRESSURES

Students were asked several questions regarding social pressures. Many of the questions at this point were open-ended, designed to explore

2   The U.S. Department of Education (2000) early childhood longitudinal study examined educational resources in children's home by racial status, economic status, family's educational level, and other demographic. Consistently, Black children and low-SES children have fewer books in their homes, are read to less often, read less often on their own, and go to the library less often than White children and higher SES children.

Table 11.1
Hours Per Week Gifted Black Students Spend in Various Activities

Activity	Mean and modal hours per week
Being with family	Mean weekly hours = 27.1 Modal weekly hours = 24
Watching TV	Mean weekly hours = 13.7 Modal weekly hours = 5
Being with friends	Mean weekly hours = 10.5 Modal weekly hours = 1
Listening to music	Mean weekly hours = 10.4 Modal weekly hours = 1
Playing sports	Mean weekly hours = 8.2 Modal weekly hours = 0
Studying and doing homework	Mean weekly hours = 8.2 Modal weekly hours = 1
Talking on telephone	Mean weekly hours = 7.2 Modal weekly hours = 1
Playing video games	Mean weekly hours = 6.5 Modal weekly hours = 0
Assigned reading	Mean weekly hours = 4.6 Modal weekly hours = 1
Personal reading	Mean weekly hours = 4.1 Modal weekly hours = 1

beneath the surface of students' responses to close-ended items. In this way, the researchers were able to gain a clearer picture and understanding of peer pressure and the characteristics that gifted Black students associate with notions such as "acting White" and "acting Black." With this in mind, students were asked the following questions:

❖ Do you know anyone who has been teased/ridiculed for doing well in school?

❖ Have *you* ever been teased/ridiculed for doing well in school? If yes, by whom?

❖ Have you ever heard of the phrase "acting White"? If yes, what does this phrase mean?

❖ Have you ever been accused of "acting White"? If yes, then by whom?

❖ Have you ever heard of the phrase "acting Black"? If yes, what does this phrase mean?

❖ Some capable (smart) students do not do well in school. Why do you think this happens?

Most students (n = 110, 66%) reported knowing someone who had been teased/ridiculed for doing well in school, and 42% (n = 69) reported that that they had been teased for doing well. One third reported being teased by classmates (n = 58, 35%); 27% (n = 44) had been teased by students in other classes; 15% (n = 25) had been teased by older students; 13% (n = 21) had been teased by their friends; 8% (n = 13) had been teased by family members; and 6% (n = 10) had been teased by younger students.

PERCEPTIONS OF "ACTING WHITE" AND "ACTING BLACK"

The majority of students were familiar with the phrases "acting White" (n = 134, 81%) and "acting Black" (n = 129, 78%). Their responses to this open-ended item were examined for patterns and themes. Relative to "acting White," four major themes were found. As reflected in Table 11.2, "acting White" is characterized by: (a) language, (b) behavior, (c) intelligence, and (d) attitude. When students mentioned terms such as "speaking properly," "using poor English," "speaking slang," and "talking loud," they were coded under the heading of "language." "Behavior" referred to actions, such as "being/acting ghetto," "being thuggish or gangsta," "acting mean," "being perfect," and "acting good." "Intelligence" referred to descriptors such as "being smart," "being astute," and "getting good grades in school." Finally, the notion of "attitude" was a recurring comment, particularly as it related to "acting White" (i.e., being "arrogant," "stuck up," and "uppity"). In essence, participants reported that they perceived that Blacks who "act White" think they are superior to others. Sample responses of student definitions of "acting White" and "acting Black" are also presented in Table 11.2.

Relative to "acting White," language was mentioned 60 times by students, behavior was mentioned 48 times, intelligence was mentioned 45 times, and having an attitude was mentioned 31 times. Further, many comments reflected blatant stereotypes about Blacks and Whites, as indicated by such statements as "Acting White is acting like a typical White person would act," "Acting White is not acting like your group,"

Table 11.2

Summary of Themes and Sample Terms Based on Gifted Black Students' Perceptions of "Acting White" and "Acting Black"

	Acting White	Acting Black

	Language (60)[a]
	Behavior and Image (48)
	Intelligence (45)
	Attitude (31)
		Behavior (119;
		    including ghetto, 61)
		Language (48;
		    including slang, 25)
		Intelligence (20)
		Dress (19)

Stereotypes	• Not acting your race • Acting like a "typical" White person	• Conforming to stereotypes placed on Blacks • Doing things that are stereotypically Black
Attitude	• Stuck up/uppity • Boogy/boogie/snobbish/ snooty • Sucking up • Not embracing Black culture	• Have an attitude/have a don't care attitude • Loose • Laid back • A wannabe
Intelligent	• Smart/being too smart • Does work/does homework • Doing well in school/gets good grades • Uptight about school/ private school uptight • Taking advanced/honors courses • Would rather study than chill	• Dumb • Uneducated • Stupid • Acting ignorant • Underachieve • Pretend not to be smart
Clothes/Dress	• Dressing preppy/not wearing urban gear/not sagging • Dressing different • Dressing White	• Sagging/saggy pants • Urban gear

[a]   The number in parenthesis indicates the number of times this theme or term was mentioned by students.

"Acting Black is not acting like your own kind," "Conforming to stereotypes placed on Blacks," and "Doing things that are stereotypically Black." These references to stereotypes were not directed toward any behavior, attitude, or language; thus, they were not placed into any of the prior themes.

"Acting Black" was most often described by gifted Black students as: (a) language, (b) intelligence, (c) behavior, and (d) dress. Behavior was mentioned 119 times by students, with ghetto being mentioned 61 of the 119 instances; language was mentioned 48 times; intelligence (lack of intelligence) was mentioned 20 times; and dress or clothes was mentioned 19 times.

Regardless of grades earned in school and effort, gifted Black students held similar perceptions of "acting White" and "acting Black." Only one of the students indicated that "acting Black" was positive. The responses suggest that students hold negative perceptions and stereotypes of acting Black, but positive perceptions of acting White. Specifically, "acting Black" was associated with negative behaviors and stereotypes: low intelligence, disinterest in school and achievement, poor language skills, and a preference for urban clothes. On the other hand, "acting White" was associated with positive behaviors and stereotypes: being intelligent, caring about school, doing well academically, being well behaved, and being perfect. "Acting White" was also associated with being arrogant or believing that one is better than others.

VIEWS REGARDING WHY SOME CAPABLE STUDENTS DO NOT PERFORM WELL

As already indicated, the gifted Black students were asked to respond to the following question: "Some capable (smart) students do not do well in school. Why do you think this happens?" Students mentioned that having other priorities, laziness, depression, overconfidence, lack of academic confidence, problems at home, and a dislike for their teachers cause students not to do well. However, the overwhelming majority of the students indicated that peer pressures contribute to students underperforming in school. Relative to peer pressures, one 11th-grade male responded: "They might be afraid to be criticized or ridiculed for their achievements." Another 10th-grade male stated:

> I think it happens because they are afraid that others, not gifted like them, will tease and ridicule them. They want to fit in so they intentionally do poorly. Some smart students just may not be good on tests, homework, class work, etc.

An eighth-grade male stated: "Because they are pressured into making the wrong decisions by their peers." Two seventh-grade females indicated: "They don't want to be teased for being smart" and "Some people are scared to show how smart they are." A sixth-grade female noted: "Some smart students don't do well in school because they may think that their friends might make fun of them for being SMART!" Two 12th-grade females responded: "I think they are scared of what their peers will think about them. They also may suffer from lack of confidence and feel they cannot succeed in school. There are other factors concerning home life, friends, and parents" and "This is because they don't want to be associated with the stigma attached with achieving and doing well; plus they try to keep up with friends and don't want to be singled out or 'played.'"

SUMMARY

This study looked at achievement—more specifically, underachievement—by examining the perceptions of gifted Black students on a number of attitudinal, social, and behavioral variables. Black students who fail to reach their potential contribute to the ever persistent achievement gap and to their underrepresentation in gifted education. The purpose of this study was to shed additional light—or new light—on the achievement gap with a population of Black students who are gifted. This population has received little attention in the achievement gap discussion and research. What can we learn about achievement and underachievement, not only from Black students, but from Black students who are also gifted?

Findings from the current study are consistent with other research on low achievement and underachievement among Black students. In other words, the gifted Black students may personify an attitude-achievement paradox (Mickelson, 1990) or paradox of underachievement (Ford, 1994a, 1994b, 1996; Ford & Harris, 1996) to the extent that: (a) one third were effort-related underachievers (or nonproducers; see Delisle, 1990; Rimm, 2001) because they do not put forth their best effort in school; (b) 15% were academic underachievers because they have less than a B average; (c) too few spent time in academic-related activities (e.g., reading, studying, doing homework) compared to nonacademic activities (e.g., sports, video games, music, television); and (d) most did not have reading or writing as a hobby (Ford, 1994a, 1994b). Paradoxically, most of the students rated their work habits as good or excellent, and most rated their academic skills (study skills, test-taking skills, time management skills, and organizational skills) as strong. This confidence in their skills, while stellar, is nonetheless troublesome, given that many teachers have expressed concerns that many gifted Black students have weaknesses in academic skills; these weaknesses often prevent teachers from referring students for gifted education screening and identification (VanTassel-Baska et al., 2004).

The literature is saturated with data indicating that Black students, especially Black males, are at the greatest risk for poor school achievement, as well as low academic engagement and commitment (Whiting, 2009). These findings hold true even when the Black students are gifted (Ford, 1994b, 1996). As in previous research on gifted Black males, those in this current study were more likely than females to underachieve. Therefore, it is unfortunate, but not surprising, that most of the under-achievers—students with low effort, students with low GPAs, students with the weakest/poorest work ethic, and students with the lowest academic commitment—are Black males.

The study is also consistent with previous research on how negative peer pressures undermine the attitudes and performance of Black students (Fordham, 1988; Fordham & Ogbu, 1986). The findings also support previous works indicating that Black students equate "acting White" with being intelligent, doing well in school, enjoying school, speaking standard English, and so forth. Although "acting White" is described with positive characteristics, it also viewed as being bourgeois or arrogant. A Black student who "acts White" is thought to be uppity, stuck up, and uptight. He or she is not popular.

Finally, the concept of "acting Black" was explored. Research on this topic is miniscule. Tragically, only *one* student indicated that "acting Black" was positive. Instead, the gifted Black students, males and females alike, believed that "acting Black" means lacking in intelligence, placing a low priority on academics, speaking poorly, behaving poorly, and dressing in ill-fitted clothes. These findings lend support to Steele's (1997) notion of stereotype threat—that gifted Black students clearly hold negative stereotypes about Blacks, namely their attitudes, behaviors, and intelligence. In this respect only, gifted Black males and females were homogeneous in their views.

When the data are taken collectively, they have important ramifications for the achievement gap. It seems obvious that gifted Black students who equate intelligence with "acting White" (and lack of intelligence with "acting Black"), who do not put forth much effort into academics, who spend more time with social life and nonacademic activities, and who succumb to peer pressures are not likely to achieve at levels compared to their White counterparts; this can and does contribute to the achievement gap.

RECOMMENDATIONS

Children are not born underachievers. Underachievement is learned, and underachievement can be unlearned. We have much work ahead of us as we strive to narrow or, preferably, eliminate the achievement gap. The achievement gap is not only social and behavioral; it is attitudinal. As Mickelson (1990) noted, the achievement gap is not likely to close until attitudes or beliefs are changed. Likewise, the gap cannot close until negative stereotypes about Blacks are eliminated (Fordham, 1988; Fordham & Ogbu, 1986; Steele, 1999). What can educators and families do to help change—improve—Black students' achievement attitudes, academic behaviors, and their views of Blacks and themselves as scholars?

RECOMMENDATIONS FOR GIFTED EDUCATORS

More research is needed in gifted education to increase our understanding of underachievement (and underrepresentation) among Black students. It is clear that students—especially Black students—who underachieve are not likely to be referred for gifted education screening (Ford, 1996; VanTassel-Baska et al., 2004). It is important that those studying the achievement gap include gifted students in their research.

Administrators, teachers, and counselors need to work together to improve the image that Black students have of themselves as learners. Prevention and intervention programs that focus on improving students' achievement ethic and related behaviors are essential. These programs must focus on helping students see—and believe—the connection between effort and success in both concrete and abstract terms (Mickelson, 1990). These programs must point out discrepancies that students exhibit in this regard. For example, educators must talk to students who exert little effort, who put little time into their school work, and who place a higher priority on sports, entertainment, or their social life at the expense of their education. These discussions can be held with students individually and in small groups.

It is important that schools develop strategies to promote an achievement ethic throughout the school district, in buildings and classrooms.

Posters, symposiums, guest speakers, and mentorships can be helpful in this area. Because these students are Black, these posters, speakers, and mentors should include Black people. Likewise, the curriculum must be multicultural, as described by Banks (2006) and Ford and Harris (1999). These authors offer sample lesson plans and activities that are culturally sensitive and responsive. Stated another way, a multicultural curriculum holds much promise for improving students' image of themselves and people of color as scholars. Finally, gifted Black students are likely to benefit from counseling to cope with peer pressures, stereotypes, and their poor identities as intelligent and capable students.

To better understand how gifted Black students view themselves as learners, educators can administer instruments to students that examine their interests, motivation, and academic image or self-concept. Relative to self-concept, counselors must be familiar with racial identity and its impact on achievement. Ponterotto et al.'s (2001) book is a comprehensive treatise on various theories of racial identity, along with prevention and intervention strategies. With this information, prevention and intervention programs can be designed. Of course, these programs must consider gender differences.

RECOMMENDATIONS FOR FAMILIES

Clearly, educators cannot bear sole responsibility for closing the achievement gap. A great deal of the responsibility rests with families. Like educators, it is essential that families focus deliberately and consistently on their children's academic identity, racial identity, and skills at coping with social pressures.

Many of the students in this study spent a lot of their time watching TV and playing video games. How do these activities influence the students' images as learners? How does this help to improve their achievement and, hence, narrow the achievement gap? Families must monitor the media their children are exposed to, as well as the friends their children spent time with. Are their friends interested in school? Do they place a high priority on learning? Or do peers exert a negative influence on students?

Families are urged to connect their children with mentors and role models who are academically oriented and who have a positive racial identity. Adults in the family must also see themselves as role models and personify a strong work ethic—an image of school being important and an image of resilience. Students need support, encouragement, and guidance in the face of whatever barriers they encounter. The achievement gap is real; the achievement gap is complex; the achievement gap is stubborn; we—educators and families—must be just as stubborn and diligent in our efforts to eliminate the gap. If we can't close the gap, who can?

> We can, whenever and wherever we choose, successfully teach all children whose schooling is of interest to us. We already know more than we need in order to do this. Whether we do must finally depend on how we feel about the fact that we haven't so far. We know that our work is not done. We continue to see evidence that poor urban students and students of color are left out of the success equation. Unless we accelerate and sustain what we know and what we do on behalf of urban children, we will not have fulfilled our mission and commitment to urban children. If we recommit to learning to lead and leading for learning, then together we will go far towards enabling all our children to use the power of their minds.
>
> —Ron Edmonds (1982)

Chapter Twelve

PROMISING PROGRAMS: REVERSING UNDERACHIEVEMENT[1]

In Chapter 5 of *In Search of the Dream: Designing Schools and Classes That Work for High Potential Students From Diverse Cultural Backgrounds* (Tomlinson, Ford, Reis, Briggs, & Strickland (2004, 2009), Briggs summarized 16 model gifted programs for culturally different[2] students. Her chapter presented brief synopses of gifted education programs that represent diversity relative to geographic representation and program design, and evidence of program success. As Briggs noted, despite increased attention to the issue of underrepresentation among culturally, linguistically, and ethnically diverse (CLED) gifted students, few educators

---

1   Parts of this chapter were reproduced from Tomlinson, C. A., Ford, D. Y., Reis, S. M., Briggs, C. J., & Strickland, C. A. (Eds.). (2004). *In search of the dream: Designing schools and classrooms that work for high potential students from diverse cultural backgrounds*. Washington, DC: National Association for Gifted Children. Reprinted with the permission of the National Association for Gifted Children.

2   In this chapter, I retain the terms used by the authors when describing students (e.g., minority, culturally and linguistically diverse, non-White).

have made widespread attempts to change this situation. Sparse research documents any current efforts in gifted programs to increase the successful participation of these groups, and few research-based guidelines are available to assist program developers in their attempts to increase the identification and participation of CLED, high-potential students in programs for the gifted and talented. Little research suggests the specific curricular practices in different program designs that would effectively meet the unique needs of CLED gifted and talented students. To address this information void, an examination was conducted of interventions and practices in gifted programs that have successfully improved the representation of CLED students.

As argued elsewhere throughout this book, whereas it is clear that students from different racial and cultural backgrounds have similar needs, it is also clear that they have different needs and face different issues than their White classmates. For example, there is the unfortunate fact that Black students experience less school success than White students and other culturally different groups, and that Black students are underreferred by educators for gifted and AP classes more than White students and other culturally different students. With this said, because of the focus on Black students in this book, only those programs described by Briggs (2004) that included or specifically targeted Black students are presented in this chapter. Twelve programs that originally appeared in Briggs (2004) are described next.[3]

CLAYTON COUNTY PUBLIC SCHOOL'S GIFTED EDUCATION SERVICES
JONESBORO, GA

GIFTED EDUCATION GOALS

❖ Identify gifted students and provide services that enable students to develop their potential to become evaluators, problem solvers, innovators, and leaders.

---

3   These program descriptions originally appeared in Briggs (2004), so some data may appear dated. However, it is assumed readers can obtain ideas and strategies from these successful programs, so they are included.

GIFTED EDUCATION SERVICE DELIVERY SYSTEM

Clayton County provides services to students in pull-out classes, self-contained classes, and traditional classrooms. Full-time resource specialists serve students in each of these service options.

GRADE LEVELS SERVED

This program provides gifted education services to identified students in grades K–12, system-wide.

CURRICULUM EMPHASIS OR PROGRAMMING MODEL

A certified gifted education teacher provides service delivery to identified gifted education students (K–12). The elementary service, focusing on research, problem-solving, critical thinking, and creative thinking skills and self-science learning, is primarily delivered via a resource (pull-out) class. Additionally, some elementary schools offer cluster groupings in general education classrooms where the teacher is also certified in gifted education. Some elementary gifted education teachers also offer an introduction of advanced content delivered in "focus groups" based on student need. The secondary gifted education service delivery offerings include resource, advanced content, and cluster group settings at the middle school level. High school service delivery is provided to students via advanced content courses, including Advanced Placement, honors, and gifted education classes.

IDENTIFICATION CRITERIA

The district conducts a comprehensive talent search each year, reviewing performance data on all students in the school system. Standardized test data are retrieved from the district database and provided to each gifted education teacher. Students who score at the 90th percentile in total reading, total math, or composite on the standardized test are automatically reviewed for need of service. Planned experiences are implemented system-wide in grades K–1 as a means of eliciting a "gifted" response. In addition, general education classroom teachers in grades 2–8 are provided with lists of characteristics of giftedness after 2 weeks of observational data on students. Teachers meet and review data with grade-level teams or In-School Review Teams to discuss students' needs for modified curriculum. The meeting results in one of the following recommendations for each student:

- ❖ no modification required,
- ❖ modifications implemented by the general education classroom teacher, and
- ❖ refer student to gifted/talented education teacher for formal identification process to determine need for service

THE FORMAL IDENTIFICATION PROCESS

The state requires four multiple-criteria assessments (one normed assessment and one performance), and this program uses:

- • mental abilities (Cognitive Abilities Test),
- • achievement test (performance: ITBS or Stanford),
- • creativity test (GIFT, grades K–3; product/performance, grades 4–12), and
- • motivation (Structured Performance Assessment, grades K–3; CAMI, grades 4–8).

EVALUATION MEASURES

As part of a continuing improvement plan for gifted education services, parent, teachers, and students complete evaluation/feedback surveys on a 5-year cycle; results are compiled and are used to examine and modify gifted education services. Clayton County student participation in the Governor's Honors Program is an additional evaluation tool. The students participating in this program are considered the best students in Georgia during the current school year. In 2002–2003, Clayton County Schools had 87 semi-finalists being considered for participation, and 60 of these were CLED students.

UNIQUENESS OF THE PROGRAM FOR TALENT DEVELOPMENT OF CULTURALLY, LINGUISTICALLY, AND ETHNICALLY DIVERSE STUDENTS

One characteristic contributing to the uniqueness of this service is that all of the teachers serving G/T students are certified in gifted education via Georgia's Professional Standards Commission, having completed college courses in gifted and talented. Teachers use a wide variety of instructional materials including Great Books, Figure It Out, Problem Solving, William and Mary Problem-Based Learning Curriculum, Interact, and Foss Science Kits. In the identification process, culturally diverse low-SES students and students with learning differences are given the opportunity to demonstrate their abilities through alternative assessments (e.g., Otis-Lennon, TOMAGS, and Naglieri Nonverbal Ability Test).

CONNECTING WORLDS/MUNDOS UNIDOS GIFTED AND TALENTED DUAL ENCOUNTERS PROGRAM
HOUSTON, TX

PROGRAM GOALS

❖ Provide subject-specific gifted program services in math, language arts, science, and social studies.
❖ Provide a continuum of services to support gifted and talented students' success in Advanced Placement courses and dual credit courses.
❖ Support student development of advanced, professional quality products, as result of participation in the continuum of services.

PROGRAM DELIVERY SYSTEM

The Encounters Program drew on the work of Dr. Dorothy Sisk's Project Step-Up, utilizing staff development to acquaint teachers with Project Success and raise student achievement through the differentiation work of Samara and Curry. A district-wide effort emerged as a result of one school successfully piloting Project Step-Up, using an open-door policy providing the opportunity for all teachers to earn 30 hours of gifted and talented strategies and training to nurture the talent of all students. The district supports a well-articulated accelerated program for qualified students where accelerated/honors students have the opportunity to be identified for the gifted and talented program.

GRADE LEVELS SERVED

The program provides services to students in grades K–12.

CURRICULUM EMPHASIS OR PROGRAMMING MODEL

The Encounters Program's curricular emphasis is on acceleration and differentiation in the four core content areas. Dr. Sandra Kaplan's work and gifted training at the state level supports the curriculum differentiation in the areas of content, process, and product and serves as an evaluation tool for curriculum development. Gifted and talented programs in Texas school districts provide identified gifted and talented students with opportunities to explore and develop depth and complexity using the state guidelines. Students demonstrate learning through the development of products or performances. The work of Dr. Bertie Kingore supported the development of an evaluation rubric, blending teachers' instructional strategies for depth and complexity with the levels of student outcomes from the strategy selected.

IDENTIFICATION

The foundation for services is based on the work of gifted education specialists' research advocating that poor and minority children can be identified as gifted using traditional methods. Students are identified through varied use of assessments including the Iowa Tests of Basic Skills and Aprenda, a standardized achievement test in Spanish. Student portfolios are also used to document strengths and interests, and teacher and parent surveys are used for further information. In the area of fine arts, students are identified through three criteria: portfolios, teacher nomination (art or music teacher), and presentations, defenses, or interviews. Students not formally identified through these procedures may be placed in an acceleration opportunity. Students identified for the accelerated program often qualify for gifted and talented identification following this group experience. Thirty-five to 40% of the students in the accelerated group are limited English proficient.

EVALUATION MEASURES

The district integrates quantitative and qualitative data in a meaningful manner when looking at students for identification and ongoing assessment of student development. Researchers at the University of Houston studied the program for growth, using 7 years of data including the PEIMS report (mastery levels of student performances). Students' growth is assessed through test data and portfolios. In 1992, only 2.8% of district students were identified as gifted, with the majority Anglo. This prompted efforts to make changes by undertaking the task of increasing the number of students identified, using traditional methods, and reflecting the district demographics. Between 1993 and 1998, the percentages of participating African American and Hispanic students increased by 30% and 80%, respectively.

UNIQUENESS OF THE PROGRAM FOR TALENT DEVELOPMENT OF CULTURALLY, LINGUISTICALLY, AND ETHNICALLY DIVERSE STUDENTS

The program serves students in different delivery systems at each level: elementary, middle, and high school. The Texas Education Agency mandates that gifted students must be given some time during the school day to work with their intellectual peers, and this program provides a broad range of instruction for G/T students, but does not group homogeneously for extended periods.

At the elementary level, students have access to accelerated content and G/T identified students are required to complete self-selected projects. All students have access to the accelerated content as their needs require. Students who are not formally identified may complete projects. Students at the middle and high school levels receive services in G/T classes or accelerated classes.

For more than a decade, the Encounters Program provided numerous staff development options to support teachers' knowledge and understanding of gifted programming. Staff development included subject-specific training to meet the specific needs of the teachers. Although every campus in the district has a schoolwide Title 1 program, each campus also has a gifted and talented program, and students and teachers benefit from the resources and services of both programs. Because a large number of parents cannot provide resources and knowledge, these schools make every effort to provide all students with technology, materials, skills, teacher mentors, community mentors, university support, and business partners.

GATEway Project
Jefferson County Schools
Gifted and Talented Office
Lakewood, CO

Program Goals

- ❖ Increase the number of gifted and talented students identified from traditionally underrepresented groups in targeted schools.
- ❖ Implement an instructional framework that is aligned to the students' strengths and culture.
- ❖ Increase student achievement in reading and writing for identified students.

Program Delivery System

Services are provided through differentiation in traditional classrooms for all students, assisted by resource teachers. Resource teachers coteach, coach traditional teachers in using the GATEway framework, and provide materials to support the differentiation process. The project was funded by a federal Javits Program grant.

Grade Levels Served

The GATEway Project provides gifted services to students in grades 1–8.

CURRICULUM EMPHASIS OR
PROGRAMMING MODEL

The program is based on the GATEway Framework to Achievement and strives to address learner characteristics described in Gardner's multiple intelligences. Learning accommodations are provided based on student strengths, and opportunities are provided to promote thinking and creativity skills, use high-level questioning strategies, provide culturally responsive learning opportunities, and support skill and process learning in all students. GATEway also provides professional development for traditional teachers to broaden their perspectives of giftedness in students, and help them to understand the process of moving from potential to achievement.

Classroom teachers receiving professional development from the resource teachers were asked to create lessons or units using the GATEway Framework to Achievement as a basis. They were to take any lesson that focused on literacy and adjust it to reflect one or more of the aspects of the framework—learner characteristics in the multiple intelligences, creativity, thinking skills, questioning strategies, strength-based strategies, or cultural responsiveness. One fourth-grade teacher's reading class (homogeneously grouped, above-level readers) had read stories about disasters. They invited a Red Cross worker to their class to talk about disaster response. Their assignment was to think about what an emergency shelter might look like and need to be stocked with. Students used critical thinking in their work, and engaged in creative thinking to describe the synthesis of their ideas.

IDENTIFICATION

Identification procedures are accomplished through the use of both formal and talent pool identification. The GATEway talent pool is comprised of students who score two or more ratings of "Definitely" on the foundation criterion for identification, the DISCOVER Assessment Process (Maker, Nielson, & Rogers, 1994) Students are observed during performance tasks, which involve problem solving in the multiple intelligences, by trained observers, and then their observed behaviors are checked against known behaviors of outstanding problem solvers in the same areas. Additional criteria are used for formal identification, including IQ scores (rarely available); student achievement; creative thinking;

leadership; arts; parental referral highlighting behavioral characteristics, leadership, and teacher recommendation; Renzulli-Hartman scales for motivation and leadership; and the Kingore Observation Inventory. The GATEway project includes a talent development plan that takes into account student strengths. The multiple criteria process increases teacher awareness of different ways giftedness could look. As a result, 48% of the identified students are non-White.

EVALUATION MEASURES

Goals are assessed through daily observations, classroom teachers conferencing with resource teachers, and resource teachers providing coaching to support traditional teachers' work. The observations utilize The National Research Center on the Gifted and Talented's classroom practices observation form recommendations and Maker's DISCOVER framework. The increase in underrepresented students in gifted services through the talent development plan serves as an evaluation point. All of the grant schools are highly impacted. In a demographically similar control school not participating in the grant, no students were identified during the first year; however, in the grant schools 20 students were identified as gifted or high potential. Student achievement is evaluated through various measures of reading level and writing scored with common rubrics.

UNIQUENESS OF THE PROGRAM FOR TALENT DEVELOPMENT OF CULTURALLY, LINGUISTICALLY, AND ETHNICALLY DIVERSE STUDENTS

The GATEway project delivers gifted services through an instructional framework used to observe student motivation and effort. The desired outcomes for the framework were to assist traditional teachers in learning how to move students from potential to achievement, address obstacles, and deepen understanding of multiple intelligences.

Teachers receive student profiles for all students identifying student strengths. Learning experiences may include the introduction of unknown problems to allow students to demonstrate problem-solving behavior. Teachers learn how to accommodate student learning preferences, developing materials to allow visual-spatial students to learn literacy in their preferred style. The resource teachers who work in the grant schools support the development of these accommodations through different strategies, such as thinking skills within the content area, questioning strategies, and creativity—what it is and isn't.

The resource teacher positions are funded by the grant. However, the resource teachers plan to provide traditional teachers with knowledge, strategies, and unit plans to support students after the grant is over.

MINORITY INITIATIVE FOR GIFTED STUDENTS
GIFTED EDUCATION RESOURCE INSTITUTE
PURDUE UNIVERSITY
WEST LAFAYETTE, IN

PROGRAM GOALS

- ❖ Facilitate academic talent development among traditionally underrepresented populations of gifted students by partnering with urban school districts and foundations to identify, recruit, and support urban minority G/T students.
- ❖ Increase the diversity of the student population in the Gifted Education Resource Institute's talent development programs by developing model minority recruitment and scholarship programs.

PROGRAM DELIVERY SYSTEM

The Minority Initiative for Gifted Students (MIGS) serves students from two regional school districts in Saturday and summer programs for talented youth sponsored by the Gifted Education Resource Institute (GERI) on the Purdue University campus. Students in grades 3–8 may attend a Saturday enrichment program for 9 weeks in the fall. The summer enrichment program on the university campus offers a day camp for younger children ages 4–5 and residential campus in one-week sessions for students in grades 5–6 and a 2-week sessions for students in grades 7–12.

GRADE LEVELS SERVED

The program serves students in grades 3–12.

CURRICULUM EMPHASIS OR PROGRAMMING MODEL

All of the classes in the Purdue talent development programs are based on the Purdue Three-Stage Model. The Purdue Three-Stage Model integrates advanced content with learning processes that stress creative and critical thinking, complex problem solving, and the creation and sharing of independent projects. All GERI talent development programs provide high-ability students with exposure to advanced topics not usually covered in the K–12 curriculum, with particular emphasis on topics in math, science, and technology.

The Super Saturday program focuses on exposure and enrichment by offering a wide variety of classes to students in grades P–8 for nine Saturdays each fall and spring. Super Summer provides similar classes in a one week, half-day format in the summer. GERI summer camps provide challenging learning of advanced topics, social and emotional growth, and career development experiences in a fun, enrichment-oriented, residential environment serving ability students in grades 5–12.

IDENTIFICATION

The MIGS school districts use district procedures to identify students for participation in GERI talent development programs. These procedures are designed to find diverse students who will benefit from and be successful in GERI classes. For example, Gary, IN, schools select the top students from their self-contained gifted program. These students have already been identified as gifted by a multiple criteria selection process and have been participating in gifted programming since kindergarten. Indianapolis Public Schools do not have consistent, districtwide gifted education programs, so they collect data on students including Indiana STEP scores and Terra Nova, requiring scores at or above the 95th percentile and strong GPAs for program participation. Once the district has selected the students, meetings are scheduled with school district staff, GERI staff, and the nominated students and their families to answer questions about the program and finalize participation decisions. Efforts to increase minority student participation have been successful: the percentage of African American students participating increased from 2% to 17% between 1998 and 2002. Students who agree to participate are provided with full scholarships. The funds for the scholarship have come from a variety of sources including the Indiana Department of Education, the Tobias Foundation, the Indianapolis Public Schools, and the Davidson Foundation.

EVALUATION MEASURES

The programs are evaluated through the use of up to five sources of information. These include student, counselor, and teacher evaluations; outside evaluator observations of the program; and parental responses to the program. Findings from 3 years of evaluation data indicate that participating students have been successful in the program both academically and socially. Return rates from year to year have been exceptionally high, indicating that students enjoy the program and want to continue to participate.

UNIQUENESS OF THE PROGRAM FOR TALENT DEVELOPMENT OF CULTURALLY, LINGUISTICALLY, AND ETHNICALLY DIVERSE STUDENTS

Both program offerings provide interest-based, enrichment exposure to all participants. Efforts are made to acknowledge and support students from diverse backgrounds through the representation of diversity in teachers and counselors in the program and multicultural training for all staff. The program also takes advantage of diversity resources on the Purdue campus such as the Purdue Black Cultural Center and encourages the celebration of diverse talents through activities like talent shows. In addition, GERI talent development programs seem to be particularly appropriate for integrating diverse students because they emphasize enrichment, intrinsic motivation, interest-based learning, creativity development, and collaborative problem solving rather than individualistic, competitive, high-stakes performances.

OPEN DOORS
JACKSON, MI

PROGRAM GOALS

❖ Target the special needs of intellectually gifted children and provide necessary instructional modifications to increase student skills in and capacity for autonomous learning; creative/productive thinking; metacognition; love of learning; developing and maintaining healthy, positive, enriching relationships; and develop appropriate expectations for and understanding of the self.

❖ Provide an environment that enables students of similar ability levels to learn from and interact with one another.

❖ Provide a curriculum that addresses the unique needs of the gifted, balancing cognitive and affective experiences.

❖ Employ multiple instructional strategies to honor and accommodate individual learning differences.

PROGRAM DELIVERY SYSTEM

The Open Doors program provides services through pull-out classes.

GRADE LEVELS SERVED

The program targets students in grades 2–6.

CURRICULUM EMPHASIS OR PROGRAMMING MODEL

The Open Doors program is based on the Mississippi State Department of Education's *Suggested Outcomes for Intellectually Gifted Program*, published by the department's Office of Gifted Education. These guidelines were adapted from a number of gifted curriculum models and emphasize analytical thinking skills, creative problem solving, research, leadership, and affective/personal growth skills. Students who qualify for the program spend at least 5 hours per week in the Open Doors pull-out classes and must maintain their traditional classwork as well. Instructional strategies include simulations, service learning, group and individual projects and presentations, concept units, arts, and experiments.

IDENTIFICATION

The process begins with nominations for screening by teachers, parents, community members, or social workers, or student self-nomination. These nominations may be made at any time during the school year but a blanket screening of all first-grade students is completed to ensure no child is overlooked.

Assessments are completed using the Otis-Lennon School Aptitude Test and/or the Raven Standard Progressive Matrices. A score in the 90th percentile on one of these assessments is required for further IQ testing as the state requires an IQ score for identification. District personnel gather information on all nominated students including results from the norm-referenced group IQ tests, norm-referenced group or individual achievement tests, characteristics of giftedness checklists, leadership checklist, and demonstration of exceptional achievement in academics, leadership, or creativity.

Parents are required to provide signed permission for additional assessments and to complete a checklist about their child's thinking style, learning pace, concentration level, shyness, problem-solving strategies, and native language. Teachers complete a similar checklist for each child. These checklists are combined with student achievement data, evidence of cultural or economic disadvantage, and the breakdown of the Otis-Lennon or Raven assessment to create an individual student profile. Further assessment choices are made for individual students by psychometrists after reviewing student profiles, and every effort is made after reviewing student profiles to match the best assessment tool for each child. Students are assessed with a variety of instruments including the Universal Nonverbal Intelligence Test, Stanford-Binet-IV, Leiter-R, Wechsler Intelligence Scales for Children (WISC-III), or the Kaufman Assessment Battery for Children (KABC). All completed student profiles and assessment results are submitted to the gifted program office, and the district screening team reviews the data and determines eligibility or ineligibility for gifted programs and services.

Services begin in grade 2 and all identified students are reevaluated at the close of each school year by the local school committee to determine

Table 12.1
Diversity Increase in a 5-Year Period (216%)

February 1997	595 CLED students in the program
February 2002	1,881 CLED students in the program
February 2003	2,250 CLED students in the program

whether it is appropriate to continue placement in the gifted program during the following year.

EVALUATION MEASURES

The program has yet to undergo a formal diversity evaluation. The teachers, parents, and students evaluate the success of the program in meeting its goals by completing surveys. The program has been successful in increasing the numbers of students served, as in the first 5 years of the program there was a 216% growth in diversity (see Table 12.1).

UNIQUENESS OF THE PROGRAM FOR TALENT DEVELOPMENT OF CULTURALLY, LINGUISTICALLY, AND ETHNICALLY DIVERSE STUDENTS

The curriculum in the pull-out class provides a wide range of learning opportunities, including thinking skill training, project-based learning, and creative arts. Students work on research projects, using Creative Problem Solving (CPS) strategies or service learning. The service-learning component is unique as it is directed by the students who identify community problems, research the problems, create plans of action, raise money to support their work, collect any necessary signatures for their project, and present their proposal and outcomes to an authentic audience. Some of the projects have included: (a) collecting can goods for a food bank; (b) collecting organ donor cards; and (C) creating and marketing art projects for world hunger relief.

The goal of the service-learning experiences is for the students to learn the importance of being involved in their community and to increase students' ability to identify real problems. The Open Doors program has improved the representation of CLED students in gifted programs in direct proportion to their enrollment. The second phase of the process is finding the best ways to meet the needs of all students. Experts in the field of gifted education and diversity provide professional development offerings to help achieve this goal.

PRIMARY TALENT DEVELOPMENT
BALTIMORE COUNTY PUBLIC SCHOOLS
TOWSON, MD

PROGRAM GOALS

❖ Model best practices of learning experiences that enable all K–2 children to have opportunities to develop advanced learning capabilities.

❖ Identify strengths of students and collect observational data over time to build student profiles, guide instructional decisions, and recognize students who may be in need of gifted and talented educational services.

❖ Provide enrichment and differentiation for students who traditionally have been underserved in gifted and talented education programs.

❖ Provide primary teachers with practical resources and staff development for implementing differentiated and performance-based instruction that extends and enriches grade-level curriculum.

PROGRAM DELIVERY SYSTEM

The program provides services in traditional classroom settings through the use of modules and differentiated instruction at each grade level.

GRADE LEVELS SERVED

The Primary Talent Development (PTD) program serves students in grades K–2.

CURRICULUM EMPHASIS OR PROGRAMMING MODEL

Students are provided with a different series of open-ended, science-based, constructivist approach modules at each grade level with students having opportunities to learn through open-ended problems. Teachers have autonomy and make decisions about matching the needs of their students. Learning experiences occur over time, and teachers have the freedom to choose how they will lead their students to any experience offered. All instruction integrates best practices in gifted education and early childhood, including pacing within the traditional classroom and observation of student behaviors within the learning environment. Each module is designed to stand alone but questioning and brainstorming strategies are embedded in all of the modules. The primary purpose for these modules is as an entry point for teachers to provide a different learning environment for all students. The PTD modules seek to change from a remediation model to an enriching, accelerated model where students can have access to higher level thinking projects even if their skills are not well developed. The program is predicated upon expanded views of intelligence and theoretical models including Vygotsky's zone of proximal development and Piaget's study of child thought.

IDENTIFICATION

Access to PTD program services does not require testing or a screening process. Access is available to all K–2 students in district schools choosing to use the PTD curriculum models. Teachers provide differentiated instruction for their students and document the demonstration of certain behaviors in all of their students. The behaviors are communication, creativity, inquisitiveness, perception, resourcefulness, leadership, and persistence. Anecdotal data are gathered on students as work samples. The data are evaluated using a continuum including readiness, emergent, progressing, and independent. This process occurs during primary education years and creates a cumulative documentation of students' learning behaviors. Formal gifted identification occurs in the third grade and PTD data are important to this process.

EVALUATION MEASURES

The PTD program was developed as a strategy to address the under-representation of minority students in the district's gifted and talented education program. In 2001–2002, gifted and talented minority enrollment in grade 3 increased 2% from the previous year. A researcher specializing in the identification of gifted diverse students reviewed the PTD as part of a district evaluation of a gifted handbook and provided very positive feedback on the program design and goals.

UNIQUENESS OF THE PROGRAM FOR TALENT DEVELOPMENT OF CULTURALLY, LINGUISTICALLY, AND ETHNICALLY DIVERSE STUDENTS

This program provides early access for all students to higher level thinking and problem-based learning. Opportunities for enriching experiences are provided to all students. Curriculum modules are designed to enable students to have a broad range of ways to demonstrate their learning. In addition to the PTD program, a summer science program is offered for students completing grade 2. Students who participate in this early exposure program gain access to complex science curriculum during the following school year.

PROGRAM FOR ARTISTICALLY GIFTED MIDDLE SCHOOL STUDENTS
WOODROW WILSON MIDDLE SCHOOL
SIOUX CITY, IA

PROGRAM GOALS

- ❖ Ensure an equitable school environment that maximizes learning for all students.
- ❖ Support student achievement as demonstrated by districtwide assessments in reading, math, and science.

PROGRAM DELIVERY SYSTEM

The Program for Artistically Gifted Middle School Students serves sixth- and seventh-grade students and was designed to address the under-representation of culturally diverse and economically disadvantaged students in district gifted programs. The traditional gifted and talented program operates concurrently with the Artistically Gifted program. The goal is to meet the needs of visual-spatial gifted students through services provided in a pull-out elective art course.

GRADE LEVELS SERVED

The program serves sixth- and seventh-grade students at the middle school level.

CURRICULUM EMPHASIS OR PROGRAMMING MODEL

Gifted and talented (TAG) art classes meet every other day for the entire school year. The program's instructional strategies emphasize the development of artistic technical skills, art criticism, art history, personal reflection, and aesthetics. The curriculum used for the program was developed by the TAG art specialist and revised to meet the needs and achievement of students from year to year. The curriculum is based on the philosophy of differentiation allowing students to work on different projects, with all activities differentiated based on their needs.

IDENTIFICATION

Screening for the TAG art program begins with a nomination process by parents, teachers, peers, and students. Data are gathered for nominated students including CAT achievement test scores, grades, academic record, and an art assessment to identify artistic abilities and creativity. The academic data are used more for diagnostics and to provide the TAG art teacher with a complete profile of a student, but does not affect access to the TAG art program. The art assessment provides insight about the student's originality, fluency, creativity, and artistic development. The scored assessment, along with the nomination, enables the staff to identify students for the program.

EVALUATION MEASURES

Three data points are used for assessing this program: parent and student questionnaires, student portfolios, and district assessment that measure student gains. The test results have shown student improvement in reading as indicated by the district measurements. In addition, program data indicate that discipline referrals have been reduced and attendance is improved for TAG art students. Several of the TAG art students have received art awards in state and regional competitions.

UNIQUENESS OF THE PROGRAM FOR TALENT DEVELOPMENT OF CULTURALLY, LINGUISTICALLY, AND ETHNICALLY DIVERSE STUDENTS

The development of artistic technical skills, art criticism, art history knowledge, and aesthetics are enhanced in this program to develop leadership qualities, improve motivation, and encourage independent work. The TAG art teacher develops the curriculum and modifies it to meet the specific needs of the students. The TAG art program supports the core content areas while teaching art elements. One strategy is the use of vocabulary flip cards in which each student has a ring of vocabulary cards divided into four quadrants. Quadrant 1 contains the word and its definition. In Quadrants 2 and 3, the student writes a synonym and antonym. In Quadrant 4, the student illustrates the word. During the TAG art class, one might observe a small group of students working on flip cards, writing about their art project, or creating an art project.

An art project required the students to create a series of activities based on their creating a portrait displaying emotion. Students begin the project using the digital camera to take a black and white picture, focusing on portraying an emotion. Second, students create a portrait of emotion using charcoal. The goals of this project are to utilize the students' artistic talents and interests, strengthen critical thinking skills, and work critically and creatively. Finally, they are required to write about an event when this emotion has occurred in their life experience. Students may use paper and pencils, laptops, or record their ideas on tape.

PROJECT EXPLORE
CHATTANOOGA, TN

PROGRAM GOALS

❖ Project Explore is one program in a four-pronged initiative of the county designed to increase the number of minority students in gifted programs and increase enrichment programs in school buildings.

PROGRAM DELIVERY SYSTEM

Project Explore is a summer program developed to decrease the underrepresentation of minorities in advanced classes. Over a period of 4 years, as a result of the initiatives, the African American population increased from 19 to 150 participating students.

GRADE LEVELS SERVED

The program serves students from elementary and middle grades from Title I schools. A high school program was approved in 2003.

CURRICULUM EMPHASIS OR PROGRAMMING MODEL

The program's curriculum focuses on changing the effects of poverty on student achievement and works as a mediated learning program through hands-on experiences, thematic units, technology, and other activities that are designed to increase cognitive skills of children who live in poverty. Students receive enrichment opportunities through exposure to local and regional people, places, and events that relate to the current year's theme. Project Explore is funded by Title I and small grants. All curricular and programming decisions are based on the theory of cognitive modifiability and mediated learning as espoused by Feuerstein and Vygotsky.

IDENTIFICATION

Students are selected for participation in the program in their home schools, using criteria such as achieving at the top of their class, enjoying learning, maximizing potential, pursuing opportunities provided to them, and success in spite of less than optimal environments.

EVALUATION MEASURES

The program is evaluated using a summative evaluation. The following models are incorporated into the evaluation: management-oriented, expertise-oriented, and participant-oriented including intuitionist-pluralist evaluation and the objectives-oriented approach. This evaluation is used to plan for future program decisions and validate specific curricular approaches and teaching techniques as they relate to the theories of Feuerstein and Vygotsky. Measurement tools used include outside observations; structured interviews with students, teachers, and parents; and GATES and TerraNova scores (standardized testing).

The Project Explore coordinator reported an increase in the number of minority students eligible as gifted, from 19 in 1998 to 161 to 2003. Teachers report what they consider a significant increase in cognitive skills, level of motivation, alertness, and general enthusiasm for the program for students who have attended for more than 2 years. Although it is difficult to show statistical data supporting the program, the students came into Project Explore as high-ability learners and therefore traditional measures of increased levels of achievement are not statistically significant. However, parent, student, and teacher enthusiasm has grown almost geometrically as Title I teachers have returned to their schools implementing mediated learning strategies. The sheer increase in minority students within the system indicates that Project Explore is effective.

UNIQUENESS OF THE PROGRAM FOR TALENT DEVELOPMENT OF CULTURALLY, LINGUISTICALLY, AND ETHNICALLY DIVERSE STUDENTS

Three underlying ideas comprise the uniqueness of the program: actualizing ability, improving teachers' perceptions and instructional practices, and providing support to families. The first underlying idea can be described in a metaphor. Let us imagine that an egg represents the intellectual ability of a child. That egg must be broken or cracked when the child is young in order for his or her ability to be actualized. For many children who live in poverty, that egg is not broken. In fact, its shell becomes harder and harder, fossilizing the child's ability inside the shell. The second underlying idea is that we can change perceptions about the abilities of students from poverty and that through the training and experience provided in Project Explore, teachers will return to their building with improved instructional practices. The third underlying idea is that parents can be supported to believe that their children do not have to remain in poverty.

SCHOOL DISTRICT OF PALM BEACH COUNTY, FLORIDA
WEST PALM BEACH, FL

PROGRAM GOALS

❖ Increase the number of historically underrepresented students who successfully participate in gifted education programming options.

PROGRAM DELIVERY SYSTEM

The School District of Palm Beach County provides services though one of three methods:

❖ Full-time centers: Self-contained classrooms with gifted education endorsed teachers.
❖ Resource: Students pulled out of traditional classes; times vary by school.
❖ Inclusive: Gifted instruction provided within the traditional classroom.

Each school within the district can design a program to meet its demographic needs.

GRADE LEVELS SERVED

Services are provided to students in grades K–10.

CURRICULUM EMPHASIS OR PROGRAMMING MODEL

Each of the 10 pilot schools chooses the content focus and program design. There are three program design options. The first is a full-time center where students are served in gifted classes with a G/T certified teacher for the entire day. The second is a resource design. For this option, students are sent out of their traditional classes for 1–1.5 hours per day. The final option is an inclusive design where students are served within their traditional classrooms.

IDENTIFICATION

The new state identification procedure is divided into two paths, Plan A and Plan B. Student populations who had traditionally been adequately identified for G/T programs used Plan A with a required IQ score of 130, reading or math achievement scores at the 90% level, and a gifted characteristics checklist. Plan B is based on the use of a different matrix and includes eight criteria, nonverbal IQ test, math achievement, reading achievement, written language report card, reading grade (report card), math grade, checklist, and portfolio. For example, in place of using the Wechsler or the Stanford-Binet to assess IQ, Plan B assessed students' cognitive ability using one of the following:

- ❖ Naglieri Nonverbal Ability Test (NNAT),
- ❖ Universal Nonverbal Intelligence Test (UNIT),
- ❖ Leiter International, or
- ❖ Differential Abilities Scale (DAS).

Another criteria used in Plan B is an individual portfolio that can include sections from a menu of examples of students' past performance. Some of the options include:

- ❖ reading running records;
- ❖ English language proficiency tests;
- ❖ Florida state assessments for grades 3–5, 6–8, 9–10;
- ❖ writing samples;

❖ other test scores;

❖ creative projects; and

❖ individual projects.

A student's portfolio is evaluated by the Child Study Team using a rubric. A gifted and talented characteristics checklist must also be completed. This was developed by the district through modifications to the original gifted and talented checklist and cross-referencing the stems with research on checklists for underrepresented groups. The findings showed validation of the district stems. In addition to the two identification plans, educators in the district created an additional component for kindergarten students. Because kindergarten students do not have previous performance information available, an achievement checklist was developed to assess students' knowledge of areas including letter recognition, numbers, and shapes.

Once all of the data are gathered, a Child Study Team meets to determine eligibility for the program. If a student received 30–40 points (75%), and it is important to note that all criteria have equal weight, they were eligible for the program services. In the Fall of 2002, the state board eliminated any race-based nomination or referrals. The only groups receiving any special consideration are those who receive free or reduced lunch or are identified as limited English proficient.

A talent pool was developed in the 10 pilot schools using the screening program that considers every K–2 student for gifted potential. This process helped to identify more culturally, linguistically, and ethnically diverse students for gifted services.

EVALUATION

In 1998, an external evaluator considered to be an international expert in the area of program evaluation was hired to conduct a comprehensive evaluation. The evaluation team reviewed program philosophy, student identification and assessment, staff development, curriculum and instruction, and program design. The evaluation resulted in a 47-page report that served as a basis for program improvement. Student performance contributes to program evaluation as 97% of the students participating in the G/T program scored at grade level or higher on the state assessment.

Table 12.2
School and Gifted and Talented Enrollment

School Year	African American	Latino	European American
	% in GT / % in district	% in GT / % in district	% in GT / % in district
1994–1995	6.02 / .95	5.44 / 1.89	83.62 / 6.63
1998–1999	6.76 / 1.07	8.45 / 2.54	77.22 / 7.09
2001–2002	11.61 / 2.03	12.25 / 3.37	66.11 / 7.29

UNIQUENESS OF THE PROGRAM FOR TALENT DEVELOPMENT OF CULTURALLY, LINGUISTICALLY, AND ETHNICALLY DIVERSE STUDENTS

The pilot schools raised the identification of underrepresented students (see Table 12.2). Most of the students found in the pilot schools shared a background that is in vast contrast to those in White or upper middle-class students. This does not necessarily mean that they are not eligible for public school programs serving gifted students. The numbers demonstrate that hard work and commitment to equity and access had paid off. More than 400 students have gone through a comprehensive nomination, screening, and testing process to become eligible for gifted education.

It is very likely that these students would have never had the opportunity if not for the decision to impact those participating schools. The gifted programs have transformed the schools themselves—moving from the stereotype of having students who cannot learn, to the reality of having a program that offers hope and encouragement to their most able students.

SEM Gifted Services
St. Paul Public Schools
St. Paul, MN

Program Goals

- ❖ Provide a comprehensive, flexible plan for providing gifted and talented services.
- ❖ Challenge students in their strength areas on a regular basis.
- ❖ Strive to enable underachieving students to reach their potential.

Program Delivery System

The SEM program in St. Paul Public Schools serves students through pull-out classes, small-group Type II and III enrichment, academic competitions, and in collaboration with the traditional classroom. The program design differs in each of the 65 schools providing services.

Grade Levels Served

The program serves students in grades K–8.

Curriculum Emphasis or Programming Model

The program is based on the Schoolwide Enrichment Model created by Joe Renzulli. Programming services are based on student interests and strengths and a continuum of services is provided at each school. The goal is to provide all students with enrichment opportunities and support them in their explorations and product development. Specifically, talent development and curriculum differentiation opportunities are available to challenge high-ability, high-potential students. SEM specialists are trained in the model and use a common enrichment language.

IDENTIFICATION

The district uses the Naglieri Nonverbal Abilities Test (NNAT) as its formal identification assessment and offers the assessment starting at the kindergarten level. The district has a G/T magnet requirement of an NNAT score for admission, as well as a portfolio review process. For students remaining in the SEM schools, some are formally identified for state documentation purposes, but others are identified for services through the portfolio review process and on their interests and strengths. All students are reported to the state as either *identified* or *served*.

EVALUATION MEASURES

There are plans to develop a rubric to evaluate the services offered and program results but nothing is available at this time. The SEM specialists frequently discuss and evaluate the strengths and needs of their individual programs, and parent comments expressing their pleasure in what students have accomplished are available.

UNIQUENESS OF THE PROGRAM FOR TALENT DEVELOPMENT OF CULTURALLY, LINGUISTICALLY, AND ETHNICALLY DIVERSE STUDENTS

This program serves diverse populations, including limited English proficient, African American, Hispanic, and Muong students, through an inclusive model. Students have access to services based on interests and areas of strength. SEM specialists make no distinction between those students formally identified and those identified based on the topic offered. Although the numbers of gifted students served in the district must be reported to the state, the SEM specialist provides services to students interested in topics presented, whether identified gifted or not.

SUPPORTING TARGETED-AUDIENCE REFERRALS TO GIFTED AND TALENTED EDUCATION (STARGATE) MATHEMATICS
BALTIMORE COUNTY PUBLIC SCHOOLS
TOWSON, MD

PROGRAM GOALS

❖ Support students referred for gifted and talented education through an environment that provides validation and affirmation of students' strengths, affiliation with students with similar strengths, and affinity through challenge.

❖ Provide students with opportunities to enhance achievement behaviors in the dimensions of facing challenges, accepting responsibility, valuing the importance of achievement, developing independence, and demonstrating respect for self and others.

❖ Provide academic challenge for students.

❖ Actively involve parents as program partners.

❖ Provide the local school with data on student performance.

❖ Establish a network of teachers who have experience meeting the social, emotional, and academic needs of students who are referred for gifted education services.

PROGRAM DELIVERY SYSTEM

The STARGATE Mathematics program provides services to students during a summer session.

GRADE LEVELS SERVED

Students served in the program are between the third and fourth grades.

CURRICULUM EMPHASIS OR PROGRAMMING MODEL

The STARGATE program is based on a constructivist approach and built around math concepts, specifically multiplication, division, fractions, and geometry, and includes manipulative problem solving and open-ended questions. The curriculum seeks to fill in the holes in students' math knowledge and provide opportunity for students to take their math thinking beyond traditional requirements.

IDENTIFICATION

An in-school PACE math program serves as the starting point for identifying students to attend the STARGATE program. In the 24 schools participating in this program, teachers recommend students using observations and completing a checklist. They watch and document the following behaviors: gifted characteristics, leadership, curiosity, problem-solving skills, and the ability to work from concrete to abstract. The teachers focus on students who are doing well in math but not necessarily identified as gifted. From this data, at least 10 students are selected from each of the 24 schools to attend STARGATE. All nominated students are invited to attend.

EVALUATION MEASURES

The evaluation of the STARGATE program involves a number of data sources to determine program effectiveness including student questionnaires, student performance assessments, student evaluations (journals), teacher evaluations (behavioral checklists, anecdotal records, and gifted and talented recommendations), parent questionnaires, student academic growth (rubrics and performance tasks), leadership, and motivation (district's achievement behavior checklist).

All students who attend STARGATE are tested prior to entering the program and at the conclusion with questions about math enjoyment and word problems to qualify growth. Eighty-seven percent of the students attending the STARGATE program increased their posttest scores by 12 percentage points or more. Eighty-two percent of the STARGATE students were identified for fourth-grade gifted and talented math in the fall, creating an increased participation in gifted math classes. The students and teachers involved in this program are very positive. When teachers begin to teach a new concept during the school year, students reflect on their STARGATE experiences with comments such as, "I remember the way we learned this in STARGATE and it makes math easy."

A total of 74 students attended STARGATE Math in 2001. Of this total, 58 (78%) were recommended for screening by their home school for grade 4 gifted and talented math (G/T 4 Math). At the end of grade 4, of the 58 who were recommended for screening, 43 (74%) had successfully completed G/T 4 Math. The five students from one school who were recommended were never screened by the home school, and six students who were recommended for screening are no longer attending a Baltimore County Public School.

A total of 45 students attended STARGATE Math in 2000. Of this total, 30 (66%) were recommended for screening by their home school for G/T 4 Math. At the end of grade 5, of the 30 who were recommended, 14 (47%) had successfully completed G/T 4 and 5 math. There were six (20%) students who no longer attended a Baltimore County Public School.

UNIQUENESS OF THE PROGRAM FOR TALENT DEVELOPMENT OF CULTURALLY, LINGUISTICALLY, AND ETHNICALLY DIVERSE STUDENTS

STARGATE instruction focuses on math concepts, manipulative problem solving, and open-ended questions. Teamwork is emphasized. At the beginning of each summer program, students are divided into teams and throughout the 2 weeks of the summer program, these teams work for rewards. Rewards are given to teams who demonstrate characteristics of achievement and work well as a group. Many culturally diverse students have never had their learning abilities affirmed, nor have they been in a classroom where risk taking is encouraged and even rewarded. STARGATE does both.

Also, research has shown that culturally diverse students learn better when they can work cooperatively on open-ended, untimed questions, an important component of the content and delivery of STARGATE.

EXEMPLARY GENERAL EDUCATION PROGRAMS FOR CULTURALLY DIVERSE LEARNERS

In Chapter 6 of *In Search of the Dream,* Cindy A. Strickland (2004) summarized several exemplary general education programs that appear successful in their quest to guide culturally diverse and/or students from low-economic backgrounds to improved academic success. The programs range in the age span served, from preschool to college, and in the type(s) of programming emphasized, comprehensive reform or single subject-focused. The majority of these programs operate during the school day, but a few are designed to provide tutoring and/or mentoring support to supplement school offerings. The programs selected for inclusion in Chapter 6 of *In Search of the Dream* repeatedly surfaced in the research conducted in preparation for the literature review and had credible evidence available to support their claims of increased student achievement and/or satisfaction. Several programs are described below.[4]

AN ACHIEVABLE DREAM

Grade Levels Served: K–12

Program Goal:
❖ Give children who are at risk of failure in school, due to socioeconomic factors, a chance to succeed.

Program Description: An Achievable Dream (AAD) is a partnership between the business community and Newport News Public Schools in Virginia that serves more than 1,000 students in a K–8 magnet school and a high school component. The program is designed to offer students a nurturing environment in which they form a strong relationship with caring adult. AAD students have the opportunity to engage in enrichment activities both during and outside of school through an incentive program supported in part by the business community. A strong emphasis on discipline, including both character and moral development, is

---

4   Again, these program descriptions originally appeared in Strickland (2004), so some data may appear dated. However, it is assumed readers can obtain ideas and strategies from these successful programs, so they are included.

designed to teach students to focus on setting goals and on the personal and decision-making skills needed to meet those goals. AAD provides students with a curriculum that challenges them and encourages them to have high expectations. The curriculum includes a major focus on reading; business English, or "speaking green" (the color of money); accelerated math courses; and etiquette. Students are required to take tennis instruction as a vehicle for teaching discipline, fairness, and other life skills needed to succeed. Classes are small, with low student-teacher ratios. Tutoring is provided for those students who need it.

Evaluation Measures and Results: An Achievable Dream has received several honors, detailed on its website (http://www.achievabledream. org). Other indicators of success:

- ❖ On the 2001 Virginia Standards of Learning (SOL) tests, Achievable Dreamers (96% are African American) closed the achievement gap to just 8 percentage points.
- ❖ Preliminary results on the 2002 SOL tests indicate that An Achievable Dream Academy was on target to meet the state's standards for "full accreditation."

AVID: Advancement Via Individual Determination

Grade Levels Served: Middle and high school

Program Goals:

- ❖ Support students who are capable of a rigorous college preparatory program such as honors and Advanced Placement classes, but who would not normally choose to enroll in such a program.
- ❖ Provide high expectations, encouragement, day-to-day help, and guidance in how to navigate through the system.
- ❖ Help students develop the social as well as academic habits and skills necessary to success, including good study habits and academic survival skills.
- ❖ Foster positive attitudes toward higher education; a vision of college as attainable.

❖ Enroll 100% of AVID graduates in colleges and universities, with 80% of these at 4-year institutions.

Program Description: Students are placed in advanced classes alongside high-achieving students and are provided the help they need to support their success in this setting through an AVID elective class that meets every day. The AVID class provides instruction and encouragement in the development of academic survival skills and college entry skills, provides scheduled tutoring time in a variety of subject areas, and offers motivational activities to support college and career exploration. The class stresses a collaborative approach to learning, an emphasis on the skills and habits of inquiry, and writing as a tool for learning. Teachers and students work together to provide a strong sense of community that expects and rewards hard work, perseverance, and academic achievement. Adults in the program both nurture and support students as well as advocate for them in the school setting. Students and parents are required to sign a contract agreeing to program requirements. The strength of the AVID program appears to be its emphasis on supporting students socially and academically once they enroll in college preparatory courses. The required AVID class ensures that students meet every day with caring adults and a peer group with whom they can share their challenges and celebrate their successes. AVID programs serve 85,000 students each year across 23 states and 15 countries. Students are admitted based on the following criteria:

❖ *Ability*: Academic potential to succeed in college preparatory courses and college (with support); usually a B+–C grade average in middle or high school.

❖ *Desire and determination*: Desire to attend college; willingness to undertake demanding academic program.

❖ *Membership in an underserved group (historically unlikely to attend college)*: Low-income households as defined by eligibility for free or reduced price lunch; first generation in family to attend college.

Evaluation Measures and Results: The AVID website (http://www.avid.org) lists numerous articles that provide information about research studies involving AVID programs and sites. Both internal and external research is included. Sample research findings include:

❖ AVID increases the enrollment of underserved students in colleges and universities.

- ❖ AVID students overcome the negative effect of parental income and education on student achievement.
- ❖ AVID helps school personnel raise the level of expectation that they have for these students.
- ❖ AVID students are less likely to drop out of school.
- ❖ AVID students are successful in college.

BRIGHT BEGINNINGS

Grade Levels Served: Pre-K (4-year-olds)

Program Goals:
- ❖ Support the school district's goal to have 85% of third-grade students reading at or above grade level.
- ❖ Provide a rich, child-centered, literacy-focused program to ensure that all children in Mecklenburg County enter kindergarten ready to learn.
- ❖ Provide experiences, especially in the areas of language and early literacy development, that lay the foundation for early school success.

Program Description: Bright Beginnings served approximately 3,000 students in 157 classrooms in the Charlotte-Mecklenburg (North Carolina) School System. The program has detailed goals in the following areas:
- ❖ social and personal development,
- ❖ language and literacy,
- ❖ mathematical thinking,
- ❖ scientific thinking,
- ❖ social studies,
- ❖ creative arts,
- ❖ physical education, and
- ❖ technology.

Bright Beginnings operates on a set of beliefs that recognize that cognitive, social, emotional, and physical development are interrelated in young children, and all developmental areas must be addressed according to the unique needs of individual children.

Evaluation Measures and Results:

❖ In a district comparison study, 1997–1998 Bright Beginnings participants outperformed eligible nonparticipants.

❖ End-of-grade test scores in literacy and math show significant and sustained benefits from participation in the program.

COCA-COLA VALUED YOUTH PROGRAM

Grade Levels Served: Elementary–middle school

Program Goals:

❖ Set up and coordinate a tutoring program in which secondary students tutor elementary students.

❖ Have a positive impact on students, tutors, families, and schools.

❖ Help schools and communities see the inherent value and potential of each child.

Program Description: The Coca-Cola Valued Youth Program is an in-school mentoring program that targets middle school students who are at risk of dropping out and pairs them with elementary students at least 4 years younger who need tutoring. The tutoring experience is set up to increase the self-esteem of the tutors and their sense of self-efficacy and connection to school. Tutors work 4 days a week at an elementary site, a commitment that encourages school attendance. On the fifth day, they attend a special class that focuses on building their general literacy skills, self-awareness and pride, and expertise in tutoring. Students receive a stipend for participating in the program, which also includes field trips and guest speakers. The program is based on the following tenets:

❖ All students can learn.

❖ The school values all students.

❖ All students can actively contribute to their own education and to the education of others.

❖ All students, parents, and teachers have the right to participate fully in creating and maintaining excellent schools.

❖ Excellence in schools contributes to individual and collective economic growth, stability, and advancement.

❖ Commitment to educational excellence is created by including students, parents, and teachers in setting goals, making decisions, monitoring progress, and evaluating outcomes.

❖ Students, parents, and teachers must be provided extensive, consistent support in ways that allow students to learn, teachers to teach, and parents to be involved.

The program has been in more than 240 schools in 25 cities across the United States. Since its inception in 1984, the program has kept more than 11,500 at-risk students in school.

Evaluation Measures and Results: The Coca-Cola Valued Youth Project has received numerous awards and honors. Internal evaluations are conducted yearly to provide both formative and summative feedback. Evaluations consist of quantitative and qualitative measures. Selected findings that benefit tutors include:

❖ Improved grades, achievement test scores, attendance, self-concept, and attitudes toward school.

❖ Fewer disciplinary referrals.

❖ A less than 2% dropout rate for its participants.

COGNITIVELY GUIDED INSTRUCTION

Grade Levels Served: Elementary

Program Goals:

❖ Improve elementary mathematics instruction and achievement.

❖ Develop student problem solving in the early elementary grades.

Program Description: The Cognitively Guided Instruction (CGI) model was developed by the Wisconsin Center for Education Research. CGI combines high standards for student achievement in mathematics with professional development for teachers. CGI focuses on helping teachers understand how primary-grade students solve mathematics problems and use reasoning for learning. Professional development helps teachers learn about the ways in which young children think about mathematics and how they go about solving problems. Teachers are taught to recognize the strategies students are using and then encourage their acquisition and use of more advanced strategies.

Evaluation Measures and Results: CGI has a strong research base, particularly concerning its use with at-risk students. Selected results include:

❖ Teacher change in practices and attitudes concerning math instruction; less reliance on textbooks, more on observation of student thinking.

❖ Increased student basic skills knowledge, problem-solving, and reasoning skills, and self-confidence.

❖ Significantly better math achievement scores, particularly in solving advanced problems.

CORE KNOWLEDGE

Grade Levels Served: K–8

Program Goal:

❖ Provide access to a specific sequenced body of shared and lasting knowledge that should form the core of a preschool–grade 8 curriculum.

Program Description: The Core Knowledge Program has been in use in at least 30 states, and is especially strong in Colorado, with more than 50 schools having used the curriculum. The program asserts that, in order to ensure academic excellence, fairness to all students, and higher rates of literacy, schools need access to a solid, specific, and shared core curriculum that helps them establish strong foundations of knowledge at each grade level. Detailed grade-by-grade sequences are offered in language arts, social studies, science, mathematics, visual arts, and music.

Evaluation Measures and Results: Numerous internal and external studies have been carried out to determine direct and indirect effects of the Core Knowledge program. Selected results include:

❖ Core Knowledge fosters equity and excellence.

❖ Significantly better achievement scores on both norm and criterion based standardized tests.

- Increased teacher satisfaction.
- Increased student enthusiasm for learning.
- Improved coordination and consistency of curriculum across grade levels.

DIFFERENT WAYS OF KNOWING

Grade Levels Served: K–12

Program Goal:
- Improve student achievement by improving classroom practices.

Program Description: Different Ways of Knowing (DWOK) is an initiative of the Galef Institute in Los Angeles that provides a range of field-tested and research-validated services to schools. Those services vary according to the needs of individual schools or districts. Services typically include assistance in conducting a comprehensive self-study, staff development opportunities (including leadership training for administrators), onsite coaching, and access to classroom resources. The program, which has worked with more than 600 schools since 1989, is grounded in six best practices designed to increase student achievement:
- use of "big ideas" to ground curriculum;
- focus on inquiry and self-directed learning;
- reading, writing, and math strategies designed to close the achievement gap;
- integrated arts component;
- partnerships with communities and families; and
- leadership training.

Evaluation Measures and Results: DWOK prides itself on a solid research base aided by outside evaluations. Selected findings include:
- Significant gains in reading, math, science, and social studies.
- Increased student achievement and motivation.
- Increased opportunities for students to engage in creative and critical thinking.

GRADUATION REALLY ACHIEVES DREAMS (PROJECT GRAD)

Grade Levels Served: K–16

Program Goals:
- ❖ Improve grades, achievement scores, and attitudes toward school.
- ❖ Improve teacher training and ongoing support.
- ❖ Increase parent involvement.
- ❖ Reduce disciplinary referrals.
- ❖ Increase college enrollment.
- ❖ Improve access to financial aid and scholarships for college.

Program Description: Project GRAD is designed to work in the lowest performing schools in low-income neighborhoods to improve the academic achievement and college enrollment rates of students. More than 90% of the students in Project GRAD schools meet the federal poverty guidelines for special assistance. Project GRAD is set up to encompass a high school and all of the feeder schools for that high school, providing both horizontal and vertical consistency of the program for students and teachers.

A number of components make up the Project GRAD curriculum. MOVE-IT math is a program that emphasizes student discovery, reasoning, and communication centered on math concepts. Success for All is a research-based reading and writing program of intervention and acceleration to ensure all students succeed in reading in elementary school. Consistency Management and Cooperative Discipline provide a research-based management system that emphasizes consistency of classroom organization and student self-discipline. Communities in Schools provides community outreach, dropout prevention, and social service supports through the provision of full-time case workers and project managers.

The high school program adds activities and services to prepare students to apply and succeed in college. Project GRAD has recently expanded to a total of five feeder systems in Houston that enroll more than 50,000 students in 74 schools. At the time of this writing, Project GRAD had sites in Atlanta, Brownsville, Cincinnati, Columbus, Akron,

Knoxville, Los Angeles, Newark, and Roosevelt (New York) and had served a total of more than 130,000 children in 198 schools.

Evaluation Measures and Results: Project GRAD undergoes both internal and external evaluations. Selected results include:

❖ By the end of the first 2–3 years of implementation, in most feeder schools, Project GRAD produced significant evidence of measurable impact on student achievement, including improved test scores in reading and math.

❖ Since 1992, college enrollment for Project GRAD students at Houston's Davis High school increased 62% versus the district average of 13%.

HELPING ONE STUDENT TO SUCCEED

Grade Levels Served: K–12

Program Goals:

❖ Accelerate learning in language arts and mathematics.

❖ Provide teachers with research-based strategies that improve student learning.

Program Description: Helping One Student to Succeed (HOSTS) is a highly structured tutoring program in which volunteers are paired with students who are at risk of school failure. This tutoring is typically offered as either a pull-out or afterschool program. Lesson plans are drawn from the HOSTS database and are matched to students based on tests of reading comprehension. The HOSTS program also offers a variety of professional development resources to help teachers improve their skills in teaching reading and math. Specific tools help teachers make data-driven decisions and design interventions to maximize student learning. HOSTS learning systems have operated in more than 1,600 schools in the United States, Puerto Rico, and El Salvador. In addition, HOSTS has reported that it has trained more than 100,000 mentors annually.

Evaluation Measures and Results: Numerous internal and external studies that include the collection of both quantitative and qualitative data are conducted annually. Selected results include:

❖ Significant improvement in achievement scores.

❖ Positive impacts on learning, self-esteem, and school attendance.

❖ Positive impact on mentors, particularly residents of retirement facilities and peer and high school mentors.

HIGH SCHOOLS THAT WORK

Grade Levels Served: High school

Program Goals:

❖ Raise the achievement of all students in all classes.

❖ Encourage students to take challenging coursework.

❖ Graduate students who have completed a challenging academic core curriculum with a concentration in an academic or technical area.

Program Description: High Schools That Work (HSTW) is a school improvement initiative sponsored by the Southern Regional Education Board. It provides a framework of goals, key practices, and key conditions for accelerating learning and setting high standards. The initiative targets high school students who are seldom challenged due to unengaging instruction and/or low expectations. The program aims to encourage students to take challenging courses, to provide them with teaching that motivates them to learn the rigorous content in these courses, and to provide the necessary extra help and attention that will enable students to succeed in that environment. In 2004, there were more than 1,100 HSTW sites in 27 states. Key practices include:

❖ High expectations for students.

❖ Increased access to challenging vocational and academic studies.

❖ Integrated school-based system of work and school-based learning.

❖ Organizational structure to encourage collaboration between vocational and academic faculty.

❖ Guidance and advising system for students and parents.

❖ Extra help for students lacking necessary background for success.

Evaluation Measures and Results: HSTW uses both student assessment and internal and external program evaluation data to continuously improve their programming. Selected findings include:

- ❖ Significantly increased percentages of seniors who meet the HSTW achievement goals in mathematics, science, and reading and the percentages of students in their senior classes who completed the HSTW-recommended program of study.
- ❖ Increased use of best practices by teachers.

PROJECT SEED, INC.: STUDENTS DISCOVERING MATHEMATICS SUCCESSFULLY

Grade Levels Served: Elementary and middle school

Program Goals:

- ❖ Increase the number of at-risk urban youth majoring in, and pursuing careers in, mathematics and related fields by exposing them to advanced, conceptually oriented mathematics.
- ❖ Increase students' academic self-confidence, develop their problem-solving and critical thinking skills, and raise their mathematics achievement levels.

Program Description: Project SEED has four key components:

- ❖ Classroom instruction base on a nonlecture, Socratic, group-discovery format.
- ❖ Staff development to train teachers in the curriculum and in communication and management skills.
- ❖ Family involvement that includes workshops to help families learn how to reinforce the curriculum at home.
- ❖ Curriculum developed by Project SEED staff that is tailored to the needs of the adopting school district.

Project SEED classes are conducted by project staff and supplement regular mathematics instruction. The classroom teacher participates in the lesson along with the students, allowing them to observe quality instructional methodology. Workshops and one-on-one consultation add to the professional development component.

Evaluation Measures and Results: Project SEED has received many honors and has undergone both internal and external evaluations. Selected results include:

- ❖ Increased scores on standardized tests that were cumulative and persistent.
- ❖ Enrollment in more upper division mathematics courses in high school.
- ❖ Fewer retentions.

SUCCESS FOR ALL

Grade Levels Served: K–5

Program Goal: To ensure that virtually all children can read and write at or above grade level by grade 5.

Program Description: Success for All (SFA) is a comprehensive approach to restructuring elementary schools to ensure the success of every child. SFA schools are typically those with a high percentage of minority students, students designated as economically disadvantaged, and/or students with limited English proficiency. The SFA program includes the following components:

- ❖ reading and writing programs,
- ❖ 8-week assessments,
- ❖ tutors,
- ❖ early learning (preschool and kindergarten),
- ❖ cooperative learning,
- ❖ family support team,
- ❖ facilitator,
- ❖ staff support teams,
- ❖ professional development,
- ❖ leadership academy, and
- ❖ experienced sites conferences.

At the heart of the SFA program is a 90-minute block of uninter-
rupted daily reading instruction. Students are grouped cross grade by
reading level, and frequent assessments ensure that adequate progress is
being made and student placement remains appropriate. Schools must
apply to the SFA program. Requirements include a staff fully aware of
what the program entails, the availability of resources to implement the
program successfully, and a serious commitment to implementation of
the program. The Success for All Foundation reports that it has served
about 1,500 schools in 48 states, as well as assisted with related projects
in at least five other countries.

Evaluation Measures and Results: The Success for All reading program
has been evaluated in more than 20 studies at eight research institutions.
Links to numerous research reports are available at the SFA website
(http://www.successforall.net). Selected findings include:

- SFA students generally perform 3–12 months ahead of control
  group peers in grade equivalency measures; achievement effects
  seem to be particularly strong for students in the lowest quartile.
- Fewer special education placements among SFA students.
- A narrowing of the achievement gap between Whites and
  African Americans.

CHAPTER THIRTEEN

SUMMARY AND DIRECTIONS FOR THE FUTURE

Gifted students are highly inquisitive beings who normally should become "high achievers" as a result of their curiosity, experimentation, discoveries, assimilation-organization-use of information, perceptions, relationships, and memory. Gifted children are made into underachievers as a result of specific handicaps—a dull, meager curriculum that destroys the motivation to achieve in school, inappropriate learning styles, or a lack of adult assistance to the child in need of learning how to handle socio-emotional conflict, to gain self-control, and to set realistic expectations.

—Whitmore (1980, p. 132)

There is a great deal of burden placed on students identified as gifted to achieve to the highest levels and to levels set by others, be they realistic or not. Black students who are gifted often find themselves in a quandary or facing a pyrrhic victory—they frequently win *and* lose socially (Fordham, 1988; Fordham & Ogbu, 1986).

Gifted students almost always face high expectations. Conversely, Black students almost always face low expectations and negative stereotypes, regardless of their ability and potential. So, where do Black students who are gifted fit into the aforementioned positive stereotypes and expectations placed upon gifted students in general? Based on superficial, arbitrary characteristics, like skin color, Black students are highly likely to be subjected to negative stereotypes by society at large, educators, family members, and other students. This is a heavy and certainly unneces-sary burden placed upon these students.

As noted previously, underachievement is learned; I am convinced that no child is born underachieving. Instead, gifted students are made into underachievers as a result of specific social/external or handicapping conditions: a dull, meager curriculum that destroys the motivation and desire to achieve in school, incompatible teaching and learning styles, and/or a lack of adult (teacher, parent, caregiver) assistance to those in need of learning how to effectively manage and cope with social, school, familial, and personal/psychological conflict(s) and problems.

Academic achievement is dependent on more than individual/per-sonal abilities, resources, and aspirations, and those of primary caregivers and educators. The social environment in which learning takes place can enhance or diminish the attitudes, values, and behaviors that lead to high and/or optimal achievement. The school is a microcosm of the society. Therefore, the racial, class, and gender-role stereotypes, prejudices, and biases prevalent in society find their way into school or educational set-tings (Scott-Jones & Clark, 1986).

Underachievement is a symptom of a variety of causes and corre-lates, and its etiology is debatable and open to interpretation. Living with one or more risk factors contributes to or worsens underachievement for gifted Black students. School practices must be addressed, including the instruments used for the identification of giftedness and underachieve-ment, the cutoff scores used for labeling and placement, and the per-vasive colorblind, ethnocentric curriculum, for they all play vital roles in underachievement among gifted Black students. These same factors hinder the successful identification of Black students as gifted and/or underachieving.

For gifted Black students, particularly those who perform poorly on standardized tests, underachievement is a ubiquitous concept. To reit-erate, such students, by virtue of taking tests normed on middle-class White students, tend to perform poorly on such tests and may, therefore, not be identified as gifted and/or gifted underachievers. The heavy and sometimes exclusive reliance on test scores to predict ability and poten-tial, as well as the faith placed in tests by educators and decision makers, can be (and often are) educationally harmful for many underachieving and gifted Black students.

Test makers and their products fail to consider many factors, includ-ing the direct and indirect effects of gender, race, income, SES, lan-guage, experience, quality of instruction, expectations, health, teaching and learning style preferences, test anxiety, language differences, nonintellectual/noncognitive variables (such as motivation, interest, and task commitment), and test-taking conditions on test performance and outcomes. All of the issues affect, in meaningful ways, the validity and reliability of the instruments and, accordingly, the usefulness and efficacy of such scores or performance.

There is no single, universally accepted view of intelligence, be it a definition, model, or theory. Intelligence is socially and culturally defined and valued. Frankly and unfairly, the status quo determines such decisions. To understand and appreciate individual differences in the context of testing and achievement, educators must gather information about how gifted Black students learn, communicate, and express themselves, as well as provide equitable or culturally responsive options for these students to demonstrate their abilities or potential, and learning opportunities at home, school, and the larger society.

BLACK STUDENTS: ALMOST INVISIBLE IN GIFTED PROGRAMS AND AP CLASSES

Gifted programs and AP classes represent the most segregated programs in public schools. They are disproportionately White and middle class, and they value, identify, and serve primarily intellectually and academically gifted students. The underrepresentation of Black students in programs for the gifted has been well-documented and many barriers have been identified. Findings reveal that two of the most neglected populations in gifted education and AP classes are: (a) students whose talents may not be actualized because they are culturally different from the mainstream, and (b) socially and culturally different individuals (VanTassel-Baska et al., 1989). In many cases, these students are overlooked for gifted education programs whose identification procedures are inappropriate and/or have a disparate impact. The following list sets forth several reasons for not overlooking, that is, for supporting and nurturing this population:

❖ *The makeup of the academy is changing.* Perhaps one of the most noticeable trends in American education has been the increase in the racial and cultural makeup of the nation's schools. As already noted, in 1972, 21% of public students were either American

Indian, Black, Hispanic, or Asian Pacific Islander (Planty et al., 2009). By the year 2020, racially different students are expected to comprise half of all school-age students from ages 5 to 17 (Hodgkinson, 1988, 2007; Planty et al., 2009). The increasing number of such students requires and demands that educators delve beneath the surface of what may easily be referred to as an abysmal state of education in America, and gifted education is not exempt from this moral and professional obligation.

❖ *The underrepresentation of Black students in gifted programs and AP classes is often unsubstantiated by data and not addressed with equitable means.* Their representation is limited by the restrictions placed on the meaning of "gifted," identification instruments, policies and procedures, and, just as importantly, philosophies about gifted students and Black students. Historically, middle- and upper-class Whites have predominated gifted programs and AP classes (VanTassel-Baska et al., 1989), and making changes threatens those families in power and those families and students who benefit from the status quo. Gallagher and Weiss (1985) found no substantial body of evidence to suggest that gifted-ness is genetically determined; rather, it is "genetics married to opportunity that produces gifted students" (p. 32). Genes are not destiny.

❖ *Traditional tests are inadequate for assessing intelligence or giftedness among Blacks.* Identification often relies heavily upon standard-ized tests and scores found to be questionable or inapplicable for Black students. These tests include, for example, the WISC-IV, the Cognitive Abilities Test, and the Stanford-Binet IV. The literature presents data and criticism indicating that such tests, standardized on White, middle-class norms, show bias or unfair-ness in favor of White students (Baldwin, 1987; Ford, 1996, 2004; Frasier, García, & Passow, 1995; Haney & Madaus, 1989; Renzulli & Stoddard, 1980; Sternberg, 2007). According to the U.S. Department of Education (Planty et al., 2009), although low-income and low-SES students—many of whom are Black—represent some 20% of public school enrollment, they constitute only 4% of students who perform at the 95th percentile or above on standardized tests.

❖ *Traditional definitions and theories of gifted are inappropriate for use with Black students.* Giftedness has been defined and identified by performance on intelligence tests whose unquestionable analogy is "the higher the IQ score, the higher the intelligence." However, Gallagher and Weiss (1985) argued that each culture defines giftedness in its own image, and Sternberg (2007) noted that giftedness in one culture may be different for another culture.

❖ *Cultural differences influence pedagogical approaches, which influence student achievement.* Pedagogical or instructional factors include different teaching and learning styles, values, and attitudes that frequently conflict with those of the mainstream. Educators working with gifted Black students must understand at least two facts here: First, by virtue of being gifted, Black students exhibit characteristics of gifted students (e.g., creativity, inventiveness, high level of abstraction, critical thinking) to varying degrees; and second, gifted Black students may have markedly different frames of reference from the dominant culture (Stronge, Lynch, & Smith, 1987). VanTassel-Baska et al. (1989) asserted that, even when such students are identified, little attention is given to how their cultural and social backgrounds influence the learning process and academic achievement. A consideration of students' cultural background is vital because it may inhibit their academic achievement and subsequent placement in gifted programs and AP classes. In essence, schools, AP classes, and gifted programs must acknowledge and affirm student differences and individuality.

❖ *Peer group pressure to resist academic success hinders students' motivation to achieve and academic performance.* To repeat from previous chapters, peer pressure from both Black and White students contribute to underachievement and the low representation of Black students in gifted programs and AP classes. Black students who are gifted and high achieving are likely to be accused of "acting White" and rejecting the Black culture when they achieve in school and/or are well-behaved. Black students may intentionally underachieve to avoid being ostracized by Black and White peers.

❖ *Parental resistance among Blacks to the educational process carries important implications for gifted education.* Oppressive environmental forces influence how Black parents live and rear their students. Too many Black parents may be distrustful of the educational process, and view it as an instrument of the dominant culture that strips Blacks of their own cultural values, beliefs, norms, and attitudes. Those parents who hold this point of view may resist placing their children in gifted programs and AP classes. They wind up sacrificing academics for the social and psychological health of their children—again, a type of pyrrhic victory.

❖ *Environmental or social forces, including stereotypes and injustice, are commonplace in some schools and interfere with the learning process.* Despite law and awakening modernity, racism and discrimination persist (Baldwin, 1985; Dovidio et al., 2005; Hilliard, 1979; Ogbu, 1983, 1988, 2003). Moreover, teacher expectations and the cultural deficit perspective continue to cloud the thinking of some educators. Jensen (1969) argued that Blacks are innately less intelligent than Whites, and that education will not improve their school achievement. Herrnstein and Murray (1994) proposed a similar argument, but from a polemic and sociological perspective. Conversely, some educators contend that it is the social system rather than the testing instrument that is prejudiced against racial minorities (Mistry & Rogoff, 1985). *I strongly concur.* As stated by Boykin (1986),

poor performance relative to mainstream students and a high incidence of school dropout are still the rule rather than the exception for these Black students, despite two decades of national concern. We must ask why there has been so little progress toward solving this problem, in spite of the apparent best of intentions and the commitment of very considerable resources. (p. 57)

The problems continue because we have not addressed adequately the determinants of academic underachievement among this population. This book is humbly offered as a contribution to the limited data available relating school, social, familial, cultural, and psychological factors to achievement among gifted Black students. Research that seeks to understand and then address social, school, psychological, and cultural barriers to academic achievement is in great demand in our urban schools (actually, in all school types), AP classes, and gifted programs.

Gifted underachievers are among the most misunderstood and educationally neglected students in schools; no other group of students, except Black students, has suffered so much from lack of interest in them as persons (Whitmore, 1980). It has been reiterated here and elsewhere (Witty, 1978) that for gifted Black students to receive an equal educational opportunity, there must be (a) early identification with attention to special needs; (b) careful programming in light of their strengths, characteristics, and learning and living styles; (c) intelligent and caring teaching that is free of limiting expectations; (d) wide-range counseling programs; and (e) and community support services.

We will continue to see very capable Black students underachieve if we do not close the credibility gap between schools and Black students. There is also a need for quantitative changes in research on gifted Black students and their families, which must be accompanied by qualitative changes. Research is not a neutral process (Ford & Whiting, 2009; Whiting & Ford, 2009). In many ways, the study of Black students and their families is very personal, despite researchers' beliefs that they approach their subjects with great objectivity (Dilworth-Anderson & McAdoo, 1988). Stated differently, the theoretical and conceptual perspectives of researchers are influenced by their personal life history, family of origin, value orientations, and group identification. One's social position, income, class, generation, occupation, values, and ethos all affect the production of knowledge. The baggage researchers bring into learning situations is packed with group and personal ideologies and experiences.

Krasner and Houts (1984) proposed that behavioral scientists operate from value-laden perspectives. Theoretical perspectives reflect basic value assumptions of researchers themselves rather than logical fact finding. Value-laden research compromises and threatens the conceptual and theoretical integrity of a science or discipline.

In 1978, Allen described the limited applicability of theories of Black family life. Too often, it was argued, theories and research fail to capture the strengths and uniqueness of Black people. They do not focus, Allen maintained, on the dynamic, change-oriented, adaptive perspectives of Black family life.

Ethnocentric research, whether on Black students or their families, reflect findings of the larger, predominant society. For example, income, occupational status, family structure, and parents' educational levels are deemed the primary determinants of family functioning and the quality of family life. When Black families deviate from the prevailing or acceptable norms, they are often viewed as deviant or pathological, as noted in Chapter 8; when Black students deviate from norms of giftedness established on middle-class White students, they are not identified as gifted. Focusing on gifted students in nuclear families only and ignoring racial and cultural variables in research promises to yield fruitless data, information that carries little external validity and generalizability in this multicultural society. If gifted Black students are to prosper in school and life, educators and researchers cannot continue to promote a knowledge-base that is culturally insensitive, unresponsive, and even irresponsible. Future research must consider the multitude of variables important in the lives of Black families, including achievement orientations, beliefs, and values, along with customs, norms, and traditions.

REFERENCES

Abi-Nader, J. (1990). "A house for my mother": Motivating Hispanic high school students. *Anthropology & Education Quarterly, 21,* 41–58.

Adler, A. (1964). *Social interest: A challenge to mankind.* New York, NY: Capricorn Books.

Albert, R. S. (1969). Genius: Present-day status of the concept and its implications for the study of creativity and giftedness. *American Psychologist, 24,* 743–753.

Allen, W. (1978). The search for applicable theories of Black family life. *Journal of Marriage and the Family, 40,* 117–131.

Allington, R. C. (1980). Teacher interruption behaviors during primary grade oral reading. *Journal of Educational Psychology, 72,* 371–377.

Allport, G. (1954). *The nature of prejudice.* Reading, MA: Addison-Wesley.

Allport, G. (1979). *The nature of prejudice* (Updated ed.). Reading, MA: Addison-Wesley.

Alpert, R., & Haber, R. N. (1960). Anxiety in academic achievement situations. *Journal of Abnormal and Social Psychology, 10,* 207–215.

Alvino, J. R. (1991). An investigation into the needs of gifted boys. *Roeper Review, 13,* 174–180.

Alvino, J. R., McDonnel, R. C., & Richert, S. (1981). National survey of identification practices in gifted and talented education. *Exceptional Children, 48,* 124–132.

American Association of Colleges of Teacher Education. (1984, November 28). Public dilemma: Equity vs. excellence. *Education Week, 20.*

American Association of Colleges of Teacher Education, Commission on Multicultural Education. (1973). No one model American. *Journal of Teacher Education, 24,* 264–265.

American Association of Colleges of Teacher Education, Committee on Multicultural Education. (2006). *Educators' preparation for cultural and linguistic diversity: A call to action.* Washington, DC: Author.

American Association of University Women. (1992). *How schools shortchange girls.* Washington, DC: National Education Association Professional Library.

American Association of University Women. (2006). *Where the girls are: The facts about gender equity in education.* Baltimore, MD: Author.

American Association of University Women Educational Foundation Commission on Technology, Gender, and Teacher Education. (2004). *Under the microscope: A decade of gender equity projects in the sciences.* Washington, DC: Author.

American Educational Research Association, American Psychological Association, and National Council on Measurement in Education. (1985). *Standards for educational and psychological testing.* Washington, DC: American Psychological Association.

American Psychological Association. (1974). *United Nations draft program for a decade of action to combat racism and racial discrimination.* Washington, DC: Author.

American Psychological Association. (2006). *Resolution against racism and racial discrimination and their adverse impacts on mental health.* Washington, DC: Author.

American School Counselor Association. (2007). *Position stated: Gifted programs.* Retrieved from http://asca2.timberlakepublishing.com//files/PS_Gifted.pdf.

American Speech and Hearing Association. (1983). *Social dialects* (Position paper). Retrieved from http://www.asha.org/docs/html/PS1983-00115.html

Anderson, K. L., & Allen, W. R. (1984). Correlates of extended household structure. *Phylon, 45,* 144–157.

Angus, S. F. (1989). Three approaches to stress management for children. *Elementary School Guidance & Counseling, 23,* 228–233.

Applebee, A. (1989). *A study of book-length works taught in high school English courses.* Albany, NY: Center for the Learning and Teaching of Literature, State University of New York, School of Education.

Archambault, F. X., Westberg, K. L., Brown, S. W., Hallmark, B. W., Zhang, W., & Emmons, C. L. (1993). Classroom practices used with gifted third and fourth grade students. *Journal for the Education of the Gifted, 16,* 103–119.

Arnold, K. D. (1993). Undergraduate aspirations and career outcomes of academically talented women: A discriminant analysis. *Roeper Review, 15,* 169–175.

Aronson, J. (2004). The threat of stereotype: To close the achievement gap, we must address negative stereotypes that suppress student achievement. *Educational Leadership, 62*(3), 14–19.

Aronson, J., Fried, C., & Good, C. (2002). Reducing the effects of stereotype threat on African American college students by shaping theories of intelligence. *Journal of Experimental Social Psychology, 38,* 113–125.

Ashton, P. T., & Webb, R. B. (1986). *Making a difference: Teachers' sense of efficacy and student achievement.* White Plains, NY: Longman.

Atkinson, D. R., Jennings, R. G., & Liongson, I. (1990). Minority students' reasons for not seeking counseling and suggestions for improving services. *Journal of College Student Development, 31*, 342–305.

Atkinson, J. W. (1964). *An introduction to motivation*. Princeton, NJ: Van Nostrand.

Atkinson, J. W. (1980). Motivational effects in so-called tests of ability and educational achievement. In L. J. Fyans (Ed.), *Achievement motivation: Recent trends in theory and research* (pp. 92–114). New York, NY: Plenum.

Aud, S., Hussar, W., Planty, M., Snyder, T., Bianco, K., Fox, M., . . . Drake, L. (2010). *The condition of education 2010* (NCES 2010-028). Washington, DC: National Center for Education Statistics, Institute of Education Sciences, U.S. Department of Education.

Aylward, G. P. (1994). *Practitioner's guide to developmental and psychological testing*. New York, NY: Plenum Medical Book Co.

Baldwin, A. Y. (1987). Undiscovered diamonds. *Journal for the Education of the Gifted, 10*, 271–286.

Baldwin, A. Y. (1994). The seven plus story: Developing hidden talent among students in socioeconomically disadvantaged environments. *Gifted Child Quarterly, 38*, 80–84.

Baldwin, A. Y., & Vialle, W. (1999). *The many faces of giftedness: Lifting the masks*. Belmont, CA: Wadsworth.

Bandura, A. (1977). *Social learning theory*. Englewood Cliffs, NJ: Prentice Hall.

Banks, C. A. M. (2010). Communities, families, and educators working together for school improvement. In J. A. Banks & C. A. M. Banks (Eds.), *Multicultural education: Issues and perspectives* (7th ed., pp. 417–438). Hoboken, NJ: John Wiley & Sons.

Banks, J. A. (1979). *Teaching strategies for ethnic studies* (2nd ed.). Boston, MA: Allyn & Bacon.

Banks, J. A. (1993). Multicultural education: Historical development, dimensions, and practice. In L. D. Darling-Hammond (Ed.), *Review of research in education* (pp. 3–49). Washington, DC: American Educational Research Association.

Banks, J. A. (2006). *Cultural diversity and American education*. Boston, MA: Allyn & Bacon.

Banks, J. A. (2010). Approaches to multicultural curriculum reform. In J. A. Banks & C. A. M. Banks (Eds.), *Multicultural education: Issues and perspectives* (7th ed., pp. 233–258). Hoboken, NJ: John Wiley & Sons.

Banks, J. A., & Banks, C. A. M. (Eds.). (1993). *Multicultural education: Issues and perspectives* (2nd ed.). Boston, MA: Allyn & Bacon.

Banks, J. A., & Banks, C. A. M. (Eds.). (2010). *Multicultural education: Issues and perspectives* (7th ed.). Hoboken, NJ: John Wiley & Sons.

Barbe, W. B. (1956). A study of the family background of the gifted. *Journal of Educational Psychology, 47*, 302–309.

Barnette, E. L. (1989). A program to meet the emotional and social needs of gifted and talented adolescents. *Journal of Counseling and Development, 67*, 525–528.

Bartley, R. (1980). *An analysis of secondary students' educational aspiration, school satisfaction and self-satisfaction in the Seattle Public Schools* (Report No. 80-9). Seattle, WA: Washington Department of Planning, Research, and Evaluation. (ERIC Document Reproduction Service No. ED209399)

Barton, P. E. (2003). *Parsing the achievement gap: Baselines for tracking progress*. Princeton, NJ: Educational Testing Services.

Barton, P. E., & Coley, R. J. (2009). *Parsing the achievement gap II.* Princeton, NJ: Educational Testing Services.

Bempechat, J., & Ginsburg, H. P. (1989). *Underachievement and educational disadvantage: The home and school experience of at-risk youth.* New York, NY: ERIC Clearinghouse on Urban Education.

Benbow, C. P., & Arjmand, O. (1990). Predictors of high academic achievement in mathematics and science by mathematically talented students: A longitudinal study. *Journal of Educational Psychology, 82,* 430–441.

Berk, R. A. (1983). Learning disabilities as a category of underachievement. In L. S. Fox, L. Brody, & D. Tobin (Eds.), *Learning disabled/gifted children: Identification and programming* (pp. 51–76). Baltimore, MD: University Park Press.

Bernal, E. M. (1981, February). *Special problems and procedures for identifying gifted minority students.* Paper presented at the Council for Exceptional Children's Conference on the Bilingual Child, New Orleans, LA. (ERIC Document Reproduction Service No. ED203652)

Bernard, M. E. (1990). Rational-emotive therapy with children and adolescents: Treatment strategies. *School Psychology Review, 19,* 294–303.

Bernstein, J. (1982, April 12). Who was Christy Matherson? *New Yorker,* 152–153.

Biggs, B. E., & Felton, G. S. (1977). *Up from underachievement.* Springfield, IL: Charles C. Thomas.

Billingsley, A. (1968). *Black families in White America.* Englewood Cliffs, NJ: Prentice-Hall.

Binet, A., & Simon, T. (1905). Methodes nouvelles pour le diagnostic du niveau intellectual des anormaux. *Anne Psychologique, 11,* 191–244.

Bitting, P. F., Cordeiro, P. A., & Baptiste, H. P., Jr. (1992). Philosophical and conceptual issues related to students at risk. In H. C. Waxman, J. Walker de Felix, J. E. Anderson, & H. P. Baptiste, Jr. (Eds.), *Students at risk in at-risk schools: Improving environments for learning* (pp. 17–32). Newbury Park, CA: Corwin Press.

Blackwell, J. E. (1975). *The Black community: Diversity and unity.* New York, NY: Harper & Row.

Blankenstein, A. M. (2004). *Failure is not an option: Six principles that guide student achievement in high-performing schools.* Thousand Oaks, CA: Corwin Press.

Blistein, R. (2009, July/August). Racism's hidden toll. *Miller-McClune,* 48–57.

Bloom, B. S. (1964). *Stability and change in human characteristics.* New York, NY: John Wiley and Sons.

Bloom, B. S. (Ed.). (1985). *Developing talent in young people.* New York, NY: Ballantine.

Board of Education of Hendrick Hudson Central School District v. Rowley, 458 U.S. 176 (1982).

Bonner, F. A., II. (2001). *Academically gifted African-American male college students: A phenomenological study.* Storrs: University of Connecticut, The National Research Center on the Gifted and Talented..

Bonner, F. A., II. (2003). To be young, gifted, African American, and male. *Gifted Child Today, 26*(2), 26–34.

Bonner, F. A., II. (2010). *Academically gifted African American male college students.* Westport, CT: Greenwood.

Books, S. (2004). *Poverty and schooling in the U.S.* New York, NY: Routledge.

Borland, J. H. (1978). Teacher identification of the gifted: A new look. *Journal for the Education of the Gifted, 2,* 13–22.

Bourdieu, P. (1977). Cultural reproduction and social reproduction. In J. Karabel & A. H. Halsey (Eds.), *Power and ideology in education* (pp. 487–510). New York, NY: Oxford University Press.

Boutte, G. S. (1992). Frustrations of an African-American parent: A personal and professional account. *Phi Delta Kappan, 73*, 786–788.

Boutte, G. (1999). *Multicultural education: Raising consciousness.* Belmont, CA: Wadsworth.

Bowie, R. L., & Bond, C. L. (1994). Influencing future teachers' attitudes toward Black English: Are we making a difference? *Journal of Teacher Education, 45*, 112–118.

Bowles, S., & Gintis, E. (1976). *Schooling in capitalist America: Educational reform and the contradictions of economic life.* New York, NY: Routledge.

Boy, A. V., & Pine, G. J. (1988). *Fostering psychosocial development in the classroom.* Springfield, IL: Charles C. Thomas.

Boyd-Franklin, N. (2003). *Black families in therapy: Understanding the African American perspective* (2nd ed.). New York, NY: Guilford.

Boyer, E. L. (1983). *High school.* New York, NY: Harper & Row.

Boykin, A. W. (1983). The academic performance of Afro-American children. In J. Spence (Ed.), *Achievement and achievement motives* (pp. 321–371). San Francisco, CA: W. Freeman.

Boykin, A. W. (1986). The triple quandary and the schooling of Afro-American children. In U. Neisser (Ed.), *The school achievement of minority children* (pp. 57–91). Hillsdale, NJ: Lawrence Erlbaum.

Boykin, A. W. (1994). Afrocultural expression and its implications for schooling. In E. R. Hollins, J. E. King, & W. C. Hayman (Eds.), *Teaching diverse populations: Formulating a knowledge base* (pp. 225–273). New York, NY: State University of New York Press.

Boykin, A. W., Albury, A., Tyler, K. M., Hurley, E. A., Bailey, C. T., & Miller, O. A. (2005). Culture-based perceptions of academic achievement among low-income elementary students. *Cultural Diversity and Ethnic Minority Psychology, 11*, 339–350.

Boykin, A. W., Tyler, K. M., & Miller, O. A. (2005). In search of cultural themes and their expressions in the dynamics of classroom life. *Urban Education, 40*, 521–549.

Boykin, A. W., Tyler, K. M., Watkins-Lewis, K. M., & Kizzie, K. (2006). Culture in the sanctioned classroom practices of elementary school teachers serving low-income African American students. *Journal of Education of Students Placed At-Risk, 11*, 161–173.

Bradley, R. H., Rock, S. L., Caldwell, B. M., Harris, P. T., & Hamrick, H. M. (1987). Home environment and school performance among Black elementary school children. *Journal of Negro Education, 56*, 499–509.

Brice Heath, S. (1983). *Ways with words.* Cambridge, UK: Cambridge University Press.

Bricklin, B., & Bricklin, P. M. (1967). *Bright child, poor grades: The psychology of underachievement.* New York, NY: Delacorte Press.

Bridgeland, J. M., DiIulio, J. J., Jr., & Morison, B. (2006). *The silent epidemic: Perspectives of high school dropouts.* Washington, DC: Civic Enterprises.

Briggs, C. J. (2004). Gifted programs of note for culturally diverse learners. In C. A. Tomlinson, D. Y. Ford, S. M. Reis, C. J. Briggs, & C. A. Strickland (Eds.), *In search of the dream: Designing schools and classrooms that work for high potential students from diverse cultural backgrounds* (pp. 147–188). Washington, DC: National Association for Gifted Children.

Britton, G., & Lumpkin, M. (1983). Females and minorities in basal readers. *Interracial Books for Children Bulletin, 14*(6), 4–7.

Bronfenbrenner, U. (1979). *The ecology of human development: Experiments by nature and design.* Cambridge, MA: Harvard University Press.

Bronfenbrenner, U. (1986). Ecology of the family as a context for human development: Research perspectives. *Developmental Psychology, 22,* 723–742.

Bronson, J., & Merryman, A. (2009, Sept. 5). See babies discriminate. *Newsweek.* Retrieved from http://www.newsweek.com/2009/09/04/see-baby-discriminate.html

Brookover, W. B., & Lezotte, L. W. (1979). *Changes in school characteristics coincident with change in student achievement* (Occasional Paper No. 17). East Lansing: Michigan State University, Institute for Research on Teaching.

Brophy, J. (1986). *On motivating students* (Occasional Paper No. 101). East Lansing: Michigan State University, Institute for Research on Teaching.

Brophy, J., & Good, T. (1974). *Teacher-student relationships: Causes and consequences.* New York, NY: Holt, Rinehart & Winston.

Brophy, J., & Good, T. (1986). Teacher behavior and student achievement. In M. C. Wittrock (Ed.), *Handbook of research on teaching* (3rd ed., pp. 328–375). New York, NY: McMillan.

Brown v. Board of Education of Topeka, Kansas, 347 U.S. 483 (1954).

Bullivant, B. M. (1993). Culture: Its nature and meaning for education. In J. A. Banks & C. A. M. Banks (Eds.), *Multicultural education: Issues and perspectives* (2nd ed., pp. 29–47). Boston, MA: Allyn & Bacon.

Bureau of Labor Statistics. (1983). *Consumer expenditure survey, 1982–1983: Diary survey.* Retrieved from http://www.icpsr.umich.edu/icpsrweb/NACDA/studies/8599;jsessionid=4A51F41F9D39966355716CDB2C10FB6F?author=United+States+Department+of+Labor.+Bureau+of+Labor+Statistics&paging.startRow=1

Burney, V. H., & Beilke, J. R. (2008). The constraints of poverty on high achievement. *Journal for the Education of the Gifted, 31,* 295–321.

Burt, C. L. (1972). Inheritance of general intelligence. *American Psychologist, 27,* 175–190.

Burton, N. W., Burgess Whitman, N., Yepes-Baraya, M., Cline, F., & Kim, R. M. (2002). *Minority student success: The role of teachers in Advanced Placement Program (AP) courses* (Research Report No. 2002-8). New York, NY: College Entrance Examination Board.

Butler-Por, N. (1987). *Underachievers in school: Issues and intervention.* Hoboken, NJ: John Wiley & Sons.

Byrnes, D. A. (1984). Social isolates and the teacher. *Educational Forum, 48,* 373–381.

Calabrese, R. L. (1990). The public school: A source of alienation for minority parents. *Journal of Negro Education, 59,* 148–154.

Caldwell, C. H., Kohn-Wood, L. P., Schmeelk-Cone, K. H., Chavous, T. M., & Zimmerman, M. A. (2004). Racial discrimination and racial identity as risk or protective factors for violent behaviors in African American young adults. *American Journal of Community Psychology, 33,* 91–105.

Callahan, C. M. (1991). An update on gifted females. *Journal for the Education of the Gifted, 14,* 284–311.

Callahan, C. M., & McIntyre, J. A. (1994). *Identifying outstanding talent in American Indian and Alaska Native students.* Washington, DC: U.S. Department of Education.

Callahan, C. M., Tomlinson, C. A., & Pizzat, P. M. (1993). *Contexts for promise: Noteworthy practices and innovations in the identification of gifted students.* Charlottesville: The University of Virginia, The National Research Center on the Gifted and Talented.

Campbell, C. A. (1991). Group guidance for academically under-motivated children. *Elementary School Guidance & Counseling, 25,* 302–306.

Carnegie Corporation of New York. (1984/1985). Renegotiating society's contract with the public schools. *Carnegie Quarterly, 29/30,* 1–4, 6–11.

Carroll, A., Gurski, G., Hinsdale, K., & McIntyre, K. (1977). *Culturally appropriate assessment: A sourcebook for practitioners.* Los Angeles, CA: Regional Resource Center.

Carter, K. (1984). Do teachers understand principles for writing tests? *Journal of Teacher Education, 35,* 57–60.

Carter, S. C. (2000). *No excuses: Lessons from 21 high-performing high-poverty schools.* Washington, DC: Heritage Foundation.

Carter, T. P., & Chatfield, M. L. (1986). Effective bilingual schools: Implementation for policy and practice. *American Journal of Education, 95,* 200–232.

Casas, J. M., Ponterotto, J. G., & Gutierrez, J. M. (1986). An ethical indictment of counseling research and training: The cross-cultural perspective. *Journal of Counseling and Development, 64,* 347–349.

Cassidy, J., & Hossler, A. (1992). State and federal definitions of the gifted: An update. *Gifted Child Today, 15*(1), 46–53.

Castellano, J. A. (2003). *Special populations in gifted education: Working with diverse gifted learners.* Boston, MA: Allyn & Bacon.

Castellano, J. A., & Frazier, A. D. (2011). *Special populations in gifted education: Understanding our most able students from diverse backgrounds.* Waco, TX: Prufrock Press.

Chaplin, J. P. (1975). *Dictionary of psychology.* New York, NY: Dell.

Childers, J. H., & Fairman, M. (1986). The school counselor as facilitator of organizational health. *The School Counselor, 33,* 332–337.

Children's Defense Fund. (2008). *Cradle to grave pipeline fact sheet.* Washington, DC: Author.

Ciha, T. E., Harris, R., Hoffman, C., & Potter, M. W. (1974). Parents as identifiers of giftedness: Ignored but accurate. *Gifted Child Quarterly, 18,* 191–195.

Citizens Policy Center for Oakland. (1984). *Voices from the classroom: Students and teachers speak out on the quality of teaching in our schools.* San Francisco, CA: Rosenberg Foundation.

City of Richmond v. J. A. Croson Co., 488 U.S. 469 (1989).

Civil Rights Act of 1964, Pub. Law 88-352 (July 2, 1964).

Clance, P. R., & Imes, I. M. (1978). The imposter phenomenon in high achieving women: Dynamics and therapeutic intervention. *Psychotherapy: Theory, Research and Practice, 15,* 241–247.

Clark, B. (1991). *Growing up gifted: Developing the potential of children at home and school.* New York, NY: Macmillan.

Clark, K. B., & Clark, M. K. (1940). Skin color as a factor in racial identification of Negro preschool children. *Journal of Social Psychology, 11,* 159–169.

Clark, R. (1983). *Family life and school achievement: Why poor Black children succeed and fail.* Chicago, IL: University of Chicago Press.

Clewell, B. C., Anderson, B., Bruschi, B., Joy, M., & Meltzer, M. (1994). *Conditions conducive to success in minority-dominant schools with strong Advanced Placement programs* (Unpublished final report submitted to Advanced Placement Program). Princeton, NJ: Educational Testing Service.

Cline, S., & Schwartz, D. (Eds.). (1999). *Diverse populations of gifted children: Meeting their needs in the regular classroom and beyond.* Columbus, OH: Merrill/Prentice Hall.

Colangelo, N. (1988). Families of gifted children: The next ten years. *Roeper Review, 11,* 16–18.

Colangelo, N. (1991). Counseling gifted students. In N. Colangelo & G. A. Davis (Eds.), *Handbook of gifted education* (pp. 271–284). Needham Heights, MA: Allyn & Bacon.

Colangelo, N., & Davis, G. A. (1991). *Handbook of gifted education.* Boston, MA: Allyn & Bacon.

Colangelo, N., & Davis, G. A. (2003). *Handbook of gifted education* (3rd ed.). Boston, MA: Allyn & Bacon.

Colangelo, N., & Dettman, D. F. (1983). A review of research on parents and families of gifted children. *Exceptional Children, 50,* 20–27.

Colangelo, N., Kerr, B. A., Christensen, P., & Maxey, J. (1993). A comparison of gifted underachievers and gifted high achievers. *Gifted Child Quarterly, 37,* 155–160.

Coleman, J. M., & Fults, B. A. (1985). Special-class placement, level of intelligence, and the self-concepts of gifted children: A social comparison perspective. *Remedial and Special Education, 6,* 7–11.

Coleman, J. S. (1987). Families and schools. *Educational Researcher, 16*(6), 32–38.

Coleman, J. S. (1994). *Foundations of social theory.* Cambridge, MA: Harvard University Press.

Coleman, J. S., Campbell, E. Q., Hobson, C. J., McPartland, J., Mood, A. M., Weinfeld, F. D., & York, R. L. (1966). *Equality of educational opportunity.* Washington, DC: U.S. Government Printing Office.

Coleman, M. R., & Gallagher, J. J. (1992a). *Report on state policies related to the identification of gifted students.* Chapel Hill, NC: Gifted Education Policy Studies Program at the University of North Carolina at Chapel Hill.

Coleman, M. R., & Gallagher, J. J. (1992b). State policies for identification of nontraditional gifted students. *Gifted Child Today, 15*(1), 15–17.

Coley, P. (2003). *Parsing the achievement gap: Baselines for tracking progress.* Princeton, NJ: Educational Testing Services.

Coley, R. J., & Casserly, P. L. (1992). *A study of AP students in high school with large minority populations* (Advanced Placement Program report). Princeton, NJ: Educational Testing Service.

College Board. (1985). *Equity and excellence: The educational status of Black Americans.* New York, NY: Author.

College Board. (2002). *Opening classroom doors: Strategies for expanding access to AP.* New York, NY: Author.

College Board. (2008). *The 4th annual AP report to the nation.* Washington, DC: Author.

College Board. (2009). *The 5th annual AP report to the nation.* Washington, DC: Author.

Comer, J. P. (1989). Racism and the education of young children. *Teachers College Press, 90,* 352–361.

Comer, J. P. (1990). Recreating our school communities for youth: The Comer School Development Program. *Partnership: A Journal for Leaders in Education, 15*(1), 14–18.

Condran, J. G. (1979). Changes in White attitudes toward Blacks: 1963–1977. *Public Opinion Quarterly, 43,* 463–476.

Cooley, M. R., Cornell, D. G., & Lee, C. C. (1991). Peer acceptance and self-concept of Black students in a summer gifted program. *Journal for the Education of the Gifted, 14,* 166–177.

Cooper, S. E., & Robinson, D. A. G. (1987). The effects of a structured academic support group on GPA and self-concept of ability. *Techniques: A Journal for Remedial Education and Counseling, 3*, 260–264.

Corder, L. J., & Quisenberry, N. L. (1987). Early education and Afro-Americans: History, assumptions and future implications for the future. *Childhood Education, 63*, 154–158.

Cornell, D. G. (1989). Child adjustment and parent use of the term "gifted." *Gifted Child Quarterly, 33*, 59–64.

Council for Exceptional Children. (1994). Statistical profile of special education in the United States, 1994 (Supplement). *Teaching Exceptional Children, 26*(3), 1–4.

Council for Exceptional Children, & National Association for Gifted Children. (2006). *CEC-NAGC initial knowledge & skill standards for gifted and talented education*. Washington, DC: Author.

Cox, J., Daniel, N., & Boston, B. (1985). *Educating able learners*. Austin, TX: University of Texas Press.

Crawley, B. (1988). Black families in a neo-conservative era. *Family Relations, 37*, 415–419.

Cross, T. L. (2004). *On the social and emotional lives of gifted children: Issues and factors in their psychological development* (2nd ed.). Waco, TX: Prufrock Press.

Cross, W. E., Jr. (1971, July). Toward a psychology of Black liberation: The Negro-to-Black conversion experience. *Black World, 20*, 13–27.

Cross, W. E., Jr. (1989). Nigrescence: A nondiaphanous phenomenon. *The Counseling Psychologist, 17*, 273–276.

Cross, W. E., Jr., & Vandiver, B. J. (2001). Nigrescence theory and measurement: Introducing the Cross Racial Identity Scale (CRIS). In J. G. Ponterotto, J. M. Casas, L. A. Suzuki, & C. M. Alexander (Eds.), *Handbook of multicultural counseling* (2nd ed., pp. 30–44). Thousand Oaks, CA: Sage.

C. S. Mott Children's Hospital, the University of Michigan Department of Pediatrics and Communicable Disease, and the University of Michigan Child Health Evaluation and Research Unit. (2010). *National poll on children's health*. Retrieved from http://www.med.umich.edu/mott/npch/pdf/081610report.pdf

Csikszentmihalyi, M., & McCormack, J. (1986). The influence of teachers. *Phi Delta Kappan, 67*, 415–419.

Curry, R. L. (1961). Certain characteristics of under-achievers and over-achievers. *Peabody Journal of Education, 39*, 41–45.

Dabrowski, K. (1972). *Psychoneurosis is not an illness*. London, England: Gryf.

Damico, S. B. (1989, March). *Staying in school: Social learning factors which lead to retention*. Paper presented at the Annual Meeting of the American Educational Research Association, San Francisco, CA. (ERIC Document Reproduction Service No. ED324776)

Dana, R. H., & Baker, D. H. (1961). High school achievement and the Bell Adjustment Inventory. *Psychological Reports, 8*, 353–356.

Dandy, E. B. (1988, April). *Dialect differences: Do they interfere?* Paper presented at the annual meeting of the Minority Advising Program and Minority Recruitment Advising Officers, Savannah, GA. (ERIC Document Reproduction Services No. ED294240)

Davidson Institute for Talent Development. (2009). *Gifted education policies*. Retrieved from http://www.davidsongifted.org/db/StatePolicy.aspx

Davis, G. A., & Rimm, S. B. (1989). *Education of the gifted and talented* (2nd ed.). Englewood Cliffs, NJ: Prentice-Hall.

Davis, G. A., & Rimm, S. B. (1994). *Education of the gifted and talented* (3rd ed.). Boston, MA: Allyn & Bacon.

Davis, G. A., & Rimm, S. B. (2004). *Education of the gifted and talented* (5th ed.). Boston, MA: Allyn & Bacon.

Davis, G. A., Rimm, S. B., & Siegle, D. (2010). *Education of the gifted and talented* (6th ed.). Boston, MA: Allyn & Bacon.

Davis, J. L. (2009). Exalting our children: The role of families in the achievement of low-income African American gifted learners. In B. MacFarlane & T. Stambaugh (Eds.), *Leading change in gifted education: The festschrift of Dr. Joyce VanTassel-Baska* (pp. 161–168). Waco, TX: Prufrock Press.

Davis, W. E., & McCaul, E. J. (1990). *At-risk children and youth: A crisis in our schools and society.* Orono: University of Maine.

Delgado-Gaitan, C., & Trueba, H. T. (1985). Ethnographic study of the participant structures in task completion: Reinterpretation of "handicaps" in Mexican children. *Learning Disability Quarterly, 8,* 67–75.

Delisle, J. R. (1990). *Underachieving gifted students.* Washington, DC: ERIC Clearinghouse on Disabilities and Gifted Education. (ERIC Digest E478)

Delisle, J. R. (1992). *Guiding the social and emotional development of gifted youth: A practical guide for educators and counselors.* New York, NY: Longman.

Delisle, J. R., & Galbraith, J. (2002). *When gifted kids don't have all the answers: How to meet their social and emotional needs.* Minneapolis, MN: Free Spirit.

DellaValle, J. C. (1984). *An experimental investigation of the relationship between preference for mobility and the word-pair recognition scores of seventh-grade students to provide supervisory and administrative guidelines for the organization of effective instructional environments* (Unpublished doctoral dissertation). St. Johns University, New York, NY.

Delpit, L. (1995). *Other people's children: Cultural conflict in the classroom.* New York, NY: The New Press.

Delpit, L. (2006). *Other people's children: Cultural conflict in the classroom* (2nd ed.). New York, NY: The New Press.

DeMarrais, K., & LeCompte, M. D. (1995). *The way schools work: A sociological analysis of education* (2nd ed.). White Plains, NY: Longman.

Demo, D. H., & Acock, A. C. (1991). The impact of divorce on children. In A. Booth (Ed.), *Contemporary families: Looking forward, looking back* (pp. 162–191). Minneapolis, MN: National Council on Family Relations.

DeVaul, S., & Davis, J. (1988, September). *Whole family: Whole child. Broken family.* Paper presented at the conference of the West Virginia Association for Gifted and Talented, Parkersburg, WV. (ERIC Document Reproduction No. ED305776)

Devine, P. G. (1989). Stereotypes and prejudice: Their automatic and controlled components. *Journal of Personality and Social Psychology, 56,* 5–18.

Dewey, J. (1963). *Experience and education.* New York, NY: Collier.

Diana v. California State Board of Education, CA 70 RFT (N.D. Cal. 1970).

Dillard, J. L. (1972). *Black English: Its history and usage in the United States.* New York, NY: Random House.

Dillard, J. L. (1992). *A history of American English.* New York, NY: Longman.

Dilworth, M. E. (Ed.). (1992). *Diversity in teacher education: New expectations.* San Francisco, CA: Jossey-Bass.

Dilworth-Anderson, P., & McAdoo, H. P. (1988). The study of ethnic minority families: Implications for practitioners and policymakers. *Family Relations, 37,* 265–267.

Dirkes, M. A. (1985). Anxiety in the gifted: Pluses and minuses. *Roeper Review, 8,* 13–15.

Donenberg, G. R. (2004). *Traditional and alternative families: Strengths and challenges.* Retrieved from http://www.psych.uic.edu/hd/NonTradFam_hand.pdf

Donovan, M. S., & Cross, C. T. (Eds.). (2002). *Minority students in special and gifted education.* Washington, DC: National Academy Press, National Research Council Panel on Minority Students in Special and Gifted Education.

Dorr-Bremm, D. W., & Herman, J. L. (1986). *Assessing student achievement: A profile of classroom practices.* Los Angeles: University of California, Center for the Study of Evaluation.

Dovidio, J. F., & Gaertner, S. L. (Eds.). (1986). *Prejudice, discrimination, and racism.* Orlando, FL: Academic Press.

Dovidio, J. F., Glick, P. G., & Rudman, L. (Eds.). (2005). *On the nature of prejudice: Fifty years after Allport.* Malden, MA: Blackwell.

Dunn, R., Beaudry, J. A., & Klavas, A. (1989). Survey of research on learning styles. *Educational Leadership, 46*(6), 50–58.

Dunn, R., DeBello, T., Brennan, P., Krimsky, J., & Murrain, P. (1981). Learning style researchers define differences differently. *Educational Leadership, 38,* 372–375.

Dunn, R., & Dunn, K. (1992). *Teaching elementary students through their individual learning styles.* Boston, MA: Allyn & Bacon.

Dunn, R., Dunn, K., & Price, G. E. (1984). *Learning style inventory.* Lawrence, KS: Price Systems.

Dunn, R., Gemake, J., Jalali, F., Zenhausern, R., Quinn, P., & Spiridakis, J. (1990). Cross-cultural differences in the learning styles of fourth-, fifth-, and sixth-grade students of Afro, Chinese, Greek, and Mexican heritage. *Journal of Multicultural Counseling and Development, 18,* 68–93.

Dusek, J. B. (1980). The development of test anxiety in children. In I. G. Sarason (Ed.), *Test anxiety: Theory, research and applications* (pp. 87–110). Hillsdale, NJ: Erlbaum.

Dweck, C. S. (1975). The role of expectations and attributions in the alleviation of learned helplessness. *Journal of Personality and Social Psychology, 31,* 674–685.

Dweck, C. S. (1999). *Self theories: Their role in motivation, personality, and development.* Philadelphia, PA: The Psychology Press.

Dweck, C. S., & Elliott, S. (1983). Achievement motivation. In P. Mussen (Ed.), *Handbook of child psychology: Socialization, personality, and social development* (Vol. 4, pp. 643–691). New York, NY: John Wiley & Son.

Eastland, T., & Bennett, W. J. (1979). *Counting by race.* New York, NY: Basic Books.

Eato, L. E., & Lerner, R. M. (1981). Relations of physical and social environment perceptions to adolescence self-esteem. *Journal of Genetic Psychology, 139,* 143–190.

Eccles, J. (1985). Why doesn't Jane run? Sex differences in educational and occupational patterns. In F. D. Horowitz & M. O'Brien (Eds.), *The gifted and talented: Developmental perspectives* (pp. 251–295). Washington, DC: American Psychological Association.

Eccles, J. S. (1989). Bringing young women to math and science. In M. Crawford & M. Gentry (Eds.), *Gender and thought: Psychological perspectives* (pp. 36–57). New York, NY: Springer-Verlag.

Edelman, M. W. (1985). The sea is so wide and my boat is so small: Problems facing Black children today. In H. P. McAdoo & J. L. McAdoo (Eds.), *Black children: Social, educational, and parental environments* (pp. 72–84). Newbury Park, CA: Sage.

Edmonds, R. R. (1979). *Effective schools for the urban poor.* In U. Neisser (Ed.), *The school achievement of minority children* (pp. 93–104). Hillsdale, NJ: Lawrence Erlbaum.

Edmonds, R. R. (1982). Programs of school improvement: An overview. *Educational Leadership, 40*(3), 4–11.

Education for All Handicapped Children Act, 20 U.S.C. § 1401 et seq. (1975).

Education Trust. (2006). *The funding gaps 2006.* Washington, DC: Author.

Education Trust. (2009). *Education watch: Tracking achievement, attainment, and opportunity in America's public schools.* Washington, DC: Author.

Edwards, B. L. (2006). The impact of racism on social function: Is it skin deep? In L. V. Blitz & M. Pender Greene (Eds.), *Racism and racial identity: Reflections on urban practice in mental health* (pp. 31–46). New York, NY: Routledge.

Eisen, P. (1978). Children under stress. *Australian and New Zealand Journal of Psychiatry, 13,* 197–204.

Eisenberg, S., & O'Dell, F. (1988). Teaching children to trust in a non-trusting world. *Elementary School Guidance & Counseling, 22,* 264–267.

Eisenhardt, K. M. (1989). Building theories from case study research. *Academy of Management Review, 14,* 532–550.

Elementary and Secondary Education Act of 1965, 20 U.S.C. § 236.

Elementary and Secondary Education Act of 1969, 20 U.S.C. § 863.

Elementary and Secondary Education Amendments of 1970, Pub. L. No. 91-230, 84 Stat. 121 (1970).

Ellis, A. (1962). *Reason and emotions in psychotherapy.* New York, NY: Lyle Stuart.

Ellis, A., & Harper, R. (1975). *A new guide to rational living.* Englewood Cliffs, NJ: Prentice-Hall.

Epps, E. G. (1969). Correlates of academic achievement among Northern and Southern urban Negro students. *Journal of Social Issues, 25,* 55–70.

Epstein, J. L., & Dauber, S. L. (1991). School programs and teacher practices of parent involvement in inner-city elementary and middle schools. *The Elementary School Journal, 91,* 289–304.

Erickson, F. (2010). Culture in society and in educational practice. In J. A. Banks & C. A. M. Banks (Eds.), *Multicultural education: Issues and perspectives* (7th ed., pp. 33–53). Hoboken, NJ: John Wiley & Sons.

Erikson, E. (1968). *Identity: Youth and crisis.* New York, NY: Norton.

Estes, T. H., Estes, J. J., Richards, H. C., & Roettger, D. M. (1981). *Estes Attitude Scales: Manual for administration and interpretation.* Austin, TX: Pro-Ed.

Exum, H. A. (1979). Facilitating psychological and emotional development of gifted Black students. In N. Colangelo & R. T. Zaffrann (Eds.), *New voices in counseling the gifted* (pp. 312–320). Dubuque: IA: Kendall/Hunt.

Exum, H. A. (1983). Key issues in family counseling with gifted and talented Black students. *Roeper Review, 5,* 28–31.

Fantini, M., & Weinstein, G. (1968). *Making urban schools work.* New York, NY: Holt, Rinehart, & Winston.

Fantuzzo, J. W., Polite, K., & Grayson, N. (1990). An evaluation of reciprocal peer tutoring across elementary school settings. *Journal of School Psychology, 28,* 309–323.

Farqhuar, W. W., & Payne, D. A. (1964). A classification and comparison of techniques used in selecting under- and over-achievers. *Personnel and Guidance Journal, 42,* 874–884.

Federal Bureau of Investigation. (2008). *Hate crime statistics.* Retrieved from http://www.fbi.gov/ucr/hc2008/index.html

Federal Interagency Forum on Child and Family Statistics. (2009). *America's children: Key national indicators on child well-being.* Retrieved from http://childstats.gov/americaschildren

Feingold, A. (1988). Cognitive gender differences are disappearing. *American Psychologist, 43,* 95–103.

Feldhusen, J. F., & Kroll, M. D. (1985). Parent perceptions of gifted children's educational needs. *Roeper Review, 7,* 249.

Ferguson, R. (2002). Addressing racial disparities in high-achieving suburban schools. *NCREL Policy Issues, 1,* 3–11.

Festinger, L. (1954). A theory of social comparisons. *Human Relations, 2,* 117–140.

Filla, T., & Clark, D. (1973). *Human relations resource guide on in-service programs.* St. Paul, MN: Minnesota Department of Education.

Fine, B. (1967). *Underachievers: How they can be helped.* New York, NY: Dalton.

Fine, M. (1986). Why urban adolescents drop into and out of public high school. In G. Natriello (Ed.), *School dropouts: Patterns and policies* (pp. 52–69). New York, NY: Teachers College Press.

Fine, M., & Pitts, B. (1980). Interventions with underachieving gifted children: Rationale and strategies. *Gifted Child Quarterly, 24,* 51–55.

Finney, B. C., & Van Dalsem, E. (1969). Group counseling for gifted underachieving high school students. *Journal of Counseling Psychology, 16,* 87–94.

Fisher, D. L., & Fraser, B. J. (1993). Interpersonal teacher behavior style and school environment. In T. H. Wubbels & J. Levy (Eds.), *Do you know what you look like? Interpersonal relationships in education* (pp. 103–112). London, England: Falmer Press.

Fishman, J. A. (Ed.). (2001). *Handbook of language and ethnic identity.* New York, NY: Oxford University Press.

Flanagan, D. P., & Ortiz, S. O. (2001). *Essentials of cross-battery assessment.* New York, NY: Wiley Press.

Flanagan, D. P., Ortiz, S. O., & Alfonso, V. C. (2007). *Essentials of cross-battery assessment* (2nd ed.). New York, NY: Wiley Press.

Fleming, M., & Chambers, B. (1983). Teacher-made tests: Windows on the classroom. In W. E. Hathaway (Ed.), *Testing in the schools: New directions for testing and measurement* (pp. 29–38). San Francisco, CA: Jossey-Bass.

Ford, B. A. (1992). Multicultural education training for special educators working with African-American youth. *Exceptional Children, 59,* 107–114.

Ford, D. Y. (1991). *Self-perceptions of social, psychological, and cultural determinants of achievement among gifted Black students: A paradox of underachievement* (Unpublished doctoral dissertation). Cleveland State University, Cleveland, OH.

Ford, D. Y. (1992). Determinants of underachievement as perceived by gifted, above-average, and average Black students. *Roeper Review, 14,* 130–136.

Ford, D. Y. (1993a). An investigation into the paradox of underachievement among gifted Black students. *Roeper Review, 16,* 78–84.

Ford, D. Y. (1993b). Black students' achievement orientation as a function of perceived family achievement orientation and demographic variables. *Journal of Negro Education, 62,* 47–66.

Ford, D. Y. (1993c). Support for the achievement ideology and determinants of underachievement as perceived by gifted, above-average, and average Black students. *Journal for the Education of the Gifted, 16,* 280–298.

Ford, D. Y. (1994a). An exploration of perceptions of alternative family structures among university students. *Family Relations, 43,* 68–73.

Ford, D. Y. (1994b). Nurturing resilience in gifted Black youth. *Roeper Review, 17,* 80–85.

Ford, D. Y. (1995). Desegregating gifted education: A need unmet. *Journal of Negro Education, 64,* 52–56.

Ford, D. Y. (1996). *Reversing underachievement among gifted Black students: Promising practices and programs.* New York, NY: Teachers College Press.

Ford, D. Y. (1998). The under-representation of minority students in gifted education: Problems and promises in recruitment and retention. *The Journal of Special Education, 32,* 4–14.

Ford, D. Y. (1999). *A study of factors affecting the recruitment and retention of minority teachers in gifted education.* Storrs: University of Connecticut, The National Research Center on the Gifted and Talented.

Ford, D. Y. (2004). *Intelligence testing and cultural diversity: Concerns, cautions, and considerations.* Storrs: University of Connecticut, The National Research Center on the Gifted and Talented.

Ford, D. Y. (2006). Closing the achievement gap: How gifted education can help. *Gifted Child Today, 29*(4), 14–18.

Ford, D. Y. (2007a). Diamonds in the rough: Recognizing and meeting the needs of gifted children from low SES backgrounds. In J. VanTassel-Baska & T. Stambaugh (Eds.), *Overlooked gems: A national perspective on low-income promising learners* (pp. 37–42). Washington, DC: National Association for Gifted Children.

Ford, D. Y. (2007b). Intelligence testing and cultural diversity: The need for alternative instruments, policies, and procedures. In J. L. VanTassel-Baska (Ed.), *Alternative assessments with gifted and talented students* (pp. 107–128). Waco, TX: Prufrock Press.

Ford, D. Y. (2010). Recruiting and retaining gifted students from diverse ethnic, cultural, and linguistic backgrounds. In J. A. Banks & C. A. M. Banks (Eds.), *Multicultural education: Issues and perspectives* (7th ed., pp. 371–389). Hoboken, NJ: John Wiley & Sons.

Ford, D. Y., Grantham, T. C., & Harris, J. J., III. (1997). The recruitment and retention of minority teachers in gifted education. *Roeper Review, 19,* 213–220.

Ford, D. Y., Grantham, T. C., & Whiting, G. W. (2008a). Another look at the achievement gap: Learning from the experiences of gifted Black students. *Urban Education, 43,* 216–239.

Ford, D. Y., Grantham, T. C., & Whiting, G. W. (2008b). Culturally and linguistically diverse students in gifted education: Recruitment and retention issues. *Exceptional Children, 74,* 289–308.

Ford, D. Y., & Harris, J. J., III. (1991). On discovering the hidden treasure of gifted and talented African-American children. *Roeper Review, 13,* 27–33.

Ford, D. Y., & Harris, J. J., III. (1995a). Exploring university counselors' perceptions of distinctions between achievement among gifted Black and gifted White students. *Journal of Counseling and Development, 73,* 443–450.

Ford, D. Y., & Harris, J. J., III. (1995b). Underachievement among gifted African-American students: Implications for school counselors. *The School Counselor, 42,* 196–203.

Ford, D. Y., & Harris, J. J., III. (1996). Perceptions and attitudes of Black students toward school, achievement, and other educational variables. *Child Development, 67,* 1141–1152.

Ford, D. Y., & Harris, J. J., III. (1999). *Multicultural gifted education.* New York, NY: Teachers College Press.

Ford, D. Y., Harris, J. J., III, & Schuerger, J. M. (1993). Racial identity development among gifted Black students: Counseling issues and concerns. *Journal of Counseling and Development, 71,* 409–417.

Ford, D. Y., Harris, J. J., III, & Turner, W. L. (1990/1991). The extended African-American family: A pragmatic strategy that blunts the blades of injustice. *The Urban League Review Policy Research Journal, 14,* 71–83.

Ford, D. Y., Harris, J. J., III, Tyson, C. A., & Frazier Trotman, M. (2002). Beyond deficit thinking: Providing access for gifted African American students. *Roeper Review, 24,* 52–58.

Ford, D. Y., Harris, J. J., III, Webb, K. S., & Jones, D. L. (1994). Rejection or confirmation of racial identity: A dilemma for high-achieving Blacks? *Journal of Educational Thought, 28,* 7–33.

Ford, D. Y., Harris, J. J., III, & Winborne, D. G. (1991). The coloring of IQ testing: A new name for an old phenomenon. In D. J. Jones (Ed.), *Prescriptions and policies: The social well-being of African Americans in the 1990s* (pp. 99–112). New Brunswick, NJ: Transaction.

Ford, D. Y., Howard, T. C., & Harris, J. J., III. (1999). Using multicultural literature in gifted education classrooms. *Gifted Child Today, 22*(4), 14–21.

Ford, D. Y., & Kea, C. D. (2009). Creating culturally responsive instruction: For students' and teachers' sake. *Focus on Exceptional Children, 41*(9), 1–16.

Ford, D. Y., & Milner, H. R. (2005). *Teaching culturally diverse gifted students.* Waco, TX: Prufrock Press.

Ford, D. Y., Moore, J. L., III, & Whiting, G. W. (2006). Eliminating deficit orientations: Creating classrooms and curriculums for gifted students from diverse cultural backgrounds. In M. G. Constantine & D. W. Sue (Eds.), *Addressing racism: Facilitating cultural competence in mental health and educational settings* (pp. 173–193). Hoboken, NJ: Wiley.

Ford, D. Y., & Trotman Scott, M. (2010). Under-representation of African American students in gifted education: Nine theories and frameworks for information, understanding, and change. *Gifted Education Press Quarterly, 24*(3), 2–6.

Ford, D. Y., Tyson, C. A., Howard, T. C., & Harris, J. J., III. (2000). Multicultural literature and gifted Black students: Promoting self-understanding, awareness, and pride. *Roeper Review, 22,* 235–240.

Ford, D. Y., & Whiting, G. W. (2008). Cultural competence: Preparing gifted students for a diverse society. *Roeper Review, 30,* 1–7.

Ford, D. Y., & Whiting, G. W. (2009). Racial identity and peer pressures among gifted African-American students: Issues and recommendations. In H. A. Neville, B. M. Tynes, & S. O. Utsey (Eds.), *Handbook of African American psychology* (pp. 223–236). Thousand Oaks, CA: Sage.

Ford, D. Y., Wright, L. B., Grantham, T. C., & Harris, J. J., III. (1998). Achievement levels, outcomes, and orientation of Black students in single and two-parent families. *Urban Education, 33,* 360–384.

Fordham, S. (1986). *Blacked out: Dilemmas of race, identity, and success at Capital High.* Chicago, IL: The University of Chicago Press.

Fordham, S. (1988). Racelessness as a strategy in Black students' school success: Pragmatic strategy or pyrrhic victory? *Harvard Educational Review, 58,* 54–84.

Fordham, S., & Ogbu, J. U. (1986). Black students' school success: Coping with the "burden of 'acting White.'" *The Urban Review, 18,* 176–203.

Fox, L. H., & Turner, L. D. (1981, Spring). Gifted and creative females in the middle school years. *American Middle School Education,* 17–23.

Franklin, J. H. (1988). A historical note on Black families. In H. P. McAdoo (Ed.), *Black families* (2nd ed., pp. 23–26). Newbury Park, CA: Sage.

Frantz, C. S., & Prillaman, D. (1993). State certification endorsement for school counselors: Special education requirements. *The School Counselor, 40,* 375–379.

Fraser, B. J. (1994). Research on classroom and school climate. In D. Gabel (Ed.), *Handbook of research on science teaching and learning* (pp. 493–541). New York, NY: Macmillan.

Frasier, M. M. (1989). A perspective on identifying Black students for gifted programs. In C. J. Maker & S. W. Schiever (Eds.), *Critical issues in gifted education: Defensible programs for cultural and ethnic minorities* (Vol. II, pp. 213–255). Austin, TX: Pro-Ed.

Frasier, M. M. (1992). Ethnic/minority children: Reflections and directions. In *Challenges in gifted education: Developing potential and investing in knowledge for the 21st century* (pp. 41–48). Columbus: Ohio State Department of Education.

Frasier, M. M., García, J. H., & Passow, A. H. (1995). *A review of assessment issues in gifted education and their implications for identifying gifted minority students* (RM95204). Storrs: The National Research Center on the Gifted and Talented, University of Connecticut.

Frasier, M. M., Hunsaker, S. L., Lee, J., Finley, V. S., García, J. H., Martin, D., & Frank, E. (1995). *An exploratory study of the effectiveness of the staff development model and the research-based assessment plan in improving the identification of gifted economically disadvantaged students* (RM95224). Storrs: The National Research Center on the Gifted and Talented, University of Connecticut.

Frasier, M. M., Hunsaker, S. L., Lee, J., Mitchell, S., Cramond, B., Krisel, S., . . . Finley, V. S. (1995). *Core attributes of giftedness: A foundation for recognizing the gifted potential of minority and economically disadvantaged students* (RM95210). Storrs: The National Research Center on the Gifted and Talented, University of Connecticut.

Frasier, M. M., Martin, D., García, J. H., Finley, V. S., Frank, E., Krisel, S., & King, L. L. (1995). *A new window for looking at gifted children* (RM95222). Storrs: The National Research Center on the Gifted and Talented, University of Connecticut.

Frasier, M. M., & Passow, A. H. (1994). *Toward a new paradigm for identifying talent potential* (RM94112). Storrs: The National Research Center on the Gifted and Talented, University of Connecticut.

Frederico, P. A., & Landis, D. B. (1980, August). *Are cognitive styles independent of ability and aptitude?* Paper presented at the annual conference of the American Psychological Association, Montreal, Canada.

Freeman, J. (1983). Emotional problems of the gifted child. *Journal of Child Psychology and Psychiatry, 24,* 66–70.

Friere, P. (1970). *Pedagogy of the oppressed.* New York, NY: Continuum Publishing.

Gabelko, N. H. (1988). Prejudice reduction in secondary schools. *Social Education, 52,* 276–279.

Gagné, F. (1989). Peer nominations as a psychometric instrument: Many questions asked but few answered. *Gifted Child Quarterly, 33,* 53–58.

Galbraith, J. (1985). The eight great gripes of gifted kids: Responding to special needs. *Roeper Review, 8,* 15–17.

Gallagher, J. J. (1979). Issues on the education of the gifted. In A. H. Passow (Ed.), *The gifted and talented: Their education and development* (pp. 28–44). Chicago, IL: University of Chicago Press.

Gallagher, J. J. (1988). National agenda for educating gifted students: Statement of priorities. *Exceptional Children, 55,* 107–114.

Gallagher, J. J., & Gallagher, S. A. (1994). *Teaching the gifted child* (4th ed.). Needham Heights, MA: Allyn & Bacon.

Gallagher, J. J., & Kinney, L. (Eds.). (1974). *Talent delayed—talent denied: A conference report.* Reston, VA: Foundation for Exceptional Children.

Gallagher, J. J., & Weiss, P. (1985). *The education of gifted and talented students: A history and prospectus.* Washington, DC: Council for Basic Education.

Gallup Poll finds public support for programs for gifted students. (1992, December 9). *Education Week,* 2.

García Coll, C. T., Sepkoski, C., & Lester, B. M. (1981). Cultural and biomedical correlates of neonatal behavior. *Developmental Psychobiology, 14,* 147–154.

Garcia, R., & Walker de Felix, J. (1992). The dropout issue and school reform. In H. C. Waxman, J. Walker de Felix, J. E. Anderson, & H. P. Baptiste, Jr. (Eds.), *Students at risk in at-risk schools: Improving environments for learning* (pp. 43–60). Newbury Park, CA: Corwin Press.

Gardner, H. (1983). *Frames of mind: The theory of multiple intelligences.* New York, NY: Basic Books.

Gardner, H. (1985). *The mind's new science: A history of the cognitive revolution.* New York, NY: Basic Books.

Gay, G. (1990). Achieving educational equality through curriculum desegregation. *Phi Delta Kappan, 72,* 56–72.

Gay, G. (2000). *Culturally responsive teaching: Theory, research, & practice.* New York, NY: Teachers College Press.

Gay, G. (2002). Preparing for culturally responsive teaching. *Journal of Teacher Education, 53,* 106–116.

Gay, J. E. (1978). A proposed plan for identifying Black gifted children. *Gifted Child Quarterly, 22,* 353–359.

Gelbrich, J. A., & Hare, E. K. (1989). The effects of single parenthood on school achievement in a gifted population. *Gifted Child Quarterly, 33,* 115–117.

Gender equity issue continued and meeting the special needs of gifted males [Special issue]. (1991). *Roeper Review, 13*(4).

Gerler, E. R., Jr., Bland, M., Meland, P., & Miller, D. (1986). The effect of small-group counseling on underachievers. *Elementary School Guidance & Counseling, 20,* 303–305.

Gerler, E. R., Jr., Drew, N. S., & Mohr, P. (1990). Succeeding in middle school: A multimodal approach. *Elementary School Guidance & Counseling, 24,* 263–271.

Gerler, E. R., Jr., Kinney, J., & Anderson, R. F. (1985). The effects of counseling on classroom performance. *Humanistic Education and Development, 23,* 155–165.

Gifted and Talented Children's Education Act of 1978, 20 U.S.C. § 3311.

Ginsberg, G., & Harrison, C. H. (1977). *How to help your gifted child: A handbook for parents and teachers.* New York, NY: Monarch Press.

Giroux, H. (1983). Theories of reproduction and resistance in the new sociology of education: A critical analysis. *Harvard Educational Review, 53,* 257–293.

Glasser, W. (1965). *Reality therapy: A new approach to psychiatry.* New York, NY: Harper & Row.

Glasser, W. (1986). *Control theory in the classroom.* New York, NY: Harper & Row.

Goddard, H. H. (1912). *The Kallikak family: A study in the heredity of feeble-mindedness.* New York, NY: Macmillan.

Goleman, D. (1995). *Emotional intelligence.* New York, NY: Bantam Books.

Gollnick, D. M., & Chinn, P. C. (1998). *Multicultural education in a pluralistic society* (5th ed.). Upper Saddle River, NJ: Merrill.

Good, C., Dweck, C. S., & Rattan, A. (2008). *The effects of perceiving fixed-ability environments and stereotyping on women's sense of belonging to math.* Unpublished manuscript, Barnard College, Columbia University.

Good, T. L., & Brophy, J. E. (1987). *Looking into classrooms* (4th ed.). New York, NY: Harper & Row.

Goodlad, J. I. (1983). Access to knowledge. *Teachers College Record, 84,* 787–800.

Goodlad, J. I. (1984). *A place called school: Prospects for the future.* New York, NY: McGraw-Hill.

Goodlad, J. I., & Oakes, J. (1988). We must offer equal access to knowledge. *Educational Leadership, 45*(5), 16–22.

Goodwin, A. L., & King, S. H. (2002). *Culturally responsive parental involvement: Concrete understanding and basic strategies.* New York, NY: AACTE.

Gould, S. J. (1991). *The mismeasure of man.* New York, NY: Norton.

Gould, S. J. (1995). *The mismeasure of man* (Rev. ed.). New York, NY: Norton.

Governors' Commission on Socially Disadvantaged Black Males. (1989). *Call to action* (Vol. 2). Columbus, OH: Author.

Gowan, J. C. (1957). Intelligence, interests, and reading ability in relation to scholastic achievement. *Psychology Newsletter, 15/16,* 22–36.

Granat, D., Hathaway, P., Saleton, W., & Sansing, J. (1986). Blacks and Whites in Washington: How separate? How equal? A special report. *Washingtonian, 22,* 152–182.

Grantham, T. C. (1994). *Improving achievement outcomes for African American students: An organizational effectiveness study.* The University of Virginia, Charlottesville, VA.

Grantham, T. C. (1997). *The under-representation of Black males in gifted programs: Case studies of participation motivation* (Unpublished doctoral dissertation). The University of Virginia, Charlottesville, VA.

Grantham, T. C. (2004a) Multicultural mentoring to increase Black male representation in gifted programs. *Gifted Child Quarterly, 48,* 232–245.

Grantham, T. C. (2004b). Rocky Jones: A case study of a gifted high-achieving Black male's participation motivation in gifted programs. *Roeper Review, 26,* 208–215.

Gratz v. Bollinger, 539 U.S. 244 (2003).

Gray, J. (1985, March). A Black American princess. New game, new rules. *The Washington Post,* pp. E1, E5.

Green, K., Fine, M. J., & Tollefson, N. (1988). Family systems characteristics and underachieving gifted adolescent males. *Gifted Child Quarterly, 32,* 267–272.

Green, V. M. (1981). Blacks in the United States: The creation of an enduring people. In G. P. Castile & G. Kusher (Eds.), *Persistence peoples: Cultural enclaves in perspective* (pp. 69–77). Tucson: University of Arizona Press.

Greenfield, P. (1997). You can't take it with you: Why ability assessments don't cross cultures. *American Psychologist, 52,* 1115–1124.

Gregorc, A. F. (1984). *Gregorc Style Delineator: Development technical and administration manual.* Maynard, CA: Gabriel Systems.

Griggs v. Duke Power Co., 401 U.S. 424 (1971).

Griggs, S. A., & Dunn, R. S. (1984). Selected case studies of the learning style preferences of gifted students. *Gifted Child Quarterly, 28,* 115–119.

Griggs, S. A., & Dunn, R. (1989). The learning styles of multicultural groups and counseling implications. *Journal of Multicultural Counseling and Development, 1,* 146–155.

Grites, T. J. (1979). Between high school counselor and college advisor—A void. *The Personnel and Guidance Journal, 58,* 200–204.

Gross, M. U. M. (1989). The pursuit of excellence or the search for intimacy? The forced-choice dilemma of gifted youth. *Roeper Review, 11,* 189–193.

Groth-Marnat, G. (1997). *Handbook of psychological assessment* (3rd ed.). New York, NY: John Wiley & Sons.

Groth-Marnat, G. (2003). *Handbook of psychological assessment* (4th ed.). New York, NY: John Wiley & Sons.

Grutter v. Bollinger, 539 U.S. 306 (2003).

Gubbins, E. J., Siegle, D., Renzulli, J. S., & Brown, S. W. (1993, Fall). Assumptions underlying the identification of gifted and talented students. *The National Research Center on the Gifted and Talented Newsletter,* 3–5.

Guggenheim, F. (1969). Self-esteem and achievement expectations for White and Negro children. *Journal of Projective Techniques and Personality Assessment, 33,* 63–71.

Gullickson, A. R., & Ellwein, M. C. (1985). Post hoc analysis of teacher-made tests: The goodness of fit between prescriptions and practice. *Educational Measurement: Issues and Practice, 4*(1), 15–18.

Haggard, E. A. (1957). Socialization, personality, and academic achievement in gifted children. *The School Review, 65,* 388–414.

Hale, J. E. (2001). *Learning while Black: Creating educational excellence for African American children.* Baltimore, MD: Johns Hopkins University Press.

Hale-Benson, J. (1986). *Black children: Their roots, culture, and learning styles.* Baltimore, MD: Johns Hopkins University Press.

Hall, E. T. (1959). *The silent language.* New York, NY: Doubleday.

Hall, E. T. (1976). *Beyond culture.* New York, NY: Doubleday.

Hall, E. T. (1983). *The dance of life, the other dimension of time.* New York, NY: Doubleday.

Hammill, D. D. (1990). On defining learning disabilities: An emerging consensus. *Journal of Learning Disabilities, 23,* 74–91.

Handwerk, P., Tognatta, N., Coley, R. J., & Gitomer, D. H. (2008). *Access to success: Patterns of Advanced Placement in U.S. high schools.* Princeton, NJ: Educational Testing Service.

Haney, W., & Madaus, G. (1989). Searching for alternatives to standardized tests: Whys, whats, and whithers. *Phi Delta Kappan, 70,* 683–687.

Hansen, J. B., & Linden, L. W. (1990). Selecting instruments for identifying gifted and talented students. *Roeper Review, 13,* 10–15.

Hargis, C. H. (1989). *Teaching low achieving and disabled students.* Springfield, IL: Charles C. Thomas.

Harmon, D. A. (2002). They won't teach me: The voices of gifted African American inner-city students. *Roeper Review, 24,* 68–75.

Harmon, D. A. (2004). Improving test performance among culturally diverse gifted students. *Understanding Our Gifted, 16*(4), 18–22.

Harper, F. D., Terry, L. M., & Twiggs, R. (2009). Counseling strategies with Black boys and Black men: Implications for policy. *Journal of Negro Education, 78,* 216–232.

Harrington, J., Harrington, C., & Karns, E. (1991). The Marland Report: Twenty years later. *Journal for the Education of the Gifted, 15*, 31–43.

Harris, J. J., III, & Ford, D. Y. (1991). Identifying and nurturing the promise of gifted Black students. *Journal of Negro Education, 60*, 3–18.

Harry, B. (1992). *Cultural diversity, families, and the special education system: Communication and empowerment.* New York, NY: Teachers College Press.

Hart, B., & Risley, T. R. (1995). *Meaningful differences in the everyday experiences of young American children.* Baltimore, MD: Paul H. Brookes.

Hart-Hester, S., Heuchert, C., & Whittier, K. (1989). The effects of teaching reality therapy techniques to elementary students to help change behaviors. *Journal of Reality Therapy, 8*(2), 13–18.

Harter, S. (1982). The Perceived Competence Scale for Children. *Child Development, 53*, 87–97.

Haynes, N. M., Comer, J. P., & Hamilton-Lee, M. (1989). School climate enhancement through parent involvement. *Journal of School Psychology, 27*, 87–90.

Haynes, N. M., & Hamilton-Lee, M. (1986). *The school climate survey.* New Haven, CT: Yale University, Child Study Center.

Haynes, N. M., Hamilton-Lee, M., & Comer, J. P. (1988). Differences in self-concept among high, average, and low achieving high school sophomores. *The Journal of Social Psychology, 128*, 259–264.

Hébert, T. P. (1991). Meeting the affective needs of bright boys through bibliotherapy. *Roeper Review, 13*, 207–212.

Hébert, T. P. (1998). Fostering emotional growth in young gifted children through bibliotherapy. In S. M. Reis, S. M. Baum, & L. R. Maxfield (Eds.), *Nurturing the gifts and talents of primary grade students* (pp. 309–327). Mansfield Center, CT: Creative Learning Press.

Hébert, T. P. (2009). Guiding gifted teenagers to self-understanding through biography. In J. VanTassel-Baska, T. L. Cross, & F. R. Olenchak (Eds.), *Social-emotional curriculum with gifted and talented students* (pp. 259–287). Waco, TX: Prufrock Press.

Hébert, T. P., Long, L. A., & Speirs Neumeister, K. L. (2005). Using biography to counsel gifted young women. In S. K. Johnsen & J. Kendrick (Eds.), *Teaching and counseling gifted girls* (pp. 89–118). Waco, TX: Prufrock Press.

Helms, J. E. (1989). Considering some methodological issues in racial identity counseling research. *The Counseling Psychologist, 17*, 227–252.

Helms, J. E. (1992). Why is there no study of equivalence in standardized cognitive-ability testing? *American Psychologist, 47*, 1083–1101.

Helms, J. E. (1994). Racial identity in the school environment. In P. Pedersen & J. C. Carey (Eds.), *Multicultural counseling in schools: A practical handbook* (pp. 19–37). Boston, MA: Allyn & Bacon.

Henry J. Kaiser Family Foundation. (2006). *Race, ethnicity, and health care: Young African American men in the United States.* Retrieved from http://kff.org/minority-health/update/7541.pdf

Herrnstein, R. J., & Murray, C. (1994). *The bell curve: Intelligence and class structure in American life.* New York, NY: Free Press.

Herskovitz, M. J. (1958). *The myth of the Negro past.* Boston, MA: Beacon Press.

Heuchert, C. M. (1989). Enhancing self-directed behavior in the classroom. *Academic Therapy, 24*, 295–303.

High, M. H., & Udall, A. J. (1983). Teacher ratings of students in relation to ethnicity of students and school ethnic balance. *Journal for the Education of the Gifted, 6*, 154–166

Hill, R. (1971). *The strengths of Black families*. New York, NY: Emerson Hall.

Hilliard, A. G., III. (1976). *Alternatives to IQ testing: An approach to the identification of gifted "minority" children*. Sacramento, CA: California State Department of Education.

Hilliard, A. G., III. (1979). Standardization and cultural bias as impediments to the scientific study and validation of "intelligence." *Journal of Research and Development in Education, 12*, 47–58.

Hilliard, A. G., III. (Ed.). (1991). *Testing African American students*. Morristown, NJ: Aaron Press.

Hilliard, A. G., III. (1992). Behavioral style, culture, and teaching and learning. *Journal of Negro Education, 61*, 370–377.

Hilliard, A. G., III. (1997). *SBA: The reawakening of the African mind*. Gainesville, FL: Marare Press.

Hitchcock, M. E., & Tompkins, G. E. (1987). Are basal reading textbooks still sexist? *The Reading Teacher, 41*, 288–292.

Hobson v. Hansen, 269 F. Supp. 401 (D.D.C. 1967), off'd sub nom. Smuck v. Holson, 408 F. 2d 175 (D.C. Cir. 1969).

Hochschild, J. L. (1984). *The new American dilemma: Liberal democracy and school desegregation*. New Haven, CT: Yale University Press.

Hodgkinson, H. (1988). An interview with Harold Hodgkinson: Using demographic data for long-range planning. *Phi Delta Kappan, 70*, 166–170.

Hodgkinson, H. (2007). Leaving too many children behind. In J. VanTassel-Baska & T. Stambaugh (Eds.), *Overlooked gems: A national perspective on low-income promising learners* (pp. 7–20). Washington, DC: National Association for Gifted Children.

Hofstede, G. (2001). *Culture's consequences: Comparing values, behaviors, institutions and organizations across cultures* (2nd ed.). Thousand Oaks, CA: Sage.

Holahan, C. K., & Stephan, C. W. (1981). When beauty isn't talent: The influence of physical attractiveness, attitudes toward women, and competence on impression formation, *Sex Roles, 7*, 867–876.

Hollinger, C., & Fleming, E. (1992). Project CHOICE: The emerging roles and careers of gifted women. *Roeper Review, 15*, 156–160.

Hollingworth, L. S. (1926). *Gifted children: Their nature and nurture*. New York, NY: MacMillan.

Hollingworth, L. S. (1942). *Children above 180 IQ (Stanford-Binet)*. Yonkers-on-Hudson, NY: World Book Company.

Horner, M. S. (1972). Toward an understanding of achievement related conflicts in women. *Journal of Social Issues, 28*, 157–175.

Horowitz, F. D., & O'Brien, M. (Eds.). (1985). *The gifted and talented: Developmental perspectives*. Washington, DC: American Psychological Association.

Howard, J., & Hammond, R. (1985, September 9). Rumors of inferiority: The hidden obstacle to Black student success. *The New Republic*, 16–21.

Hoy, W. K., Tarter, C. J., & Kottkamp, R. B. (1991). *Open schools/healthy schools: Measuring organizational climate*. Beverly Hills, CA: Sage.

Hrabowski, F. A., III. (1998). *Beating the odds: Raising academically successful African American males*. New York, NY: Oxford University Press.

Hrabowski, F. A., III. (2001). The Meyerhoff Scholars Program: Producing high-achieving minority students in mathematics and science. *Notices of the AMS, 48*(1), *26–28*.

Hundeide, K. (1992). Cultural constraints on cognitive development. In P. S. Klein & A. J. Tannenbaum (Eds.), *To be young and gifted* (pp. 52–69). Norwood, NJ: Ablex.

Hutchinson, R. L., & Reagan, C. A. (1989). Problems for which seniors would seek help from school counselors. *The School Counselor, 36,* 271–280.

Hyman, H. H., & Sheatsley, P. B. (1956). Attitudes toward desegregation. *Scientific American, 195*(6), 35–39.

Hyman, H. H., & Sheatsley, P. B. (1964). Attitudes toward desegregation. *Scientific American, 211*(1), 16–23.

Individuals with Disabilities Education Act, 20 U.S.C. § 1401 et seq. (1990).

Irvine, D. J. (1991). Gifted education with a state mandate: The importance of vigorous advocacy. *Gifted Child Quarterly, 35,* 196–199.

Irvine, J. J. (2002). *In search of wholeness: African American teachers and their culturally specific classroom practices.* New York, NY: Palgrave/St. Martin's Press.

Irvine, J. J. (2003). *Educating teachers for diversity: Seeing with the cultural eye.* New York, NY: Teachers College Press.

Jackson, J. L., & Moore, J. L., III. (2006). African American males in education: Endangered or ignored? *Teachers College Record, 108,* 201–205.

Jackson, P. (1968). *Life in classrooms.* New York, NY: Holt, Rinehart & Winston.

Jacobs, J. C. (1971). Effectiveness of teacher and parent identification of gifted children as a function of school levels. *Psychology in the Schools, 8,* 140–142.

Janos, P. M. (1983). The psychological vulnerabilities of children of very superior intellectual ability. *Dissertation Abstracts International, 44,* 1030A. (University Microfilms No. AAC 8318377)

Janos, P. M., & Robinson, N. M. (1985). Psychological development in intellectually gifted children. In F. D. Horowitz & M. O'Brien (Eds.), *The gifted and talented: Developmental perspectives* (pp. 149–195). Washington, DC: American Psychological Association.

Jencks, C., & Phillips, M. (Eds.). (1998). *The Black-White test score gap.* Washington, DC: The Brookings Institute.

Jenkins, L. E. (1989). The Black family and academic achievement. In G. L. Berry & J. K. Asamen (Eds.), *Black students: Psychological issues and academic achievement* (pp. 138–152). Newbury Park, CA: Corwin Press.

Jenkins, M. D. (1936). A socio-psychological study of Negro children of superior intelligence. *Journal of Negro Education, 5,* 175–190.

Jenkins, M. D. (1950). Intellectually superior Negro youth: Problems and needs. *Journal of Negro Education, 19,* 322–332.

Jensen, A. R. (1969). How much can we boost IQ and scholastic achievement? *Harvard Educational Review, 39,* 1–123.

Jensen, A. R. (1979). *Bias in mental testing.* New York, NY: Free Press.

Johnson, P. D. (2006). Counseling African American men: A contextualized humanistic perspective. *Counseling and Values, 50,* 187–195.

Jones, J. M. (1981). The concept of racism and its changing reality. In B. J. Bowser & R. G. Hunt (Eds.), *Impacts of racism on White Americans* (pp. 27–49). Beverly Hills, CA: Sage.

Jones, R. L. (1988). *Psychological assessment of minority group children: A casebook.* Berkeley, CA: Cobbs & Henry.

Kahle, J. B. (1986). *Equitable science education: A discrepancy model.* Perth, Western Australia: Science and Mathematics Education Center, Curtin University of Technology.

Kahle, J. B., & Meece, J. (1994). Research on gender issues in the classroom. In D. L. Gable (Ed.), *Handbook on research in science education* (pp. 542–557). New York, NY: MacMillan.

Karnes, F. A., & Marquardt, R. G. (1991). *Gifted children and the law.* Dayton, OH: Ohio Psychology Press.

Karnes, F. A., & Whorton, J. E. (1991). Teacher certification and endorsement in gifted education: Past, present, and future. *Gifted Child Quarterly, 35,* 148–150.

Katz, I., Roberts, S. O., & Robinson, J. M. (1965). Effects of task difficulty, race of administrator, and instructions on digit-symbol performance of Negroes. *Journal of Personality and Social Psychology, 2,* 53–59.

Katz, P. A. (1976). The acquisition of racial attitudes in children. In P. A. Katz (Ed.), *Toward the elimination of racism* (pp. 125–150). New York, NY: Pergamon Press.

Kaufmann, F. A. (1981). The 1964–1968 presidential scholars: A follow-up study. *Exceptional Children, 48,* 164–169.

Kaufmann, F. A., & Sexton, D. (1983). Some implications for home-school linkages. *Roeper Review, 6,* 49–51.

Kay, S. I., & Subotnik, R. F. (1994). Talent beyond words: Unveiling spatial, expressive, kinesthetic, and musical talent in young children. *Gifted Child Quarterly, 38,* 70–74.

Keat, D. (1979). *Multimodal therapy with children.* New York, NY: Pergamon Press.

Keefe, J. W. (1979). Learning style: An overview. In *Student learning styles: Diagnosing and proscribing programs* (pp. 1–17). Reston, VA: National Association of Secondary School Principals.

Keirouz, K. S. (1990). Concerns of parents of gifted children: A research review. *Gifted Child Quarterly, 34,* 56–63.

Kerr, B. A. (1985). *Smart girls, gifted women.* Columbus, OH: Ohio Psychology Publishing.

Kerr, B. A. (1991). *A handbook for counseling the gifted and talented.* Alexandria, VA: American Counseling Association.

Kerr, B. A., Colangelo, N., Maxey, J., & Christensen, P. (1992). Characteristics of academically talented minority students. *Journal of Counseling and Development, 70,* 606–609.

Kershner, K. M., & Connolly, J. A. (Eds.). (1992). *At-risk students and school restructuring* (pp. 5–11). Washington, DC: Office of Educational Research and Improvement.

Kessler, J. W. (1963). My son, the underachiever. *PTA Magazine, 58,* 12–14.

Kinder, D. R. (1986). The continuing American dilemma: White resistance to racial change 40 years after Myrdal. *Journal of Social Issues, 42,* 151–171.

Kirsch, I., Braun, H., Yamamoto, K., & Sum, A. (2007). *America's perfect storm: Three forces changing our nation's future.* Princeton, NJ: Educational Testing Service.

Kitano, M. K. (1991). A multicultural educational perspective on serving the culturally diverse gifted. *Journal for the Education of the Gifted, 15,* 4–19.

Klausmeier, K., Mishra, S. P., & Maker, C. J. (1987). Identification of gifted learners: A national survey of assessment practices and training needs of school psychologists. *Gifted Child Quarterly, 31,* 135–137.

Kline, B. E., & Short, E. B. (1991). Changes in emotional resilience: Gifted adolescent boys. *Gifted Child Quarterly, 33,* 135–137.

Kohlberg, L. (1972, November/December). A cognitive-developmental approach to moral education. *The Humanist, 32,* 72–77.

Kohlberg, L. (1975). The cognitive-developmental approach to moral education. *Phi Delta Kappan, 56,* 670–677.

Kolb, A. Y., & Kolb, D. A. (2005). *Learning styles and learning spaces: Enhancing experiential learning in higher education.* Cleveland, OH: Experience-Based Learning Systems, Case Western Reserve University.

Korman, M. (1974). National conference on levels and patterns of professional training in psychology: Major themes. *American Psychologist, 29,* 301–313.

Kozol, J. (2005). *The shame of the nation: The restoration of apartheid schooling in America.* New York, NY: Crown.

Kranz, B. (1981). *Kranz Talent Identification Instrument.* Moorhead, MN: Moorhead State College.

Krasner, L., & Houts, A. (1984). A study of the "value" systems of behavioral scientists. *American Psychologist, 39,* 840–850.

Kulieke, M. J., & Olszewski-Kubilius, P. (1989). The influence of family values and climate on the development of talent. In J. L. VanTassel-Baska & P. Olszewski-Kubilius (Eds.), *Patterns of influence on gifted learners: The home, the self, and the school* (pp. 40–59). New York, NY: Teachers College Press.

Kunjufu, J. (1993, February). *Maximizing African-American male academic achievement.* Paper presented at the fifth annual Equal Educational Opportunity Conference, Louisville, KY.

Kunjufu, J. (2001). *State of emergency: We must save African American males.* Chicago, IL: African American Images.

Labov, W. (1969). *The study of nonstandard English.* Washington, DC: National Council of Teachers of English.

Labov, W. (1972). *Language in the inner city.* Philadelphia, PA: University of Pennsylvania.

Labov, W. (1976). Some sources of reading problems for Negro speakers of nonstandard English. In A. Frazier (Ed.), *New directions in elementary English* (pp. 140–167). Champaign, IL: National Council of Teachers of English.

Labov, W. (1985). The logic of nonstandard English. In P. P. Giglioli (Ed.), *Language and social context* (pp. 179–215). New York, NY: Viking Penguin.

Ladson-Billings, G. (1990a). Culturally relevant teaching: Effective instruction for Black students. *The College Board Review, 155,* 20–25.

Ladson-Billings, G. (1990b). Like lightning in a bottle: Attempting to capture the pedagogical excellence of successful teachers of Black students. *Qualitative Studies in Education, 3,* 335–344.

Ladson-Billings, G. (1994). Who will teach our children? Preparing teachers to successfully teach African American students. In E. R. Hollins, J. E. King, & W. C. Hayman (Eds.), *Teaching diverse populations: Formulating a knowledge base* (pp. 129–158). New York: State University of New York Press.

Ladson-Billings, G. (2006). From the achievement gap to the education debt: Understanding achievement in U.S. schools. *Educational Researcher, 35*(7), 3–12.

Ladson-Billings, G. (2009). *Dreamkeepers: Successful teachers for African-American children* (2nd ed.). San Francisco, CA: Jossey-Bass.

Langdon, C. A. (1991). Comment: So long, June and Ward. *Educational Horizons, 69,* 170.

Laosa, L. M. (1977). Inequality in the classroom: Observation research on student-teacher interactions. *Aztlán: A Journal of Chicano Studies, 8*(1–2), 51–67

Larry P. v. Riles (1979, October). NO. C-712270 RFP (N. C. Cal.).

Lazarus, A. A. (Ed.). (1985). *Casebook of multimodal therapy.* New York, NY: Guilford.

Lee, C. C. (1984). An investigation of psychosocial variables related to academic success for rural Black adolescents. *Journal of Negro Education, 53,* 424–433.

Lee, C. C., & Workman, D. J. (1992). School counselors and research: Current status and future direction. *The School Counselor, 40,* 15–19.

Lee, V. E., & Burkham, D. T. (2002). *Inequality at the starting gate: Social background differences in achievement as children begin school.* Washington, DC: Educational Policy Institute.

Levin, H. M. (1990). The educationally disadvantaged are still among us. In J. G. Bain & J. L. Herman (Eds.), *Making schools work for underachieving minority students* (pp. 3–11). New York, NY: Greenwood.

Lewin, K. (1936). *Principles of topological psychology.* New York, NY: Basic Books.

Li, A. K. F. (1988). Self-perception and motivational orientation in gifted children. *Roeper Review, 10,* 175–180.

Lightfoot, S. (1983). *The good high school.* New York, NY: Basic Books.

Lindstrom, R. R., & Van Sant, S. (1986). Special issues in working with gifted minority adolescents. *Journal of Counseling and Development, 64,* 583–586.

Locke, D. C. (1989). Fostering the self-esteem of African-American children. *Elementary School Guidance & Counseling, 23,* 254–259.

Louis, B., & Lewis, M. (1992). Parental beliefs about giftedness in young children and their relation to actual ability level. *Gifted Child Quarterly, 36,* 27–31.

Lubienski, S. T. (2001, April). *A second look at mathematics achievement gaps: Intersections of race, class, and gender in NAEP data.* Paper presented at the American Educational Research Association conference, Seattle, WA.

Lubienski, S. T. (2007). What we can do about achievement disparities. *Educational Leadership, 65*(3), 54–59.

Lubienski, S. T. (2008). On "gap gazing" in mathematics education: The need for gaps analyses. *Journal for Research in Mathematics Education, 39,* 350–356.

Lubienski, S. T., & Bowen, A. (2000). Who's counting? A survey of mathematics education research 1982–1998. *Journal for Research in Mathematics Education, 31,* 626–633.

Lubienski, S. T., & Gutiérrez, R. (2008). Bridging the "gaps" in perspectives on equity in mathematics education. *Journal for Research in Mathematics Education, 39,* 365–371.

Mackler, B. (1970). Blacks who are academically successful. *Urban Education, 5,* 210–237.

MacLeod, J. (1987). *Ain't no makin' it: Leveled aspirations in a low-income neighborhood.* Boulder, CO: Westview Press.

MacLeod, J. (1995). *Ain't no makin' it: Leveled aspirations in a low-income neighborhood* (2nd ed.). Boulder, CO: Westview Press.

Maker, C. J., Nielson, A. B., & Rogers, J. A. (1994). Giftedness, diversity, and problem-solving: Multiple intelligences and diversity in educational settings. *Teaching Exceptional Children, 27*(1), 4–19.

Maker, C. J., & Schiever, S. W. (Eds.). (1989). *Critical issues in gifted education: Defensible programs for cultural and ethnic minorities* (Vol. II). Austin, TX: Pro-Ed.

Mallett, S. D., Kirschenbaum, D. S., & Humphrey, L. L. (1983). Description and subjective evaluation of an objectively successful improvement program. *Personnel and Guidance Journal, 61,* 341–345.

Manaster, G. J., & Powell, P. M. (1983). A framework for understanding gifted adolescents' psychological maladjustment. *Roeper Review, 6,* 70–73.

Mandel, H. P., & Marcus, S. I. (1988). *The psychology of underachievement: Differential diagnosis, differential treatment.* New York, NY: Wiley & Sons.

Mandel, H. P., Friedland, J. G., & Marcus, S. I. (1996). *Achievement motivation profile.* Los Angeles, CA: Western Psychological Association.

Mandler, G., & Sarason, S. B. (1952). A study of anxiety and learning. *Journal of Abnormal and Social Psychology, 47,* 166–173.

Manning, M. L., & Baruth, L. G. (2010). *Multicultural education of children and adolescents* (5th ed.). Boston, MA: Allyn & Bacon.

Marion, R. L. (1980). Communicating with parents of culturally diverse exceptional children. *Exceptional Children, 46,* 616–623.

Marion, R. L. (1981). Working with parents of the disadvantaged or culturally different gifted. *Roeper Review, 4,* 32–34.

Marks, B. T., Settles, I. H., Cooke, D. Y., Morgan, L., & Sellers, R. M. (2004). African American racial identity: A review of contemporary models and measures. In R. L. Jones (Ed.), *Black psychology* (4th ed., pp. 383–404). Hampton, VA: Cobb & Henry.

Marland, S. P., Jr. (1972). *Education of the gifted and talented: Report to the Congress of the United States by the U.S. Commissioner of Education and background papers submitted to the U.S. Office of Education,* 2 vols. Washington, DC: U.S. Government Printing Office. (Government Documents, Y4.L 11/2: G36).

Marsh, H. W. (1990). *Self-Description Questionnaire, II.* San Antonio, TX: The Psychological Corporation.

Maslach, C., & Jackson, S. E. (1981). *Maslach Burnout Inventory* (Research ed.). Palo Alto, CA: Consulting Psychologist Press.

Maslach, C., Jackson, S. E., & Leiter, M. (1996). *Maslach Burnout Inventory manual* (3rd ed.). Palo Alto, CA: Consulting Psychologist Press.

Maslow, A. H. (1954). *Motivation and personality.* New York, NY: Harper & Row.

Maslow, A. H. (1962). *Toward a psychology of being.* Princeton, NJ: Van Nostrand.

Maslow, A. H. (1968). *Toward a psychology of being* (2nd ed.). Princeton, NJ: Van Nostrand.

Mason, J. (1996). *Cultural competence self-assessment questionnaire.* Portland, OR: JLM & Associates.

Matter, D. E., & Matter, R. M. (1985). Children who are lonely and shy: Action steps for the counselors. *Elementary School Guidance & Counseling, 20,* 129–135.

McAdoo, H. P. (Ed.). (1988). *Black families* (2nd ed.). Newbury Park, CA: Sage.

McAdoo, H. P. (Ed.). (1993). *Family ethnicity: Strength in diversity.* Newbury Park, CA: Sage.

McAdoo, H. P. (Ed.). (2001). *Black children: Social, educational, and parental environments* (2nd ed.). Thousand Oaks, CA: Sage.

McAdoo, H. P. (Ed.). (2006). *Black families* (4th ed.). Thousand Oaks, CA: Sage.

McAdoo, H. P., & McAdoo, J. L. (Eds.). (1985). *Black children: Social, educational and parental environments.* Beverly Hills, CA: Sage.

McAdoo, H. P., & Younge, S. Y. (2009). Black families. In B. M. Tynes, H. A. Neville, & S. O. Utsey (Eds.), *Handbook of African American psychology* (pp. 103–125). Thousand Oaks, CA: Sage.

McBee, M. T. (2006). A descriptive analysis of referral sources for gifted identification screening for race and socioeconomic status. *Journal of Secondary Gifted Education, 17,* 103–111.

McCall, R., Applebaum, M., & Hogarty, P. (1973). Developmental changes in mental performance. *Monographs of the Society for Research in Child Development Series, 150*(3).

McCall, R. B., Evahn, C., & Kratzer, L. (1992). *High school underachievers: What do they achieve as adults?* Newbury Park, CA: Sage.

McCarthy, B. (1990). Using the 4MAT system to bring learning styles to schools. *Educational Leadership, 48*(2), 31–37.

McClelland, D. (1961). *The achieving society*. Princeton, NJ: Van Norstrand.

McClelland, D. C., Atkinson, J. W., Clark, R. A., & Lowell, E. L. (1953). *The achievement motive*. Princeton, NJ: Van Nostrand.

McDavid, R. I. (1964). Dialectology and the teaching of reading. *The Reading Teacher, 18,* 206–213.

McIntosh, P. (1988). *White privilege and male privilege: A personal account of coming to see correspondences through work in women's studies* (Working Paper #189). Wellesley, MA: Wellesley College Center for Research on Women.

McIntosh, P. (1992). *White privilege: Unpacking the invisible knapsack*. Retrieved from http://www.nymbp.org/reference/WhitePrivilege.pdf

McLeod, J., & Crophy, A. (1989). *Fostering academic excellence*. New York, NY: Pergamon Press.

McLoyd, V. C. (1990). The impact of economic hardship on Black families and children: Psychological distress, parenting, and socioeconomic development. *Child Development, 61,* 311–346.

McQuary, J. P., & Truax, W. E. (1955). An underachievement scale. *Journal of Educational Research, 47,* 393–399.

Mech, E. V. (1972, September). *Achievement motivation patterns among low income Anglo American, Mexican American, and Negro youth*. Paper presented at the annual American Psychological Association meeting, Honolulu, HI.

Menacha, M. (1997). Early racist discourses: The roots of deficit thinking. In R. Valencia (Ed.), *The evolution of deficit thinking: Educational thought and practice* (pp. 13–40). New York, NY: Falmer Press.

Mendaglio, S., & Peterson, J. S. (Eds.). (2007). *Models of counseling gifted children, adolescents, and young adults*. Waco, TX: Prufrock Press.

Mercer, D. C. (1986). Learning disabilities. In N. G. Haring & L. McCormick (Eds.), *Exceptional children and youth* (4th ed., pp. 119–159). Columbus, OH: Charles E. Merrill.

Merton, R. K. (1938). Social structure and anomie. *American Sociological Review, 3,* 672–682.

Merton, R. K. (1968). *Social theory and social structure*. New York, NY: The Free Press.

Metropolitan Life Insurance Company. (2009). *MetLife study of the American dream*. New York, NY: Author.

Mickelson, R. (1984). *Race, class, and gender differences in adolescents' academic achievement attitudes and behaviors* (Unpublished doctoral dissertation). University of California, Los Angeles.

Mickelson, R. (1990). The attitude-achievement paradox among Black adolescents. *Sociology of Education, 63,* 44–61.

Milgrim, R. M. (Ed.). (1993). *Counseling gifted and talented children: A guide for teachers, counselors, and parents*. Norwood, NJ: Ablex.

Milgrim, R. M., Dunn, R., & Price, G. E. (Eds.). (1993). *Teaching and counseling gifted and talented adolescents: An international learning style perspective*. London, England: Praeger.

Miller, J. G. (1996). A cultural-psychological perspective on intelligence. In R. J. Sternberg & E. L. Grigorenko (Eds.), *Intelligence, heredity, and environment* (pp. 269–302). New York, NY: Cambridge University Press.

Mills v. Board of Education of the District of Columbia, 348 F. Supp. 886 (D. D.C. 1972).

Milsom, A., & Peterson, J. (2006). Introduction to special issue: Examining disability and giftedness in schools. *Professional School Counseling, 10*(1), 1–2.

Mistry, J., & Rogoff, B. (1985). The gifted and talented from a cross-cultural perspective. In F. D. Horowitz & M. O'Brien (Eds.), *The gifted and talented: A developmental perspective* (pp. 125–144). Washington, DC: American Psychological Association.

Montgomery, A., & Rossi, R. (1994). Becoming at risk of failure in America's schools. In R. Rossi (Ed.), *Students and schools at risk: Context and framework for positive change* (pp. 3–22). New York, NY: Teachers College Press.

Moos, R. H. (1979). *Evaluating educational environments.* San Francisco, CA: Jossey-Bass.

Morawska, A., & Sanders, M. R. (2009). Parenting gifted and talented children: Conceptual and empirical foundations. *Gifted Child Quarterly, 53,* 163–173.

Morse, L. A. (1987). Working with young procrastinators: Elementary school students who do not complete school assignments. *Elementary School Guidance & Counseling, 21,* 221–228.

Moynihan, D. (1965). *The Negro family: The case for national action.* Washington, DC: U.S. Department of Labor, Office of Planning and Research.

Murray, H. (1938). *Explorations in personality.* New York, NY: Oxford University Press.

Myrdal, G. (1944). *An American dilemma: The Negro problem and modern democracy.* New York, NY: Harper & Bros.

Nairn, A. (1980). *The reign of ETS: The corporation that makes up minds.* Washington, DC: Ralph Nader.

National Association for Gifted Children. (1997). *Position paper on testing.* Washington, DC: Author.

National Association for Gifted Children. (2000). *Nurturing social and emotional development of gifted children.* Retrieved from http://www.nagc.org/uploadedFiles/Information_and_Resources/Position_Papers/affective%20needs%20position%20paper.pdf

National Association for Gifted Children. (2009). *State of the states in gifted education: National policy and practice data 2008–2009.* Washington, DC: National Association for Gifted Children and The Council of State Directors of Programs for the Gifted.

National Center for Health Statistics. (1983). *Advanced report of final natality statistics: 1978* (Monthly vital statistics report 31(8) supplement). Washington, DC: U.S. Government Printing Office.

National Commission on Excellence in Education. (1983). *A nation at risk: The imperative for educational reform.* Washington, DC: United States Department of Education.

National Opinion Research Center. (1980–1987). *General social surveys: Cumulative codebook.* Storrs: University of Connecticut, Roper Public Opinion Research Center.

National Urban League. (2007). *The state of Black America, 2009.* Retrieved from http://www.nul.org/thestateofblackamerica.html

Neihart, M., Reis, S. M., Robinson, N. M., & Moon, S. M. (Eds.). (2002). *The social and emotional development of gifted children: What do we know?* Waco, TX: Prufrock Press.

Neill, D. M., & Medina, N. J. (1989). Standardized testing: Harmful to educational health. *Phi Delta Kappan, 70,* 688–697.

New America Media. (2007). *Deep divisions, shared destiny: A poll of Black, Hispanic, and Asian Americans on race relations.* San Francisco, CA: Author.

Newman, C. I., Dember, C. F., & Krug, O. (1973). He can but he won't: A psychodynamic study of so-called "gifted underachievers." *Psychoanalytic Study of the Child, 28,* 83–129.

Newmann, F. M., Rutter, R. A., & Smith, M. S. (1989). Organizational factors that affect school sense of efficacy, community, and expectations. *Sociology of Education, 62,* 221–238.

Newton, A. (1994). *Using cinematherapy to meet the social and emotional needs of gifted and underachieving students.* Unpublished class project, Curry School of Education, The University of Virginia, Charlottesville, VA.

Nguyen, H. H., & Ryan, A. M. (2008). Does stereotype threat affect cognitive ability test performance of minorities and women? A meta-analytic review of experimental evidence. *Journal of Applied Psychology, 93,* 1314–1335.

Nicholls, J. G. (1984). Conceptions of ability and achievement motivation. In R. Ames & C. Ames (Eds.), *Research on motivation in education: Student motivation* (Vol. 1, pp. 39–73). New York, NY: Academic Press.

No Child Left Behind Act (NCLB), 107th Cong., 1st sess. HR 1, P.L. 107–110. (2001).

Noble, K. D. (1987). The dilemma of the gifted woman. *Psychology of Women Quarterly, 11,* 367–378.

Noble, K. D. (1989). Living out the promise of high potential: Perceptions of 100 gifted women. *Advanced Development, 1,* 57–75.

Nobles, W. W. (1985). *Africanicity and the Black family: The development of a theoretical model* (2nd ed.). Oakland, CA: Institute for the Advanced Study of Black Family Life and Culture.

Nobles, W. W. (1989). Psychological Nigrescence: An Afrocentric review. *The Counseling Psychologist, 17,* 253–257.

Noguera, P. A. (2008). *The trouble with Black boys . . . and other reflections on race, equity, and the future of public education.* New York, NY: Jossey-Bass.

Oakes, J. (1982). The reproduction of inequity: The content of secondary school tracking. *Urban Review, 14,* 107–120.

Oakes, J. (1983). Tracking and ability grouping in American schools: Some constitutional questions. *Teachers College Record, 84,* 801–819.

Oakes, J. (1985). *Keeping track: How schools structure inequality* (2nd ed.). New Haven, CT: Yale University Press.

Oakes, J. (1987). Curriculum inequality and school reform. *Equity and Excellence, 23*(1–2), 8–14.

Oakes, J. (1988). Tracking: Can schools take a different route? *National Education Association, 6,* 41–47.

Oakes, J. (2005). *Keeping track: How schools structure inequality* (2nd ed.). New Haven: Yale Press.

Oakes, J. (2008). Keeping track: Structuring equality and inequality in an era of accountability. *Teachers College Record, 110,* 700–712.

Oberg, K. (1954). *Culture shock* (Report No. A-329). Indianapolis, IN: Bobbs-Merrill Series in the Social Sciences.

Oberg, K. (1960). Adjustment to new cultural environments. *Practical Anthropology, 7,* 170–179.

Ogbu, J. U. (1983). Minority students and schooling in pluralistic societies. *Comparative Education Review, 27,* 168–170.

Ogbu, J. U. (1987). Variability in minority school performance: A problem in search of anexplanation. *Anthropology and Education Quarterly, 18,* 321–334.

Ogbu, J. U. (1988). Human intelligence testing: A cultural-ecological perspective. *Phi Kappa Phi Journal, 68,* 23–29.

Ogbu, J. U. (1990). Minority education in comparative perspective. *Journal of Negro Education, 59,* 45–57.

Ogbu, J. U. (1993). Differences in cultural frame of reference. *International Journal of Behavioral Development, 16,* 483–506.

Ogbu, J. U. (1994). From cultural differences to differences in cultural frame of reference. In P. M. Greenfield & R. R. Cocking (Eds.), *Cross-cultural roots of minority child development* (pp. 372–391). Hillsdale, NJ: Lawrence Erlbaum.

Ogbu, J. U. (2003). *Black American students in an affluent suburb: A study of academic engagement.* Mahwah, NJ: Lawrence Erlbaum.

Ogbu, J. U. (2004). Collective identity and the burden of "acting White" in Black history, community, and education. *The Urban Review, 36,* 1–35.

Ogbu, J. U. (2008). *Minority status, oppositional culture & schooling.* London, England: Routledge.

Ohlsen, M. M., & Gazda, G. M. (1965). Counseling underachieving bright pupils. *Education, 86,* 78–81.

Oldfield, D. (1986). The effects of the relaxation response on self-concept and acting out behavior. *Elementary School Guidance & Counseling, 20,* 255–260.

Olszewski, P. M., Kulieke, M., & Buescher, T. (1987). The influence of the family environment on the development of talent: A literature review. *Journal for the Education of the Gifted, 2,* 6–28.

Olszewski-Kubilius, P. M., & Scott, J. M. (1992). An investigation of the college and career counseling needs of economically disadvantaged minority gifted students. *Roeper Review, 14,* 141–148.

Omizo, M. M. (1981). Relaxation training and biofeedback with hyperactive elementary school children. *Elementary School Guidance & Counseling, 15,* 329–332.

Omizo, M. M., Hershberger, J. M., & Omizo, S. A. (1988). Teaching children to cope with anger. *Elementary School Guidance & Counseling, 22,* 241–245.

Omnibus Budget Reconciliation Act of 1981, Pub. Law 97-35 (August 13, 1981).

Onwuegbuzie, A. J., & Daley, C. E. (2001). Racial differences in IQ revisited: A synthesis of nearly a century of research. *Journal of Black Psychology, 27,* 209–220.

Ordovensky, P. (1988, April 13). Test bias aids boys in scholarship. *USA Today,* p. 10.

Orfield, G. (2001). *Schools more separate: Consequences of a decade of resegregation.* Cambridge, MA: The Civil Rights Project, Harvard University.

Orfield, G., & Frankenberg, E. (2007). *Lessons in integration: Realizing the promise of racial diversity in American schools.* Charlottesville: University of Virginia Press.

Orfield, G., & Lee, C. (2007). *Historic reversals, accelerating resegregation, and the need for new integration strategies.* Los Angeles, CA: UCLA Civil Rights Project.

O'Tuel, F. S. (1994). APOGEE: Equity in the identification of gifted and talented students. *Gifted Child Quarterly, 38,* 75–79.

Parham, T. A., & Brown, S. (2003). Therapeutic approaches with African American populations. In F. D. Harper & J. McFadden (Eds.), *Culture and counseling: New approaches* (pp. 81–98). Boston, MA: Allyn & Bacon.

Parham, T. A., & Helms, J. E. (1985). Relation of racial identity attitudes to self-actualization and affective states of Black students. *Journal of Counseling Psychology, 32,* 431–440.

Passow, A. H. (1972). The gifted and the disadvantaged. *The National Elementary Principal, 51*(5), 24–41.

Patchen, M. (Ed.). (1982). *Black-White contact in schools: Its social and academic effects.* West Lafayette, IN: Purdue University Press.

Patton, J. M., & Sims, S. J. (1993). A schematic guide to the assessment and identification of African American learners with gifts and talents. *The National Research Center on the Gifted and Talented Newsletter,* 8–9.

Pearson, J. L., Hunter, A. G., Ensminger, M. E., & Kellam, S. G. (1990). Black grandmothers in multi-generational households: Diversity in family structure and parenting involvement in the Woodlawn Community. *Child Development, 61,* 434–442.

Peterson, J. S. (1990). Noon-hour discussion: Dealing with the burdens of capability. *Gifted Child Today, 13*(4), 17–22.

Peterson, J. S. (2009). *Gifted at risk: Poetic profiles.* Scottsdale, AZ: Great Potential Press.

Peterson, J. S., Duncan, N., & Canady, K. (2009). A longitudinal study of negative life events, stress, and school experiences of gifted youth. *Gifted Child Quarterly, 53,* 34–49.

Peterson, J. S., & Morris, C. W. (2010). Preparing school counselors to address concerns related to giftedness: A study of accredited counselor preparation programs. *Journal for the Education of the Gifted, 33,* 163–188.

Pegnato, C. W., & Birch, J. W. (1959). Locating gifted children in junior high school: A comparison of methods. *Exceptional Children, 25,* 300–304.

Pelligrini, A. D., & Glickman, C. D. (1990). Measuring kindergartners' social competence. *Young Children, 45*(4), 40–44.

Pennsylvania Association for Retarded Children v. Commonwealth of Pennsylvania, 334 F. Supp. 1257 (E.D. Pa. 1971).

Pennsylvania Association for Retarded Children v. Commonwealth of Pennsylvania, 343 F. Supp. 279 (E.D. Pa. 1972).

Peske, H. G., & Haycock, K. (2006). *Teacher inequality. How poor and minority students are shortchanged on teacher quality.* Washington, DC: Education Trust.

Peterson, J. S. (1983). *Making the grade: Report of the Twentieth Century Task Force on Federal Elementary and Secondary Education Policy.* New York, NY: The Twentieth Century Fund.

Petroni, F. A., & Hirsch, E. A. (1970). *Two, four, six, eight, when you gonna integrate?* New York, NY: Behavioral Publications.

Pettigrew, T. F. (1981). The mental health impact. In B. J. Bowser & R. G. Hunt (Eds.), *Impacts of racism on White Americans* (pp. 97–118). Beverly Hills, CA: Sage.

Phillips, B. N., Pitcher, G. D., Worsham, M. E., & Miller, S. C. (1980). Test anxiety and the school environment. In I. G. Sarason (Ed.), *Test anxiety: Theory, research, and applications* (pp. 326–343). Hillsdale, NJ: Lawrence Erlbaum.

Phinney, J. S., & Rotherham, M. J. (Eds.). (1987). *Children's ethnic socialization: Pluralism and development.* Newberry Park, CA: Sage.

Piers, E. V., Harris, D. B., & Herzberg, D. S. (2002). *Piers-Harris Children's Self-Concept Scale* (2nd ed.). Los Angeles, CA: Western Psychological Services.

Plake, B. S., Ansorge, C. J., Parker, C. S., & Lowry, S. B. (1982). Effects of item arrangement, knowledge of arrangement, test anxiety and sex performance. *Journal of Educational Measurement, 19,* 49–57.

Planty, M., Hussar, W., Snyder, T., Kena, G., KewalRamani, A., Kemp, J., . . . Dinkes, R. (2009). *The condition of education 2009* (NCES 2009-081). Washington, DC: National Center for Education Statistics, Institute of Education Sciences, U.S. Department of Education.

Ponterotto, J. G., Casas, J. M., Suzuki, L. A., & Alexander, C. M. (Eds.). (2001). *Handbook of multicultural counseling* (2nd ed.). Thousand Oaks, CA: Sage.

Ponterotto, J. G., & Pedersen, P. B. (1993). *Preventing prejudice: A guide for counselors and educators.* Newbury Park, CA: Sage.

Ponterotto, J. G., & Pedersen, P. B. (2006). *Preventing prejudice: A guide for counselors and educators* (2nd ed.). Newbury Park, CA: Sage.

Prom-Jackson, S., Johnson, S. T., & Wallace, M. B. (1987). Home environment, talented minority youth, and school achievement. *Journal of Negro Education, 56,* 111–121.

Raph, J. B., Goldberg, M. L., & Passow, A. H. (1966). *Bright underachievers.* New York, NY: Teachers College Press.

Rathvon, N. W. (1991). Effects of a guidance unit in two formats on the examination performance of underachieving middle school students. *The School Counselor, 38,* 294–304.

Read, C. R. (1991). Achievement and career choices: Comparisons of males and females. *Roeper Review, 13,* 188–193.

Regents of the University of California v. Bakke, 438 U.S. 265 (1978).

Reis, S. M. (1987). We can't change what we don't recognize: Understanding the special needs of gifted females. *Gifted Child Quarterly, 31,* 83–88.

Reis, S. M. (1991). The need for clarification in research designed to examine gender differences in achievement and accomplishment. *Roeper Review, 13,* 193–198.

Reis, S. M. (2002). Toward a theory of creativity in diverse creative women. *Creativity Research Journal, 14,* 305–316.

Reis, S. M. (2003). Gifted girls, twenty-five years later: Hopes realized and new challenges found. *Roeper Review, 25,* 154–158.

Reis, S. M. (2005). Feminist perspectives on talent development: A research-based conception of giftedness in women. In R. J. Sternberg & J. E. Davidson (Eds.), *Conceptions of giftedness* (pp. 217–245). New York, NY: Cambridge University Press.

Reis, S. M. (2007). Social and emotional issues faced by gifted girls in elementary and secondary school. *KAGE Update, 3,* 1, 8–9.

Reis, S. M., & Callahan, C. M. (1989). Gifted females: They've come a long way—or have they? *Journal for the Education of the Gifted, 12,* 99–117.

Reis, S. M., & Renzulli, J. S. (2009). Developing talents and gifted behaviors in children. In B. MacFarlane & T. Stambaugh (Eds.), *Leading change in gifted education: The festschrift of Dr. Joyce VanTassel-Baska* (pp. 107–115). Waco, TX: Prufrock Press.

Rensberger, B. (1984). Margaret Mead: An indomitable presence. In A. L. Hammond (Ed.), *A passion to know: 20 profiles in science* (pp. 37–38). New York, NY: Simon & Schuster.

Renzulli, J. S. (1977). *The Enrichment Triad Model: A guide for developing defensible programs for the gifted and talented.* Mansfield Center, CT: Creative Learning Press.

Renzulli, J. S. (1986). The three-ring conception of giftedness: A developmental model for creative productivity. In R. J. Sternberg & J. E. Davidson (Eds.), *Conceptions of giftedness* (pp. 53–92). New York, NY: Cambridge University Press.

Renzulli, J. S. (1987). The difference is what makes differentiation. *Journal for the Education of the Gifted, 10,* 265–266.

Renzulli, J. S. (1997). *The Schoolwide Enrichment Model: A guide for developing defensible programs for the gifted and talented.* Mansfield Center, CT: Creative Learning Press.

Renzulli, J. S. (2002). Expanding conceptions of giftedness to include co-cognitive traits and to promote social capital. *Phi Delta Kappan, 84,* 33–40, 57–58.

Renzulli, J. S. (2003). A rising tide lifts all ships: Applying gifted education know-how to the development of high potential in all students. *The Korean Journal of Thinking & Problem Solving, 13,* 83–110.

Renzulli, J. S., & Park, S. (2000). Gifted dropouts: The who and the why. *Gifted Child Quarterly, 44,* 261–271.

Renzulli, J. S., Reis, S. M., Hébert, T. P., & Diaz, E. I. (1994). The plight of high ability students in urban schools. In M. C. Wang & M. C. Reynolds (Eds.), *Making a difference for students at risk* (pp. 61–98). Thousand Oaks, CA: Corwin Press.

Renzulli, J. S., & Stoddard, B. (1980). *Gifted and talented education in perspective.* Reston, VA: Council for Exceptional Children.

Ridley, C. R. (1989). Racism in counseling as an adverse behavioral process. In P. B. Pedersen, J. G. Draguns, W. J. Lonner, & J. E. Trimble (Eds.), *Counseling across cultures* (3rd ed., pp. 55–77). Honolulu, HI: University of Hawaii Press.

Rimm, S. B. (2001). Underachievement: A continuing dilemma. In J. F. Smutny (Ed.), *Underserved gifted populations* (pp. 349–360). Cresskill, NJ: Hampton Press.

Rimm, S., & Lowe, B. (1988). Family environments of underachieving gifted students. *Gifted Child Quarterly, 32,* 353–359.

Rogers, C. R. (1951). *Client-centered therapy: Its current practice, implications, and theory.* Boston, MA: Houghton Mifflin.

Rogers, C. R. (1961). *On becoming a person: A therapist's view of psychotherapy.* Boston, MA: Houghton Mifflin.

Rogers, J. A., & Nielson, A. B. (1993). Gifted children and divorce: A study of the literature on the incidence of divorce in families with gifted children. *Journal for the Education of the Gifted, 16,* 251–267.

Roome, J. R., & Romney, D. M. (1985). Reducing anxiety in gifted children by inducing relaxation training. *Roeper Review, 7,* 177–179.

Rosenholtz, S. J. (1985). Effective schools: Interpreting the evidence. *American Journal of Education, 9,* 352–388.

Rosenthal, R., & Jacobson, L. (1968). *Pygmalion in the classroom: Teacher expectation and pupils' intellectual development.* New York, NY: Holt, Rinehart, & Winston.

Rosenthal, R., & Jacobson, L. (1979). *Pygmalion in the classroom: Teacher expectations and pupils' intellectual development* (2nd ed.). Baltimore, MD: Johns Hopkins University Press.

Rosenthal, R., & Jacobson, L. (1992). *Pygmalion in the classroom: Teacher expectations and pupils' intellectual development* (Expanded ed.). New York, NY: Irvington.

Roth, R. M. (1970). *Underachieving students and guidance.* New York, NY: Houghton Mifflin.

Ruben, A. M. (1989). Preventing school dropouts through classroom guidance. *Elementary School Guidance & Counseling, 24,* 21–29.

Rumberger, R. W. (1983). Dropping out of high school: The influence of race, sex and family background. *American Educational Research Journal, 20,* 199–220.

Rumberger, R. W. (1987). High school dropouts: A review of issues and evidence. *Review of Educational Research, 57,* 101–121.

Ryan, J. S. (1983). Identifying intellectually superior Black children. *Journal of Educational Research, 76,* 153–156.

Sadker, M., & Sadker, D. (1982). *Sex equity handbook for schools.* New York, NY: Longman.

Sadker, M., Sadker, D., & Klein, S. (1986). Abolishing misperceptions about sex equity in education. *Theory Into Practice, 25,* 220–226.

Sadker, M., Sadker, D., & Long, L. (1993). Gender and educational quality. In J. A. Banks & C. A. M. Banks (Eds.), *Multicultural education: Issues and perspectives* (2nd ed., pp. 111–128). Boston, MA: Allyn & Bacon.

Sadker, M., Sadker, D., & Steindam, S. (1989). Gender equity and educational reform. *Educational Leadership, 46*(6), 44–47.

Salomone, R. C. (1986). *Legal rights and federal policy: Equal education under law.* New York, NY: St. Martin's Press.

Samuda, R. J. (1998). *Psychological testing of American minorities: Issues and consequences* (2nd ed.). Thousand Oaks, CA: Sage.

Samuda, R. J., Feuerstein, R., Kaufman, A. S., Lewis, J. E., & Sternberg, R. J. (1998). *Advances in cross-cultural assessment.* Thousand Oaks, CA: Sage.

Samuda, R. J., Kong, S. L., Cummins, J., Lewis, J., & Pascual-Leone, J. (1991). *Assessment and placement of minority students.* Lewiston, NY: Hogrefe and ISSP.

Sanborn, M. P. (1979). Working with parents. In N. Colangelo & R. T. Zaffrann (Eds.), *New voices in counseling the gifted* (pp. 396–400). Dubuque, IA: Kendall/ Hunt.

Sanchez, A. R., & King, M. (1986). Mexican Americans' use of counseling services: Cultural and institutional factors. *Journal of College Student Personnel, 27,* 344–349.

Sandhu, D. S., & Aspy, C. B. (1997). *Counseling for prejudice prevention and reduction.* Alexandria, VA: American Counseling Association.

Saracho, O. N. (1989). Cognitive style in the play of young children. *Early Childhood Development and Care, 51,* 65–76.

Saracho, O. N., & Gerstl, C. K. (1992). Learning differences among at-risk minority students. In H. C. Waxman, J. Walker de Felix, J. E. Anderson, & H. P. Baptiste, Jr. (Eds.), *Students at risk in at-risk schools: Improving environments for learning* (pp. 105–136). Newbury Park, CA: Corwin Press.

Sarason, I., Pederson, A., & Nyman, B. (1968). Test anxiety and the observation of models. *Journal of Personality, 36,* 493–511.

Sarason, L. G., & Ganzer, V. J. (1962). Anxiety, reinforcement, and experimental instructions in a free verbalization situation. *Journal of Abnormal and Social Psychology, 65,* 300–307.

Sarason, S. B., Davidson, K. S., Lighthall, F. F., & Waite, R. R. (1958). A test anxiety scale for children. *Child Development, 29,* 105–113.

Sarason, S. B., Davidson, K. S., Lighthall, F. F., Waite, R. R., & Ruebush, B. K. (1960). *Anxiety in elementary school children.* New York, NY: Wiley.

Sattler, J. M. (1992). *Assessment of children* (Rev. ed.). San Diego, CA: Jerome M. Sattler.

Saurenman, D. A., & Michael, W. B. (1980). Differential placement of high-achieving and low-achieving gifted pupils in grades, four, five, and six on measures of field dependence-field independence, creativity, and self-concept. *Gifted Child Quarterly, 24,* 81–86.

Sax, G. (1989). *Principles of educational and psychological measurement and evaluation* (3rd ed.). Belmont, CA: Wadsworth.

Schlosser, L. K. (1992). Teacher distance and student disengagement: School lives on the margin. *Journal of Teacher Education, 43,* 128–140.

Schmader, T., Johns, M., & Barquissau, M. (2004). The costs of accepting gender differences: The role of stereotype endorsement in women's experience in the math domain. *Sex Roles: A Journal of Research, 50,* 835–850.

Schmitz, C. C., & Galbraith, J. (1985). *Managing the social and emotional needs of the gifted: A teacher's survival guide.* Minneapolis, MN: Free Spirit.

Schott Foundation for Public Education. (2006). *A positive future for Black boys: Building the movement.* Cambridge, MA: Author.

Schott Foundation for Public Education. (2007). *Schott 2007 annual report.* Cambridge, MA: Author.

Schott Foundation for Public Education. (2008). *Given half a chance: The school 50 state report on public education and Black males* (Executive Summary). Cambridge, MA: Author.

Schott Foundation for Public Education. (2009). *Lost opportunity: A 50 state report on the opportunity to learn in America.* Cambridge, MA: Author.

Schuler, H., Thornton, G. C., III., Frintrup, A., Mueller-Hanson, R. (2002). *Achievement Motivation Inventory (AMI).* Göttingen, Germany: Hans Huber.

Schultz, T. W. (1961). Investment in human capital. *American Economic Review, 52,* 13–32.

Schuster, D. T. (1990). Fulfillment of potential, life satisfaction, and competence: Comparing four cohorts of gifted women at midlife. *Journal of Educational Psychology, 82,* 471–478.

Scott, M. S., Perou, R., Urbano, R., Hogan, A., & Gold, S. (1992). The identification of giftedness: A comparison of White, Hispanic, and Black families. *Gifted Child Quarterly, 36,* 131–139.

Scott-Jones, D., & Clark, M. L. (1986). The school experiences of Black girls: The interaction of gender, race, and socioeconomic status. *Phi Delta Kappan, 67,* 520–526.

Search Institute. (2010). *40 developmental assets.* Retrieved from http://www.search-institute.org/assets

Sears, S. J. (1993). The changing scope of practice of the secondary school counselor. *The School Counselor, 40,* 384–388.

Sebring, A. D. (1983). Parental factors in the social and emotional adjustment of the gifted. *Roeper Review, 6,* 97–99.

Seeley, K. R. (1984). Perspectives on adolescent giftedness and delinquency. *Journal for the Education of the Gifted, 8,* 59–72.

Seeley, K. R., & Mahoney, A. R. (1981). Giftedness and delinquency: A small beginning toward some answers. In R. E. Clasen et al. (Ed), *Programming for the gifted, talented and creative: Models and methods* (2nd ed., pp. 247–258). Madison, WI: University of Wisconsin Extension.

Serwatka, T. S., Deering, S., & Stoddard, A. (1989). Correlates of the under-representation of Black students in classes for gifted students. *Journal of Negro Education, 58,* 80–87.

Shade, B. J. (1978). Social-psychological characteristics of achieving Black children. *Negro Educational Review, 29,* 80–87.

Shade, B. J. (1994). Understanding the African American learner. In E. R. Hollins, J. E. King, & W. C. Hayman (Eds.), *Teaching diverse populations: Formulating a knowledge base* (pp. 175–189). New York: State University of New York Press.

Shade, B. J. (1997). *Culture, style and the educative process: Making schools work for racially diverse students* (2nd ed.). Springfield, IL: Charles C. Thomas.

Shade, B. J., & Edwards, P. A. (1987). Ecological correlates of the educative style of Afro-American children. *Journal of Negro Education, 56,* 88–99.

Shade, B. J., Kelly, C., & Oberg, M. (1997). *Creating culturally responsive classrooms.* Washington, DC: American Psychological Association.

Shade, B. J., & New, C. A. (1993). Cultural influences on learning: Teaching implications. In J. A. Banks & C. A. M. Banks (Eds.), *Multicultural education: Issues and perspectives* (2nd ed., pp. 317–331). Boston, MA: Allyn & Bacon.

Shantideva, A. (1976). *A guide to the Bodhisatva's way of life*. Dharmasala, India: Library of Tibetan Works and Archives.

Shavelson, R. J., Bolus, R., & Keesling, J. W. (1980). Self-concept: Recent developments in theory and methods. In D. A. Payne (Ed.), *Recent developments in affective measurement* (pp. 25–43). San Francisco, CA: Jossey-Bass.

Shaw, F. W., II. (1986). Identification of the gifted. *Urban Education, 21,* 42–61.

Shaw, M. C., & McCuen, J. T. (1960). The onset of academic underachievement in bright children. *Journal of Educational Psychology, 51,* 103–108.

Shaw, M. C., & McCuen, J. T. (1960). The onset of academic underachievement in bright children. *Journal of Educational Psychology, 86,* 551–583.

Sheldon, P. (1954, February). The families of highly gifted children. *Marriage and Family Living,* 59–67.

Shmoop University. (2010). *Reverse discrimination?* Retrieved from http://www.shmoop.com/equal-protection/reverse-discrimination.html

Shuy, R. W. (1969). A linguistic background for developing beginning reading materials for Black children. In J. C. Baratz & R. W. Shuy (Eds.), *Teaching Black children to read* (pp. 117–137). Washington, DC: Center for Applied Linguistics.

Silverman, L. K. (1989). Invisible gifts, invisible handicaps. *Roeper Review, 12,* 37–42.

Silverman, L. K. (Ed.). (1993). *Counseling the gifted and talented*. Denver, CO: Love.

Sinclair, R. L., & Ghory, W. J. (1987). Becoming marginal. In H. T. Trueba (Ed.), *Success or failure* (pp. 169–184). Cambridge, MA: Newbury House.

Sinclair, R. L., & Ghory, W. J. (1992). Marginality, community, and the responsibility of educators for students who do not succeed in school. In H. C. Waxman, J. Walker de Felix, J. E. Anderson, & H. P. Baptiste, Jr. (Eds.), *Students at risk in at-risk schools. Improving environments for learning* (pp. 33–42). Newbury Park, CA: Corwin Press.

Sizer, T. R. (1984). *Horace's compromise: The dilemma of the American high school*. Boston, MA: Houghton Mifflin.

Slaughter, D. T., & Epps, E. G. (1987). The home environment and academic achievement of Black American children and youth: An overview. *Journal of Negro Education, 56,* 3–20.

Slaughter, D. T., & Kuehne, V. S. (1988). Improving Black education: Perspectives on parent involvement. *Urban League Review, 11,* 59–75.

Smith, E. M. J. (1989). Black racial identity development. *Counseling Psychologist, 17,* 277–288.

Smith, J., LeRose, B., & Clasen, R. E. (1991). Underrepresentation of minority students in gifted programs: Yes! It matters! *Gifted Child Quarterly, 35,* 81–83.

Smitherman, G. (1977). *Talking and testifying: The language of Black America*. Boston, MA: Houghton Mifflin.

Smitherman, G. (1983). Language and liberation. *Journal of Negro Education, 52,* 15–23.

Smitherman, G. (1999). *Talkin that talk: Language, culture and education in African Americans*. New York, NY: Routledge.

Snyderman, M., & Rothman, S. (1987). Survey of expert opinion on intelligence and aptitude testing. *American Psychologist, 42,* 137–144.

Solomon, D., Houlihan, K. A., & Parelius, R. (1969). Intellectual achievement responsibility in Negro and White children. *Psychological Reports, 24,* 479–483.

Spearman, C. (1927). *The abilities of man*. London, England: Macmillan.

Spencer, M. B., & Markstrom-Adams, C. (1990). Identity process among racial and ethnic minority children in America. *Child Development, 61,* 290–310.

St. John, N. (1969). Thirty-six teachers: Their characteristics and outcomes for Black and White pupils. *American Educational Research Journal, 8,* 635–647.

Stambaugh, T. (2009). Promising students of poverty: Pathways and perils to success. In B. MacFarlane & T. Stambaugh (Eds.), *Leading change in gifted education: The festschrift of Dr. Joyce VanTassel-Baska* (pp. 135–148). Waco, TX: Prufrock Press.

Stanovich, K. E. (1986). Matthew Effects in reading: Some consequences of individual differences in the acquisition of literacy. *Reading Research Quarterly, 21,* 360–407.

Staples, R. (Ed.). (1986). *The Black family: Essays and studies.* Belmont, CA: Wadsworth.

Staples, R. (1987). Social structure and Black family life: An analysis of current trends. *Journal of Black Studies, 17,* 267–286.

Staples, R., & Johnson, L. R. (1993). *Black families at the crossroads: Challenges and prospects.* San Francisco, CA: Jossey-Bass.

Steele, C. M. (1997). A threat in the air: How stereotypes shape the intellectual identities and performance of women and African Americans. *American Psychologist, 52,* 613–629.

Steele, C. M. (1999). Thin ice: "Stereotype threat" and Black college students. *Atlantic Monthly, 284*(2), 50–54.

Steele, C. M., & Aronson, J. (1995). Stereotype threat and the intellectual test performance of African-Americans. *Journal of Personality and Social Psychology, 69,* 797–811.

Sternberg, R. J. (1982). *Handbook of human intelligence.* New York, NY: Cambridge University Press.

Sternberg, R. J. (1985). *Beyond IQ: A triarchic theory of human intelligence.* Cambridge: Cambridge University Press.

Sternberg, R. J. (2007). Cultural concepts of gifted. *Roeper Review, 29,* 160–165.

Sternberg, R. J., & Davidson, J. E. (Eds.). (1986). *Conceptions of giftedness.* Cambridge: Cambridge University Press.

Sternberg, R. J., & Detterman, D. K. (1986). *What is intelligence? Contemporary viewpoints on its nature and definition.* Norwood, NJ: Ablex.

Sternberg, R. J., & Kolligian, J. (Eds.). (1990). *Competence reconsidered.* New Haven, CT: Yale University Press.

Stockard, J., & Mayberry, M. (1992). *Effective educational environments.* Newbury Park, CA: Sage.

Storti, C. (1999). *The art of crossing cultures.* Yarmouth, MN: Intercultural Press.

Strickland, C. A. (2004). Exemplary general education programs for culturally diverse learners. In C. A. Tomlinson, D. Y. Ford, S. M. Reis, C. J. Briggs, & C. A. Strickland (Eds.), *In search of the dream: Designing schools and classrooms that work for high potential students from diverse cultural backgrounds.* Washington, DC: National Association for Gifted Children.

Strom, R., Collinsworth, P., Strom, S., Griswold, D., & Strom, P. (1992). Grandparent education for Black families. *Journal of Negro Education, 61,* 554–569.

Strom, R., Strom, S., Collinsworth, P., & Griswold, D. (1993). Helping Black grandparents help three generations. *The Educational Digest, 59,* 43–46.

Stronge, J. H., Lynch, C. K., & Smith, C. R. (1987). Educating the culturally disadvantaged gifted student. *The School Counselor, 34,* 336–344.

Sue, D. W. (2003). *Overcoming our racism: The journey to liberation.* San Francisco, CA: Jossey-Bass.

Sue, D. W., & Sue, D. (1990). *Counseling the culturally different: Theory & practice* (2nd ed.). New York, NY: Wiley & Sons.

Sue, D. W., Arrendondo, P., & McDavis, R. J. (1992). Multicultural counseling competencies and standards: A call to the profession. *Journal of Counseling and Development, 70,* 477–486.

Sue, D. W., Capodilupo, C. M., Torino, G. C., Bucceri, J. M., Holder, A. M. B., Nadal, K. L., & Esquilin, M. (2007). Racial microaggressions in everyday life: Implications for clinical practice. *American Psychologist, 62,* 271–286.

Supplee, P. L. (1990). *Reaching the gifted underachiever: Program strategy and design.* New York, NY: Teachers College Press.

Swicord, B. (1988). Maximizing the relationship between self-esteem and independent study in an urban gifted program. *Roeper Review, 11,* 31–33.

Tagiuri, R., & Litwin, G. I. (Eds.). (1968). *Organizational climate: Exploration of a concept.* Boston, MA: Harvard University, Division of Research, Graduate School of Business Administration.

Tannenbaum, A. J. (1983). *Gifted children: Psychological and educational perspectives.* New York, NY: MacMillan.

Tannenbaum, A. J. (1992). Early signs of giftedness: Research and commentary. In P. S. Klein & A. J. Tannenbaum (Eds.), *To be young and gifted* (pp. 3–32). Norwood, NJ: Ablex.

Tan-Williams, C., & Gutteridge, D. (1981). Creative thinking and moral reasoning of academically gifted secondary school adolescents. *Gifted Child Quarterly, 25,* 149–153.

Tatum, A. W. (2005). *Teaching reading to Black adolescent males: Closing the achievement gap.* Portland, ME: Stenhouse.

Tatum, A. W. (2007a). Building the textual lineages of African American male adolescents. In K. Beers, R. Probst, & L. Rief (Eds.), *Adolescent literacy: Turning promise into practice* (pp. 81–85). Portsmouth, NH: Heinemann.

Tatum, A. W. (2007b). Literacy development of African American males. In A. Berger, L. Rush, & J. Eakle (Eds.), *Secondary school reading and writing: What research reveals* (pp. 184–202). Urbana, IL: National Council of Teacher Educators.

Tatum, A. W. (2008a). African American males at risk: A researcher's study of endangered males and literature that works. In S. Lehr (Ed.), *Shattering the looking glass: Issues, controversy, and trends in children's literature* (pp. 137–153). Norwood, MA: Christopher Gordon.

Tatum, A. W. (2008b). Discussing texts with adolescents in culturally responsive ways. In. K. Hinchman & H. K. Sheridan-Thomas (Eds.), *Best practice in adolescent literacy instruction* (pp. 3–19). New York, NY: Guilford.

Tatum, A. W. (2008c). Toward a more anatomically complete model of literacy instruction: A focus on African American male adolescents and texts. *Harvard Educational Review, 78,* 155–180.

Tatum, A. W. (2008d). Adolescents and texts: Overserved or underserved? A focus on adolescents and texts. *English Journal, 98*(2), 82–85.

Tatum, A. W. (2009). *Reading for their life: (Re)building the textual lineage of African American adolescent males.* Portsmouth, NH: Heinemann.

Tatum, A. W., & Fisher, T. A. (2008). Nurturing resilience among adolescent readers. In S. Lenski & J. Lewis (Eds.), *Addressing the needs of struggling middle level and high school readers* (pp. 58–73). New York, NY: Guilford.

Taylor, C. W., & Ellison, R. L. (1968). *Manual for Alpha Biographical Inventory.* Salt Lake City, UT: Institute for Behavioral Research in Creativity.

Taylor, J. B. (1983). Influence of speech variety on teachers' evaluation of reading comprehension. *Journal of Educational Psychology, 75,* 662–667.

Terman, L. M. (1925). *Genetic studies of genius: Vol. 1. Mental and physical traits of a thousand gifted children.* Stanford, CA: Stanford University Press.

Terman, L. M., & Oden, M. H. (1947). *The gifted child grows up: Twenty-five year's follow-up of a superior group: Genetic studies of genius, Vol. 4.* Stanford, CA: Stanford University Press.

Tetreault, M. K., & Schmuck, P. (1985). Equity, educational reform and gender. *Issues in Education, 3,* 45–67.

Thompson, C. L., & Rudolph, L. B. (1992). *Counseling children* (3rd ed.). Pacific Grove, CA: Brooks/Cole.

Thorndike, R. L. (1963). *The concepts of over- and under-achievement.* New York, NY: Teachers College Press.

Tinsley, B. R., & Parke, R. D. (1984). The contemporary impact of the extended family on the nuclear family: Grandparents as support and socialization agents. In M. Lewis & L. Rosenblum (Eds.), *Social connection: Beyond the dyad* (pp. 161–194). New York, NY: Plenum Press.

Title IV, Part B. [Jacob K. Javits Gifted and Talented Students Education Act of 1988], Elementary and Secondary Education Act of 1988, 20 U.S.C. § 3061 et seq.

Tittle, C. K., & Zytowski, D. G. (Eds.). (1978). *Sex-fair interest measurement and implication.* Washington, DC: National Institute of Education Research.

Toch, T. (2006). *Margin of error: The education testing industry in the No Child Left Behind era.* Washington, DC: Education Sector.

Toldson, I. A. (2008). *Breaking barriers: Plotting the path to academic success for school-aged African American males.* Washington, DC: Congressional Black Caucus Foundation.

Tomlinson, C. A., Ford, D. Y., Reis, S. M., Briggs, C. J., & Strickland, C. A. (Eds.). (2004). *In search of the dream: Designing schools and classrooms that work for high potential students from diverse cultural backgrounds.* Washington, DC: National Association for Gifted Children.

Tomlinson, C. A., Ford, D. Y., Reis, S. M., Briggs, C. J., & Strickland, C. A. (Eds.). (2009). *In search of the dream: Designing schools and classrooms that work for high potential students from diverse cultural backgrounds* (2nd ed.). Washington, DC: National Association for Gifted Children.

Tomlinson, T. (1992). *Issues in education: Hard work and high expectations: Motivating students to learn.* Washington, DC: U.S. Department of Education, Office of Educational Research and Improvement.

Torrance, E. P. (1973). What gifted disadvantaged children can teach their teachers. *Gifted Child Quarterly, 17,* 243–249.

Torrance, E. P. (1977). *Discovery and nurturance of giftedness in the culturally different.* Reston, VA: Council on Exceptional Children.

Torrance, E. P. (1978). Ways of discovering gifted Black children. In A. Y. Baldwin, G. H. Gear, & L. J. Lucito (Eds.), *Educational planning for the gifted: Overcoming cultural, geographic and socioeconomic barriers* (pp. 29–33). Reston, VA: Council for Exceptional Children.

Turner, J., & McGann, C. S. (1980). Black studies as an integral tradition in African-American intellectual history. *Journal of Negro Education, 49,* 52–59.

Tuttle, F. B., Becker, L. A., & Sousa, J. A. (1988). *Characteristics and identification of gifted and talented students* (3rd ed.). Washington, DC: National Education Association.

U.S. Census Bureau. (1982). *Characteristics of the population below poverty level: 1980.* Washington, DC: Government Printing Office.

U.S. Census Bureau. (1983). *Money, income, and poverty status of families and persons in the United States: 1982 advanced report.* Washington, DC: Government Printing Office.

U.S. Census Bureau. (1984). *Persons in institutions and other group quarters: 1980 Census of populations, PC 80-2-40.* Washington, DC: Government Printing Office.

U.S. Census Bureau. (1986). *Household and family characteristics: March 1985.* Washington, DC: Government Printing Office.

U.S. Census Bureau. (1990). *Summary of population and housing characteristics, West Virginia.* Washington, DC: Government Printing Office.

U.S. Census Bureau. (1992). *Money income of households, families, and persons in the United States.* Washington, DC: Government Printing Office.

U.S. Census Bureau. (2006). *United States educational attainment: 2006 American community survey.* Washington, DC: Government Printing Office.

U.S. Department of Education. (1993). *National excellence: A case for developing America's talent.* Washington, DC: Office of Educational Research and Improvement.

U.S. Department of Education. (2002). *2002 Elementary and Secondary School Survey.* Washington, DC: Office U.S. for Civil Rights.

U.S. Department of Education. (2003). *Status and trends in the education of Blacks.* Washington, DC: National Center for Education Statistics.

U.S. Department of Education. (2004). *2004 Elementary and Secondary School Survey.* Washington, DC: Office U.S. for Civil Rights.

U.S. Department of Education. (2006a). *Twenty-sixth annual report to Congress on the implementation of the Individuals with Disabilities Education Act.* Washington, DC: Office of Special Education Programs.

U.S. Department of Education (2006b). *2006 Elementary and Secondary School Survey.* Washington, DC: Office for Civil Rights.

U.S. Department of Education (2008). *Annual report to Congress of the Office for Civil Rights, Fiscal year 2007–08.* Washington, DC: Office for Civil Rights.

U.S. Department of Education. (2009). *The twenty-ninth annual report to Congress on the implementation of the Individuals with Disabilities Education Act.* Washington, DC: Office of Special Education Programs.

U.S. Department of Education, National Center for Education Statistics. (2000). *America's kindergartners* (NCES 2000-070). Washington, DC: Author.

Valencia, R. R. (Ed.). (1997). *The evolution of deficit thinking: Educational thought and practice.* New York, NY: Falmer Press.

Valencia, R. R., & Solórzano, D. (1997). Contemporary deficit thinking. In R. Valencia (Ed.), *The evolution of deficit thinking: Educational thought and practice* (pp. 160–210). New York, NY: Falmer Press.

Vandiver, B. J., Fhagen-Smith, P. E., Cokley, K. O., Cross, W. E., Jr., & Worrell, F. C. (2001). Cross Nigrescence model: From theory to scale to theory. *Journal of Multicultural Counseling and Development, 29,* 174–200.

VanTassel-Baska, J. (1989). The role of the family in the success of disadvantaged gifted learners. *Journal for the Education of the Gifted, 13,* 22–36.

VanTassel-Baska, J. (Ed.). (2010). *Patterns and profiles of promising learners from poverty.* Waco, TX: Prufrock Press.

VanTassel-Baska, J., Feng, A., Quek, C., & Struck, J. (2004). A study of educators' and students' perceptions of academic success for underrepresented populations identified for gifted programs. *Psychology Science, 46,* 363–378.

VanTassel-Baska, J., Patton, J., & Prillaman, D. (1989). Disadvantaged gifted learners at-risk for educational attention. *Focus on Exceptional Children, 22*(3), 1–16.

VanTassel-Baska, J., & Stambaugh, T. (Eds.). (2007). *Overlooked gems: A national perspective on low-income promising learners.* Washington, DC: National Association for Gifted Children.

VanTassel-Baska, J., & Willis, G. (1987). A three year study of the effects of low income on SAT scores among the academically able. *Gifted Child Quarterly, 31,* 169–173.

Vogt, L. A., Jordan, C., & Tharp, R. G. (1987). Explaining school failure, producing school success: Two cases. *Anthropology & Education Quarterly, 18,* 276–286.

Vontress, C. E., & Epp, L. R. (1997). Historical hostility in the African American client: Implications for counseling. *Journal of Multicultural Counseling and Development, 25,* 170–184.

Vontress, C. E., Johnson, J. A., & Epp, L. R. (1999). *Cross-cultural counseling: A casebook.* Alexandria, VA: American Counseling Association.

Vygotsky, L. S. (1978). *Mind in society: The development of higher psychological processes.* Cambridge, MA: Harvard University Press.

Waetgen, W. B. (1977, September). *Sex differences in learning: Some questions.* Paper presented at the fourth annual meeting of the International Society for the Study of Behavioral Development, Pavia, Italy.

Wagner, M. (1991). *Drop outs with disabilities: What do we know? What can we do?* Menlo Park, CA: SRI International.

Wagner, R. K., & Sternberg, R. J. (1985). Practical intelligence in real-world pursuits: The role of tacit knowledge. *Journal of Personality and Social Psychology, 49,* 436–458.

Walker de Felix, J. (1992). Issues confronting at-risk students. In H. C. Waxman, J. Walker de Felix, J. E. Anderson, & H. P. Baptiste, Jr. (Eds.), *Students at risk in at-risk schools. Improving environments for learning* (pp. 61–64). Newbury Park, CA: Corwin Press.

Walton, G. M., & Cohen, G. L. (2007). A question of belonging: Race, social fit, and achievement. *Journal of Personality and Social Psychology, 92,* 82–96.

Waxman, H. C. (1992). Reversing the cycle of educational failure for students in at-risk school environments. In H. C. Waxman, J. Walker de Felix, J. E. Anderson, & H. P. Baptiste, Jr. (Eds.), *Students at risk in at-risk schools. Improving environments for learning* (pp. 1–10). Newbury Park, CA: Corwin Press.

Webb, J. T., Meckstroth, E. A., & Tolan, S. S. (1982). *Guiding the gifted child: A practical source for parents and teachers.* Columbus, OH: Ohio Psychology Publishing Company.

Webb-Johnson, G. (2002). Are schools ready for Joshua? Dimensions of African-American culture among students identified as having behavioral/emotional disorders. *Qualitative Studies in Education, 15,* 653–671.

Weis, L. (1985). *Between two worlds: Black students in an urban community college.* New York, NY: Routledge.

Weiss, H. B., Kreider, H., Lopez, E. L., & Chatman-Nelson, C. (2010). *Preparing educators to engage families: Case studies using an ecological systems framework* (2nd ed.). Thousand Oaks, CA: Sage.

Welch, I. D., & McCarroll, L. (1993). The future role of school counselors. *The School Counselor, 41,* 48–53.

Wellesley College Center for Research on Women. (1992). *How schools shortchange girls.* Washington, DC: American Association of University Women Educational Foundation.

Wesman, A. G. (1968). Intelligence testing. *American Psychologist, 27,* 267–274.

West, J. D., Hosie, T. W., & Mathews, F. N. (1989). Families of academically gifted children: Adaptability and cohesion. *The School Counselor, 37,* 121–127.

Whaley, A. L. (2001). Cultural mistrust and mental health services for African Americans. *The Counseling Psychologist, 29,* 513–531.

Whiting, G. W. (2006a). Enhancing culturally diverse males' scholar identity: Suggestions for educators of gifted students. *Gifted Child Today, 29*(3), 46–50.

Whiting, G. W. (2006b). From at risk to at promise: Developing a scholar identity among Black male adolescents. *Journal of Secondary Gifted Education, 17,* 222–229.

Whiting, G. W. (2009). The Scholar Identity Institute: Guiding Darnel and other Black males. *Gifted Child Today, 32*(4), 53–58.

Whiting, G. W., & Ford, D. Y. (2009). Black students and Advanced Placement classes: Summary, concerns, and recommendations. *Gifted Child Today, 32*(1), 23–26.

Whitley, B. E., Jr., & Kite, M. E. (2006). *The psychology of prejudice and discrimination.* Belmont, CA: Wadsworth.

Whitmore, J. R. (1980). *Giftedness, conflict, and underachievement.* Boston, MA: Allyn & Bacon.

Whitmore, J. R. (1986). Understanding a lack of motivation to excel. *Gifted Child Quarterly, 30,* 66–69.

Whitmore, J. R. (1988). Gifted children at risk for learning difficulties. *Teaching Exceptional Children, 20*(4), 10–14.

Williamson, M. (1992). *A return to love: Reflections on the principles of "a course in miracles."* New York, NY: HarperPerennial.

Wilson, M. N. (1986). The Black extended family: An analytical consideration. *Developmental Psychology, 22,* 246–256.

Wilson, M. N. (1989). Child development in the context of the Black extended family. *American Psychologist, 44,* 380–385.

Winne, P. H., Woodlands, M. J., & Wong, B. Y. L. (1982). Comparability of self-concept among learning disabled, normal, and gifted students. *Journal of Learning Disabilities, 15,* 470–475.

Witkin, H. A., Oltman, P. K., Raskin, E., & Karp, S. A. (1971). *A manual for the embedded figures tests.* Palo Alto, CA: Consulting Psychologists Press.

Wittmer, J., & Myrick, R. D. (1989). *The teacher as facilitator.* Minneapolis, MN: Educational Media Corporation.

Witty, E. P. (1978). Equal educational opportunity for gifted minority group children: Promise or possibility? *Gifted Child Quarterly, 22,* 344–352.

Wolfle, J. A. (1991). Underachieving gifted males: Are we missing the boat? *Roeper Review, 13,* 181–183.

Wood, S. (2010). Best practices in counseling the gifted in schools: What's really happening? *Gifted Child Quarterly, 54,* 43–58.

Woodard, S. L. (1995). Counseling disruptive Black elementary school boys. *Journal of Multicultural Counseling and Development, 23,* 21–28.

Woodson, C. G. (1933/2000). *Miseducation of the Negro.* Chicago, IL: African American Images.

Worthen, B. R., Borg, W. R., & White, K. R. (1993). *Measurement and evaluation in the schools.* New York, NY: Longman.

Wright, W. J. (1991). The endangered Black male child. *Educational Leadership, 49*(4), 14–16.

Wygant v. Jackson Board of Education, 476 U.S. 267 (1986).

Wynn, M. (1992). *Empowering African American males to succeed: A ten step approach for parents and teachers.* Marietta, GA: Rising Sun.

Wynne, H., & Walberg, H. (1994). Persisting groups: An overlooked force for learning. *Phi Delta Kappan, 75,* 527–530.

Zill, N. (1983). *Happy, healthy, and insecure.* New York, NY: Doubleday.

Zionts, P. (1983). The rational-emotive approach: A strategy for understanding and correcting irrational beliefs in pupils. *The Pointer, 27*(3), 13–17.

Zirkel, P. A., & Stevens, P. L. (1987). The law concerning public education of gifted students. *Journal for the Education of the Gifted, 10,* 305–322.

Zuccone, C. F., & Amerikaner, M. (1986). Counseling gifted underachievers: A family systems approach. *Journal of Counseling and Development, 64,* 590–592.

APPENDIX

A few scholars in education have focused exclusively on gifted Black males, namely Tarek C. Grantham, Gilman W. Whiting, James L. Moore, III, and Fred A. Bonner, II. Collectively, their culturally responsive conceptual model and studies with gifted Black males demonstrate that they struggle in building positive relationships with their teachers and classmates. Many believe they must "fake it to make it" socially. They don the roles of class clown, athlete, gang member/leader, thug, or other socially unacceptable roles and labels to fit it. Educators (and caregivers) must expose Black males to the scholars below who have devoted their lives to gifted Black males. A few of them are described next.

TAREK C. GRANTHAM

Dr. Grantham grew up in Richmond, VA. He was raised primarily by his mother, but his father was in his life on an inconsistent basis. As a teenager, Grantham admits to making bad choices in school and failing to reach his full academic potential. Both of his parents valued education highly and challenged him to excel; however, his father did not participate in any of his school activities. In college, Dr. Grantham became more deliberate and diligent at meeting challenges, and began to overcome personal fears and distorted views of what it meant to be a successful Black man. A critical step was to forgive his father and let go of past disappointments. He believes that professional success without his family would amount to his failure as a Black man.

At the time of this writing, Dr. Tarek C. Grantham is an associate professor in the Department of Educational Psychology and Instructional Technology at the University of Georgia (UGA). He teaches courses in the Gifted and Creative Education Program and has served as Program Coordinator, providing leadership for educators in the in-field endorsement program and for graduate students enrolled in five graduate degree programs. Dr. Grantham's research addresses recruitment and retention of ethnic minority students (particularly African Americans) in programs for gifted students. In his area of research, Dr. Grantham has published on mentoring, multicultural education, motivation, and effective advocacy to recruit and retain gifted ethnic minority students. He consults on these issues within public and private schools and presents research to local, state, and national audiences (e.g., Georgia Association for Gifted Children, American Educational Research Association) to encourage proactive efforts that aim to confront underrepresentation among gifted ethnic minority students. Dr. Grantham has published in top-tier journals (e.g., *Gifted Child Quarterly*, *Exceptional Children*, *Urban Education*) on equity issues related to underrepresentation in gifted education. He has been awarded research grants sponsored by the University of Georgia College of Education and other agencies to address barriers that negatively impact the recruitment and retention within pre-K–12 gifted programs. He has served as a board member of the Education Commission and the Diversity Committee for the National Association for Gifted Children. In addition, Dr. Grantham has worked as co-coordinator of the UGA Preparing Future Faculty Program in Psychology sponsored by the American Psychological Association, working to recruit, train, and retain diverse faculty in colleges and universities in the field of educational psychology.

GILMAN W. WHITING

Gilman W. Whiting grew up in Rhode Island and was raised in a single-parent home headed by his mother. His is not only an academician but also a health advocate and fitness trainer. Like too many Black males, Dr. Whiting often faced hardships at home, in the community, and at school, but was able to overcome them. He, like other Black males profiled in this Appendix, personifies resilience. Whiting received his doctorate from Purdue University's College of Education. His areas of concentration were curriculum and instruction, vocational and technical education, as well as work and the family. At the time of this writing, Professor Whiting is an assistant professor of African American and Diaspora Studies and the Director of Undergraduate Studies in the African American and Diaspora Studies Program at Vanderbilt University. He teaches courses on the African American Diaspora, Black masculinity, race, sport, and American culture and qualitative research methods. He also teaches in the Peabody College of Education in the Department of Human Organizational Development. His areas of research include work with young Black fathers, low-income minorities, welfare reform and fatherhood initiatives, education reform, special needs populations (gifted, at-risk learners, young Black men and scholar identities), and health in the Black community. Whiting is the author of more than 30 scholarly publications relating to minority populations, especially males, in diverse publications such as *Urban Education*, the *Willamette Journal*, *Gifted Education Press Quarterly*, *Journal of Secondary Gifted Education*, *Gifted Child Today*, and the *Midwestern Educational Research Journal*. He is editor of the forthcoming volume, *On Manliness: Black American Masculinities*, and author of a book-in-progress entitled *Fathering from the Margins: Young Black Fathers, Outlaw Culture, and Welfare Reform*. He consults with school districts nationally on various issues related to psychosocial behavior and motivation among young students. Whiting is the creator of the Scholar Identity Model™ and codirects the Scholar Identity Institute for young Black males.

JAMES L. MOORE, III

James L. Moore, III grew up in a nuclear family in Lyman, SC, a small town outside of Spartanburg. He was a football star in high school and college. Growing up in the traditional family structure did not inoculate him from social injustices. He was persistent and determined to excel and it has paid off. Moore received his B.A. in English education from Delaware State University and earned both his M.A.Ed. and Ph.D. in counselor education from Virginia Polytechnic Institute and State University. He is currently an associate professor in counselor education in the College of Education and Human Ecology at The Ohio State University and is the coordinator of the School of Counseling Program. At this time of this writing, Dr. Moore is the inaugural director of the Todd Anthony Bell National Resource Center on the African American Male and has faculty affiliations with the Ohio Collaborative, John Glenn Institute, and Criminal Justice Research Center at The Ohio State University.

Dr. Moore has a research agenda that focuses on (a) how educational professionals, such as school counselors, influence the educational/career aspirations and school experiences of students of color (particularly African American males); (b) sociocultural, familial, school, and community factors that support, enhance, and impede academic outcomes for K–16 African American students (e.g., elementary, secondary, and postsecondary); (c) recruitment and retention issues of students of color, particularly African Americans, in K–12 gifted education and high-potential college students in STEM majors; and (d) social, emotional, and psychological consequences of racial oppression for African American males and other people of color in various domains in society (e.g., education, counseling, workplace, athletics). In 9 years, he has made significant contributions in school counseling, gifted education, urban education, higher education, multicultural education/counseling, and STEM education.

Moore is listed in *Outstanding Young Men in America* (1998 edition), *Academic Keys Who's Who in Education* (2003 edition), *Manchester Who's Who Among Professionals in Counseling and Development* (2005/2006 edition), *Prestige International Who's Who Registries of Outstanding Professionals* (2007 edition), and *Who's Who in Black Columbus* (2008 and 2009 editions). He is also the recipient of the Brothers of the Academy's National Junior Scholar Award (2003), The Ohio State University's College of Education Distinguished Scholar Award (2004),

North Central Association for Counselor Education and Supervision's Research Award (2004), Ohio School Counselor Association's Research Award (2004), American Educational Research Association—Division E Early Career Award in Counseling (2005), Ohio School Counselors Association's George E. Hill Counselor Educator Award (2005), Counselors for Social Justice's Ohana Award (2006), Phi Delta Kappa's Emerging Leaders Award (2007–2008), American Educational Research Association Distinguished Scholar Award in Counseling–Division E (2008), National Association for Gifted Children's Early Scholar Award (2009), Institute for School-Based Family Counseling's Outstanding Contributions to School-Based Family Counseling (2009), and is an inducted member in numerous professional and honor societies, including Alpha Kappa Mu, Phi Kappa Phi, Phi Delta Kappa, Kappa Delta Pi, and Chi Sigma Iota.

FRED A. BONNER, II

Fred A. Bonner, II is a 1987 honor graduate of Jefferson High School in Jefferson, TX. Dr. Bonner grew up in a two-parent, middle-class family structure in his East Texas community. Bonner was raised in a family of educators—his grandmother taught secondary English; his father who initially served as a coach and athletic director later became a high school assistant principal; and his mother who served as a high school coach also served as an English, physical education, and physical science teacher at the secondary level. Bonner currently serves as professor of higher education administration and Associate Dean of Faculties at Texas A&M University—College Station. He received a B.A. degree in chemistry from the University of North Texas in 1991, an M.S.Ed. in curriculum and instruction from Baylor University in 1994, and an Ed.D. in higher education administration and college teaching from the University of Arkansas-Fayetteville in 1997. Dr. Bonner has been the recipient of the American Association for Higher Education Black Caucus Dissertation Award and the Educational Leadership, Counseling, and Foundation's Dissertation of the Year Award from the University of Arkansas, College of Education. Bonner has published articles and book chapters on academically gifted African American male college students, teaching in the multicultural college classroom, diversity issues in student affairs, and success factors influencing the retention of students of color in higher education. He serves, at the time of this writing, as an assistant editor for the *National Association of Student Affairs Professionals Journal*, and has completed three summers as a research fellow with the Yale University Psychology Department (PACE Center), focusing on issues that impact academically gifted African American male college students. Bonner has authored a book that highlights the experiences of postsecondary gifted African American male undergraduates in predominantly White and Historically Black college contexts. He spent the 2005–2006 year as an American Council on Education Fellow in the Office of the President at Old Dominion University in Norfolk, VA.

ABOUT THE AUTHOR

Donna Y. Ford, Ph.D., is Professor of Education and Human Development at Vanderbilt University. She teaches in the Department of Special Education. Dr. Ford conducts research primarily in gifted education and multicultural/urban education. Specifically, her work focuses on: (a) minority student achievement and underachievement; (b) recruiting and retaining culturally diverse students in gifted education; (c) multicultural and urban education; and (d) family involvement. Dr. Ford is cofounder of the Scholar Identity Institute for Black Males.

Dr. Ford's work has been recognized by various professional organizations, including the Research Award from the Shannon Center for Advanced Studies; the Early Career Award and the Career Award from the American Educational Research Association; Senior Scholar Award and Early Scholar Award from the National Association for Gifted

Children; and the Esteemed Scholarship Award from the National Association of Black Psychologists. She is the author of several books and more than 100 articles and chapters, and presents nationally at professional conferences and school districts. She has served as a board member of the National Association for Gifted Children and on numerous editorial boards.

INDEX